APOLOGETIC DISCOURSE
AND THE SCRIBAL TRADITION

Society of Biblical Literature

Text-Critical Studies

Editor
James R. Adair, Jr.

Volume 5
APOLOGETIC DISCOURSE
AND THE SCRIBAL TRADITION

APOLOGETIC DISCOURSE AND THE SCRIBAL TRADITION

Evidence of the Influence of Apologetic Interests on the Text of the Canonical Gospels

Wayne C. Kannaday

Society of Biblical Literature
Atlanta

APOLOGETIC DISCOURSE
AND THE SCRIBAL TRADITION

Wayne C. Kannaday

Library of Congress Cataloging-in-Publication Data

Kannaday, Wayne Campbell.
  Apologetic discourse and the scribal tradition : evidence of the influence of apologetic interests on the text of the canonical gospels / by Wayne C. Kannaday.
      p. cm. — (Society of Biblical Literature text-critical studies)
  Includes bibliographical references and index.
  ISBN 1-58983-101-2 (pbk. : alk. paper)
  1. Bible—Canon. 2. Apologetics—History—Early church, ca. 30-600. I. Title. II. Series: Text-critical studies.

BS465.K35 2004
226'.0486—dc22

                            2004016238

08 07 06 05 04   5 4 3 2 1

Printed in the United States of America
on acid-free paper

To
Helen and Christopher

ἀγάπη πρὸς γυναίκαν μου καὶ υἱόν

CONTENTS

ACKNOWLEDGMENTS

My deep thanks are due those whose influence, encouragement, and effort have contributed to the publication of this volume. Although many more persons than I can name here deserve to be mentioned, I would be remiss if I did not recognize some of those without whose assistance and support this book would not have come into print.

Great thanks are due Elizabeth Clark, Paul Meyer, Zlatko Plese, and Moody Smith who were dutiful and helpful in their challenges and suggestions regarding this work in its previous life as my dissertation for the University of North Carolina at Chapel Hill. Not enough can be said about the dedicated and tireless labors of my doctoral advisor and mentor, Bart D. Ehrman, whose many and able capacities as a teacher, editor, scholar, debater, wordsmith, textual critic, and motivator have left an indelible mark upon this work. My efforts to emulate his patient direction, erudite scholarship, and disciplined encouragement, like those of a scribe following his exemplar, may readily be discerned in the pages that follow.

I also wish to thank members of the staff of the Society of Biblical Literature responsible for bringing this book to press, especially Jimmy Adair for promoting the Text-Critical Studies series in which this volume appears, and Leigh Anderson for her capable editorial assistance and patience. Also, let me express my deep appreciation to Ellen Roueche, who with diligence and perspicacious attention to detail produced the camera-ready manuscript. Of course, responsibility for the inevitable deficiencies of this study rest solely with me, and serve as yet another instance of "textual corruption."

My colleagues at Newberry College, in particular Mike Beggs, Russell Kleckley (now of Augsburg College), Garth Kemmerling (retired), and Jesse Scott, have also contributed to this book in numerous ways, not least of which was their willingness to be saddled with additional departmental responsibilities in order to afford me time to complete this study.

Finally, I am compelled to declare my appreciation to my remarkable wife, Helen, and my wonderful son, Christopher, by dedicating this book to them. They have borne much in the way of burden and responsibility as I have labored over the keyboard to bring this volume to a conclusion, but they have responded consistently with love and humor.

LIST OF ABBREVIATIONS

AB	Anchor Bible
ABD	*Anchor Bible Dictionary*
ABRL	Anchor Bible Reference Library
ANF	*Ante-Nicene Fathers*
ANRW	*Aufstieg und Niedergang der römischen Welt.* Edited by H. Temporani and W. Haase. Berlin and New York: Walter de Gruyter, 1972-
ANTC	Abingdon New Testament Commentaries
AthR	*Anglican Theological Review*
Bib	*Biblica*
BJRL	*Bulletin of the John Rylands University Library of Manchester*
CSCO	Corpus scriptorum christianorum orientalium. Edited by I. B. Chabot et al. Paris, 1903-
ExpTim	*Expository Times*
FC	Fathers of the Church. Washington, DC, 1947-
GCS	Die griechischen christlichen Schriftsteller der ersten [drei] Jahrhunderte
HeyJ	*Heythrop Journal*
HibJ	*Hibbert Journal*
HTR	*Harvard Theological Review*
ICC	International Critical Commentary
IGNTP	International Greek New Testament Project
JBL	*Journal of Biblical Literature*
JECS	*Journal of Early Christian Studies*
JJS	*Journal of Jewish Studies*
JQR	*Jewish Quarterly Review*
JTS	*Journal of Theological Studies*
LCL	Loeb Classical Library
NICNT	New International Commentary on the New Testament
NIGTC	New International Greek Testament Commentary
NovT	*Novum Testamentum*
NovTSup	Novum Testamentum Supplements
NTS	*New Testament Studies*
NTTS	New Testament Tools and Studies
OECT	Oxford Early Christian Texts. Edited by H. Chadwick. Oxford, 1970-
RB	*Revue biblique*
RelSRev	*Religious Studies Review*
SBL	Society of Biblical Literature
SBLMS	Society of Biblical Literature Monograph Series
SBLNTGF	Society of Biblical Literature The New Testament in the Greek Fathers
SBLSP	*Society of Biblical Literature Seminar Papers*
SC	Sources chrétiennes. Paris: Cerf, 1943-
SD	Studies and Documents
SecCent	Second Century

SJT	*Scottish Journal of Theology*
SNTSMS	Society for the Study of the New Testament Monograph Series
SP	Sacra Pagina
StPatr	Studia Patristica
ThH	Théologie historique
TS	Texts and Studies
TU	Texte und Untersuchungen
TWNT	Gerhard Kittel, et al., eds. *Theological Dictionary of the New Testament*. 10 Volumes. Geoffrey W. Bromiley, trans.; Grand Rapids, MI: Eerdmans, 1964-1976. German edition *Theologisches Wörterbuch zum Neuen Testament*. Stuttgart: W. Kohlhammer Verlag.
TZ	*Theologische Zeitschrift*
VC	*Vigiliae Christianae*
WH	Westcott and Hort. Westcott, B. F., and Hort, F. J. A. *Introduction to the New Testament in the Original Greek*. New York: Harper & Brothers, 1882. Reprinted Peabody, MA: Hendrickson, 1988.
WUNT	Wissenschaftliche Untersuchungen zum Neuen Testament
ZNW	*Zeitschrift für die neutestamentliche Wissenschaft und die Kunde der älteren Kirche*
ZTK	*Zeitschrift für Theologie und Kirche*

1

THE PEN AND THE SWORD: APOLOGETIC DISCOURSE AND THE TEXT OF THE NEW TESTAMENT

Even in Roman antiquity, the pen sometimes proved mightier than the sword. With the same intentions as those sticks and stones first cast at Stephen or Saul, sharp words and piercing polemic drafted during the second and third centuries by pagan intellectuals were hurled against the early Christian movement. In a world where capital punishment could be executed in response to innuendo and rumor as swiftly as on the basis of evidence gleaned from interrogation and reliable information,[1] the negative impressions propagated among the elite and the masses by literate and vocal critics of the new faith constituted grave danger to the movement and its adherents.

In point of fact, this war of words was waged on a variety of fronts. For example, Jewish antagonists, representing the religious and cultural wellspring of Christianity, opposed the new movement on the grounds that Jesus was a sorcerer,[2] and that the new faith constituted an apostatized form of Judaism, an incorrigible prodigal child.[3] Even within Christianity itself, civil conflicts broke out in the guise of doctrinal controversies and internecine factions, later to be identified by the dominant orthodox

---

[1]See, e.g., Pliny's correspondence with Trajan, in which Pliny reports his willingness to execute Christians on the basis of protocol despite the fact that his own investigation suggested to him that Christians constituted nothing more than an innocuous superstition. *Ep.* 96. For English translations of the relevant texts and an insightful discussion of this correspondence, see also Stephen Benko, "Pagan Criticism of Christianity during the First Two Centuries A. D." *Aufstieg und Niedergang der römische Welt* II.23.2 H. Temporani and W. Haase, eds. Berlin and New York: Walter de Gruyter, 1980: 1055–1118.

[2]As reported in Justin Martyr, *Dial.* 69 and the Babylonian Talmud, *Sanhedrin* 43a. See the discussion in John P. Meier, *A Marginal Jew*, Vol. I (ABRL; New York: Doubleday, 1991), 93–98.

[3]This is a frequently plowed field. See, however, with direct relationship to this current work Eldon J. Epp, *The Theological Tendency of Codex Bezae Cantabrigiensis* (Cambridge: Cambridge University Press, 1966).

party as "heresies."[4] Nascent Christianity, however, drew perhaps its most formidable opposition from pagans and Romans, particularly from among intellectual writers.

It is with this aspect of the campaign—with the vigorous exchange that was generated by some of the greatest minds and most enduring profiles of the second, third, and fourth centuries—that this present study is most chiefly concerned. In particular, it gives attention, first of all, to those who took it upon themselves to direct criticism toward this new movement, to challenge the intellectual underpinnings of this new faith, to ridicule its narrative inconsistencies, and to accuse its lack of moral character; and, second, to those believers who assumed a posture of defense against those verbal opponents. In short, for the purposes of this present work, I am interested in the dynamic between defenders of the faith and those pagan intellectuals who hurled the gauntlet in the face of this novel religion, declaring that its idiosyncracies were to be disdained and that Christianity would not find in the Roman world—at least not among its literate elite citizens—fertile soil for the *logos spermatikos*.[5]

Those who first addressed the cultured despisers of Christianity and offered for their new faith a reasoned defense are generally identified among scholars of antiquity as Christian apologists.[6] To present such a defense, however, required these spokespersons to engage pagan intellectuals on disadvantageous ground as they attempted to argue the merits of their faith within the rational parameters and rhetorical devices of Greco-Roman philosophy.[7] This strategy was, of course, in large measure reactionary, provoked by the published criticisms of such formidable minds as Galen, Marcus Aurelius, Fronto, and Celsus, and the far-reaching negative perceptions represented in such historical works as the *Annals* of Tacitus and Suetonius' *Lives of the Emperors*, the clever satires of Lucian and Apuleius, and the official correspondence between Pliny and Trajan.

---

[4]For more on this see the classic work of Walter Bauer, *Rechtglaübigkeit und Ketzerei im ältesten Christentum*. BHT, 10 (Tübingen: J. C. B. Mohr/Paul Siebeck, 1934); English translation of Second Edition (1964, ed. by George Strecker), *Orthodoxy and Heresy in Earliest Christianity* (Trans. Robert Kraft, et al.; ed. Robert Kraft and Gerhard Krodel; Philadelphia: Fortress, 1971); and, with direct implications for this study, Bart D. Ehrman, *The Orthodox Corruption of Scripture* (New York and Oxford: Oxford University Press, 1993).

[5]This phrase belongs to Justin Martyr, although he may have been indebted for it to Philo. For the discussion see H. Chadwick, "Justin Martyr's Defence of Christianity," *BJRL* (47) 1965, 275–97, esp. 296.

[6]A useful introduction and overview to Christian apologists, particularly those most relevant to this study, belongs to Robert M. Grant, *Greek Apologists of the Second Century* (Philadelphia: Westminster, 1988).

[7]Measuring Christianity as a "philosophy," the physician Galen determined that their need for parables rather than reasoned arguments pointed to their inferiority as a philosophical school or movement. On the other hand, Galen found cause to affirm Christians for their self-discipline and courage in the face of death. For texts and discussion see Richard Walzer, *Galen on Jews and Christians* (London: Oxford University Press, 1949), 13–16.

So challenged, however, Christian advocates arose in the form of literary apologists and began, in spite of the hardships and consequences, to cultivate that unwelcoming earth. Amazingly—somewhat miraculously Justin would say—the seed sprouted and, like kudzu in southern climates, spread until, in the fourth century, it won favor with the emperor and thereby conquered his empire. Between Augustus and Constantine, however, much water would go under the bridge, much ink would be spilled, and much blood would be shed. Attacks against adherents of this new religion would be staged in two distinct spheres by two very different kinds of assailants —writers and warriors; but the dynamic between them would be symbiotic and would proceed in both directions. In no particular order, the war of words would spark the clash of kingdoms, which would further fuel the duel between the apologists and their antagonists. Pagan intellectuals would publish criticisms and satires; provincial governors would issue arrest warrants and death sentences. Still, this Jesus movement survived; and, in time, under the emblem of the cross, it conquered (*in hoc signo vinces*).

Despite the fact that history is generally written—and preserved—by the winners (eventual winners in this case), it is fortunate that the exigencies of the past have bequeathed to us direct accounts of some of the most important of these critics. Writings have endured to the present from the pens of the younger Pliny, the historians Suetonius and Tacitus, the Stoics Epictetus and Marcus Aurelius, Hadrian, Crescens, Marcus Cornelius Fronto, the satirist Lucian of Samosata, the novelist Lucius Apuleius, Aelius Aristides, the physician Galen of Pergamum, and, in the quotations of his respondent Origen, Celsus.[8]

Meanwhile, certain Christian writings were gaining popularity and authoritative status within the spreading movement. Gradually, an authoritative canon of distinctively Christian writings began forming, although the familiar twenty-seven books would not gain official canonical status until late in the fourth century.[9] Among

---

[8]Stephen Benko, "Pagan Criticism of Christianity," 1055–1118. See also Robert Wilken, *The Christians as the Romans Saw Them* (New Haven: Yale University Press, 1984).

[9]The history of the New Testament canon consists of a complex tale that has merited the abundant literature on the subject. Well into the second century, when Christians spoke of "scripture" they had in mind the Jewish sacred writings, the Tanak. In time, the letters of Paul were brought together as a collection. In an effort to codify the revered Jesus-traditions, gospels continued to be composed well into the second century, but the familiar four were held in particularly high esteem, although when Montanists began to appeal to John dispute over the Fourth Gospel arose for a time in the West. Following the Eastern disposition to exclude Revelation, only twenty-six books were recognized as canonical at the Council of Laodicea held in 363. It was not until four years later, in the Easter letter composed by Bishop Athanasius and broadcast among the churches of his jurisdiction, that the twenty-seven books current today were first prescribed as authoritative. Even then, it would remain for the Councils of Hippo in 393 and Carthage in 397 to embrace those same twenty-seven books, even after acknowledging that Hebrews was not the product of Paul's pen. For more on the New Testament canon see, e.g., the full scale treatments of Harry Y. Gamble, *The New Testament Canon: Its Making and Meaning* (Philadelphia: Fortress, 1985); and Bruce M. Metzger, *The Canon of the New Testament*

these writings, exactly four Gospels—a number Irenaeus believed to be divinely appointed—found acceptance across the church.[10] As these writings became sacred scripture, copyists became engaged in the labor of duplicating and transmitting these texts for use among the dispersed faith communities. Though less is known about these mostly anonymous scribes than is required to pen a thoroughgoing history of New Testament transmission, the legacy of their handiwork is enough to inform us of the critical role they played in the expansion of Christianity and the evolution of the New Testament.[11] Textual scholars, therefore, are compelled to study not only manuscripts and paleography, but are also required to consider the authors and copyists that produced those texts. Thus, textual criticism is not only a literary enterprise; it is also a historical discipline.

Yet, for all but the last century, laborers in this field have focused almost exclusively on the literary aspects of the task. Although the importance of historical influence on the text of the New Testament has more recently begun to generate increased interest and is generally recognized today, a measure of the resources allocated toward this aspect of textual criticism betrays that old habits die hard.

The limits of knowledge and the lack of resources notwithstanding, there is a sense in which this present project could not have come together until there was first a convergence of two luminary bodies, until the two related but separate disciplines of New Testament Textual Criticism and the History of Early Christianity began together to illuminate the primary sources that constitute the raw material of this study. In the following survey of the major scholarship that has gradually brick by brick formed a foundation for this present work, I will make an effort to trace the evolutionary process that has produced an emerging recognition that New Testament textual criticism is, in addition to its primary task as a reconstructive literary discipline, also a serviceable tool for the historian.[12] Following this *Forschungsbericht*, I will include a brief

---

(Oxford: Oxford University Press, 1987). For briefer treatments and overviews see, e.g., Harry Y. Gamble, "The Canon of the New Testament," in *The New Testament and Its Modern Interpreters*, Eldon J. Epp and George W. MacRae, eds. (Atlanta: Scholars Press, 1989), 201–43; Helmut Koester, *History and Literature of Early Christianity*, vol. 2 (New York and Berlin: Walter de Gruyter, 1987), 1–15; and the astute questions of James D. G. Dunn in his *Unity and Diversity in the New Testament: An Inquiry into the Character of Earliest Christianity* (Second Edition; London: SCM Press, 1990), 374–88.

[10]*Adv. Haer.* 3.11.8.

[11]For a useful and provocative study on scribes in antiquity see Kim Haines-Eitzen, *Guardians of Letters: Literacy, Power, and the Transmitters of Early Christian Literature* (Oxford/ New York: Oxford University Press, 2000).

[12]It is unnecessary here, however, to reinvent the wheel. Several fine *Forschungsberichte* exist already and are best deferred to rather than reworked. See especially J. Neville Birdsall, "The Recent History of New Testament Textual Criticism (from Westcott and Hort, 1881, to the Present)," *ANRW* II.26.1., 99–197; Jacobus H. Petzer, "The History of the New Testament Text—Its Reconstruction, Significance, and Use in New Testament Textual Criticism," in B. Aland and J. Delobel, eds., *New Testament Textual Criticism, Exegesis, and Church History: A*

introduction to the principle historical figures whose writings establish the parameters and contours of pagan opposition and apologetic response, before moving on in subsequent chapters to an examination of how features of this discourse show themselves in the activity of some of the parties responsible for transmitting the text of the New Testament.

SCRIBAL INTENTIONALITY AND THE NEW TESTAMENT TEXT:
A *FORSCHUNGSBERICHT*

RELEVANT TEXT-CRITICAL WORKS

The need for textual criticism of the New Testament stems from a combination of factors.[13] Most fundamental is the historical fact that the autographs, probably written on papyrus, have all perished; thus, we do not possess in any single manuscript form the "original" New Testament. In addition, during the subsequent 1400 years in which the New Testament was copied exclusively by hand and thereby transmitted, those very copyists (scribes) frequently introduced into the text (and then further transmitted) errors of accident or omission. In some instances—probably with the idea of "correcting" them—scribes also intentionally altered their exemplars.

There are now extant, in whole or in part, some 5,500 Greek manuscripts of the New Testament, almost 2400 of which contain some part of the Gospels.[14] In addition

---

Discussion of Methods (Kampen: Pharos, 1994), 11–36. Dated but rich bibliographies worth mining are located in Bruce M. Metzger, *Annotated Bibliography of the Textual Criticism of the New Testament, 1914–1939* (Copenhagen, 1955) and idem, *Chapters in the History of New Testament Textual Criticism* (Leiden and Grand Rapids, 1963). In addition to these are the overviews located in primers of textual criticism, notably Bruce M. Metzger, *The Text of the New Testament: Its Transmission, Corruption, and Restoration* (Third Enlarged Edition; New York and Oxford: Oxford University Press, 1992), Part Two, 93–146; and Kurt and Barbara Aland, *The Text of the New Testament* (Second Edition, trans. Erroll F. Rhodes; Grand Rapids, MI: Eerdmans, 1995), 3–47. See also the recent volume of essays generated in honor of Bruce M. Metzger in Bart D. Ehrman and Michael W. Holmes, eds. *The Text of the New Testament in Contemporary Research: Essays on the* Status Quaestionis (Grand Rapids, MI: Eerdmans, 1995). These essays represent the efforts of top textual scholars to summarize and report on the current state of various issues related to the discipline of New Testament textual criticism.

[13]For a fuller discussion see the primers on textual criticism by B. M. Metzger and K. and B. Aland referred to in the previous note.

[14]Exact numbers are hard to come by. "The total number of manuscripts now stands at 5,487 according to the official registry of manuscripts maintained by Aland in the Institute for New Testament Textual Research," it states in K. and B. Aland, *Text of the New Testament*, 73. More recently, D. C. Parker amended that number upward. He reports that the present catalogue consists of ninety-five papyri (forty-five of which contain Gospel material), 196 majuscules that contain Gospel material (he does not provide a total number), 2,856 minuscules (2,145 of which contain Gospel material), and 2,403 lectionaries, "the majority of which contain Gospel readings." Idem, *The Living Text of the Gospels* (Cambridge: Cambridge University Press,

there exist hundreds of copies of ancient translations of Christian scriptures (not counting over 8000 copies of the Latin Vulgate)—"Versional Witnesses" they are labeled—plus the evidence from the citations of the New Testament in the writings of early church fathers. In practical terms, however, these constitute a poverty of riches, for—except for the smallest fragments—no two manuscripts anywhere in existence are exactly alike.[15]

The task of the textual critic, therefore, initially, is to sift through all this material, carefully collating each manuscript or source with all the others. This is done in order to detect and recognize possible errors and changes in the text, with an eye toward determining which variant reading at any given point is more likely to be the "original."[16]

Textual criticism, then, is typically identified, as in these words of Gordon Fee, as "the science that compares all known manuscripts of a given work in an effort to trace the history of variations within the given text so as to discover its original form."[17] Fee further recognizes that textual criticism interests the biblical interpreter in at least three ways. First, textual criticism attempts to determine the authentic words of the author. The question the exegete must ask prior to "What does the text mean?" is "What does the text say?" Secondly, since most readers have access to the text only in translation, a translator's first concern must be that she or he is translating the actual words the author wrote. Third, a knowledge of the history of textual variation will also help the

---

1997), 8–13

[15]Bart D. Ehrman, *The New Testament: A Historical Introduction to the Early Christian Writings* (Second Edition; New York and Oxford: Oxford University Press, 2000), 443.

[16]Yet, some practitioners of this discipline, for good reason, deny the possibility of obtaining the "original" text. For a forthright and compelling discussion of the problems related to the term "original" and the historical restrictions that limit the text scholars can realistically reconstruct see William L. Petersen, "What Text Can New Testament Textual Criticism Ultimately Reach?" in *New Testament Textual Criticism, Exegesis, and Early Church History*, B. Aland and J. Delobel, eds. (Kampen: Pharos, 1994), 136–52. In that same volume see also Jacobus Petzer, "The History of the New Testament Text—Its Reconstruction, Significance and Use in New Testament Textual Criticism," 11–36, where he notes that the identity of the "original" text has not received its due attention within the practice of the discipline, and adds, "What is certain, is that we are not reconstructing the "autographs," for New Testament scholarship is slowly but certainly coming to realize that "autograph" is a much more complex concept than generally anticipated" (36). In regard for the complexities of this issue, I will throughout this work distinguish this use of the term "original" by enclosing it within quotation marks.

[17]Gordon Fee, "Textual Criticism of the New Testament," in Eldon Epp and Gordon Fee, eds. *Studies in the Theory and Method of New Testament Textual Criticism.* (Grand Rapids, MI: Eerdmans, 1993), 3. Over the years textual criticism has commonly been known as "lower" criticism in contrast to the so-called "higher" (historical and literary) criticism. Although this distinction was intended to refer to the foundational nature of textual criticism, i.e., that one cannot analyze a text literarily or historically until one has determined what that text is, in practice textual criticism was frequently looked upon as a necessary but tedious and underappreciated sub-specialty of New Testament studies.

interpreter see how a passage was understood during the early history of the church. In many instances variant readings are a reflection of a scribe's or a church's theological interests, and sometimes such changes put one in direct contact with historical exegesis.

It is Fee's third point that represents a presumably secondary task for the textual critic, but one which is steadily gaining attention within the discipline. For example, Eldon Epp, in his appraisal of the influence of history upon text, declared, "For too long the text of the New Testament has been conceived in static terms."[18] In the fashion of a storm, he described the tumultuous context in which the text arose, and insisted that copies of New Testament books were circulating within these complex situations and were interactive with them.

> It is within this background of dynamic movement, development, and controversy that the earliest New Testament manuscripts must be examined, for—as has long been asserted but too little exercised—the text of the NT in its earliest stages was a vibrant, living text that functioned dynamically within the developing church. Textual criticism, therefore, can never be understood apart from the history of the church.[19]

This added impulse within the discipline, however, did not begin to bud until the early part of the twentieth century.

Prior to 1881, textual criticism was dominated by the Elzivir edition of Erasmus' 1516 collation of the Greek New Testament, the so-called "Textus Receptus" (TR). To be sure, there were occasional forays against that dominance, as attested by the pioneering efforts of Johannes Albrecht Bengel (1687–1752) and J. J. Griesbach (1745–1812), both of whom published important editions of the Greek New Testament. Although Bengel (1734) for the most part reproduced the text of Erasmus, he introduced a critical apparatus that classified and evaluated variant readings. On this basis, some scholars credit him with the birth of modern scientific textual criticism.[20] Griesbach's edition (1775–77) was noteworthy because it departed, for the first time in Germany, from dependence on the TR. For the most part, however, whatever fresh insights crept into the discipline were usually the result of newly discovered manuscripts unearthed by such pioneers as Constantine von Tischendorf (1815–1874).

---

[18]Eldon J. Epp, "The Significance of the Papyri for Determining the Nature of the New Testament Text in the Second Century: A Dynamic View of Textual Transmission," in William Petersen, ed. *Gospel Traditions of the Second Century* (Notre Dame and London: University of Notre Dame Press, 1989), 75. For later reference, it should be noted that here Epp contends against the position of Kurt Aland that there existed by the early third century three identifiable text-types.

[19]E. Epp, "Significance of the Papyri," 75.

[20]See, e.g., their informing comparison of the relative contributions of Bengel and Griesbach, which conclude to the advantage of Bengel, in K. and B. Aland, *Text of the New Testament*, 9–11. But for the view that the importance of Griesbach cannot be overestimated see B. M. Metzger, *Text of the New Testament*, 119–121.

Although the true measure of Tischendorf's labors on behalf of the enterprise of New Testament textual criticism can never be calculated fully, most scholars agree that his fame rests more upon his collection of textual evidence than in his compiled editions. Still, the critical apparatus of his final edition of *Novum Testamentum Graece, editio octava critica maior* remains unsurpassed, probably not to be finally outdone until the completion of the apparatus being assembled under the auspices of the International Greek New Testament Project (IGNTP).

In that watershed year of 1881, however, after twenty-eight years of collaborative labor, Fenton John Anthony Hort and Brooke Foss Westcott published a bold new edition they brashly labeled "The New Testament in the Original Greek," a version based on a much more numerous and widely diverse collection of manuscripts than had been at the disposal of Erasmus. Published the following year to accompany this new compilation was an *Introduction* that articulated the theoretical foundation underpinning their work and that proved to be a trail blazing epic.[21] Their masterful knowledge and treatment of the documents, arduous attention to detail, creative assertion of ground-breaking theory, and eloquent prose represented a pinnacle of scholarship seldom attained in any discipline, and certainly one that cast a redefining spell upon New Testament textual criticism, the influence of which continues to the present.

Despite their erudition and methodological precision, however, the work of Westcott and Hort was plagued by two ill-determined presuppositions. One was their veneration of their so-called "Neutral" text, which in large measure consisted of the confluence of the Codices Sinaiticus (ℵ) and Vaticanus (B). So devoted to this textual tradition were they that, when confronted with a few shorter texts in the "Western" tradition that appeared "original" with respect to the modified Neutral readings, they could not bring themselves to label them as "Neutral Interpolations" or "Non-Western Interpolations," but gave them the clumsy appellation, "Western Non-interpolations."[22]

A second and, for this project, more misleading assertion consisted of their sure pronouncement that

---

[21]B. F. Westcott and F. J. A. Hort, *Introduction to the New Testament in the Original Greek* (Peabody, MA: Hendrickson, 1988; Originally published in New York: Harper & Brothers, 1882).

[22]Discussions on the topic of "Western Non-Interpolations" have become a cottage industry for textual scholars. Several of these readings will be considered in the frame of this study. For a sampler of treatments see Westcott and Hort, *Introduction*, 175–77; B. M. Metzger, *Text*, 134; Kurt Aland, "Die Bedeutung des P^{75} für den Text des Neuen Testaments: Ein Beitrag zur Frage des 'Western non-interpolations,'" in *Studien zur Überlieferung des Neuen Testaments und seines Textes*, Kurt Aland, ed. (Berlin: Walter de Gruyter, 1967), 155–72 and idem and Barbara Aland, *Text*, 33, 37, 236, 311 (both of which offer a consistently negative appraisal of WH throughout); Joseph A. Fitzmyer, *The Gospel According to Luke (I–IX)* (AB 28; Garden City, NY: Doubleday, 1981), 130–31; and Bart D. Ehrman, *The Orthodox Corruption of Scripture* (New York and London: Oxford University Press, 1993), 223–28.

there are no signs of deliberate falsification of the text for dogmatic purposes. The license of paraphrase occasionally assumes the appearance of wilful corruption, where scribes allowed themselves to change language which they thought capable of dangerous misconstruction; or attempted to correct apparent errors which they doubtless assumed to be due to previous transcription; or embodied in explicit words a meaning which they supposed to be implied....Accusations of wilful tampering are accordingly not unfrequent in Christian antiquity: but, with a single exception [later identified as Marcion], wherever they can be verified they prove to be groundless, being in fact hasty and unjust inferences from mere diversities of inherited text.[23]

Here Hort, the chief architect of the Introduction and the greater genius behind the project, leaned too far in the conservative direction. In playing his hand so close to the vest, he wagered wrongly that scribes constituted benign participants in the transmission of the New Testament text. It will be seen again in the course of this study, as has been ably demonstrated previously by others, that scribes were sentient beings living in a world that was hostile to the text they were charged with duplicating. Usually, to be sure, they carried out their work as passive transmitters; it has even been shown that a copyist could presumably reproduce a text even when he could not read or understand it.[24] Sometimes, however, scribes took on the unsupervised role of creative consultant, and transposed their exemplars in accord with a tune pulsating in their minds. Thus, in the same sense that "the hand that rocks the cradle is the hand that rules the world," from the perspective of the historian, the scribe's pen was mightier than the evangelist's word. No autograph has survived the exigencies of history. Only transmitted copies of the Christian scriptures have made their way into the third millennium. It is the products of scribes, not those of the evangelists, that have endured.

Still, until the turn of the century, textual critics were driven almost exclusively by the singular ambition to reconstruct the "original" text of the New Testament. Like accountants poring over spreadsheets, scholars collated manuscripts, scrolled, screened and scrutinized variants according to the canons of the discipline and in light of external evidence and internal probabilities, and, all too finally, selected one reading as the most likely representative of the autograph. All the rest of the variants were summarily dismissed, like so many wood chips at a carpenter's bench, as scribal

---

[23]WH, 282–3. To be fair to Hort, though, he was able to acknowledge, at least, that "dogmatic preferences to a great extent determined theologians, and probably scribes, in their choice between rival readings already in existence" (283). It would have been a short walk, then, had a scholar of the magnitude of Hort been confronted with some of the evidence and studies in currency today for him to have reversed his path on this position. Also on this quote by Hort, see the insightful discussion of Hort on this point in Epp, *Theological Tendency*, 1–4.

[24]See Kim Haines-Eitzen, *Guardians of Letters*, e.g. 36, particularly with reference to her discussion of the visionary command given the Shepherd of Hermas to copy a book and his response that "...I copied everything letter by letter because I could not find the syllables" (*Shep.*, *vis.* 2.1.4).

infelicities. Scribes were viewed as disinterested copyists, albeit very human ones, capable of errors of omission and commission born of fatigue, tedium, and visual or mental lapses.

As early as 1904, scholars began to question the assertion of Westcott and Hort and sense the potential value of examining such scribal debris for the clues it might offer.[25] J. Rendel Harris was a leader among those, and his treatment of certain variant readings began to challenge Hort's claim to a lack of dogmatic influence on the transmission of the New Testament text. In the early part of the twentieth century he published two articles in which he identified variant readings that he argued were the product of theological concerns and anti-Jewish attitudes.[26] For example, Harris discerned in the scribal changes to Luke 4:16 a clear example where dogmatic (Marcionite) influence had left an enduring mark on the text, and he followed Vogels in arguing that Jesus' prayer of forgiveness from the cross (Luke 23:34) owed its secondary excision to an anti-Judaic reaction prevalent in the second century.[27] Such evidence led Harris to voice with astute candor:

> The evangelical stream is demonstrably discolored by the media through which it passes. The Bible of any given church becomes affected by the church in which it circulates. The people who handle the text leave their finger-prints on the pages, and the trained detective can identify the criminal who made the marks.[28]

For generations, however, scholarship was slow to advance the baton past the quarter run by Harris. One notable exception was Burnett Hillman Streeter, who published in 1924 the first of eleven impressions of his classic work, *The Four Gospels.*[29] Although this volume is best known for its influential treatment of the Synoptic

---

[25]Kirsopp Lake, *The Influence of Textual Criticism on the Exegesis of the New Testament* (Oxford: Parker and Sons, 1904), 1–27. This small book consists of Lake's inaugural lecture at the University of Leiden, delivered on January 27, 1904. Best known as the lecture in which he called Westcott and Hort's efforts to construct the "Original Greek" of the New Testament text "a failure, though a splendid one," the substance of the lecture dealt with a series of variant readings which he argued were the products of doctrinally motivated adaptation on the part of scribes. Specifically, Lake brings into question the Trinitarian baptismal formula in Matthew 28:19, as well as two other texts that prescribe baptism as incumbent for Christian initiates: Mark 16:16 (a spurious text) and John 3:5 (with regard to which Lake argues that "of water and" have been added to the verse to impose baptismal doctrine on the verse). I confine this material to the notes because it is not directly related to apologetic interests, but I preserve it nevertheless for its keen insight.

[26]J. Rendel Harris, "New Points of View in Textual Criticism," *The Expositor* 8/7 (1914) 316–34; and idem, "Was the Diatessaron Anti-Judaic?" *HTR* 18 (1925) 103–09.

[27]J. R. Harris, *HTR*, 104 and 106.

[28]J. R. Harris, *HTR*, 103.

[29]B. H. Streeter, *The Four Gospels: A Study of Origins Treating of the Manuscript Tradition, Sources, Authorship, and Dates* (London: Macmillan, 1924; Eleventh Edition; New York: St. Martin's Press, 1964).

Problem, Streeter sought to lay the foundation for his arguments in an interface of
specialities, including textual criticism, source analysis, and the cultural background of
early Christianity.[30] With a strategy not unlike that later used by Walter Bauer in
Orthodoxy and Heresy, the first tool Streeter employed in his analysis of textual traditions
was a map. He proposed a theory of "local texts," in which he associated specific
textual traditions with particular localities, usually major urban centers important to
Christianity. Streeter, along with Kirsopp Lake and his associates, was largely
responsible for identifying the "Caesarean" text, of which Codex Koridethi (Θ) was
said to be its best representative.[31] In prefaces to subsequent editions of his magnum
opus, Streeter discussed how recent manuscript discoveries and scholarship had served
to confirm their notions about the Caesarean text. He labored also, with the utmost
respect for the epoch-making character of the accomplishments of Westcott and Hort,
to refine and correct their work. For example, where they labeled as "Neutral" the
textual tradition represented by Sinaiticus (ℵ) and Vaticanus (B), Streeter identified it
as the local text of Alexandria.[32]

Streeter discerned that there existed a symbiotic connection between the history
of the text, the establishment of the canon, and the formulation of doctrine. On the
basis of this inseparable association, Streeter asserted that three questions always face
the textual critic:

> (1) He must account for the great divergence between the types of text current in the
> second, third and fourth centuries. (2) He must explain the origin of the Byzantine
> standard text and the process by which it replaced the other types. (3) Finally, in the
> light of the conclusions reached on these two points, he must endeavour to
> determine which of these types of text, or what kind of combination of them, will
> represent most nearly the text of the Gospels as they left the hands of their several
> authors. The third problem is of course much the most important; but he cannot
> hope to solve it rightly unless he has first found a reasonably satisfactory solution to
> the other two.[33]

Represented in Streeter's work, then, was a clear sense that any investigation into
the textual tradition of the New Testament, the development of the Christian canon,
or the evolution of the church necessitated, in fact, the study of a mutual history.

D. W. Riddle also saw the wisdom of treating textual criticism as a historical
enterprise as well as a literary labor.[34] Heralding with bold expression a view ahead of
its time, Riddle asserted:

---

[30]B. H. Streeter, *Four Gospels*, xxvii.
[31]B. H. Streeter, *Four Gospels*, vii–x, 77–107.
[32]B. H. Streeter, *Four Gospels*, 27 f., 54–64. See p. 34, for his estimation of Hort, about
whom he states, "There is no greater name in the history of Textual Criticism."
[33]B. H. Streeter, *Four Gospels*, 30–31.
[34]D. W. Riddle, "Textual Criticism as a Historical Discipline," *AngThR* 18 (1936) 220–33.

The legitimate task of textual criticism is not limited to the recovery of approximately the original form of the documents, to the establishment of the "best" text, nor to the "elimination of spurious readings." It must be recognized that every significant variant records a religious experience which brought it into being. This means that there are no "spurious readings": the various forms of the text are sources for the study of the history of Christianity.[35]

The train of thought put into motion by Harris and fueled by Riddle gained added momentum near the middle of the century. During the Schweich Lectures he delivered in 1946, Günther Zuntz in rendering an appraisal of the current state of textual criticism, declared, "The recovery of the original text, if it is to be attempted scientifically, depends upon the illumination of its history in the second century."[36] A. F. J. Klijn, in 1949, similarly insisted that no final judgment could be made on the original text "until each reading in it was checked for its linguistic, tendentious, or other peculiarities."[37] During that same decade, E. L. Titus completed his unpublished but frequently cited dissertation in which he investigated what motivations lay behind modifications made to the New Testament by two early Greek apologists, Justin and Clement of Alexandria.[38]

The fifties saw others once again hoist the banner previously borne by Riddle. C. S. C. Williams introduced his study of variant readings in the Synoptic Gospels and Acts with the statement, "The possibility that many of the variant readings of the text of our New Testament are due to intentional alteration by scribes does not seem to have received the attention that it deserves."[39] In the course of his study he attributed certain variant readings to various motivations, including harmonization, grammar and style, clarification, the effort to avoid offense, and various tendentious or reverential purposes. Merrill Parvis identified all variant readings (here he was not referring to accidents or errors) to be products of Christian thought and therefore clues to its history. He went so far as to label them "interpretations," and he noted that they were considered significant enough somewhere by someone to be incorporated into the

---

[35]D. W. Riddle, "Textual Criticism as a Historical Discipline," 221.

[36]G. Zuntz, *The Text of the Epistles: A Disquisition Upon the Corpus Paulinum* (London: Oxford University Press, 1953), 11.

[37]A. F. J. Klijn, *A Survey of the Researches into the Western Text of the Gospels and Acts* (Utrecht, 1949), 168.

[38]E. L. Titus, "The Motivation of Changes Made in the New Testament Text by Justin Martyr and Clement of Alexandria: A Study in the Origin of New Testament Variation" (Unpublished Ph.D. thesis, University of Chicago, 1942).

[39]C. S. C. Williams, *Alterations to the Text of the Synoptic Gospels and Acts* (Oxford: Basil Blackwell, 1951). Williams also contributed an in-depth treatment of a number of significant variant readings, many of which possess relevance for this study and will be discussed in context below.

sacred scriptures.[40] He even theorized the possibility of realigning textual affinities on the basis of certain specific doctrines reflected within the manuscripts.

That same year Leon Wright went to press with a study of modifications to the words of Jesus as they were presented in various second-century writings, including apostolic fathers and Christian apologists.[41] Wright classified his findings under the following headings: Prudential Motivation, Contextual Adaptation, Harmonistic, Stylistic, Explanatory, Ethical and Practical, Dogmatic, and Heretical Adaptation. Each category represented for him a motivating force that had been at work reshaping the New Testament voice of Jesus. In preparing his readers for what they would find in his book, Wright declared, "We shall observe in this material, also, the ubiquitous operation of special interests competing for priority in the maturing life of the Christian church."[42]

The impact such studies were making on the field had not overtaken the field, but they were gaining ground. On one hand, as late as the sixties, there continued to appear in primers on the New Testament and on Textual Criticism statements that echoed the sentiments of Hort.[43] To illustrate, wrote Harold Greenlee, "No Christian doctrine...hangs upon a debatable text."[44] On the other hand, this decade produced works that were giving greater attention and increasing importance to the historical implications of textual studies. Kenneth W. Clark's published presidential address to the 1965 meeting of the Society of Biblical Literature serves as a case in point.[45] He declared that, although scribes should not be accused of falsification and fraud, the insistence that textual variation never resulted from the influence of doctrinal interests upon scribes represented a "false assurance."[46] Clark went on to identify the phantom nature of the "original" text, arguing that such a text never existed in such a way as to

---

[40]Merrill M. Parvis, "The Nature and Tasks of New Testament Textual Criticism: An Appraisal," *JRel* 32 (1952), 165–74, esp. 172.

[41]Leon Wright, *Alterations of the Words of Jesus As Quoted in the Literature of the Second Century* (Cambridge, MA: Harvard University Press, 1952).

[42]L. Wright, *Alterations to the Words of Jesus*, 13.

[43]See, e.g., J. Harold Greenlee, *Introduction to New Testament Textual Criticism* (Grand Rapids, MI: Eerdmans, 1964); Howard C. Kee, Franklin W. Young, and Karlfried Froelich, *Understanding the New Testament* (2nd edition; Englewood Cliffs, NJ: Prentice-Hall, 1965).

[44]J. H. Greenlee, *Introduction to New Testament Textual Criticism*, 68.

[45]Kenneth W. Clark, "The Theological Relevance of Textual Variation in Current Criticism of the Greek New Testament," *JBL* 85 (1966) 1–16.

[46]K. W. Clark stated:

Many of the denials that textual variation is harmful to the faith are truly denials of allegations never made. We can agree with Hort that "perceptible fraud" is not evident in textual alteration....But these are heinous faults we should never allege and these are not the terms that we should employ. Willful and deliberate, yes. But not tampering, falsification, and fraud. Alteration, yes; but not corruption. Emendation, yes; but not in bad faith.

Idem, "Theological Relevance of Textual Variation," 5.

become established and fixed. Moreover he joined those who recognized the historically revealing significance of those readings determined *not* to be the "original."

> The textual critic must recognize the fluidity and theological vitality in Scriptural accounts, and move on from isolated words to the broader context....Furthermore, our attention to original text must not eclipse the valuable theological insight in textual deviation early and late.[47]

Clark saw this opportunity as a call to reorganize the labors of the distinct disciplines of textual criticism, ecclesiastical history, and theological studies into more collaborative enterprises.

Relevant and useful insights materialized from corners outside textual criticism, as well. Many of the ideas C. F. D. Moule expressed with regard to *Tendenzkritik* and Form Criticism may apply equally well to certain scribal modifications. I am thinking here of his statement:

> If it can be established that a document was written with a clear propagandistic purpose, then it becomes probable (other things being equal) that its writer bent the facts, or made a tendentious selection from among them, to fit his purpose; and it is therefore necessary to make allowances for such distortion, in any attempt to get back to the truth about what actually happened. Accordingly, a question of prime importance for the historian in interpreting a document and estimating its worth is, What was this document for? What did its author hope to achieve by it? [48]

Moule's questions may be especially useful if redirected to those textual variants determined to be intentional in origin. After all, an intentional variant, it may be argued, is no longer the act of a scribe but an author. In considering transcriptional probabilities, then, the textual critic should do more than measure the greater likelihood of scribal activity; she or he should also consider the breadth of options for why that scribe may have composed that reading. Although it is inevitable that some conjecture will creep into the calculus, in many cases the hypothesis can be weighed against more reliable constants. As will be seen in the course of this study, I have made an effort to balance conjectural possibilities with reasoned plausibilities and, in a few important cases, transparent certainties. As a further example, Moule explains the form critical principle that when the apparent purpose in the life of the church of a specific form unit appears to be apologetic or propagandistic, then "one must reckon with the possibility that the contents of the unit were shaped and modified so as to enhance its force: the size of a miracle or the effect of a polemical saying may be exaggerated; and so forth."[49]

---

[47]K. W. Clark, "Theological Relevance of Textual Variation," 16.
[48]C. F. D. Moule, "Some Observations on *Tendenzkritik*," in Ernst Bammel and idem, eds. *Jesus and the Politics of His Day* (Cambridge: Cambridge University Press, 1984), 91.
[49]C. F. D. Moule, "Some Observations on *Tendenzkritik*," 91–100.

By 1966 the stars finally achieved complete alignment when Eldon J. Epp presided over the union of Textual Criticism and Early Christian History in the publication of his study of the text of Acts in Codex Bezae Cantabrigiensis.[50] In reporting the findings of his full-scale investigation into what he perceived to be a theological tendency in Codex D, Epp argued that nearly forty percent of the variant readings in this codex's reproduction of Luke's second volume could be attributed to an anti-Judaic bias.

Epp's contention, though carefully configured and thoughtfully argued, was not embraced by the academy with unanimous consent. C. K. Barrett, for example, revisited Epp's thesis and concluded that he overstated the case. First of all, Barrett claimed that many of the modifications to Acts located in Codex D could best be explained as efforts "simply to increase interest, heighten tension, to make descriptions more vivid, in a word, to brighten the colours of Luke's narrative, where no theological, ecclesiastical, racial, or any such interest in involved."[51] Second, in disagreeing with Epp's particular claim of locating in Bezae an anti-Judaic tendency, Barrett asserted that the tendency to anti-Judaism resides already in Luke, and that the essential characteristic of Codex D is its tendency to exaggerate tendencies that already exist in the text. In this sense, Barrett believed, the canonical text of Acts in Bezae shared much in common with the apocryphal Acts.

In my judgment, Barrett's detailed reflection serves us well in issuing a caveat with regard to the temptation to reduce or define the product of any single scribe or Codex or text-type to any single tendency or bias. Moreover, we must be wary of simply finding what we go out searching for, whether that be scribal products born of anti-Judaic tendencies or those wrought by apologetic interests. That said, there are times when Barrett's disagreement with Epp seems semantic if not superficial. Epp is not attempting to restrict all anti-Judaic language to the scribe responsible for Codex Bezae; what he is trying to do is gather a number of variant readings that, in his estimation, can be explained best as the result of an anti-Judaic bias on the part of the copyist. Like Barrett, some scholars may take exception to his treatment of a particular variant, but there is hardly sufficient reason to dismiss his thesis. Indeed, for the most part, current scholarship continues to refer to Epp's volume with due recognition of its insights. Some scribes in the act of transcribing the text of the New Testament did, in fact, alter their exemplars out of some conscious bias or deliberate motive, and, as Epp's research sufficiently shows, one of these conscious motives leading some copyists to "corrupt" the text was that of an anti-Judaic bias. Epp's work is best understood, as he himself says, as seeking to uncover reasons for deviations within the

---

[50]Eldon J. Epp, *The Theological Tendency of Codex Cantabrigiensis in Acts* (Cambridge: Cambridge University Press, 1966).

[51]C. K. Barrett, "Is There a Theological Tendency in Codex Bezae?" in *Text and Interpretation; Studies in the New Testament presented to Matthew Black.* Ernest Best and R. McL. Wilson, eds. (Cambridge: Cambridge University Press, 1979), 15–27. The quotation stems from p. 22.

broader work of reconstructing the history of the transmission of the text. Thus, he states that, even if the "original" text of the New Testament was suddenly located, the discipline of textual criticism would not cease.

> But with variant texts, there would remain the valid task of tracing the development of the variants in the history of textual transmission and of attempting to uncover reasons for the deviations. After all, these variant texts were for some Christians at some time and place the "original" text; it would be a denial of history to ignore them under any circumstances.[52]

This fresh collaboration between historical inquiry and textual criticism has also provided illumination for recent investigation into the relationship of women to the early church. Current scholarship generally agrees that, although the early church admitted women into positions of authority and leadership, by early in the second century a concerted effort was under way within evolving Christianity to suppress women.[53] Investigation into a number of textual variants shows support for this contention. For example, Elisabeth Schüssler Fiorenza cites a number of passages from Acts that betray an agenda on the part of some scribes to reconfigure by way of reduction the place of women in the stories of Christian scripture.[54] Also, two brief but important studies by Ben Witherington have exposed additional textual data that reflects this bias against women.[55] For example, Witherington argues that the shift in pronoun from singular to plural by some copyists of Luke 8:3 represents a deliberate effort on the part of some scribes to redefine the role of the women listed there. Rather than being persons who served "him" (Jesus) as his financial benefactors, the reassignment of their service to "them" (the disciples) relegated the women to more traditional roles within the home and as caretakers of "the menfolk."

Another of these interdisciplinary studies has shown that internecine theological controversies also affected the transmission of the New Testament text. In his 1993 monograph entitled *The Orthodox Corruption of Scripture*, Bart Ehrman demonstrated with compelling force that a large number of variant readings in the canonical text were the products of scribes attuned to the christological controversies of the second and third centuries.[56] He argued that scores of intentional readings were generated in direct

---

[52]E. J. Epp, *Theological Tendency*, 13.

[53]See, e.g., Karen Jo Torjesen, *When Women Were Priests: Women's Leadership in the Early Church and the Scandal of their Subordination in the Rise of Christianity* (San Francisco: HarperSanFrancisco, 1993).

[54]E. S. Fiorenza, *In Memory of Her* (New York: Crossroad, 1994).

[55]Ben Witherington, "On the Road with Mary Magdalene, Joanna, Susanna, and Other Disciples—Luke 8:1–3," *ZNW* 70 (1979), 243–48; and idem, "The Anti-Feminist Tendency in the Western Text in Acts," *JBL* 103 (March, 1984) 82–84.

[56]Bart D. Ehrman, *The Orthodox Corruption of Scripture: The Effect of Early Christological Controversies on the Text of the New Testament* (New York and London: Oxford University Press, 1993).

response to various "heresies," and could thus be recognized and classified on the basis of their precipitating motivation as anti-docetic, anti-separationist, anti-adoptionist, and anti-patripassianist. Based on his study, he concluded that copiers of the text who subscribed to "proto-orthodox" beliefs altered the text to make it say what they already thought it meant.[57] That same year, Peter Head discussed a series of variant readings that he argued reflected what he called "a reverential motivation" on the part of the scribes who generated them.[58]

Even more recently, D. C. Parker contributed a volume dedicated to underscoring and understanding the causes behind "the incidence of conscious alteration to the text."[59] One of the many fruitful avenues he pursued in this book was his insistence that the responsibilities assigned text critics must not be restricted to the singular purpose of reconstructing the "original" New Testament. For him,

> The task of textual criticism consists of collecting evidence and evaluating it. Its contribution in gathering information about early Christian documents is beyond question. It is evidently important then to discern the appropriate question and ask it of the data.[60]

This insistence of Parker that textual critics must evaluate as well as collect textual evidence has been taken to heart in the pages that follow. Indeed, the textual data adduced in this volume consists of nothing new; textual critics before me have uncovered the manuscript evidence and variant readings that will be considered. What *is* new here, however, is the set of questions that will be posed to this data for the purpose of scrutiny and discovery. Driving all of them is this question: "Are any of the variant readings located in the canonical Gospels best explained as the product of scribes acting intentionally to modify their exemplars under the influence of apologetic interests?" The constellation of variants that have been adduced here along with the arguments I have contributed offer in response to this question a resounding yes. Moreover, I seek to demonstrate that apologetic motivation was not an insignificant influence on the New Testament text. Such a study, however, presses us beyond the confines of the discipline of textual criticism, and requires us to explore also something about the dynamics that existed between pagan critics and early Christian apologists.

---

[57]Ehrman employs the term "proto-orthodox" in an effort to avoid any sense of historical determinism, and, by it, simply means those ideological progenitors of the doctrinal stances that had not yet but would subsequently come to occupy the dominant theological position of the Church, and thereby achieve the claim to "orthodoxy." For his more detailed discussion of the issues related to nomenclature see idem, *Orthodox Corruption*, 11–15 and 37, n. 43.

[58]Peter Head, "Christology and Textual Transmission: Reverential Alterations in the Synoptic Gospels," *NovT* 35 (1993) 105–29.

[59]D. C. Parker, *The Living Text of the Gospels*, 2.

[60]D. C. Parker, *The Living Text of the Gospels*, 7.

RELEVANT WRITINGS PERTAINING TO EARLY CHRISTIAN APOLOGETICS

Alongside these developments within textual criticism, important studies were also appearing related to the field of the History of Early Christianity and, in particular, Christian apologetics, particularly in Europe. In time, some of these proved to be harbingers of an approaching convergence of disciplines. The year 1907 produced two major studies in Germany that became immediate standards. Johannes Geffcken issued *Zwei griechischen Apologeten*, which consisted of critical editions for the apologetic works of Athenagoras and Aristides, the two Greek apologists of the title, but added to his edition his own composite of the historical setting out of which these works were issued.[61] That same year the academic giant Walter Bauer released a probing study of how the narrative of the life of Jesus evolved in the early church, particularly during the period of the New Testament apocrypha.[62]

The year 1934 welcomed the completion by Pierre Champagne de Labriolle of a magisterial work that represented the first thoroughgoing treatment of the pagan intellectual response to nascent Christianity.[63] Labriolle's thorough investigation into the sources demonstrated that the earliest decades of the Christian movement elicited very little interest or response—in fact, virtually no mention at all—from pagan intellectual circles. The fastidious social observers of the day, Martial and Juvenal, he noted, never even mentioned Christians. The second half of the second century, however, began to see a change.

Here he described how pagan indifference to the Jesus movement soon begot discomfort and sarcasm, and, in time, bred an all-out assault, both polemical and political, against adherents of the new faith. Concerned pleas for conformity gave way to harsh tirades of rational criticism and bitter accusation. By this time, the Christian movement showed signs of vitality across the empire. Conservative intellectuals like Celsus, who prized the Roman order, began to see the dangers inherent in the movement. He recognized that the new faith had continued to spread despite public ridicule and persecution, and came to believe that the only way to put an end to this infectious malady was to expose its presumably sandy foundations to the storm of informed assault. Although Labriolle concentrated his narrative on Celsus, Porphyry, and Julian, he also managed to locate others to go along with the usual suspects.

Much more could be said about Labriolle, but the constraints of this study demand summary. For our purposes, it is important to recognize that it was Labriolle who first carved into the stem of historical inquiry the contextual contours onto which one could graft the writings of pagan critics like Celsus and Porphyry. Also, with direct bearing on this present work, Labriolle recognized that Celsus, and, to an even greater

---

[61]Johannes Geffcken, *Zwei griechischen Apologeten* (Leipzig and Berlin: Teubner, 1907).

[62]Walter Bauer, *Das Leben Jesu im Zeitalter der neutestamentlichen Apocryphen* (Tübingen: Mohr (Siebeck), 1907; Reprinted, Darmstadt: Wissenschaftliche Buchgesellschaft, 1967).

[63]Pierre de Labriolle, *La Réaction païenne: Étude sur la polémique antichrétienne du Ier au VI e siècle* (Paris: L'Artisan du Livre, 1934).

extent, Porphyry were well acquainted with New Testament writings, and he further realized that apologetic respondents to such informed critics required, at times, a defense of the scriptures.[64] Labriolle, as we shall observe below in treating his discussion of Origen's response to pagan criticism related to the reported eclipse at Jesus' crucifixion, even wandered at points into text-critical grounds.[65]

Henry Chadwick's critically-acclaimed 1953 translation of Origen's *Contra Celsum* not only included an informative introduction and valuable footnotes, but it also inspired the ground-breaking study by Carl Andresen, *Logos und Nomos*.[66] The fresh contribution of Andresen was to juxtapose the works of Celsus and Justin, recognize how their work was similarly informed by middle Platonism, and draw upon that philosophical background to gain nuances into both of these important second century writers. His investigation brought him to the conclusion that in large measure Celsus had written Ἀληθὴς Λόγος as a direct response to the arguments forged by Justin. Parts of this volume read like an exegesis of Celsus' *True Doctrine* interpreted through the lens of middle Platonism. Andresen summarized the arguments of Celsus under four main points. As the first of these, consisting of Books I.28–II.79, he recognized Celsus' contrary stance against the Christian contention that Jesus was a son of God; he insisted that Jesus was only a man (*nur ein Mensch*). Second, recapitulating the content of Books III–IV, Andresen took note of Celsus' charge that Christianity was, in fact, the product of a split with Judaism and constituted a new religion, one that lacked an adequate foundation ("...*das Christentum keine 'der Sache angemessene Grundlage' hat.*"). Here Celsus articulated his great disfavor with the practice of Christian missionaries (*Missionspraxis*) in propagating features of an oriental doctrine that stood in sharp relief to the teachings of the ancient and timeless truths (*alte Logos*) which Celsus believed lay at the foundation of all human civilization. This led to the third *Hauptteil*, featured in Books V.2–VII.61, in which Celsus turned his attention to the dogma—the *Nomos* of Andresen's title—of the new religion. Christianity appeared to Celsus as a perversion (*Abart*), Andresen stated, on the basis that although Christians claimed to be monotheists, in practice, they worshiped two deities. It was in his analysis of this section that Andresen summarized Celsus' appraisal of the new religion as a world without reason (*Welt ohne Logos*) and a world without dogma (*Welt ohne Nomos*). Celsus argued that Christians behaved out of a misunderstanding of Greek wisdom. Christians lacked *Logos* and *Nomos* because they had rejected the perennial truths of the ancients. Finally, Books VII.62–VIII.75 constituted the fourth and final section of the work, in which Celsus confronted believers for rejecting their duty to tradition (*Bilderdienst*) and the popular cult (*Dämonenkult*).[67]

---

[64]P. Labriolle, *La Réaction païenne*, e.g., 128 and 251–56.

[65]P. Labriolle, *La Réaction païenne*, 204–220.

[66]Henry Chadwick, *Origen: Contra Celsum* (Oxford: Clarendon Press, 1953). Carl Andresen, *Logos und Nomos: Die Polemik des Kelsos wider das Christentum* (Berlin: Walter de Gruyter, 1955).

[67]C. Andresen, *Logos und Nomos*, 39–43.

Andresen recognized that Celsus shared much in the way of world view with the Christian apologist Justin. Both, he believed, embraced a common philosophical underpinning, which he identified as middle Platonism. Both shared an understanding of such concepts as Logos and Nomos. Andresen hypothesized that Celsus was not so much attempting to construct a vindictive polemic against Christians, as he was seeking to preserve the cherished values of his Hellenistic ancestors (*das griechische "Vätergesetz"*).

More recently, two studies by Stephen Benko replowed the ground first tilled by Labriolle, but with a distinctive focus on the first two Christian centuries.[68] His 1980 article surveyed the primary sources of the pagan critics of Christianity from Pliny the Younger to Celsus, thirteen in all, and gathered his findings into what he credibly termed "a kaleidoscopic view of how pagans looked at Christians in the first two centuries."[69] His useful summary merits reporting. Benko lists his insights under six headings. First, he says that pagans understood Christianity to be a Jewish sect, an appraisal that conveyed both blessings and curses. On the one hand, this identification enabled Christians to enjoy some of the privileges afforded Jews by Roman authorities, mainly on the basis of their antiquity as a religion. On the other hand, however, Christians were viewed with the same suspicion directed toward Jews as a result of the several insurgent revolts led by Jewish extremists such as Simeon Bar Kochba. Second, Christians were labeled a superstition, and accused of engaging in magic and many of the immoral and heinous behaviors associated with its practice. This attitude was supported by apparent similarities that existed between features of Christian worship and certain magical practices. Third, Christianity, on account of shared habit of nocturnal meetings with the outlawed Bacchanalia, was deemed in some circles a conspiracy. Fourth, Christian meetings resembled civic associations (ἐταιρεία in Greek, *collegium* in Latin), in particular, burial associations. After Trajan proclaimed such associations against the law, Christian gatherings were, as Celsus noted, operating illegally. Fifth, Christianity was likened to the mystery religions which were becoming common during this period. Finally, some pagans, notably Galen, compared Christianity to a philosophical movement, albeit an inferior one.[70]

Scholars have occasionally questioned whether or not scribes would have been at all concerned about how sacred texts would have been perceived by pagans and other outsiders. Data that constitute a tenable response to this question, however, were previously adduced by Pierre de Labriolle.[71] He noted that by the second century pagan critics were combing the Christian scriptures for weaknesses they could exploit in their

---

[68]Stephen Benko, "Pagan Criticism of Christianity During the First Two Centuries A.D." *ANRW* II.23.2 (H. Temporani and W. Haase, eds.; Berlin and New York: Walter de Gruyter, 1980), 1055–1118; and idem, *Pagan Rome and Early Christians* (Bloomington: Indiana University Press, 1984).

[69]S. Benko, "Pagan Criticism of Christianity," 1108.

[70]S. Benko, "Pagan Criticism of Christianity," 1108–10.

[71]Labriolle, *La Réaction païenne*, 128 and 204 f.

assaults on the new movement. Celsus, for example, in his assault against Christianity, founded many of his arguments upon evidence gleaned from his own perusal of Christian sacred texts. "However, these objections come from your own writings," says Celsus' Jewish alter-ego, "and we need no other witnesses; for you provide your own refutation."[72] In addition, Origen contended that Celsus conveniently believed the scriptures when it was to his advantage to do so, but dismissed them when he wished to avoid the divine character of the books.[73] Also, the criticisms drafted by Porphyry demonstrated that he had read at least some of the Christian scriptures, most certainly the Gospels. Moreover, B. H. Streeter recognized in the evolution of the Gospel narratives from the canonicals to the second-century *Gospel of Peter* the shaping influence of apologetic motivation.[74] So did E. C. Colwell, who detailed the apologetic reshaping of the Jesus narrative he believed to be inherent in the Fourth Gospel.[75]

The evidence is ample, therefore, that Christian scribes *did* have cause to be concerned with how their sacred books were perceived by outsiders. The text of the New Testament was in a potential sense an ammunition magazine, a common store of gunpowder and musket balls critical to victory in the campaign being waged by both pagan intellectuals and apologetic defenders. As such it was also a battleground. Pagans sought to use Christian sacred writings to score rhetorical points against them, in much the same way that Christian protagonists attempted to draft Plato or Homer in support for their own cause. Therefore, as stated in the words of Bart Ehrman:

> Christians of the second and third centuries were involved in a wide range of theological disputes about the nature of God, the disposition of the material world, the person of Christ, and the status of scripture. Scribes were not isolated from the implications of these disputes. Theological polemics played a significant role in the texts of the "New" Testament that were circulating, particularly among Christians who represented views that were later to be championed by the victorious party, the so-called "orthodox" believers who determined the shape of the creed and established the contours of the canon. Especially in this early era, when the allegedly apostolic writings were just beginning to be seen as authoritative, scribes who reproduced them were not at all disinclined to modify what they had received so as to make them more serviceable in their polemical milieu.[76]

I conclude this review with the work of another scholar whose views bring us back by way of contrast to the views of F. J. A. Hort. Kim Haines-Eitzen in the year 2000 published the first thoroughgoing study of the scribes who copied the New

---

[72]*Cels.* II.74, Chadwick, 122; see also I.12, II.77.
[73]*Cels.* I.63–64.
[74]B. H. Streeter, *Four Gospels*, 360.
[75]E. C. Colwell, *John Defends the Gospel.*
[76]B. Ehrman, "The Cup, The Bread...," 576–91, esp. 591.

Testament and other Christian literature during the second and third centuries.[77] Her work located among Christian scribes a characteristic that distinguished them from most other copyists of Greco-Roman antiquity. Where among most other scribes there was a distinction between scribes and users, those who copied Christian texts also read and studied them.

> Although it was customary in the Graeco-Roman world to hire a scribe or enlist the services of one's own slave-scribe to produce a copy of a literary text, a similar distinction between producers and users does not appear in the context of early Christian text transmission. What emerges from the historical record is precisely the opposite: the producers of copies of early Christian literature, the scribes, were also the users of this literature.[78]

This marriage of identity and function, she further noted, bred profound consequences. Because the reproducers were also readers, they were not disinterested copyists—the human Xerox machines they are often portrayed to be; rather, they were invested, sentient laborers who were sensitive to heretical discord and polemic disdain swirling about them as they conscientiously (and consciously) went about their tasks. Also, undoubtedly, they recognized the power at their disposal. Issues connected to written texts were issues they could profoundly affect. Their ability to write meant they could correct, clarify, buttress, or interpret a text, and, in so doing, impose with enduring effect their own ideas onto their exemplars and, in turn, those controversies that sought out authority or information in Christian sacred writings.[79] Christian scribes who read the text were by definition interpreters of the text. In turn, it was as interpreters that they also engaged in the labor of reproducing texts, so that, at times, they imposed their interpretation upon the text by editing and altering it. To be sure, often enough to discern it, there was sometimes ideology in the ink. Haines-Eitzen summarizes the point succinctly and well:

> Scholars have become increasingly attuned to the ways in which variant readings suggest the intersection of ideology and text reproduction. For example, studies have shown that certain changes made by scribes in the process of copying appear to have been motivated by anti-Jewish sentiments; others seem influenced by a certain animosity toward women; others by apologetic concerns; and still others can be explained by theological, especially Christological, concerns. Such studies have seriously countered Hort's famous statement: "even among the numerous

---

[77]Kim Haines-Eitzen, *Guardian of Letters.*

[78]K. Haines-Eitzen, *Guardians of Letters*, 130.

[79]Haines-Eitzen is aware that her arguments contradict traditionally held views that copyists worked mechanically, as well as the widely-held supposition that written modes of communication appear fixed while it is oral forms that are fluid and flexible. Yet, her arguments are thoughtfully considered and, in my judgment, compelling. See idem, *Guardians of Letters*, 176, n. 3.

unquestionably spurious readings of the New Testament there are no signs of deliberate falsification of the text for dogmatic purposes."[80]

Although Hort's genius and legacy remain undiminished, Haines-Eitzen usefully summarizes evidence that indicates that on this point he was in error. For dogmatic, as well as other tendentious purposes, Christian scribes engaged in the act of transmitting the text of the New Testament occasionally changed their exemplar in order to produce a text that resonated with the tuning fork of the copyist's own ideology. Among those purposes was a concern to defend the faith, in the community of which they were personally invested and for the purposes of which they copied these sacred writings in the first place.

In summary, across time studies have reached greater clarity with regard to the nature and impulse of intentional scribal manipulations of the text of the New Testament. Where J. Rendel Harris began the last century speaking of locating the fingerprints of such textual handlers, it does not seem an overstatement to ascribe to studies current at the dawn of this new millennium—such as those of Eldon Epp, Elizabeth Schüssler Fiorenza, Bart Ehrman, and Kim Haines-Eitzen—credit for catching scribes in the act of altering the scriptures for tendentious purposes.

Thus, the New Testament we have today consists of a product that is something between an academic mélange and an old family recipe. The published text represents a selection of the finest raw ingredients available, which have been roasted in the oasts of scholarly scrutiny and distilled by genealogical speculations and the evaluation of reasoned eclecticism. In any given year, it is the best vintage our best-equipped scholars can produce. Yet, at any given time that we raise in toast this filtered nectar, it is incumbent upon us to remember that somewhere out there are those who with devoted persistence are tampering with the recipe.

Such was true also in the earliest centuries of the Christian movement. Then, the sacred text was forged in a crucible of Roman hegemony, Jewish apocalypticism, internecine controversy, local persecution, individual zeal, corporate piety, and death-defying conviction. Persons who were living in a volatile age and who were shaped by its energies in turn defended and shaped the faith and its text. It is that intersection between historical discourse and textual transmission that constitutes the content of this study. So now we turn to examine and stencil the characteristic features of the discourse that has survived between pagan critics and Christian defenders toward the end of forming a matrix against which we can compare selected textual variants in the canonical Gospels.

PAGAN OPPOSITION AND CHRISTIAN APOLOGETIC RESPONSE

Because of the polemical character of the subject sources of this study, our search for intersections is destined to be a collision course. In one direction, pagan critics

---

[80]K. Haines-Eitzen, *Guardians of Letters*, 112.

hurled pejorative lances at Christians, accusing them of immorality, atheism, impiety, and treason; on the other, Christian apologists invoked every conceivable defense to fortify their faith and shield the faithful against intellectual assault. We must not be deceived that because it was a war of words it lacked weapons. The consequences of this conversation were real. Pagan polemicists were concerned to safeguard their revered and stable way of life against this upstart cult. Where they once viewed Christians as a benign novelty, pagans by the second century looked upon them nervously with suspicion, contempt, and even fear. What was at stake for the apologists was the life of a fragile, fledgling religious movement. Christianity did not yet have a foothold in the imperial court; it was not yet sustained by the benevolence of Constantine and most of his successors. Its tenets and practices were still evolving, and the movement remained vulnerable from within as well as from without. For both sides, a way of life hung in the balance. So the sources make clear.

PAGAN OPPOSITION TO CHRISTIANITY

The dearth of sources we encounter on the pagan side is due in part to the vitriolic zeal with which post-Constantinian Christians at the request of their bishops or under orders from the emperor stoked their bonfires with anti-Christian writings.[81] Ironically, much of the substantial pagan critique that survived the ravages of Fahrenheit 451 did so in the guise of quotations located in the apologetic literature that was intended to refute them—so many wolves, as it were, cloaked in the garments of sheep.

The ready availability of several excellent thoroughgoing surveys and studies that serve well to introduce and provide analysis of the primary sources written by pagan opponents of Christianity eliminates the need to recite that information here. What follows here is intended simply to establish a context for the sources and authors we will be examining in the chapters below.[82]

Pliny, Governor of Bithynia-Pontus. To date, no mention of Jesus of Nazareth has been located in a pagan source written prior to the year 112 C.E. The first occurs in official

---

[81]Efforts to destroy pagan polemical writings was highly successful. Porphyry's *Against the Christians*, for example, was ordered burned along with the heretical writings of Nestorius by Emperor Theodosius II in the year 448 C.E. No complete manuscript has survived to the present. All we know of this work, as is also true of Celsus' *True Word*, are those allusions and quotations cited by Christian writers, usually with the mind to refute them. See W. H. C. Frend, *The Rise of Christianity* (London: Darton, Longman, and Todd, 1984), 442.

[82]The work of P. Labriolle, *La Réaction païenne* is not only a classic, but remains a rich and comprehensive survey of these sources. More recently there is the work of S. Benko, "Pagan Criticism of Christianity During the First Two Centuries A.D.," *ANRW* II.23.2, 1055–1118; and the more popular (but still very useful) treatment of the subject by Robert L. Wilken, *Christians as the Romans Saw Them* (New Haven/London: Yale University Press, 1984). I rely heavily upon these sources not only in this section but throughout this study.

correspondence that was issued between the seated governor of Bithynia-Pontus, Pliny the Younger (c. 61–113 C.E.), and his emperor, Trajan.[83] From this famous correspondence we learn much about how a provincial governor regarded and treated Christians who resided within his jurisdiction.

It is his apparent uncertainty about what to do with Christians that prompts Pliny to contact the emperor. His curiosity is invoked, in part, by the issue of whether or not he should discriminate on the basis of age or penitence in issuing sentence; but the larger question is whether there is something inherent in the very name Christian that deserves capital punishment, or whether it is for crimes associated with the name that sentence is warranted. He is content meanwhile to carry out judgment, based on his own contention that "stubbornness and inflexible obstinacy should be punished." The governor's interim procedure is as simple as it is ruthless: he asks them if they are in fact Christians, and if they answer affirmatively—or deny it, but will not show due reverence to the emperor or curse Christ—he executes them. Pliny here shows Roman justice to be both swift and coldly efficient. Still, something about this procedure appears to have proved unsatisfactory to Pliny. In writing Rome, he also informs Trajan of his orders to torture some Christian women in order to learn more of their activities and intentions. What data he is able to obtain from this exercise leads him to conclude that Christians constitute by and large a harmless lot, fairly innocuous in their practice of a "depraved and excessive superstition."[84] Many of the elements we locate in Pliny are echoed by later pagan polemicists, and are addressed by Christian apologists. In fact, the issue of whether Christians should be judged on the basis of their name alone or for specific crimes becomes an apologetic standard.

Two Pagan Historians: Tacitus and Suetonius. From two pagan historians roughly contemporary with Pliny, we gain confirmation of this attitude against Christians held by Romans. Tacitus (c. 55–117 C.E.) viewed Christians as a disruptive social force. In his *Annals* (15.44), where he described the torching of Rome under Nero, he reports how the emperor was able to shift responsibility for the fire from himself onto the *Christiani*, a group consisting of a "vulgar mob...hated for their crimes." Tacitus goes on to explain, however, that many of them were convicted not for setting the blaze but because of their *odium humani generis*, hatred of the human race.[85] Suetonius (c. 70–160 C.E.), in his account of the reign of Nero (*Nero* 16.2), reports among other things, "Punishment was inflicted on the Christians, a class of men given to a new and mischievous superstition." Both P. Labriolle and S. Benko rightly observe that what

---

[83]See P. Labriolle, *La Réaction païenne*, 28–35; S. Benko, "Pagan Criticism of Christianity," 1066–70.

[84]Pliny, *Ep.* 96.10; Translation by S. Benko, "Pagan Criticism of Christianity," 1068–69.

[85]See P. Labriolle, *La Réaction païenne*, 36–41; S. Benko, "Pagan Criticism of Christianity," 1062–63.

appears to disturb him most about Christians is the novelty of their superstition, and how it stands opposed to the old and correct religion.[86]

Other Early Second-Century Sources. From Epictetus (c. 50–130), a former slave and noted Stoic philosopher, we catch only a glimpse of his perceptions regarding Christians (he identified them as Galileans), but for the most part his appraisal was positive. Most notably, he attributed their lack of fear before authorities to the sort of "habit" that philosophers should seek to engender within others.[87] Yet another famous Stoic, the emperor Marcus Aurelius (121–180 C.E.), was less generous in his appraisal of Christians. He attributed their boldness in the face of death to stubbornness more than courage or reasoned decisiveness.[88]

Only two ancient references speak of the second-century Roman Crescens.[89] Justin's *Second Apology* identified him as a Cynic philosopher whom the apologist characterized as a "lover of bravado and boasting" famous for publicly attacking Christians. Justin avowed that Crescens' charges of impiety and atheism against Christians resulted from his failure to study the teachings of Christ.[90] Tatian in his reference to him claimed that Crescens coveted money and indulged in pederasty.[91] Beyond what can be read between the lines of these polemical appraisals of his intellect and character, only one more thing can be said concerning the Cynic. Both Justin and Tatian implied that Crescens posed a danger to them, so it may be possible that Crescens played a role in the death of Justin Martyr (165 C.E.).[92] Despite how little we can confidently assert about Crescens, it is clear that he sowed hostility toward Christians, presumably because they failed to show due reverence to the traditional deities of Rome.

Satirists: Lucian of Samosata and Apuleius of Madaura. Among the numerous characters satirized by Lucian (c. 115–200 C.E.) was a certain Peregrinus (c. 100–165 C.E.), who Lucian tells us claimed for himself the moniker Proteus.[93] In "Death of Peregrinus," the author portrays the title character as a great pretender, one who skips through life

---

[86]S. Benko, "Pagan Criticism of Christianity," 1056–62, esp. 1061.; P. Labriolle, *La Réaction païenne*, 44.

[87]Epictetus, *Discourses* 4.7.1–6. See S. Benko, "Pagan Criticism of Christianity," 1077–78.

[88]*Meditations* XI.3. For the citation and discussion of the text, see S. Benko, "Pagan Criticism of Christianity," 1092; also George Long, trans., *Marcus Aurelius: Meditations* (Amherst,, NY: Prometheus, 1991, 105–106.

[89]S. Benko, "Pagan Criticism of Christianity," 1078.

[90]Justin, *Ap.* II.3, 11.

[91]Tatian, *Or.* 19.

[92]Along with the above references see the discussion in P. Labriolle, *La Réaction païenne*, 63–5.

[93]For a brief introduction to Lucian and translations in English of his writings, see Lionel Casson, ed. and trans., *Selected Satires of Lucian* (New York/London: W. W. Norton, 1962. See also the comments of S. Benko, "Pagan Criticism of Christianity," 1093–97.

preying on the gullibility of others. Suspected of murdering his father, Peregrinus fled to Palestine and where it was said that he converted to Christianity and very quickly attained high rank in the church. He gained also quite a small fortune when, upon being imprisoned for his beliefs, Christian visitors offered him gifts. In time, though, his practice of eating meat offered to idols led to his estrangement from the church, and he traveled on to Egypt and Italy, encountering Cynicism and achieved a reputation as a philosopher. He became best remembered, however, for his spectacular demise. At the Olympic games held in 165 C.E., Peregrinus after much fanfare leaped headlong into a bonfire, thus terminating his career in a blazing suicide. So sensational was this act that it was recalled frequently, even by Christian writers such as Athenagoras and Tertullian.[94] In this story, gullibility appears as the most defining characteristic Lucian attaches to Christians. Here they are seen as persons all too ready to fall for a charismatic charlatan, even one so transparent as Lucian depicts Peregrinus. Yet, as can be seen in another of his tales, Lucian was not always consistent in offering this evaluation of those associated with the Jesus movement.

Another brief reference to Christians occurs in Lucian's exposé of a religious charlatan in Abonoteichus entitled "Alexander the False Prophet." Commissioned by an Epicurean gentleman, the work was addressed to a certain "Celsus," a fact that has given rise to speculation by some that this Celsus might have been the same person who penned *True Doctrine*.[95] This satirical narrative relates the tale of a schemer named Alexander who designs an elaborate ruse to pass himself off as an oracle. Despite the almost whimsical tone of the piece, some historical kernel underlies the story. Coins minted by proud Abonoteichans can be found in museums today that bear the image of their shrine's serpentine deity.

Lucian portrays Alexander as the most brazen of scoundrels, declaring him to be as great a villain as Alexander the Great was a hero. He explains that as a youth Alexander parlayed his genuine good looks into a lucrative career as a prostitute, during which time he engaged as a lover a certain quack magician who tutored him in the arts of incantations and chicanery. When the bloom of his youth was spent, he partnered with a fellow swindler in fleecing various people of means, one of whom was a woman from Pella. There they became familiar with a breed of large but gentle serpent, fierce in appearance but completely docile in manner. Sight of this reptile recalled for them tales of Zeus taking the guise of a snake before impregnating Olympius with Alexander the Great, and provided the impetus for their most sinister plot—to grow prosperous by establishing their own oracle, employing such a snake as a leading character in the

---

[94]See Athenagoras, *Leg.* 26 and Tertullian, *Mart.* 4, both of which are cited in translation in S. Benko, "Pagan Criticism of Christianity," 1095, n. 153.

[95]Origen equated the author of *True Logos* with this same friend of Lucian. James Francis has fashioned a case for giving some degree of credence to this claim in idem, *Subversive Virtue: Asceticism and Authority in the Second-Century Pagan World* (University Park, PA: Pennsylvania State University, 1995), 133–5. C. Andresen, however, asserted that there was little to be gained in establishing this connection (idem, *Logos und Nomos*, 5).

ruse. After selecting Abonoteichus as the perfect location for carrying out their plot, Alexander and his partner managed to convince the citizenry there that the sudden appearance of their pet snake represented a visitation from the god Asclepius. Once the gullible masses fell prey to this deceit, the success of the next step in their plan was guaranteed. Alexander wound the serpent around him in such a way to fashion the look of a serpent's body with a human face, and then invited people to write and seal questions of import for which divine guidance or forewarning would prove beneficial. Then, upon delivery, Alexander by various tricks was able to open the questions, offer either easy or vague responses, and then return them sealed to an amazed audience. Praising this god—freshly dubbed Glycon—the masses formed a ready clientele, happily trading hard-earned coins for easily-dispensed oracles; and thereby Alexander and his growing entourage realized a substantial fortune, and managed to solicit sexual favors from young women and boys.

The episode of this narrative that possesses particular interest for our current discussion, however, concerns that minority of citizens who began to unmask the charlatan and his tricks. Lucian describes these "men of sense"as Epicureans, but quickly adds that Alexander's campaign of intimidation against them was also directed at atheists and Christians, as well.[96] A bit later, Lucian writes, Alexander designed his own mystery ritual that began with an initial proclamation, part of which declared, "If any atheist, Christian, or Epicurean has come here to spy, let him be gone....Christians, begone!...Epicureans, begone!"[97] What is striking here is that Lucian's treatment of Christians in this story stands in sharp contrast to his portrayal of them in the tale of Peregrinus. Where Christians proved gullible to the charms of Proteus in "Death of Peregrinus," in the tale of Alexander they are grouped in company with Lucian's esteemed Epicureans and generic atheists as those who, alone, demonstrated the good sense not to fall victim to the machinations of this charlatan. Thus, it would appear that Lucian did not consistently hold a poor opinion of Christians. Still, perhaps his view should not be seen as entirely neutral. In describing the audience that Alexander attracted in Abonoteichus, Lucian glibly reports that the crowd consisted of practically the whole town, but then he adds, "women, old men, children...." Where this formula—old men, women, and children—clearly serves Lucian here as a pejorative characterization of the citizenry of Abonoteichus, it is almost the same formula he used in "Death of Peregrinus" to characterize Christians. "Gray-haired widows and orphan children," he reports, hung around the prison, while "bigwigs of the sect" (old men?) bribed jailers in order to spend the night with Proteus.[98] If pressed, I am inclined to venture the opinion that Lucian did not hold a high opinion of Christians; he merely, it would seem, held an even lower opinion of Alexander.

Brief and passing as these references to Christians in Lucian's writings are, they do offer us some input for arriving at a composite of how pagans perceived Christians.

---

[96]Lucian, "Alexander the Quack Prophet," 25. See Lionel Casson, *Selected Satires*, 281.
[97]Lucian, "Alexander the Quack Prophet," 38. See Lionel Casson, *Selected Satires*, 286–7.
[98]Lucian, "Death of Peregrinus," 12–13. See Lionel Casson, *Selected Satires*, 368–9.

Lucian clearly sees them as gullible enough to be conned by Proteus, but astute enough not to fall prey to Alexander. He repeats the notion we find frequently among ancient critics of Christianity that they are counted among the atheists. Also, even though he details the activities of widows, old women and orphans when he describes Christians, he acknowledges that there are, in fact, men possessing some status among their ranks.[99]

The familiar story of a dabbler in magic, Lucius, who accidentally transforms himself into an ass also includes a brief description that many scholars believe is a reference to Christianity. Lucius Apuleius of Madaura (c. 123–?), author of this tale entitled *Metamorphoses* (more commonly referred to as *The Golden Ass*), described the wife of a baker as a woman wicked to the core and possessing a heart that lacked no vice. All of this prompted Lucius, at this point in the tale incarnate as an ass, to pity her husband. With regard to this study, the key phrase in her characterization is, "She scorned and spurned the gods of heaven; and in the place of true religion she professed some fantastic blasphemous creed of a God whom she named the One and Only God."[100] If the scholars who read this as a reference to Christianity are accurate, Jack Lindsay is probably correct that an underlying anti-Christian polemic runs through this book of Apuleius.[101] S. Benko is a bit more reserved in his assessment that Apuleius is speaking of Christians here, but he considers the possibility strong. He reflects:

> This description could fit a Jewish proselyte, i.e., a θεοσεβής (=god-fearer), but it could also fit a Christian: the baker's wife worshiped one god, rejected polytheism, enjoyed wine in the early morning—which could be a reference to the early morning Eucharist, and she was promiscuous—which may reflect the popular charge about the Christians' immoral behavior as contained in the "Octavius." Apuleius presented the baker's wife as a wicked woman, quite in line with the uncritical contemptuous view of Christianity of his day.[102]

Apart from their distinctive literary contributions to the second century, the writings of these two satirists offer insights for historians of early Christianity, as well. Because their remarks in these instances are supplementary rather than topical, they

---

[99]Lucian, "Death of Peregrinus," 12–13; Once again see Lionel Casson, *Selected Satires*, 368, where he identifies them as "bigwigs of the sect," possibly indicating persons, probably male, who were well to do.

[100]Apuleius, *Metam.* 9.14. Here I am using the translation of Jack Lindsay, trans., *Apuleius: The Golden Ass* (Bloomington, IN: Indiana University Press, 1962), 193.

[101]Lindsay points beyond this reference to the image of a Virgin triumphing on the ass in Book VII and to the recollection that Christians were said to worship a man with the head of an ass. Yet, he balances his treatment by stating that his greater concern is express a positive devotion to Isis, as well as to offer social criticism of the issue of slavery in antiquity. See J. Lindsay, *Golden Ass*, 21–22.

[102]S. Benko, "Pagan Criticism of Christianity," 1090.

probably convey a fairly accurate reflection of how these writers appraised Christianity, and, more generally, of the opinions of some other pagan intellectuals toward the Jesus movement. As such, these two articulate pagan voices portray early second-century Christians as gullible and easily manipulated, obstinate, cruel, impious (with regard to pagan deities), given to drink and perversity, and sexually profligate. Too, they highlight the association of women—particularly those who are aged, unsophisticated, or promiscuous—in the movement and present them as indicative of its membership. Such descriptions applied to Christians will be met again and often in pagan discourse, particular in the citation of one Marcus Fronto, a contemporary of Apuleius, recorded in the *Octavius* of Minucius Felix.

Marcus Cornelius Fronto. The Roman intellectual Marcus Cornelius Fronto (c. 100–166 C.E.) stood recognized as one of the great rhetoricians of his day and served as one of the tutors of Marcus Aurelius.[103] Recorded in the *Octavius* (8–9) of Minucius Felix there appears a polemical discourse against Christians that is attributed to Fronto.[104] Represented in these words is a nearly exhaustive summary of the standard but wide-ranging calumnies regularly directed against the beliefs and composition of Christianity and the behavior of its adherents. Christians, according to him, consist of the "dregs of society," and theirs is a religion of fools, blasphemous conspirators, and gullible women.[105] They meet in nocturnal assemblies, participate in clandestine ceremonies and cannibalistic feasts, and overturn the lights so that they can engage in acts of unspeakable promiscuity and incest. In terms of veneration, they worship the head of an ass, the genitals of their father, and an executed criminal and his cross. As a work that informs us historically, the *Octavius* is particularly valuable for its comprehensive collection of elements of the polemical pagan portrayal of Christians around the turn of the third century. Below in subsequent chapters, I will attempt to demonstrate

---

[103]For more on Fronto see P. Labriolle, *La Réaction païenne*, 87–94.

[104]Attribution of this passage to Fronto, however, does not pass without dispute. For instance, W. H. C. Frend questions the legitimacy of tracing the legacy of the speech directly back to Fronto, although he expresses confidence that its content accurately represents widespread Roman opinion toward Christians current in the middle of the second century. See idem, *Martyrdom and Persecution*, 252–3, 269. In part, the issue lies in the fact that no such oration may be found in the extant works of Fronto. Still, S. Benko, "Pagan Criticism of Christianity," 1081–2, is optimistic in his outlook that the arguments reported by Minucius Felix do, in fact, find their basis in Fronto. The apologist himself gives credit for it to Caecilius' "illustrious friend from Cirta." See *Oct.* 9.6. G. Clarke, trans. *The Octavius of Marcus Minucius Felix* (New York: Newman, 1974). Labriolle points out an even more direct reference to Fronto in *Oct.* 31.1–2, and offers plausible reasons for connecting the reference and oration to Fronto. See P. Labriolle, *La Réaction païenne*, 91–2.

[105]For an insightful discussion of this passage from the *Octavius* with a focus on its negative treatment and appraisal of early Christian women, see Margaret Y. MacDonald, *Early Christian Women and Pagan Opinion: The Power of the Hysterical Woman* (Cambridge: Cambridge University Press, 1996), 59–67.

points in the scribal tradition at which apologetic concern with regard to these
elements prompted copyists to modify their texts. There I will cite this important
passage in full.

Celsus and Ἀληθὴς Λόγος. It is to Origen that we are indebted for preserving the
work of the conservative intellectual critic of Christianity, Celsus.[106] Around the year
172 C.E., Celsus authored a work he provocatively entitled, Ἀληθὴς Λόγος, variously
translated as "True Word," "True Logos," "True Discourse," "True Account,"or
"True Doctrine."[107] Based on our current knowledge, Celsus appears to have been the
first pagan writer who set out to compose a complete treatise against Christianity. So
far as can be determined from reconstructions based on Origen's citations, *True
Doctrine* consisted of an attempt to call Christians back from their errors and
isolationist behaviors to participate once again in the ancient traditions and practices
that he reasoned to be "true."

For Celsus, then, Christianity was based in error, and much of his book serves as
a rather extensive compendium of arguments against the religious movement.[108]
Christianity represented an inferior philosophical system (VI.1); its membership
consisted of people of low social class and limited intellectual abilities (I.62, II.46); and
believers worshiped a man Celsus variously depicted as an unsophisticated carpenter
(II.2), a wicked sorcerer (I.38, I.71, II.32, II.49, VIII.41), a liar (II.7), brigand (II.44),
vagabond (I.62, II.46), bastard (I.32), and a rightfully executed insurrectionist who

---

[106]For a detailed introduction see P. Labriolle, *La Réaction païenne*, esp. 111–169. The most
thorough analysis remains the classic work of Carl Andresen, *Logos und Nomos: Die Polemik des
Kelsos wider Das Christentum* (Berlin: Walter de Gruyter, 1955). The most exhaustive critical edition
is that of Marcel Borret, S.J., ed. *Origène. Contre Celse* (Sources Chrétiennes; Paris: Les Éditions
du Cerf, 1967), while the most popular English translation and introduction belongs to Henry
Chadwick, *Origen: Contra Celsum* (Cambridge: Cambridge University Press, 1953). A particularly
insightful study exploring the common conceptual base underlying the discussions of Jesus in
Celsus and Origen appears in Eugene Gallagher, *Divine Man or Magician? Celsus and Origen on Jesus*
(SBLDS 64; Chico, CA: Scholars Press, 1982).

[107]For example, H. Crouzel, *Origen* translates the title "True Word"; both Henry Chadwick,
Origen: Contra Celsum, and R. J. Hoffmann, *Celsus: On the True Doctrine*, favor "True Doctrine";
"True Account" is the choice of R. M. Grant, *Greek Apologists*, and M. Frede, "Origen's Treatise
Against Celsus," while the editors of the *Ante-Nicene Christian Library*, F. Crombie and W. H.
Cairns, prefer to render the title "True Discourse." J. Trigg, *Origen*, appears to embrace the
ambiguity by reading simply "True Logos." Since, except for Trigg's borrowed ambiguity, no
single one of these renderings conveys fully the complete essence of the Greek *Logos*, and the
sole use of any one of these translations would imply it seems to me an interpretation that limits
the levels of meaning that I believe Celsus intended his title to convey, I have chosen in the
course of this book to vary my translation so that the reader is constantly reminded of the
various nuances implied by the title.

[108]M. Frede, "Origen's Treatise Against Celsus," in M. Edwards, M. Goodman, and S.
Price, eds. *Apologetics in the Roman Empire: Pagans, Jews, and Christians* (Oxford: Oxford University
Press, 1999), 131–55.

showed in the face of death fear, powerlessness, and groaning despair (I.54, II.4–5, II.24). Also, to add insult to injury, Celsus claimed that Jesus was ugly (VI.75). In addition, Celsus showed familiarity with and disdain for the Christian scriptures. He found the depiction of God there to be offensively anthropomorphic (VI.61–63). Celsus found the doctrines of the incarnation and resurrection of Jesus untenable and offensive. He repeated the widely circulating rumor that Jesus was in fact not born of a virgin but was rather the illegitimate product of the union between a Roman soldier and his prostitute mother (I.32). The notion of a god becoming flesh, dying, and returning to a corporeal existence could only be described as blasphemy (VII.14).[109]

Harsh as his rhetoric could sound, the essence of his work was an appeal for Christians to repent of their errors and to re-enter the fold of traditional piety. At the heart of his argument lay the basic belief that there existed from the foundation of the world a perennial truth (this is what he meant by "true word") that was the common heritage of all humankind. The choice of Christians to estrange themselves from public festivals and rites that commemorated that eternal truth was proof that they had wandered astray.

Scholars continue to debate the long-term impact of *True Word*. Clearly something of consequence prompted his patron Ambrose to commission Origen to devote such immense energies and resources to responding point by point to Celsus. Yet, Origen in his preface to *Contra Celsum* indicates that he had never read or heard of the book prior to receiving a copy of it from Ambrose. Clarity on the matter continues to evade scholarship.

Porphyry of Tyre. Widely considered by ancients as well as current scholars one of the most formidable of the pagan critics of Christianity, it is regrettable that the works of Porphyry (c. 232–305) have been for the most part lost.[110] Surviving the first condemnation under Constantine, his works were once more ordered burned by Theodosius and Valentinian in 448 C.E.[111] This systematic torching of his writings

---

[109]The references in the preceding paragraph have been to *Contra Celsum*. Cf. S. Benko, "Pagan Criticism of Christianity," 1101–08 for his introductory comments on Celsus, many of which have been followed closely here.

[110]Eusebius (*Hist. eccl.* VI.19.2), e.g., identified Porphyry as a contemporary of his who settled in Sicily and wrote treatises (συγγράμματα) attempting to slander Christians and their sacred scriptures (τὰς θείας γραφὰς διαβάλλειν). Robert L. Wilken referred to Porphyry as "the most learned critic of all" (Idem, *Christians as the Romans Saw Them*, 126 f.).

[111]What remains of his work consists of fragments located in various Christian writers, in particular Augustine and Jerome. The standard collection of the fragments remains that of Adolf von Harnack, "Porphyrius 'Gegen die Christen,' 15 Bücher: Zeugnisse, Fragmente, und Referate," *Abhand. kön. preuss. Akad. d. Wiss.* Phil.-hist. Kl. (Berlin, 1916), although more recent scholars have seriously challenged the attribution of those fragments derived from Macarius Magnes to Porphyry himself. The current consensus among scholars is to eliminate them from consideration as authentic, but R. Joseph Hoffmann champions the minority position in his translation of the fragments of Macarius in idem, *Porphyry's Against the Christians: The Literary*

directed by emperors and church leaders suggests that something about Porphyry and his prose posed a particularly serious threat to early Christians. Moreover, the work continued to command significant attention from many of the important Christian writers of the late third, fourth and fifth centuries, including Eusebius, Methodius, Apollonaris, Jerome, and Augustine. Even more imposing, it would seem, than the volume of his *Against the Christians*—it totaled 15 volumes—was his comprehensive knowledge of Christianity and its sacred writings. In the words of B. Croke, "The superiority of Porphyry's case stemmed from the singular advantage that he argued not so much as a convinced Hellenist but from an intimate knowledge of Christian scriptures, dogma, and customs."[112] Scholars dispute the precise date of *Against the Christians*, but its publication almost certainly fell between 270 C.E. and the first decade or so of the fourth century.[113]

A. Harnack divided his collected fragments of Porphyry's writings into five divisions that serve to articulate for us a fairly accurate picture of the general character of Porphyry's criticism of Christianity.[114] The five divisions are as follows: (1) criticism of the reliability of the apostles and evangelists; (2) a critique of the Old Testament, including most especially his groundbreaking treatment of the book of Daniel; (3) a discussion of the words and deeds of Jesus;[115] (4) a criticism of the dogma of Christianity (preserved in the writings of Augustine); and (5) a discussion of the present shortcomings of the church.[116] Porphyry supported his arguments with detailed discussions with the biblical stories, e.g., attributing Paul's ability to work miracles to magic (and of a sort inferior to that wrought by Apollonius of Tyana), scandalizing the tension between Peter and Paul as evidence of Peter's errors and the existence of disharmony within the church, deriding the habit of allegorical exegesis found in such noted Christian biblical interpreters as Origen, and advancing his own chronological

---

Remains (Amherst, NY: Prometheus, 1994). For additional introduction to Porphyry and more information expressed from the perspective of the mainstream consensus see P. Labriolle, *La Réaction païenne*, 223–96; T. D. Barnes, "Porphyry Against the Christians," 424–42; A. Meredith, "Porphyry and Julian Against the Christians," *ANRW* II.23.2, 1119–1149; and Brian Croke, "The Era of Porphyry's Anti-Christian Polemic," *JRH*, 1–14.

[112]B. Croke, "Era of Porphyry's Anti-Christian Polemic," 1.

[113]Contours of the dispute may be seen in T. D. Barnes, "Porphyry's Against the Christian: Date and Attribution," 424–42 and B. Croke, "The Era of Porphyry's Anti-Christian Polemic," 1–14. Barnes argues for a later date early in the third century, and is even willing to press back the date of Porphyry's death to invite consideration of a date near 313 C.E. Croke's article challenges each point on which Barnes has made his case, and offers compelling reasons for returning to a date around 270/3 C.E. for Porphyry's authorship of *Against the Christians* during the years he spent in Sicily.

[114]A. Harnack, "Porphyrius 'Gegen die Christen.'"

[115]Much of this material, however, is derived exclusively from the *Apocriticus* of Macarius Magnes, the analysis of which has fomented doubt among many scholars as to whether these remarks should rightly be attributed to Porphyry himself. See note 112 above.

[116]A. Meredith, "Porphyry and Julian Against the Christians," 1128.

analysis to pinpoint the relative novelty of Judaism and Christianity to Phoenician religion. Anthony Meredith further depicts how Porphyry's enduring demonstration of Daniel to be a historical, pseudepigraphical work struck a blow against the perception of the book to be prophetic in character, and thus "weakened its value as an apologetic weapon in the hand of the Christian apologists."[117] Meredith, building on H. O. Schroeder, emphasizes also that the chief difference between Celsus and Porphyry in their criticisms of Christianity involved the foundations and methodologies of their arguments:

> Whereas Celsus, as H. O. Schroeder points out, bases his arguments on the learning and philosophical position of antiquity, Porphyry confronts the Christians with their own primary weapon, the Bible. By means of historical analysis and criticism, and with the help of a somewhat pedantic and literalistic approach, he tries to expose the inaccuracies, the inconsistencies and general relative character of the sacred books. He is frequently pedantic rather than profound, looking to trivial errors as a means for upsetting the trustworthiness of the gospel and its authors.[118]

However compelling or unsatisfying such trivial pursuits may prove rhetorically, Porphyry's practice of combing the text in order to confront its inconsistencies will prove particularly useful for locating data relevant to this study. In instances involving several of the very texts that Porphyry himself adduced in order to challenge the consistency and reliability of Christian scripture, we will discover scribal activity that served to eliminate the very points of contention this polemicist had raised.[119]

Pagan Opposition in Summary: One Side of the Discourse. The character and contours of the pagan criticism of Christianity was by no means monolithic. In terms of vigor and attitude, as well as rhetorical strategy and arenas of argumentation, opposition to Christianity frequently adapted its harangue, showing signs of changing with the times, modifying the scope and focus of its arguments, and deepening the intensity of the dispute as the Christian following grew in numbers and gained a disturbing momentum. Early on, members of the Roman establishment moved beyond disregard to disdain for members of the movement. In Pliny, Tacitus, Suetonius, and Marcus Aurelius one witnesses a contempt for the perceived arrogance, obstinacy, and atheism of Christians, and for their movement constituting a "novel superstition." Some intellectuals, such as Galen and Epictetus, could appreciate certain behaviors of Christians and identify them with some regard as a "philosophy," but they rated them inferior to the more traditional branches of reason. By the time Celsus took pen in hand, his concern was with an expanding movement he viewed as a legitimate threat to the established practices of piety and traditional religions that had made Rome great. He challenged the movement, in part, by deriding its founder, Jesus; and also

---

[117]A. Meredith, "Porphyry and Julian Against the Christians," 1133.

[118]A. Meredith, "Porphyry and Julian Against the Christians," 1129.

[119]See below the discussions of Mark 1:2, Matthew 13:35, and John 7:8–10.

questioned the antiquity of the faith and the acumen of its adherents. Porphyry similarly attacked the disciples of the movement, and more than any other polemicist assailed the trustworthiness of their sacred writings. The oration attributed to Marcus Fronto located in the *Octavius* delineated with rhetorical force most of the popular portrayals of Christians as persons of immoral character and disgusting religious practices. In one way or another, almost all of the pagan critics judged Christians a threat to the stability of society, if not to the primacy of Rome.

In general terms, then, the shape of the pagan assault on Christians, like carved crystal, bore many facets. For one, erudite critics fashioned a two-pronged attack rooted in the charge that both believers and the scriptures they read and trusted lacked intellectual integrity. Another of their assaults was directed at Jesus himself. Variously he was portrayed as a person of inglorious birth, common peasant upbringing, and one who possessed either poor judgment or deliberate mischief with regard to the character of the companions with whom he chose to surround himself. Where he worked miracles, they saw him to be a sorcerer. Where he was portrayed in the vernacular of a *theios aner*, he was deemed inferior to others of his ilk, such as Apollonius of Tyana. Constituting a third facet of this literary barrage, followers of Jesus were ridiculed as ignorant, gullible fools, and for consisting mainly of women and fanatics. They were said to be people who engaged in disgusting rituals, such as Thyestean feasts (cannibalism) and Oedipal orgies (incest). Finally, coming from still another direction, pagan antagonists broadcast the indictment that Christianity represented a threat to Rome.

These were the fingers of accusation that pagans pointed in the faces of Christians. Some Christians, however, rose to these challenges and crafted responses intended to defend the faith and the faithful from these pejorative assaults. To these apologetic writers we now direct our attention.

CHRISTIAN APOLOGETIC RESPONSE

With regard to this study on the Christian side, we are interested mainly in the Greek apologists of the second and third centuries. These writers addressed and formulated their discourse in light of the dominant culture of the day. Although these writings were ostensibly addressed to outsiders—frequently the emperors themselves—many scholars today remain convinced that apologetic literature would have been read almost exclusively by those who were already part of the Christian community.

The Earliest Christian Apologists: Quadratus and Aristides. Quadratus, the earliest known of these defenders of the faith, is barely known to us at all. Eusebius alone preserves a single fragment of his otherwise lost work, a copy of which the historian claims to have owned and which he indicates was addressed to Hadrian (117–138 C.E.) shortly after the death of Trajan.[120] Johannes Quasten suggests that the work was composed sometime between 123–129 C.E. and may have issued from Asia Minor.[121] The citation reads:

τοῦ δὲ σωτῆρος ἡμῶν τὰ ἔργα ἀεὶ παρῆν ἀληθῆ γὰρ ἦν, οἱ θεραπευθέντες, οἱ ἀναστάντες ἐκ νεκρῶν, οἱ οὐκ ὤφθησαν μόνον θεραπευόμενοι καὶ ἀνιστάμενοι, ἀλλὰ καὶ ἀεὶ παρόντες, οὐδὲ ἐπιδημοῦντος μόνον τοῦ σωτῆρος, ἀλλὰ καὶ ἀπαλλαγέντος ἦσαν ἐπὶ χρόνον ἱκανόν, ὥστε καὶ εἰς τοὺς ἡμετέρους χρόνους τινὲς αὐτῶν ἀφίκοντο.

But the works of our Savior were always present, for they were true. Thus, those persons who were made well and raised from the dead were seen, not only at the time when they were healed and were raised, but also as they continued to be present. Nor did they continue only while our Savior remained among us, but even after he had departed they lived a considerable time, even to the point that into our own times some of them have survived.[122]

Brief as this fragment is, several features appear here that will emerge as standard themes among apologetic writers. One is the emphasis on healing and resurrection, features which proved central to the Christian message but also provided fodder for the pagan disputants of the movement. Second is a concern for truth, presumably in juxtaposition with falsehood. Throughout the discourse between pagans and apologists, each side would claim truth for itself and lay deceit or error at the doorstep of its opponent. Finally, Quadratus declares that the effect of Jesus' miracles was an enduring one. According to him, in fact, there were still persons alive when Quadratus penned his defense of the faith who could testify to Jesus having healed them.[123] We can detect in this proclamation a testimony for both the legitimacy of Jesus' miracles (which in later writings is contrasted with charlatans who only pretend to cure) and their positive character (posed in later literature in sharp relief to the ill effects of sorcery and magic).

---

[120]Eusebius, *Hist. eccl.* 4.3.1. For text and translation see Kirsopp Lake, *Eusebius: The Ecclesiastical History* I (LCL; 2 vol.; Cambridge, MA: Harvard University Press, 1948), 306–7.

[121]J. Quasten, *Patrology* I, 190–91. For more on Quadratus see J. R. Harris, "The Apology of Quadratus," *ExpTim* 8/21 (1921), 147–60. Quasten asserts that Harris's hypothesis that other fragments of Quadratus' apology may be interspersed among the Pseudo-Clementines, Barlaam and Joasaph, the Acts of Saint Catherine of Sinai and the Chronicle of John Malalas has been proven false, but he does not elaborate.

[122]Eusebius, *Hist. eccl.* 4.3.1–2. The Greek text is located in K. Lake, *Eusebius: The Ecclesiastical History*, LCL I, 308. The translation into English is my own.

[123]Eusebius accepted this as gospel and, along with his statement that Quadratus addressed his apology to Hadrian (117–138 C.E.), provided him the necessary evidence to ascribe to him an "early date" (ἀρχαιότητα). See K. Lake, *Eusebius: The Ecclesiastical History*, LCL I, 306–7.

In the case of another apology addressed to Hadrian we are more fortunate. The work of Aristides of Athens has survived in an Armenian fragment, a complete Syriac version, and, in Greek, as part of the Greek romance, Barlaam and Joasaph.[124] In terms of content, Aristides introduces his apology with the thesis that the human population of the world falls neatly into four distinct categories: Barbarians, Greeks, Jews, and Christians. He then proceeds to fashion his argument by showing how, of those four groups, only Christians have seized upon the true idea of God. Barbarians worship the four elements, which are part of God's creation and not God himself. Attributed to the deities the Greeks worship are weaknesses and character flaws that unmask their inferiority and lack of divine status. Jews, who merit respect for their laudable moral standards and sense of God's nature, err in their reverence for angels and obsession with cultic practices, such as dietary restrictions and circumcision. Christians alone, claims Aristides, have located the truth in the revealed Trinitarian God. Theirs is an exclusive worship that leads to a pure life. Aristides goes on to describe Christians as persons who hope in the resurrection and who pursue a life of gentle, humble service.[125] He concludes with the declaration, "I do not hesitate to say that the world continues to exist only because of the prayers of supplication of the Christians."[126] This will surface in other early Christian writers as a sort of mantra in defense of the loyalty of Christians for the Roman state.

Justin Martyr. Widely regarded as the most important of the second-century Greek apologists, Justin (c. 100–165 C.E.) was born to pagan parents in Samarian Palestine, in the town of Flavia Neapolis, formerly known as Shechem.[127] The autobiographical account of his conversion reported in *Dialogue with Trypho* (somewhat suspect historically, it should be noted, since the conversion story was composed in a stylized form bearing conventions popular with many second-century writers) indicates that he spent his youth sampling the smorgasbord of philosophical schools (Stoics, Peripatetics, Pythagoreans, Platonists), none of which ultimately proved satisfying to him.[128] Along the way he was exposed to Christians and the charges of immorality

---

[124]Two major studies including critical editions of the *Apology of Aristides* are J. Rendel Harris, *The Apology of Aristides* (TS I; Cambridge: Cambridge University Press, 1893); and Johannes Geffcken, *Zwei griechischen Apologeten* (Hildesheim/New York: Georg Olms Verlag, 1970 [Originally published 1907]).

[125]*Ap. Aris.* 15.

[126]*Ap. Aris.* 16.

[127]For affirmation of this claim see Robert M. Grant, *Greek Apologists*, 50; J. Quasten, *Patrology* I, 196; L. W. Barnard, *Justin Martyr: His Life and Thought* (Cambridge: Cambridge University Press, 1967), 1; Henry Chadwick, "Justin Martyr's Defence of Christianity," *BJRL* 47 (1965), 275–297. For a representative of those whose appraisal of Justin is less flattering, however, see J. Geffcken, *Zwei griechischen Apologeten*, 97–104.

[128]R. M. Grant notes that Justin in crafting the narrative of his conversion was probably influenced by his admiration for the stylized rhetoric of Plato. Lucian and Galen number along other second-century authors who describe their search for truth as a journey from one

directed against them, but their courage in the face of death—in contrast with the reaction to the same by Marcus Aurelius—impressed him favorably.[129] What finally led to his conversion to Christianity, he says though, was a timely encounter with an old man, who convinced him to turn to the Hebrew prophets. When he did, Justin says,

> ...a flame was kindled in my soul; and a love of the prophets, and of those men who are friends of Christ, possessed me...I found this philosophy alone to be safe and profitable. Thus, and for this reason, I became a philosopher, and I could wish that all men were of the same mind as myself, not to turn from the doctrines of the Savior.[130]

Among those whose labors bear his imprint were Tatian and Irenaeus.[131] With regard to his importance, H. Chadwick asserts, "No second-century source is more informative about the way in which the first encounters between the Church and educated society looked to a thoughtful Christian."[132]

That Justin after his conversion continued to clothe himself in the *pallium*, the symbolic cloak of a philosopher, is highly appropriate in view of his apologetic style and strategy. Among Christians, he was the first serious writer to attempt to link the proclaimed elements of the fledgling faith with the well-entrenched and highly respected tenets of Greco-Roman philosophy. Indeed, much of what we label Christian apologetic writing was modeled after Socrates' own defense at his trial, an *apologia* in which he attempted to demonstrate the rationality of his position. The *First Apology* employed stylized features from Plato's works, and Justin's *Second Apology* invoked the name of Socrates several times, including a comparison of him with Jesus to the advantage of Christ (*Ap.* II.10). Justin himself called his work a προσφώνησις, "an address," a term borrowed from Hellenistic rhetoric and defined by Menander as "a speech of praise to rulers spoken by an individual."[133]

He addressed his *First Apology* to the reigning emperor, identified as Antonius Pius, and his philosopher son "Verissimus," presumably Marcus Aurelius.[134] Two

---

philosophy to another. See R. M. Grant, *Greek Apologists*, 50–51. In his *Second Apology*, Justin makes clear that the courage Christians exhibited in the face of death had a transforming effect on him (*Ap.* II.12.1).

[129] *Ap.* II.12.1.

[130] *Dial.* 8. The translation is that of J. Quasten, *Patrology* I, 196.

[131] R. M. Grant, *Greek Apologists*, identifies Justin as "Irenaeus' favorite apologist" (61) because of his bold incarnational Logos Christology, and he refers frequently to the commonly known fact that Justin was the teacher of Tatian (e.g., 124).

[132] H. Chadwick, "Justin Martyr's Defence of Christianity," 275.

[133] Justin, *Ap.* I.1. For more on Menander see R. M. Grant, *Greek Apologists*, 54.

[134] The actual address reads "To the Emperor Titus Aelius Hadrianus Antoninus Pius Caesar Augustus, and the son Verissimus, philosopher, and Lucius, philosopher, by birth son of [L. Aelius] Caesar and by adoption son of Pius and a lover of culture...." The Senate and people of Rome are also named. See the discussion in R. M. Grant, *Greek Apologists*, 52.

themes dominated this treatise. First, Justin called for justice. He sought to belie the slanderous charges of atheism, immorality, and disloyalty directed against Christians. He invited scrutiny of behavior and welcomed judgment for any crime of which a Christian might be found guilty; but he criticized the practice of condemning Christians on the basis of the name alone. This rhetorical strategy became commonplace among apologists, particularly in the writings of Athenagoras and Theophilus.[135] Second, Justin labored to demonstrate the rational basis and actual truth of Christianity. The main pillars of his argument involved identifying Jesus as the *logos*, demonstrating the superior antiquity of Christianity, emphasizing the monotheistic nature of the faith (a belief shared by Platonists), and invoking the authority of prophecy. Again, many of these themes would be reprised in later apologists.[136]

The briefer *Second Apology* appears to have been prompted by a series of condemnations enforced by the prefect of Rome, Urbicus.[137] Addressing this work to the Roman Senate, Justin attempted to call attention to the injustice represented in the execution of these three Christians and to challenge those who accuse Christians of being atheists and impious without reading their teachings or understanding their beliefs. Justin attached blame for such injustice to a brand of hatred born of demons. It was under the influence of evil demons, he explained, that earnest persons such as Socrates became imprisoned and persecuted (*Ap.* II.7).

Dialogue with Trypho differs to some extent from the two apologies, in that it is framed as a response to a Jewish critic and it relies heavily upon the Hebrew scriptures for authoritative support for its contentions. J. Quasten explains that this is due to its being addressed to "an entirely different type of reader," but I believe we need to be wary of such a declaration.[138] Justin may well be fighting on a different front, but that does not mean he is writing to a different audience. This would make it seem odd, though, as R. M. Grant notes, that he would place the story of his own conversion—clearly a model for pagan readers to follow—not in either of his apologies but in his *Dialogue with Trypho*.[139] It is not so odd, however, if one recognizes apologetic literature to be predominantly in-house reading. The church of Justin's day

---

[135] Athenagoras, *Leg.* 1–3; Theophilus, *Autol.* I.1, 12.

[136] See as a small sampling, e.g., the theme of superior antiquity in Tatian (*Or.* 31) and Theophilus (*Autol.* III.17–29); *Logos* theology in Athenagoras (*Leg.* IV.2) and Theophilus (*Autol.* I.7); authority of prophecy in Theophilus (*Autol.* I.14); emphasis on monotheism in Athenagoras (*Leg.* 4).

[137] Based on some confusion between Eusebius' list of Justin's works in comparison with the historian's description of them, some scholars find reason to wonder if the so-called *Second Apology* may in fact be part of the so-called *First Apology*. Grant considers that, if they are parts of a single work rather than two separate pieces, it would be more accurate to identify the work a *biblidion*, "petition," rather than an apology. See, R. M. Grant, *Greek Apologists*, 54–55, and, for a fuller discussion of this issue, P. Keresztes, "The 'So-Called' Second Apology of Justin," *Latomus* 24 (1965), 858–69.

[138] J. Quasten, *Patrology* I, 203.

[139] R. M. Grant, *Greek Apologists*, 51.

included converted Jews and converted pagans. Also, many of those Jewish converts were "Hellenized," highly attuned to the culture and ideas of Greek art, literature, and philosophy.[140] Moreover, it should not be assumed that pagans, particularly converts, would have been unacquainted with the Hebrew Bible. We know of pagans that were sympathizers with Jews (God-fearers), and those pagan converts who associated with the movement would undoubtedly have participated in worship wherein the Jewish scriptures were read. Readers of apologetic literature, therefore, must beware confusing the designated addressee of the apology with the genuine intended audience. In my judgment, we are more likely to ascertain the motives and strategies of the apologists if we read the bulk of their writings as open correspondence with their communities of faith and not as confidential treatises directed to pagan aristocrats. That does not mean, however, that apologists paid no attention to pagan rhetoric in constructing their works; nor does it imply that pagans never read Christian apologetic writings. It is almost certain they did.[141] Yet, Justin was defending the faith on behalf of the faith of the faithful. His arguments, like those of most apologists of any ilk, seldom sound as if they would have proved compelling beyond the confines of his like-minded camp.[142] Within that camp, however, they provided—or were intended to provide—a more secure rational foundation for what those with like minds believed and trusted, but had not yet completely "thought through" or "figured out." Justin and his successors were, most of all, strengthening the belief of believers, not convincing the antagonistic. They were offering those of like mind but fragile faith some matrix of rationality on which to pin their piety. They sought to give those whose thoughts were being swayed some reasons to stay. They were providing those who doubted some semblance of an answer to their questions.

---

[140]See R. M. Price, "'Hellenization' and Logos Doctrine in Justin Martyr," *VC* 42 (1988), 18–23. In this brief article Price warns against overstating the division that existed in Justin's day between Judaism and Hellenism. He cautions, "We should certainly acknowledge that by the time Justin came on the scene a hellenizing process had so long been proceeding within Judaism itself that Judaism no longer presented a sharply contrasting culture"(19). Although Price may have overstated his case—Judaism as a scripture-based, exclusive monotheistic religion did stand in pointed contrast to the eclectic and inclusive polytheistic religions of Greco-Roman antiquity—his caveat nevertheless bears notice.

[141]C. Andresen, for example, has argued ably that Celsus penned his *True Doctrine* in response to Justin's apologetic writings. See Idem, *Logos und Nomos*, e.g. 356–7. For Andresen, Justin is the only Christian apologist from whom the issues Celsus addresses could have been taken. In his mind, there is no way to understand Celsus without Justin. "Kelsos ohne Justin (ist) unverständlich" (357).

[142]Grant points out that Justin spends nearly half of his apology adducing Old Testament predictions that anticipate Christ. "It is hard to imagine," he says, "a Roman emperor, or even a secretary dealing with petitions, finding this kind of material convincing or impressive." Grant goes on to assert his opinion that such collections of proof texts were gathered for use within the Christian community where it was especially suited for controversies with Jews. R. M. Grant, *Greek Apologists*, 62.

THE PEN AND THE SWORD

In comparison with the two apologies, however, the *Dialogue with Trypho* embarked on a different tack against the tempestuous forces that threatened to swamp the ecclesiastical ship. Rather than drafting the authority of Socrates and Platonic philosophy, it charted a new course with the prophetic writings of the Old Testament and their purported anticipation of the incarnation of the divine Logos, Christ, serving as magnetic north. Yet, Justin did not so much denigrate Greco-Roman philosophy as he detailed how his faith superceded it. It was toward this end that he related his autobiography, describing how his journey in search of truth took him through various and many philosophies before he finally located it in Christianity. Still, the central thesis of *Dialogue with Trypho*, particularly of chapters 32–110, was that Jesus Christ constituted the fulfillment of Hebrew prophecy.

As an apologetic strategy, the importance of this theme cannot be overstated. Not only does this line of discourse permeate the *Dialogue*, but it also finds residence in a number of other apologists. Much of the insult heaped upon Jesus—particularly that related to his recent appearance, scandalous birth, and heinous execution—was defended in terms of Old Testament prophecy. So, too, the dismissive feature of Christianity as a "novel" religious movement was rebuffed by claiming a level of antiquity that went beyond that of the Romans, Greeks, or even Jews. The Old Testament figure Moses, some apologists would articulate, was older than Plato, older than Socrates, older even than Hesiod and Homer and the heroes of their writings. And Jesus, as the incarnate Logos, was older than Moses. All these arguments grew out of a strategy that was rooted in the Gospel tradition, but was first fashioned in terms of apologetic rhetoric in the works of Justin.[143] His Logos corresponded in large measure to that of Middle Platonism, the personal reason of God in which all nations could potentially partake. In this, he and Celsus could have and would have found common ground. Where they came to the proverbial fork in the road was with Justin's assertion that the whole Logos resided in Christ alone. Where for Celsus the Ἀληθὴς Λόγος ("True Word") consisted of a perennial wisdom accessible to all people, for Justin the fullness of the Logos was bound up exclusively in the proclamation of Jesus as the personified wisdom of God.[144] On this point, he and Philo might have agreed.[145]

---

[143]Perhaps the most lucid discussion of this topic as it developed in apologetic discourse is located in Arthur J. Droge, *Homer or Moses? Early Christian Interpretations of the History of Culture* (Tübingen: J. C. B. Mohr (Paul Siebeck), 1989). His discussion of Justin, in particular, on this topic of antiquity and the Christian supersession of Judaism may be found on pages 49–81. Carl Andresen also offers insight into this theme in his work on the relationship between Celsus and Justin. See idem, *Logos und Nomos*, 308 f.

[144]Compare, e.g., Justin's Logos as timeless divine principle (334) with that of Celsus' concept of the "true word" (*Wahrer Logos*) being equivalent to "an ancient word" (*alter Logos*)(112) in C. Andresen, *Logos und Nomos*, 334.

[145]Some have argued that Justin borrowed his doctrine of Logos as Sophia from Philo, but Grant takes the position that his doctrine of the Logos "was based on a doctrine of Sophia developed within Hellenistic Judaism but not taken directly from Philo of Alexandria." Grant underscores the difference by pointing out the varying familial relationship. For Philo, God is

For Justin, though, Jesus was ἕτερος ἀριθμῷ, "distinct in number" from God, different in the sense that light is different from the sun. Already for Justin we see features of evolving Christology—not yet orthodoxy but no longer lacking nuance. Jesus the Logos was both one with and distinct from God the Father. Features of his Logos theology would continue to inspire and evolve in the writings of other Christian apologists, Athenagoras and Theophilus, to name but two.[146]

Before leaving Justin, a word is in order about his knowledge and use of the New Testament writings.[147] It is well known that Justin frequently referred to τὰ ἀπομνημονεύματα τῶν ἀποστόλων, "the *memoirs* of the apostles."[148] L. W. Barnard argues that Justin's use of the term is descriptive and intentional. Since the term Gospel was already well established by Justin's day, he appears to be doing something deliberate in using this different word. While some have argued that he was merely borrowing a phrase once used by Papias, Barnard questions this on the basis that Justin nowhere else cites Papias and that their respective approaches to the faith differ. Instead, he contends that Justin was building on the popularity of a work on Socrates by Xenophon, Ἀπομνημονεύματα Σωκράτους, *Memoirs of Socrates*. In consciously employing this phrase, Justin was attempting to offer readers unfamiliar with the Gospels but acquainted with Xenophon an indication of the sort of writing these books contained. Justin indicates that these books were read in worship and served as the basis of Christian preaching.[149]

Scholars continue to debate the content of these memoirs, whether Justin knew some or all of the canonical Gospels, and/or some of the non-canonical Gospels. L. W. Barnard reports that Justin's allusions or citations correspond to parts of every chapter of Matthew's Gospel, and to all but seven chapters of Luke's Gospel.[150] Although no direct quotations from the Gospel of John appear in Justin's writings, "certain passages," states Barnard, "are most naturally explained as reminiscences of

---

Father of the created universe, while Sophia is its mother and nurse; whereas, in Justin, Jesus is Son and Logos. R. M. Grant, *Greek Apologists*, 61.

[146]Athenagoras, *Leg.* IV.2; Theophilus, *Autol.* I.7. W. R. Schoedel has even crafted the argument that Justin may have had some degree of influence on Athenagoras in the latter's development of early Trinitarian ideas. Schoedel's contention is that the doctrine of the Trinity, with its image of God being multifaceted, may have emerged, at least in part, in response to Christian monotheism attempting to portray itself in a way that could supplant the pluralistic nature of deity inherent in polytheism. See idem, "A Neglected Motive for Second-Century Trinitarianism," *JTS*, n. s. XXXI, 2 (1980), 356–67, esp. 365–7.

[147]I am following closely here the lucid and informative discussion of this topic in L. W. Barnard, *Justin Martyr*, 54–63.

[148]Once in the *First Apology* (47) and seven times in *Dialogue with Trypho* (100–104, 106), Justin speaks of "the memoirs of the apostles." Four more times in the *Dialogue* (105, 107) he speaks of "memoirs."

[149]*Ap.* I.33; *Dial.* 88, 100–104, 106.

[150]L. W. Barnard, *Justin Martyr*, 59.

the Fourth Gospel."[151] R. M. Grant expressing greater confidence declares, "it is virtually certain that he knew the Gospel of John."[152] Still, Barnard deduces, Justin's use of John's Gospel appears "tentative," and calls into question the extent to which Justin regarded this Gospel to be scripture.[153]

With regard to non-canonical writings, A. J. Bellinzoni concludes his study of the sayings of Jesus in Justin's writings asserting, "there is a considerable amount of evidence that indicates that Justin's sources were not always the canonical gospels themselves but rather post-canonical sources based on the synoptic gospels," but also that there is "no evidence to support the position that Justin is dependent on one or more non-canonical gospels."[154] Bellinzoni believes that the Martyr's citations of the sayings of Jesus most closely resemble those of a post-synoptic harmony of the Gospels, and, more specifically, appear characteristic of a *vade mecum* designed to answer and refute challenges to the faith.[155] With regard to other New Testament books, although many allusions to them appear in his authentic works, the only clearly discernible citation stems from Revelation 20:2. Otherwise the Martyr's writings contain no precise quotations from the New Testament, although scholars recognize connections with various other canonical books.[156]

Although he was not the literary or intellectual equal of Athenagoras, and certainly not of Origen, Justin Martyr stands tall in the light of historical evaluation for his pioneering efforts to integrate the rational basis of philosophical integrity with his belief in Jesus as the incarnate Logos and resurrected Christ. As such, Justin's esteemed place among the Christian apologists requires no "apology."

---

[151]L. W. Barnard, *Justin Martyr*, 61. Most notably one thinks of the apparent reference to John 3:5 in Justin, *Ap.* I.51 (see *ANF* I, 183), although, as D. Moody Smith points out, Justin here neither cites his source nor applies to it the moniker "memoirs," his typical term for Synoptic Gospels. See D. Moody Smith, *John* (Abingdon New Testament Commentaries; Nashville: Abingdon Press, 1999), 24.

[152]R. M. Grant, *Greek Apologists*, 58.

[153]L. W. Barnard, *Justin Martyr*, 60–61.

[154]A. J. Bellinzoni, *The Sayings of Jesus in the Writings of Justin Martyr* (NovTSup XVII; Leiden: E. J. Brill, 1967), 139.

[155]A. J. Bellinzoni, *The Sayings of Jesus in the Writings of Justin Martyr*, 140–41.

[156]L. W. Barnard, e.g., reports the connections between Acts 13:27, 28, 48 and *Ap.* I.49; Acts 1:8, 9, 2:33 and *Ap.* I.1; Acts 7:52 and *Dial.* 16; Acts 4:27 and *Ap.* I.40; Romans 4:10–11 and *Dial.* 23; 1 Corinthians 5:8 and *Dial.* 14, 111; 1 Corinthians 12:7–10 and *Dial.* 39; as well as 2 Thessalonians, Galatians, Colossians, Hebrews, 1 John, and possibly 1 Peter. Barnard additionally calls attention to Justin's constant reiteration of the Pauline phrase πρωτότοκος πάσης κτίσεως, and suggests that Justin's desire to take exception to Marcion indicates a familiarity on the part of Justin with Marcion's writings and the Pauline epistles as a group. Barnard concludes his observations, stating, "Only the Pastoral Epistles appear to have left no impression on Justin's writings." Idem, *Justin Martyr*, 62–3.

Tatian. As an author, we are told, Tatian was prolific; yet history has bequeathed to us portions of only two of his works. Although he is probably best known for his *Diatessaron*, a harmonized account of the Jesus narrative consisting of material edited from the four canonical Gospels, we should not overlook the fact that Tatian also wrote an apology. In fact, *Oratio ad Graecos,* or *The Discourse to the Greeks,* is his only composition that survives in full.[157] A firm date for the work remains uncertain, but Miroslav Marcovich offers reasons for dating the work between 165–172 C.E.[158] R. M. Grant, though, believes Tatian was, in part, aroused to write this work in response to the publication of and aftermath associated with Celsus' *True Word;* he, therefore, prefers to place the distribution of *Oratio* a bit later, nearer the episode of the Gallican Martyrs, which took place around 177–178 C.E.[159] On this point, however, Arthur J. Droge disagrees with Grant, acknowledging that Tatian could have known the treatise of Celsus, but avowing that the evidence is lacking to prove that Tatian had Celsus specifically in mind when he composed his defense.[160] Droge remains unconvinced that the criticisms advanced in *True Doctrine* were unique to Celsus, and proffers as the greater likelihood that Tatian was responding to ideas that were common in educated pagan circles. Despite this lack of consensus surrounding the specifics related to this work, however, *Discourse to the Greeks* heralds Tatian as more than just a harmonizer of texts; he labored as a Christian apologist. Later in this volume, in fact, I will join swords with those scholars who argue that, at least in part, apologetic motivation prompted Tatian's compilation of the *Diatessaron.*[161]

---

[157]Recent critical editions have been compiled by Molly Whittaker, ed. and trans., *Tatian: Oratio ad Graecos and Fragments* (Oxford: Clarendon Press, 1982); and Miroslav Marcovich, ed., *Tatiani: Oratio ad Graecos* (PTS 43; Berlin/New York: Walter de Gruyter, 1995).

[158]M. Marcovich, *Tatian: Oratio ad Graecos,* 2–3. Marcovich contends that the text of *Oratio* offers hints that Tatian knew of the death of Justin, which occurred around 165 C.E., and establishes the *terminus ante quem* on the basis of when, according to Eusebius, Tatian vacated Rome to return east and set up his own sect, the ascetic Encratites.

[159]R. M. Grant, *Greek Apologists,* 112–13.

[160]Arthur J. Droge, *Homer or Moses?,* 99–100.

[161]See, e.g., William L. Petersen, *Tatian's Diatessaron: Its Creation, Dissemination, Significance, and History in Scholarship* (Leiden: E. J. Brill, 1994), 26, wherein he states that along with the goal of evangelism and the wish to reproduce as fully as possible the richness of the tradition, a third factor in the design of Gospel harmonies like the Diatessaron seems to have been the "desire to disarm critics of Christianity, such as Celsus, who used the inconsistencies and contradictions in the gospels to prove that the new religion was a fraud." T. Baarda also argues persuasively for this position. See idem, "ΔΙΑΦΩΝΙΑ–ΣΥΜΦΩΝΙΑ: Factors in the Harmonization of the Gospels, Especially in the Diatessaron of Tatian," in *Gospel Traditions of the Second Century: Origins, Recensions, Text, and Transmission,* William L. Petersen, ed. (South Bend, IN: University of Notre Dame Press, 1989), 133–154.

On the other hand, Kenneth Carroll offers a slightly different view, arguing that the New Testament came into being to protect the church against the growing flood of apocryphal literature, rather than as a reaction to heretics such as Marcion or Montanus. Still, he concedes that concern for these popular heretics served as a catalyst to hasten the process. Their

Before proceeding, however, a brief word about his biography is in order. A pupil of Justin, Tatian too was born of pagan parents. He was reared somewhere in Assyria, traveled widely, and received a conventional Hellenistic education steeped in rhetoric and philosophy. In the autobiographical account of his conversion (*Or.* 29), he indicates that, after experiencing myriad cults and mystery religions and studying the Greek philosophers, he came to believe through his encounter with the sacred scriptures that Christian doctrine was the only true philosophy. Although in this he sounds much like his master, Tatian and Justin differed widely in their appraisals of the value of philosophy. Where Justin continued to maintain that features of the truth could be found there, Tatian denounced Greek philosophy in its entirety. Indeed, there is a sense in which *Discourse to the Greeks* reads, in the words of J. Quasten, "not so much as an apology for Christianity as it is a vehement, immoderate polemic treatise which rejects and belittles the whole culture of the Greeks."[162] Such severity and extremity characterizes the *Oratio*, and explains his compulsion to retire from Rome and, around 172 C.E., to return to Mesopotamia to establish a branch of the movement more exclusive and ascetic in character.[163] Known as the Encratites, members of this sect renounced marriage as adultery, refused to eat meat, denied the salvation of Adam, and reflected ideas characteristic of Christian Gnosticism. Also, their objection to drinking wine led them to substitute water in place of wine during the celebration of the Eucharist.[164]

---

contribution, though, was more negative than positive. Every New Testament that appeared in the church at the close of the second century, he observes, possessed an expanded collection of Paul's letters and a collection of four gospels, except in Syria, where Tatian's *Diatessaron* prevailed. For his full discussion see Kenneth Carroll, "Tatian's Influence on the Developing New Testament," in Boyd L. Daniels and M. Jack Suggs, eds. *Studies in the History and Text of the New Testament in honor of Kenneth Willis Clark, Ph.D.* (SD XXIX; Salt Lake City: University of Utah Press, 1967), 59–70.

[162]J. Quasten, *Patrology* I, 221.

[163]Epiphanius (*Pan.* I.3.46) indicates an earlier departure, around 150 C.E., but the later date attested by Eusebius (*Chron.* XII) seems more accurate in view of his reported relationships with Justin, Irenaeus, a certain Rhodo (an opponent of Marcion), and Clement of Alexandria, and his own leadership of the Roman school. See M. Whittaker, *Tatian: Oratio ad Graecos,* ix.

[164]Recent scholarship has sought some clarity with regard to Tatian's precise relationship to Encratism. See, e.g., the useful discussion and further bibliography in William L. Petersen, *Tatian's Diatessaron,* 76–83. Irenaeus, he explains, was the trailblazer in accusing Tatian of heresy, associating him with both the Encratism of Saturninus and Marcion as well as the Gnosticism of Valentinus. Petersen points out, however, that since Valentinians also exhibited ascetic tendencies, it is not necessary to view these charges as distinct. Tatian's affiliation with Encratism recurs in the writings of Hippolytus, Epiphanius, Ps.-Tertullian, and Jerome, while Eusebius embellishes the charge by identifying him as the founder of the Encratites. Petersen points out the error in this, though, by citing the report of Irenaeus (*Haer.* I.28.1; cf. Eusebius, *Hist. eccl.* IV.29.2) in naming Saturninus and Marcion as the wellspring for the ascetic sect. Petersen points out further that, although evidence for the charge of Encratism is virtually lacking in *Oratio*, a number of scattered verses of the *Diatessaron* lend credence to ascetic

Tatian begins *Discourse to the Greeks* with a harsh verbal assault on Greek philosophy and culture, charging that whatever is of value in Greek thought has been plagiarized from others (1–3). In the course of the treatise, he also assails mythology and astrology (8–11); sorcery and medicine (16–18); and pagan customs such as drama, gladiatorial contests, dancing, rhetoric, and legislation (22–28). With regard to Christianity, he affirms the transcendence of God and the creative *Logos* who sprang forth from God and who is in God (4–7). Perhaps the most compelling feature of *Oratio* from an apologetic perspective is Tatian's version of a chronological template designed to demonstrate the antiquity of Christian beliefs (31, 36–41). Developing a concept first introduced by his mentor Justin, Tatian draws on Greek dates for the Trojan War as well as other calendars and genealogies to construct a meticulously detailed historical proof intended to demonstrate that Moses is older than the Chaldeans, Egyptians, Phoenicians, and even Homer. As I noted with regard to Justin, this is a theme that emerges as an apologetic convention, a standard ploy for claiming the revered characteristic of antiquity for a religious movement perceived by many pagan outsiders to be "a novel superstition."[165]

Athenagoras of Athens. A contemporary of Tatian, almost nothing is known of the life of Athenagoras.[166] Among ancient sources, only one, Methodius, mentions him, and that single reference only informs us that he authored the *Plea* (or *Embassy*) *on Behalf of Christians* (*Legatio*). Two works—his apology and a work entitled *On the Resurrection of the Dead* (*De Resurrectione*)—are all that have survived him.[167] Still, from these works we

---

influence. He summarizes the contributions of D. Plooij, A. Vööbus, and Louis Leloir, all of whom have located Diatessaronic readings which, in comparison with canonical parallels, bear the imprint of an ascetically-minded redactor (79f.). Petersen concludes his discussion, "Despite the questionable character of some of the readings, there are enough solid readings...to conclude that some passages of the *Diatessaron* were modified to conform with Encratite beliefs. This tendency is one more piece of evidence—and the only piece of internal evidence—which links Tatian with the *Diatessaron*" (82).

[165]For a thoroughgoing discussion of this feature of apologetic discourse see A. J. Droge, *Homer or Moses?*, especially Chapter 4 on Tatian (pp. 82–101).

[166]Even less is certain about the lives and work of two other apologists contemporary with Tatian and Athenagoras, Miltiades and Apollinaris of Hierapolis. Miltiades is mentioned by Tertullian (*Val.* 5) and Hippolytus (Eusebius, *Hist. eccl.* V.28.4) as someone who defended Christianity against both pagans and heretics. Eusebius (*Hist. eccl.* IV.27) tells of collecting several of the works of the prolific Claudius Apollinaris, Bishop of Hierapolis, including a treatise addressed to Marcus Aurelius and five volumes *Against the Greeks*, as well as a number of anti-heretical works. Since no work by either of these apologists has survived, no further comment on these writers appears necessary or useful here. For more information and references see J. Quasten, *Patrology* I, 228–29.

[167]For more thorough introduction to Athenagoras and critical editions and translations of his apology see J. Geffcken, *Zwei griechischen Apologeten*, William R.. Schoedel, ed. and trans., *Athenagoras: Legatio and De Resurrectione* (Oxford: Clarendon Press, 1972); and Leslie W. Barnard, *Athenagoras: A Study in Second Century Christian Apologetic* (ThH 18; Paris: Beauchesne, 1972).

can discern that Athenagoras was a person of letters, an able thinker and writer, and deserving of the epithet with which he identified himself, philosopher. J. Quasten, in fact, describes him as "unquestionably the most eloquent of the early Christian apologists."[168]

The salutation of the *Plea* suggests that it was written sometime during the co-regency shared by Marcus Aurelius and Commodus, and so scholars generally assign *Legatio* a date between 176–180 C.E.[169] With Athenagoras, the question of audience is even more convoluted than usual. J. Geffcken was adamant that *Legatio* was literature and not imperial correspondence, academic and not practical.[170] Leslie W. Barnard was less skeptical, and offered a number of reasons for taking seriously Athenagoras' addressing his embassy to the emperors. Marcus Aurelius, he reported, in squelching the revolt of Cassius in 175 C.E., showed magnanimity toward the city and purportedly carried himself there like a philosopher. Barnard wondered if it was not possible that Athenagoras, upon learning of this, might well have taken the chance that the emperor would actually give his words a hearing.[171] Similarly, W. R. Schoedel observed that the author wrote as though he were actually addressing his emperors, and he recalled Philo's *Embassy* and the writings of other ancient authors as evidence that emperors did in fact receive such correspondence and treat it in a judicial manner. Such writings, though, Schoedel pointed out, usually focused on a particular incident, and Athenagoras omitted any such direct reference. So, Schoedel remained cautious in presuming that Athenagoras could have actually directed his *Embassy* toward the imperial court. He entertained the possibility that it could have been composed with the hope of being read by the imperial Secretariate assigned such responsibilities, but he concluded with greater conviction that Athenagoras "was constructing an oration in the forensic style in obedience to the rules of rhetoric."[172]

To be sure, *Legatio* is composed in a forensic style. The apology is constructed as a refutation of three accusations that Athenagoras says pagans falsely direct at Christians: atheism, Thyestean banquets (cannibalism), and Oedipean intercourse

---

[168]J. Quasten, *Patrology* I, 229.

[169]W. R. Schoedel further notes that if one interprets literally the phrase "deep peace" in *Leg.* I.2, it would probably indicate a date prior to the persecution of the Gallic Martyrs in 177–178 C.E. Marcus Aurelius died March 17, 180 C.E. He is less inclined to accept the judgment of Eusebius (*Hist. eccl.* V.1.1 ff.) that authorship of the apology was precipitated by these martyrdoms in Lyons and Vienne. W. R. Schoedel, *Athenagoras*, xi.

[170]J. Geffcken, *Zwei griechischen Apologeten*, 99, n. 1; cf. W. R. Schoedel, *Athenagoras*, xiii–xiv, and xiv, n. 17 for his consideration of and response to Geffcken on this point.

[171]See the lucid discussion by L. W. Barnard on this question in idem, *Athenagoras*, 22–4, where he concludes, "In any event, it would seem that we should not be too sceptical about the historical basis of *Leg.* II although, no doubt, Athenagoras also intended his apology to have a wider circulation in the Graeco-Roman world." (24)

[172]W. R. Schoedel, *Athenagoras*, xii–xiii.

(incest).[173] To the first charge, Athenagoras maintained that Christians were not atheists, but monotheists. It was out of devotion to their one true revealed God that they held back homage to idols, demons, and other presumed deities. Regarding cannibalism, the apologist insisted that Christians refrained not only from committing murder, but also from attending events in the arena in which murder was perpetrated as spectacle. By such restraint, he attested, Christians demonstrated a greater regard for human life than did pagans. Finally, with respect to the charge of incest, Athenagoras pleaded innocent. Christians, he explained, esteemed marriage, chastity, and even virginity. He even went so far as to label any second marriage "a gilded adultery."[174] The persistence and diligence with which Athenagoras addressed these accusations of immorality marked his attempt to meet with equal force the seriousness of the threat these frequently-voiced charges posed.[175]

Theophilus of Antioch. Eusebius informs us that Theophilus was the sixth bishop of Syrian Antioch.[176] His writings indicate that, like Justin and Tatian before him, he was born to pagan parents and became the beneficiary of a Hellenistic education. His conversion to Christianity occurred in his maturity and was prompted by his intense reading of scripture. Of his writings, only an apologetic work addressed to his pagan friend Autolycus and consisting of three volumes survives.[177] Because the chronology outlined in the third volume ceases with the death of Marcus Aurelius, scholars date the finished work just after 180 C.E.[178] The question of audience appears most sagely resolved, once again, by treating the work as a document that is addressed to a specific individual but that clearly has a wider public audience in mind.

---

[173] These charges and parodies can be located in such pagan voices as Marcus Fronto, Lucian of Samosata, and Celsus. See the relevant sections above.

[174] *Leg.* 33.4–6. The translation is that of W. R. Schoedel in idem, *Athenagoras*, 81; cf. "decent adultery," the phrase used in *ANF* 2, 146 f.

[175] As was noted above in our discussion of Marcus Fronto, Lucian of Samosata, and Celsus.

[176] *Hist. eccl.* IV.20. Yet, R. M. Grant (*Greek Apologists*, 143) points out that Eusebius apparently was unfamiliar with Book III of *Ad Autolycum*, because the historian reported the year 177 C.E. as the end of the episcopate of Theophilus, whereas *Autol.* III.27 specifically mentions the death of Marcus Aurelius. Of course, it is also possible that Eusebius was in error or that Theophilus retired as bishop but continued to write.

[177] For introduction and texts see Robert M. Grant, ed. and trans. *Theophilus of Antioch: Ad Autolycum.* (Oxford: Clarendon Press, 1970) and idem, *Greek Apologists*, 140–174; Miroslav Marcovich, ed., *Theophili Antiocheni: Ad Autolycum* (PTS 44; Berlin/New York: Walter de Gruyter, 1995); and J. Quasten, *Patrology* I, 236–42. More extensive bibliography may be located in these references.

[178] J. Quasten, *Patrology* I, 237. R. M. Grant (*Greek Apologists*, 143), however, notes that Irenaeus' familiarity with the first two books of *Ad Autolycum* suggests that they were written earlier.

Ad Autolycum features a number of themes readily recognizable as stock apologetic ploys. In Book I, for example, he defends the name "Christian" by employing a play on the word χρηστός, i.e., "good" or "useful." Theophilus states that he bears the name Christian in hopes of proving of "good use" (εὐχρηστός) to God, while he questions whether Autolycus considers himself of "no use" (ἀχρηστός) to God.[179] Also, with regard to homage due the emperor, Theophilus echoes sentiments rooted in the New Testament tradition (e.g., Rom 13:1f., 1 Cor 9:17, 1 Pet 2:15–17) and familiar in apologetic discourse as far back as Aristides.

> Accordingly, I will pay honor to the emperor not by worshiping him but by praying for him. I worship the God who is real and true God, since I know that the emperor was made by him.[180]

In Book II, Theophilus redirects his discussion in the form of an attack on the foibles of pagan religion. The bishop ridicules as absurd the idolatry and mythology of pagan religion, and, in much the same way pagan critics assail Christian scriptures, highlights inconsistencies and the lack of harmony he finds in pagan tales.[181] He then turns his attention to his scriptures, and spends much of the rest of Book II interpreting the Hebrew scriptures, especially Genesis and the creation narrative, from a Christian perspective, and often with allegorical license.[182]

Theophilus of Antioch begins Book III with a salutation that recalls Luke's address to his Theophilus at the beginnings of Luke and Acts, speaking of the many histories that speak in vain and his desire to compose a work of clarifying precision. It is within this volume that Theophilus follows in the footsteps of Justin and Tatian in laying out his own version of a chronological argument for the antiquity of the Christian faith. Like his predecessors, his concern is to demonstrate the temporal priority of Moses over all other ancient sages and writers in order to secure the benefits associated with antiquity for the Christian movement.[183] Recalling Athenagoras, Book III also contains a defense of Christian behavior against the perceptions of unchastity and incestuous promiscuity (III.4, 8, 13), cannibalism and Thyestean banquets (III.15), and atheism (III.9), as well as Theophilus' tailored response to the pejorative description of Christianity as a novel and foolish religion (III.4). Once again, not only are these patterns of discourse frequent in the apologetic corpus, but many of these themes will compel notice in some of the scribal modifications that will be examined in subsequent chapters.

---

[179] *Autol.* I.1.
[180] *Autol.* I.11.
[181] *Autol.* II.1–8.
[182] *Autol.* II.9–38.
[183] *Autol.* III.16–29.

Melito of Sardis. Bishop of Sardis in Lydia in the later second century, Melito was remembered by his contemporaries as a person of great spiritual devotion and zeal for the faith.[184] Although today he is probably best known for his severely polemical anti-Jewish *Paschal Homily*, of greater interest for this present study is another work for which he was responsible. Sometime during the decade beginning in 170 C.E., Melito addressed an apology on behalf of Christianity to Emperor Marcus Aurelius. Of this work only fragments have survived, the most important of which were preserved by Eusebius.[185] These fragments demonstrate Melito to be among the most diplomatically savvy of the Christian apologists. Laying claim to the common view that Roman piety had led to Roman power, Melito called attention to the fact that the rise to prominence of the Roman Empire coincided precisely with the incarnation of Jesus during the reign of Caesar Augustus. Indeed, he believed, it was providence more than coincidence.

> The most convincing proof that the flourishing of our religion has been a boon to the Empire thus happily inaugurated is the fact that the Empire has suffered no mishaps since the reign of Augustus, but on the contrary, everything has increased its splendor and fame in accordance with the general prayer.[186]

Melito was perhaps the most articulate spokesperson for this apologetic theme, a message crucial in a Roman world iron-fisted and swift to judge even the hint of treason. Where pagan critics fostered suspicions that Christians were subversives, Melito stood for those apologists who negotiated the far different claim that Christians were in fact a boon to the emperor and his empire. It may be from Melito that Tertullian later borrowed this notion and used it in his own apologetic discourse.[187] To be sure, this was an argument often imitated. Indeed, such diplomatic strategies, as we shall see below in Chapter 5, also left an imprint on the scribal tradition of the canonical Gospels.

---

[184]Eusebius, *Hist. eccl.* V.24.5. See also the discussions in J. Quasten, *Patrology* I, 242–48; R. M. Grant, *Greek Apologists*, 92–98. For fuller discussions of Melito and *Peri Pascha* see Alistair Stewart-Sykes, *The Lamb's High Feast: Melito, Peri Pascha, and the Quartodeciman Paschal Liturgy at Sardis* (Leiden: E. J. Brill, 1998); Idem, *On Pascha* (Crestwood, NY: St. Vladimir's Seminary Press, 2001); Idem, "Melito's Anti-Judaism," *JECS* 5 (1997): 271–83; Thomas Halton, "Stylistic Devices in Melito *Peri Pascha*," in *Kyriakon: Festschrift Johannes Quasten*, ed. Patrick Granfield and Josef A. Jungmann (Münster: Aschendorff, 1970), 249–55; A. Wifstrand, "The Homily of Melito on the Passion," *VC* 2 (1948): 201–23; and S. G. Hall, "Melito in Light of the Passover Haggadah," *JTS* n. s. 2 (1971): 29–46.

[185]Eusebius, *Hist. eccl.* IV.26. For the texts see S. G. Hall, ed., *Melito of Sardis: On Pascha and Fragments* (Oxford: Clarendon Press, 1979).

[186]Eusebius, *Hist. eccl.* IV.26.8. This is the translation of J. Quasten, *Patrology* I, 242. Cf. Kirsopp Lake, ed. and trans., *Eusebius: Ecclesiastical History,* 2 Volumes (LCL; Cambridge, MA: Harvard University Press, 1949), I.390–91.

[187]R. M. Grant believes so. Idem, *Greek Apologists*, 187–88.

Clement of Alexandria. Born around 150 C.E. probably in Athens, his pagan parents saw that Titus Flavius Clemens received a thorough Greek education.[188] His lifetime love of learning led him throughout Italy, Syria, Palestine, and Egypt as he sought to hear the most noted educators of his day. It was in Alexandria, finally, that he met Pantaenus, who mentored him prior to Clement succeeding him as head of the Alexandrian school.[189] Persecutions under Septimus Severus forced him away from Egypt to security in Cappadocia, where he died near 215 C.E.

Clement's writings appear to confirm a breadth in his education and a depth to his intellect, showing him to be conversant in poetry, philosophy, mythology and literature.[190] Allusions to biblical texts from both testaments number in the thousands, while hundreds of times he refers to the classics of Greek literature. Although it presses the boundaries of the category to identify Clement as an apologist, his *Protrepticus* (or *Exhortation to the Greeks*) does show some kinship with earlier Christian

---

[188]See J. Quasten, *Patrology* II, 5–36.

[189]Current scholarship continues to dispute whether in fact there did exist a so-called "Alexandrian School." Eusebius makes reference to the school in *Hist. eccl.* 4.11; 5.10.2; 6.3.8; 7.32.30; 15.1; and 28.1. M. Hornschuh ("Das Leben des Origenes und die Entstehung der alexandrinische Schule," *Zeitschrift für Kirchengeschichte* 71 (1960): 193–214), G. Bardy ("Aux origines de l'Ecole d'Alexandrie," *RSR* 27 (1937): 65–90), and Johannes Munck (*Untersuchen über Klemens von Alexandrien* (Stuttgart, 1933), 185) accuse Eusebius of confusing official, public catechesis with private instruction, and thereby dispute the accuracy of his description of an Alexandrian School; moreover, they express the widely held view that no "official" catechetical institution existed in Alexandria until after Clement.

André Méhat (*Étude sur les "Stromates" de Clément d'Alexandrie*, PatSor 7 (Paris, 1966), 62–70) challenged this consensus on the basis that scholars reaching this conclusion were operating with a severely restricted definition of "catechetical." Rather than insisting that "catechetical" meant public and official education leading to baptism, Méhat offered reasons for accurately applying the term "school" to the private instruction practiced in Alexandria by such notables as Pantaenus and Clement. Robert L. Wilken ("Alexandria: A School for Training in Virtue," in *Schools of Thought in the Christian Tradition*, ed. Patrick Henry (Philadelphia: Fortress, 1984), 15–30) credits Méhat with drawing attention to the continuity that existed between the early instructors and later catechists of Alexandria, but also recognizes that his work has failed to satisfy those who criticize the reports of Eusebius. Wilken, therefore, defines the phrase "school of Alexandria" as "a way of speaking of the intellectual and spiritual activity of the early teachers in Alexandria at the time Christianity first comes into historical focus there at the end of the second century" (18). R. M. Grant ("Theological Education at Alexandria," in *The Roots of Egyptian Christianity*, ed. Birger A. Pearson and James E. Goehring (Philadelphia: Fortress, 1986, 178–89)—who portrays Philo, the Therapeutae, and Valentinian Gnosticism as among the shaping influences of Alexandrian Christianity—joins Wilken in redefining Alexandrian instruction in terms of ideas and exegetical method rather than basic catechesis (180–85). Wilken succeeds in making a case for identifying the school of Alexandria as a center for "training in virtue" (19).

[190]R. M. Grant is less convinced, asserting that the brevity and scope of his citations offers reason to attribute them to Clement's use of standard anthologies rather than his mastery of vast quantities of literature. Idem, *Greek Apologists*, 180.

apologies, particularly in its ridicule of pagan mythology and assertion of greater antiquity. Indications in the volume suggest that he was acquainted with Melito and Tatian.[191] Still, as J. Quasten points out, Clement represented an evolution of thought beyond that of the earlier apologists. For him it was no longer necessary to defend the faith against defamation and trumped up charges. His task was not to defend Christians but to convince pagans to join them.[192] In this regard, he most nearly resembles Justin in his *Dialogue with Trypho* and the *Octavius* of Minucius Felix.

Origen. "Probably the greatest scholar of Christian antiquity,"[193] Origen (c. 185–254 C.E.) is almost certainly the most important source for informing the present study.[194] Undoubtedly one of the great intellectuals of his day, he labored as a prolific author,[195] skilled linguist,[196] brilliant theologian, and firm defender of the faith who was destined in time to be, by the very church he helped mold and preserve, labeled a heretic.[197] Henri Crouzel asserts that, with the possible exception of Cyprian of Carthage, more

---

[191]For references and more discussion see R. M. Grant, *Greek Apologists*, 180.

[192]J. Quasten, *Patrology* II, 8.

[193]A widely held consensus here voiced by B. Altaner, *Patrology*, 223.

[194]The amount of material published on the subject of Origen is imposing. Fine scholarly introductions may be located in the work of Henri Crouzel, *Origen* (A. S. Worrall, trans.; San Francisco: Harper & Row, 1989; original French edition, 1985) and Joseph W. Trigg, *Origen* (London and New York: Routledge, 1998). Extensive additional bibliography may be located in Henri Crouzel, *Bibliographie critique d'Origène* and *Supplements* 1 and 2 (The Hague: Martinus Nijhoff, 1971, 1982, and 1996).

[195]The volume of his literary output surpasses that of all other writers of Christian antiquity, observes B. Altaner, *Patrology*, 225.

[196]With the support of his wealthy patron Ambrose, Origen compiled the monumental *Hexapla*, a comparative edition of the Hebrew Bible in which six parallel columns reported the texts of (1) the Hebrew text; (2) the Hebrew text transliterated into Greek characters; and the Greek translations of (3) Aquila; (4) Symmachus; (5) The Septuagint (LXX); and (6) Theodotion. See B. Altaner, *Patrology*, 225–26; J. Quasten, *Patrology* II, 44–45.

[197]Dispute of his orthodoxy arose shortly after his death, and grew more fierce when Epiphanius and Theophilus of Alexandria assumed the mantle of the opposition around 400 C.E. Controversy raged off and on until Emperor Justinian I at the Council of Constantinople in 543 C.E. issued an edict condemning a certain number of theses held by Origen, an edict to which all the bishops of the Empire gave their assent. B. Altaner (*Patrology*, 163) appears correct in this assessment. J. Quasten (*Patrology* II, 40) notes the contradictions of his life, stating:

> True, he committed errors, as we shall see, but no one can doubt but that he always wanted to be an orthodox and believing Christian. He states at the beginning of his main theological work: "That alone is to be accepted as truth which differs in no respect from ecclesiastical and apostolic tradition" (*De princ.* praef. 2). He strove to follow that rule and sealed it with his blood at the end of his life.

For brief additional comments see B. Altaner, *Patrology*, 224–25, 235–44; J. Quasten, *Patrology* II, 40–43. For a thorough study on the Origenist controversies see Elizabeth A. Clark, *The Origenist Controversy: The Cultural Construction of an Early Christian Debate* (Princeton, NJ: Princeton University Press, 1992).

is known of the life of Origen than any other ante-Nicene writer.[198] Born to Christian parents in Alexandria (his father Leonidas was martyred c. 202 C.E.), his bishop Demetrius named the gifted eighteen-year-old head of the Alexandrian catechetical school after Clement was forced to flee to Cappadocia around 203 C.E. The scholarly literature on Origen is vast, and limits of both space and focus forbid a thoroughgoing analysis of him and his writings here. Yet, this is largely unnecessary. *Contra Celsum* provides the natural and obvious point of contact between Origen and this study.[199]

The pages of *Contra Celsum* are unique in form with regard to the other apologetic works we have examined thus far. Commissioned by his wealthy Christian benefactor Ambrose, the volume consists of Origen's direct rebuttal to an older work of pagan polemic against Christianity, the *True Word* of Celsus. Origen structured the book in the form of point-counterpoint, first citing a point of contention from Celsus, and then addressing it directly with the intention of refuting his argument. In one of the many ironic strokes of history, the polemical treatise of Celsus would have been completely lost, probably by the end of the fifth century, had it not been for Origen's numerous and lengthy citations in his apology. One could reasonably infer from his preface that Origen anticipated as much, when he wrote:

> Our Saviour and Lord Jesus Christ was silent when false witnesses spoke against him, and answered nothing when he was accused; he was convinced that all his life and actions among the Jews were better than any speech in refutation of the false witness and superior to any words that he might say in reply to the accusations. And, God-loving Ambrose, I do not know why you wanted me to write an answer to Celsus' false accusations in his book against the Christians and the faith of their churches. It is as though there is not in the mere facts a clear refutation better than any written reply, which dispels the false charges and deprives the accusations of any plausibility and force....Accordingly, I have no sympathy with anyone who had faith in Christ such that it could be shaken by Celsus (who is no longer living the common life among men but has already been dead a long time), or by any plausibility of argument. I do not know in what category I ought to reckon one who needs written arguments in books to restore and confirm him in his faith after it has been shaken by the accusations brought by Celsus against the Christians. But nevertheless, since among the multitude of people supposed to believe some people of this kind might be found,...we decided to yield to your demand and to compose a treatise in reply to that which you sent us.[200]

In many respects, the eight volumes of *Contra Celsum* serve as a compendium of apologetic discourse. Most of the main objections to Christianity raised by pagans and (presumably) razed by apologists can be located here. So, lest we get mired in

---

[198]H. Crouzel, *Origen*, 1.

[199]For the critical edition see Marcel Borret, *Origène: Contra Celse* (Sources Chrétiennes, 5 vols.; Paris: Les Éditions du Cerf, 1967–1976). The best known English translation is that of Henry Chadwick, *Origen: Contra Celsum* (Cambridge: Cambridge University Press, 1953).

[200]*Cels.* Preface 1, 4. Translated by H. Chadwick, *Contra Celsum*, 3–5.

redundancy, it seems prudent to truncate our review of the Greek apologists at this point. Ample opportunity for considering Origen and his *Contra Celsum* will arise during the course of our study.

Select Latin Apologists: Tertullian and Minucius Felix. Although Greek remained the *lingua franca* of the eastern empire for some time, Latin began to make inroads as the dominant language west of Rome and in Africa by the middle of the second and early third centuries.[201] Therefore, alongside these Greek authors, we should not overlook two important Latin apologists of the third century, Tertullian and Minucius Felix.[202] Their work also commands our attention here.

In terms of earlier Christian apologies, the form of the *Octavius* of Marcus Minucius Felix most closely resembles Justin's *Dialogue with Trypho.*[203] It was composed in the form of a philosophical dialogue involving three characters. One, the author, an attorney residing in Rome, assumes the role of mediator in a debate between his two friends, the pagan Caecilius and the Christian Octavius. The work was most probably directed at pagan readers, since it resists the use of scripture and refrains from discussing doctrine.[204] In the story, the three friends are traveling together when Caecilius pays homage to a statue of Serapis, the event that provokes the debate. Making his case, Caecilius contends that when faced with the choice of the invisible god of the Christians or the traditional gods of Rome, it is best to remain loyal to the tradition underlying Rome's greatness. Moreover, he passes on a vituperative depiction of Christians consisting of a harsh litany of *ad hominem* slanders, the source for which is said to be "his friend and countryman," a reference many scholars believe to be Marcus Fronto.[205] Octavius for his part offers a seriatim rebuttal to each of the arguments adduced by Caecilius. Most telling is his argument that accusations against Christian practices and behaviors consist of a slander born of demons. The debate depicted in the *Octavius* ends with the conversion of the pagan Caecilius to the Christian faith, all to the delight of Minucius Felix.

Quintus Septimus Florens Tertullianus was born in Carthage to pagan parents near the middle of the second century. The mature Tertullian (c. 155–220? C.E.) is said to have enjoyed a reputation as a skilled lawyer.[206] After his conversion about 193 C.E.,

---

[201]B. Altaner, *Patrology*, 161.

[202]For a recent introduction to Tertullian and Minucius Felix see Simon Price, "Latin Christian Apologetics: Minucius Felix, Tertullian, and Cyprian," in *Apologetics in the Roman Empire: Pagans, Jews, and Christians*, Mark Edwards, *et al.*, eds. (Oxford: Oxford University Press, 1999), 105–29.

[203]B. Altaner (*Patrology*, 163) also rightly compares it to Cicero's *De natura deorum*.

[204]B. Altaner (*Patrology*, 163) appears correct in this assessment.

[205]Minucius Felix, *Oct.* 8–9. For determining the identity of the friend from Cirta to be Fronto see the discussion in the section above.

[206]Although Eusebius speaks of Tertullian as one "skilled in Roman law" (*Hist. eccl.* 2.2.4), T. D. Barnes makes a compelling case for not identifying the Christian Tertullian with the Roman jurist of the same name, and for questioning whether he ever was a professional lawyer.

he returned to Carthage and began to employ his abilities as an advocate on behalf of the Christian cause, leaving an impressive and influential literary legacy. Although Jerome (*Vir. ill.* 53) reports that he was a priest, since Tertullian himself remains silent on the matter, whether or not he was ordained into the clergy remains disputed.[207] The year 197 saw the publication of his two most important apologetic works, *Ad nationes* (*To the Heathen*) and *Apologeticus* (*Apology*). In the first of these, a two-volume work, Tertullian offered both a defense of Christianity against pagan attacks, and his own assault on the moral and religious decay he associates with paganism.. His *Apology*, addressed to the provincial governors of the Roman Empire, represented an original contribution to apologetic theme, style, and rhetoric. Where previous apologies had been cast in the practiced language of philosophical discourse and the familiar tropes of Hellenistic rhetoric, Tertullian composed this work using judicial terminology, the language of the courts. He did so in order to convict as unjust those who accused Christians of immoral or treasonous behavior. Like Athenagoras, he addressed the specific charges of sacramental cannibalism and Thyestean banquets; but he answered those charges as an attorney rather than as a theologian or philosopher. He contended that a double standard was at work with regard to Christians that made their trials a farce. Where all other criminals received a fair trial, rumor served as the only witness necessary to condemn a Christian.[208] Tertullian's juridical skill reached its zenith when he faced what he considered the most serious charges directed against Christians: contempt for the religion of the state (which was understood as atheism) and treason. In response to these charges he constructed a formidable syllogism. Admitting that Christians did not revere the deities of the pagans, he contended that, first, what passed for pagan gods were actually deceased humans and inanimate idols, and, second, that Christians did in fact worship the one true God, revealed in scripture to be the creator of the world. Therefore, he concluded, since in truth the pagan gods were not gods at all, it was unjust to convict Christians of atheism for their failure to pay them homage.[209]

Tertullian also developed the notion we encountered earlier in Theophilus of Antioch and Melito of Sardis that the emperor and empire prosper in large measure due to the pious and frequent prayers of Christians. Speaking of the emperors, Tertullian wrote:

> He gets his sceptre where he first got his humanity; his power where he first got his breath of life. Thither we lift our eyes....Without ceasing for all our emperors we offer

---

Tertullian, in the estimation of Barnes, undoubtedly possessed a familiarity with legal idiom and an interest in certain aspects of the law, but these are easily attributable to a level of knowledge commensurate with the typical rhetorical education of his day. Cf. idem, *Tertullian: A Historical and Literary Study* (Oxford: Clarendon Press, 1971), 22–29.

[207]B. Altaner (*Patrology*, 166) is as convinced that he was not as J. Quasten (*Patrology* II, 246–47) is sure that he was.

[208]Tertullian, *Ap.* VII.13.

[209]*Ap.* XXIV.1–2.

prayer. We pray for life prolonged; for security to the empire; for protection to the imperial house; for brave armies, a faithful senate, a virtuous people, the world at rest, whatever, as man or Caesar, an emperor would wish.[210]

In my view, his writings and the structure of his arguments show that Tertullian is addressing believers within the fold to a lesser extent than any other apologist. That is to say, Tertullian is not "preaching to the choir." His words seem geared to the pagan public and are meant to persuade. He sounds like a defense attorney prepared to go to trial and determined to win his case.

Unique as Tertullian is among the apologists, however, his brand of determination and his special concern for charges of a public and political nature appear to have left an impression on certain scribes. Readers may anticipate locating in Chapter 5 evidence in the scribal tradition that coincides with Tertullian's passion for eliminating the public perception that Christians are guilty of treason against Rome.

IN SUMMARY: A PROFILE OF APOLOGETIC INTERESTS

The sages tell us that, often, what we see depends on how we see. The search for evidence of apologetic interests in the textual tradition of the canonical Gospels requires us to cultivate an ability to harvest fresh insights from fields that have been reaped and gleaned many times over. In concluding this chapter, my purpose is to introduce the features of a profile in such a way that we might recognize signs of apologetic interests when we encounter them. Sailors say that the way one locates another ship on the distant horizon is not to look at the horizon but above it, in order to see the contours of the boat against the background sky. Similarly, evidence of apologetic interests in the textual tradition can be located only by looking beyond the variant readings themselves to the discursive backdrop from which they initially arose and against which they presently, with some measure of strain, may be discerned. Thus, ours is a search for intersections, precisely the intersection of variant readings that can be determined by reason to be intentional in nature with motivations that sensibly coincide with recognizable apologetic themes, strategies, motifs, or concerns. For purposes of order and convenience, I have organized the findings of my research into four chapters, each of which represents one of the patent themes featured in the polemic discourse between pagans and Christians. Chapter Two concerns issues related to intellectual integrity, and features an analysis of scribal activities related to harmonization, correction, and efforts to buttress Christian claims to antiquity by emphasizing the prophetic foundation of the faith. Chapter Three details the pagan assault on the personality and deeds of Jesus and adduces a number of variant readings that reflect typical apologetic responses, and suggests the development of what we might with some exaggeration label, "The Gospel According to the Scribes." Chapter Four focuses on criticism directed at the followers of Jesus, namely that they consisted

---

[210]*Ap.* XXX. Translated by S. Thelwell, *ANF*, III.42.

of "Fools, Fanatics, and Females." There we will locate and examine a series of deliberately altered readings of passages related to Jesus' followers that appear to replicate apologetic rhetorical strategies. Finally, Chapter Five recalls those tensions that existed between the Roman state and Christianity, and adduces several groups of variant readings that appear to have been influenced by a desire to displace concerns about Christians meeting "in secret," to exonerate Pilate of his role in the death of Jesus, to qualify some of the "kingdom" language used in the Gospels, and to take the offensive, characterizing opponents of Christianity as evil, hypocritical, and violent.

Each of these chapters may be thought of as an ellipse drawn around two foci. First, I begin each chapter with an effort to establish the contours of apologetic interests or concerns related to the specified topic addressed therein. This requires me to offer a brief but summary characterization of representative features of both pagan criticism and apologetic response related to the content of each chapter. Second, the substance of each chapter features an examination of those variant readings I have adduced that, in my judgment, show first of all evidence of intentional scribal activity and, moreover, appear to have been modified in ways that mirror the particular apologetic themes or dynamics as previously discerned within the discourse between apologists and their pagan opponents.

Many of my treatments of these selected variant readings will strike a familiar chord with New Testament textual scholars, but in some instances it has been necessary for me to cut against the grain of scholarly consensus (or at least the opinion of the editorial committee for N-A[27]/UBS[4]) in order to demonstrate the direction of scribal activity away from the "original" text. The requisite energy for this effort has been born, in part, from an optimism that the evidence reported herein will prove compelling, and that readers will come to believe with me that *scribes engaged in the work of transmitting the canonical Gospels did indeed, in some cases, modify their exemplars under the influence of apologetic interests.*

2

ANTIQUITY, HARMONY,
AND FACTUAL CONSISTENCY:
ISSUES OF INTELLECTUAL INTEGRITY

Tertullian captured the prevailing sentiments of many in the Greco-Roman world when he wrote, "That which is truer is prior."[1] Claim to antiquity instantly afforded religious cults and philosophical schools the badge of legitimacy. Conversely, novelty was viewed with suspicion, if not disdain. The so-called "true" doctrine that provided the title for Celsus' second-century polemic against Christianity referred to what he and many of his contemporaries believed was an ancient, perennial, and universal religious truth that underlay all civilized existence and exposed as pretenders any and all latter-day religious movements.[2] As Arthur Droge so succinctly expressed it, "nothing could be both new *and* true."[3] Thus, those who pronounced something "new" were affixing a pejorative label of some consequence, and it is clear that their opponents were so challenging Christians. Some outside observers of Christianity, for example, as they heard that the founder of this sect had been born in the days of Caesar Augustus and died during Pilate's tenure as prefect, promptly and pejoratively classified the movement as "new." The opening words of the third book the Christian apologist Theophilus addressed to Autolycus are indicative of how prevalent this issue had become by the later part of the second century:

Since historians desire to write a multitude of books to no avail (πρὸς κενὴν δόξαν), some about gods or wars or chronologies and others about useless

---

[1] Tertullian, *Adv. Marc.* V.4.1, cited according to the translation of Arthur J. Droge, *Homer or Moses?* (Tübingen: J. C. B. Mohr, 1989), 10. Cf. *ANF*, Vol III, 349.

[2] See, e.g., *Cels.* I.14. The treatise survives only in quotations cited by Origen in his apologetic rebuttal *Contra Celsum*. For the critical edition see M. Borret, *Origène Contre Celse*, 5 volumes (Sources Chrétiennes; Paris: Les Éditions du Cerf, 1968). The standard English translation is Henry Chadwick, *Origen: Contra Celsum* (Cambridge: Cambridge University Press, 1953). The classic introduction is Carl Andresen, *Logos und Nomos: Die Polemik des Kelsos wider das Christentum* (Berlin: Walter de Gruyter, 1955).

[3] Droge, *Homer or Moses?*, 9. This work is a thoroughgoing treatment of how the charge of novelty represented a challenge to early Christians and how they appealed to the Old Testament and especially the prophets and Moses to substantiate their claims that Jesus was older than Moses who was older than Homer who was older than Plato, etc.

myths (μύθων ἀνωφέλων) and other pointless labours such as you yourself
have been engaged in up to the present time (you do not shrink from
enduring that labour, though after meeting us you still regard the word of
truth as silly, fancying that our scriptures are new and modern [προσφάτους
καὶ νεωτερικάς]), therefore I too will not shrink from summing up for you,
with God's help, the antiquity of our writings (τὴν ἀρχαιότητα τῶν παρ'
ἡμῖν γραμμάτων). I will make a brief memorandum for you so that you
will not shrink from reading it but will recognize the nonsense of other
writers.[4]

Theophilus went on to add, "They also say that our message has been made public
only recently (ὡς προσφάτον), and that we have nothing to say in proof of our truth
and our teaching; they call our message foolishness (μωρίαν)."[5] Tatian, as another
example, reported that his contenders accused him of introducing "new"
(καινοτομεῖ) barbarian dogma.[6]

Moreover, as pagan intellectuals began to probe the Christian scriptures in an
effort to contradict the adherents of this emerging sect, they located in these writings
what were for them fatal flaws. Factual errors, logical inconsistencies, variations in
separate witnesses, and Old Testament citations wrongly attributed all served as
lightning rods for the violent energies of Christian antagonists, in particular Porphyry.
For him, even such minor misdemeanors ranked as felonies of illogic and insinuated
the unreliability of Christian sacred writings. Inaccuracies in reference to the Hebrew
Bible were perceived as particularly egregious, since the Christian title to
antiquity—and thus legitimacy—stemmed from appeal to prophecy.[7] Challenges of
this sort constituted for those who rose to defend the faith a crisis of intellectual
integrity. In general, apologists sought to answer these charges by, first, refuting the
objection that Christianity was new, and, second, attempting to explain away those
points seen by antagonists as factual or logical inconsistencies.

In the sections that follow, I will first introduce and illustrate these apologetic
maneuvers as they are reflected in the dynamic interactions between Christian
opponents and defenders. I will then locate variant readings in the textual tradition of
the New Testament Gospels that correspond to these apologetic strategies and serve,
in my judgment, as evidence that scribes in reproducing manuscripts of the canonical
Christian Gospels occasionally did so under the influence of apologetic interests.

---

[4] *Ad Auto.* III.1, cited according to *Theophilus of Antioch: Ad Autolycum.* (Text and Translation
by Robert M. Grant; Oxford: Clarendon Press, 1970), 100–101.
    [5] *Ad Auto.* III.4. See Grant, *Theophilus*, 105.
    [6] *Or.* 35.2.
    [7] For a typical example of how Christian apologists used the Hebrew Bible "prophetically"
see Justin, *Ap.* I.30–51and *Dial.* 11–16; Porphyry's attempts to undermine such claims will be
discussed in detail below.

THE PAGAN ACCUSATION OF NOVELTY AND
THE APOLOGETIC CLAIM TO ANTIQUITY

Antagonistic denunciations directed at the novelty of Christianity were forcefully developed in the writings of Celsus. At the foundation of his criticism lay the belief that there existed "an ancient doctrine which has existed from the beginning, which has always been maintained by the wisest nations and cities and wise men."[8] His derision for the peculiarities of Judaism, therefore, reached a predetermined limit when he acknowledged that Judaism was, at least, a "traditional" religion. Tradition, however, erected no such barrier against his censure of Christianity. Christians, he maintained, sidestepped any question put to them about their origins (II.4). Jesus he described as one who "only a very few years ago" taught his doctrine (I.26), and "quite recently" wandered around shamefully in the sight of all (VI.10). Through the mouthpiece of a Jewish antagonist—a literary creation serving as his alter ego—Celsus accused Christians of severing themselves from any authoritative heritage by seceding from Judaism, stating, "You abandoned quite recently the law of our fathers" (II.4). His objection was not that they had borrowed from the past, but that they had perverted it. They had "misunderstood" (παρακούειν, III.16; VI.7), "corrupted" (παραφθείρειν, IV.21, VII.58), and "counterfeited" (παραχαράττειν, IV.41–42) ancient doctrine. Thus, he could boldly associate Christianity's revolt against the state with the introduction of "new" ideas (καινοτομία, III.5).

It was in this important regard that Eugene Gallagher gave nuance to Anna Miura-Strange's contention that Celsus and Origen subscribed to a common Hellenistic concept of a god or son of god. Where she believed this to be common ground contested by the disputants, he insisted, rather, that they differed precisely on the matter of whether a near contemporary might correctly be identified as "divine," i.e. as a god or son of god.[9] In sharp contrast to Origen's desire to sponsor Jesus for that distinction, Celsus had limited his list of nominees to principals of the distant past, "inspired men of ancient times" even earlier than Plato.[10]

In response to this denigrating characterization of their faith as "novel," Christian apologists by and large took the offensive. In varying ways and degrees of

---

[8]*Cels.* I.14.

[9]Eugene Gallagher, *Divine Man or Magician? Celsus and Origen on Jesus* (Chico, California: Scholars Press, 1982), 42.

[10]*Cels.* VII.28, 49, 58. See also the comments of Carl Andresen, *Logos und Nomos*, 138–141, 154, 179, 183.

effectiveness, Justin,[11] Tatian,[12] Athenagoras,[13] Theophilus of Antioch,[14] Origen,[15] Minucius Felix,[16] and Tertullian[17] all argued that, not only was Christianity not "new," but it was temporally prior to all other religions and philosophies. Among the early apologists, only in Aristides is this strategy absent.[18] In this as in many respects, Christian apologists in these discussions were adapting arguments adduced earlier by Jewish apologists such as Eupolemus, the anonymous Samaritan identified as Pseudo-Eupolemus, Artapanus, and Josephus, who had similarly been driven to assert the ancient origins of their religion and to defend their faith before a Hellenized audience. This they did by formulating claims that philosophy was invented by Moses or that Abraham was the founder of culture or that Judaism could be demonstrated chronologically to be temporally prior to the philosophies or religions of Babylon,

---

[11]*Ap.* I. 23, I.31–53, I. 54, I.59.

[12]*Or.* 29, 31, 36–41.

[13]*Leg.*, 17.1, where Athenagoras argues that it is the Greek gods who issue from the pens of Orpheus, Homer, and Hesiod, and are thus themselves "very recent." See *Athenagoras: Legatio and De Resurrectione* (Edited and translated by William R. Schoedel; Oxford: Clarendon Press, 1972), 35.

[14]*Ad Auto.* II.33, III.16–29.

[15]*Cels.* I.16; IV.11–14, 20–21; VI.7; VII.28

[16]*Oct.* XXXIV.5

[17]*Ap.* XIX.

[18]In his *Apology*, Aristides—a near contemporary of Celsus—takes a boldly different approach, admitting Christian novelty but attempting to use it to his advantage. "And truly this people is a new people," he writes, "and there is something divine mingled with it." He argues that truth is found only through disciplined pursuit, and it is Christians alone who so labor to become righteous and thereby draw near this knowledge. Aristides thus endorses the "great and wonderful teaching" found in Christian writings. See *Ap.* XVI, cited here in J. R. Harris, *The Apology of Aristides.* (TS I; Cambridge: Cambridge University Press, 1893), 50. See also pp. 19–23, where Harris marshals evidence to suggest the possibility that Celsus was familiar with this work of Aristides and wrote, at least in part, to refute him.

Egypt, or Greece.[19] Laying claim to these same strategies, Christian apologists traced the steps of their Jewish predecessors.

Justin Martyr, among surviving authors, was the first to contend that Christianity was antecedent to Greek culture, though his evidence consisted mainly of *literary* parallels between Plato and Moses and the prophets that demonstrated, at least to the satisfaction of Justin, that Moses was more ancient than all the Greek writers.[20] It was left to Justin's pupil, Tatian, to construct a *chronological* argument for the relative antiquity of Christian and Greek traditions. According to A. J. Droge, the conception of such a chronological blueprint was without precedent in Christian literature, and it was transmitted in the form of sincerest flattery when it was imitated in the defenses of Clement, Origen, and Eusebius.[21] At the heart of Tatian's reasoning was a comparison of Moses with Homer, whom he considered to be the most ancient of Greek poets and historians. By carefully calculating temporal references specified in Greek literary works and Phoenician, Chaldean and Egyptian histories, Tatian determined that Homer lived contemporary with the Trojan War while Moses predated the war by four hundred years. The apologist offered further "proof" that Moses lived before Cadmus introduced the alphabet, before Deucalion's flood, before the invention of agriculture, before the foundation of cities, even before the epic Prometheus. In concluding his argument he announced, "It is clear that Moses is older than heroes, cities, and demons."[22]

As further corroboration for the primitive derivation of their religion Christian apologists routinely mustered the oracles of the Hebrew prophets. As one instance, Justin declared in his *First Apology*, "We will now offer proof, not trusting mere assertions, but being of necessity persuaded by those who prophesied [of Him] before these things came to pass, for with our own eyes we behold things that have happened

---

[19]For a fuller discussion of Jewish apologetic and its foundational influence on Christian apologetic see Droge, *Homer or Moses?*, 12–48; several relevant articles in Elizabeth Schüssler Fiorenza, *Aspects of Religious Propaganda in Judaism and Early Christianity.* (Notre Dame: University of Notre Dame Press, 1976), especially Louis Feldman, "Josephus as an Apologist of the Greco-Roman World: His Portrait of Solomon," 68–98; and chapters five, six, and seven of Gregory E. Sterling, *Historiography and Self-Definition. Josephos, Luke–Acts, and Apologetic Historiography* (NovTSup 64; Leiden: E. J. Brill, 1992), 137–225, 226–310, and 311–394. Sterling is attempting to describe the discovery of a new genre, "apologetic historiography," which he defines as "the story of a subgroup of people in an extensive prose narrative written by a member of the group who follows the group's own traditions but Hellenizes them in an effort to establish the identity of the group within the setting of the larger world"(17). The extent to which he succeeds in introducing a new genre is of less interest here than is his impressive reporting on the breadth of primary source literature related to this topic, and his awareness that those persons concerned with narrating the history of a religious subculture were keenly aware of the need to recast their stories in terms palatable to the dominant forces of the Greco-Roman world.

[20]*Ap.* I.23.1, I.44.8, 54.5. See also the discussion by Droge, *Homer or Moses?*, 91–92.

[21]A. J. Droge, *Homer or Moses?*, 92.

[22]*Or.* 40.1.

and are happening just as they were predicted."[23] A tenable association with the prophets, they were convinced, served to graft immediate credibility onto nascent Christianity by rooting its heritage in the distant past.[24] Followers of the way, they explained, depending on whether they were Jewish or Gentile, had from the beginning either recognized or adopted the Jewish scriptures as their own. The prophets, in particular, proved useful in explaining otherwise problematic elements of the faith; but, in fact, Christian exegetes tended to impose a "prophetic interpretation" upon the Pentateuch, Psalms, and most of the rest of the Hebrew Bible, as well. For example, that Jesus was crucified like a common thief was a glaring scandal to both Jews and Gentiles outside the faith, but apologists customarily retained the suffering servant oracles of Isaiah to impose prophetic anticipation and rationalization upon the passion narrative.[25] Where Celsus accused Jesus of "rushing greedily to drink" the vinegar and gall offered him on the cross, Origen referenced Psalm 68:22 as a "prophecy" that accounted for his behavior.[26]

Therefore, where pagans criticized the Jesus movement by identifying it as a novel sect, Christian apologists asserted that their faith consisted of a timely historical manifestation of a timeless ancient tradition. Their messiah was the fulfillment of ancient oracles; they, indeed, were heirs of an ancient tradition of sacred scripture and religious piety. Maintaining that claim was, in the minds of most apologists, (Aristides being the lone exception) critical. Occasionally, however, this strategy ran aground when intellectual opponents observed errors in such prophetic citations. So, it caused a tremor of no mild force when astute critics surveying the Christian scriptures (from either Testament) located there some fault line, whether a lacuna of logic or an infelicity of fact.

In specific instances of this sort, of course, editorial correction of such glaring miscues in the transmission of the New Testament would have clearly buttressed the case of the apologists. Could scribes have so aided the cause? Is there any evidence to suggest that copyists of the Christian scriptures might have engaged in such scribal intervention?

---

[23]*Ap.* I.30, quoted from *ANF*, Vol. I, 172.

[24]*Ap.* I.30. To be sure, this strategy of wringing christological content out of the content of the Hebrew Bible was not unique to the apologists. Certainly to the extent that it is fair in some measure to say that the Gospels were, in part, "prophecy historicized," it is clear that the evangelists themselves turned to the Old Testament for narrative content and interpretational meaning. Still, it seems fair to describe as characteristic of apologists the way in which they drew upon the Hebrew scriptures more to defend features of the faith against assault rather than imply or inflect doctrinal meaning on the Jesus story.

[25]*Cels.*, III.2.

[26]*Cels.* II.37.

VARIANT READINGS RELATED TO PROPHECY AND ANTIQUITY

In point of fact, scribal alteration of inaccuracies associated with prophecies is widely represented in the textual tradition. The point is made conspicuous when such improvements are observed in the very texts cited by pagan opponents in order to provoke disdain for Christians and their sacred writings. Two incontrovertible instances of this dynamic may be discerned in verses recited by the formidable Christian nemesis, Porphyry.

Porphyry routinely adduced specific verses from Christian writings to document his denunciation of the faith.[27] For example, he contentiously reported that the oracle ascribed to Isaiah in Mark 1:2 was in fact the product of a conflation between Isaiah and Malachi (to be exact, Mal 3:1 and Isa 40:3).[28] Similarly, he flagged Matthew 13:35, which wrongly assigns a passage from Psalm 78:2 to Isaiah.[29] For the purposes of this study what it noteworthy is this: both of these texts that were singled out by Porphyry to demonstrate Christian ineptitude have located in their transcriptional histories textual variants that signal a concern for factual coherence. It is my contention that scribes altered these very verses to derail Porphyry's attack and to buttress the text against future assaults of this kind. Their efforts may be discerned in the variant readings that follow.

Consider the case of Mark 1:2. Variation in the manuscripts occurs with regard to attribution of the prophetic citation, whether the text is said to be located "in Isaiah the prophet" or more generally "in the prophets." The disputed portion of the verse reads, Καθὼς γέγραπται ἐν τῷ Ἡσαΐᾳ τῷ προφήτῃ [*v.l.* ἐν τοῖς προφήταις]....What follows is, in fact, a composite quotation consisting of material from Malachi 3:1 and Exodus 23:20, as well as Isaiah 40:3. Textual critics generally recognize the erroneous attribution to Isaiah as the "original" reading and the "correction" to be the product of scribal amendment. The UBSGNT[4] Committee in their evaluation so assigned the Isaianic attribution an {A} rating.[30] Commentators routinely report the variant reading to be the result of someone who recognized the defective attribution of a composite quotation to a single prophet and repaired it.[31] M.-J. Lagrange, for example, expresses confidently:

---

[27]For a useful introduction to Porphyry's criticism of Christian sacred writings see Anthony Meredith, "Porphyry and Julian Against the Christians," *ANRW* II.23.2 (H. Temporani and W. Haase, eds.; Berlin: Walter de Gruyter, 1980), 1130, along with the discussion in Pierre de Labriolle, *La Réaction païenne* (Paris: L'Artisan du Livre, 1934), especially 251–256.

[28]Fr. 5, 9. See A. Meredith, "Porphyry and Julian," 1130.

[29]Fr. 10. See A. Meredith, "Porphyry and Julian," 1130.

[30]Bruce M. Metzger, *A Textual Commentary on the Greek New Testament* (Second Edition; Stuttgart: Deutsche Bibelgesellschaft, 1994; First edition; London and New York: United Bible Societies, 1971), 62.

[31]See, for example, Morna Hooker, *The Gospel According to Saint Mark* (Black's New Testament Commentary; Peabody, MA: Hendrickson, 1991), 35.

Il n'est pas douteux que la leçon « dans le prophète Isaïe » ne soit la leçon originale, corrigée en « dans les prophètes » par certains mss. parce que, en réalité, les paroles qui suivent sont empruntées pour moitié à Malachie (III, 1) et à Isaïe (XI, 3).[32]

What lingering puzzlement has remained for scholars regarding this text has centered around the question of how the error first found its way into the Marcan Gospel. The obvious answer is that the author of Mark simply erred, or that he knowingly credited Isaiah with the saying because of the high regard in which he or his audience held this particular prophet. In ancient times, Jerome, who once declared this textual problem to be insoluble, at one time or another offered three different solutions to the conundrum.[33] The most commonly held view in antiquity was that Mark had himself joined the two texts into one, which was the view held by Origen.[34] Lagrange reports that some scholars who think this simply an error on the part of the evangelist compare Mark's confusion to a similar disorientation located in Irenaeus, while others view Mark's attribution as deliberate since it was only the Isaianic portion of this amalgamated oracle on which his concerns rested.[35] Joel Marcus acknowledges the possibility of a Marcan error, but asserts that a greater likelihood is that Mark is deliberately placing his narrative in an Isaian context. Isaiah, notes Marcus, is the only Old Testament author mentioned by name in Mark's Gospel, and his introduction teems with allusions to Second Isaiah.[36]

Another suggestion popular with commentators is that the flaw in the autograph may have resulted from the author's use of a collection of sayings from the Hebrew Bible (*testimonia*) in which the mistaken attribution already lay.[37] Hugh Anderson building on the work of Krister Stendahl even goes so far as to propose that the sayings collection in which this wrongly-attributed citation occurred could have been formulated by the disciples of John the Baptizer.[38]

---

[32]M.-J. LaGrange, *Évangile selon Saint Marc* (Paris: Libraire Lecoffre, 1966), 3.

[33]Jerome, *Epistles*, 57.9 (*solvat hanc quaestiunculam imperita praesumptio, et ego erroris veniam deprecabor*). Cited and discussed by M.-J. LaGrange, *Évangile selon Saint Marc*, 3.

[34]Origen, *Commentary on John*, VI.24, which reads ὅτι ὁ Μάρκος δύο προφητείας ἐν διαφόροις εἰρημένας τόποις ὑπὸ δύο προφητῶν εἰς ἕν συνάγων πεποίηκεν. Cited by M.-J. LaGrange, *Évangile selon Saint Marc*, 3.

[35]M.-J. LaGrange, *Évangile selon Saint Marc*, 3.

[36]Joel Marcus, *Mark 1–8* (AB 27; New York: Doubleday, 1999), 147.

[37]See, for example, J. Marcus, *Mark 1–8*, 147; John Painter, *Mark's Gospel: Worlds in Conflict*. (London/New York: Routledge, 1997), 26; Larry Hurtado, *Mark* (Good News Commentary. San Francisco: Harper & Row, 1983), 9.

[38]Hugh Anderson, *The Gospel of Mark* (New Century Bible; Greenwood, SC: Attic Press, 1976), 69. See also Krister Stendahl, *The School of St. Matthew and Its Use of the Old Testament*. (Philadelphia: Fortress, 1968), 116 and 200. Stendahl suggests that the text as it appears in Matthew 13:35 possesses a conflative texture characteristic of Jewish pesher, along the lines of the Habakkuk commentary located among the Dead Sea Scrolls.

Sailing from the opposite shore, however, V. Taylor and A. E. J. Rawlinson represent another group of critics who take the view that the words of Malachi 3:1 are themselves the gloss, and that attribution of the quote to Isaiah was correct as it read in the "original."[39] Hugh Anderson observes, in support of this position, what he considers the otherwise puzzling omission of Malachi 3:1 in the parallel texts of Matthew 3:3 and Luke 3:4.[40]

While this latter possibility is intriguing, the external evidence weighs heavily against it. The vast majority of our most reliable witnesses (including ℵ B D L Δ Θ f^1 33 565 700, and most of the Syriac tradition) as well as Irenaeus, Origen, and Epiphanius attest that the "original" text of Mark attributed this verse to the prophet Isaiah. Such an impressive array of external sources makes for a formidable deposition, one difficult to ignore or refute. Moreover, to address Anderson's point, omission of Malachi 3:1 in the parallel texts of Matthew 3:3 and Luke 3:4 is not "puzzling" if one proceeds from the premise (as most scholars do) that Matthew and Luke used Mark as their exemplar. As scribes of Mark, each of them independently could have noticed the conflated text and chosen to alleviate the problem by keeping the name of the prophet who was arguably the most important for Christians and simply omitting Malachi 3:1. This would, in effect, have produced the same result that some other later copyist(s) achieved by omitting reference to a specific prophet but leaving intact the text—namely, it would have generated a correct(ed) text.[41]

Why, though, did these scribes not follow the lead of Matthew and Luke in how they handled the text? It is widely known that scribes often assimilated Mark to Matthew. Why, if their interest was only to polish the text editorially, did these scribes not imitate Matthew and Luke? Certainly, one could argue forcefully that the transmission of sacred texts is by nature a conservative enterprise, and that scribes were less inclined to omit material than they were to correct it. Although it is true that, generally, the shorter text is considered "original" because of the scribal habit to edit by expansion rather than abbreviation (e.g., explanation and correction rather than deletion), this tendency in the textual tradition is not maintained without exception.[42]

---

[39]V. Taylor, *Mark*, 153; J. E. H. Rawlinson, *Mark*, 7 f.

[40]H. Anderson, *Mark*, 69.

[41]Morna Hooker, however, argues that this textual problem is more easily explained on the basis of Mark being written after Matthew and Luke. I fail to see the urgency or necessity of this proposal. See Hooker, *Mark*, 35.

[42]As James Royse makes clear in idem, "Scribal Tendencies in the Transmission of the Text of the New Testament," in Bart Ehrman and Michael Holmes, eds. *The Text of the New Testament in Contemporary Research: Essays on the Status Quaestionis* (Grand Rapids, MI: Eerdmans, 1995) 239–52. Drawing heavily on E. C. Colwell, "Method in Evaluating Scribal Habits: A Study of P⁴⁵, P⁶⁶, P⁷⁵," in *Studies in Methodology in Textual Criticism of the New Testament* (NTTS 9; Leiden: Brill; Grand Rapids, MI: Eerdmans, 1969) 106–24, and confirmed by Peter M. Head, "Observations on Early Papyri of the Synoptic Gospels, Especially on the 'Scribal Habits,'" *Bib* 71 (1990) 240–47, Royse asserts "that the general tendency during the early period of textual transmission was to omit" (246).

Scribes could have chosen to delete Malachi 3:1 rather than erase the name of a well-known prophetic authority. One could presumably argue that more would have been gained by correcting the text by means of excision and keeping the reference to Isaiah. Perhaps, but is there a more compelling explanation for why scribes revised the text as they did?

Recall that Porphyry, as Julian would later, sought to discredit the writings of the New Testament in part by highlighting inconsistencies that arose in the text. On the basis of surviving fragments, much of his now lost fifteen-volume polemic *Against the Christians* is thought to have consisted of reasoned criticism of the Christian scriptures.[43] Porphyry in fact represented the contradictions and errors in these revered writings as the natural product of rustic and unsophisticated followers of Jesus; their collective intellectual and moral inadequacies made them incapable of producing anything reliable or sound. On this basis Porphyry expected the scriptures to be inherently flawed, and he set about the task of demonstrating that thesis for the masses. Among his scriptural exposés, he is best known for demonstrating that the book of Daniel issued not from the era of the Babylonian exile but from the Maccabean period.[44] Although this investigation involved an Old Testament text, it seems evident that Porphyry's concern was to refute Christian chroniclers who interpreted Daniel's "seventy weeks of years" (Dan 9:24) according to a calculus that arranged the birth of Christ to coincide with the reign of Caesar Augustus. As Anthony Meredith so well summarizes:

> The aim of Porphyry's treatment of the book of Daniel is, even in the biased version that comes down to us from Jerome, fairly obvious. In the first place, by proving that Daniel is a historical, pseudepigraphical work, he is able to destroy its value as prophecy. Then he is also in a position to deny the "ahistorical" character of the narrative, by rooting it firmly in history and by confirming its statements from the writings of secular historians. Finally, by attacking the notion of the prophetic value of "Daniel" he is able to weaken its value as an apologetic weapon in the hand of Christian apologists.[45]

---

[43]See, e.g., the discussion in P. Labriolle, *La Réaction païenne*, 251–268; W. H. C. Frend, "Prelude to the Great Persecution: The Propaganda War," *JEH* 38/1 (1987), 8–14; J. Bidez, *Vie de Porphyre* (Hildesheim:Georg Olms, 1964), 73–79; A. Meredith, "Porphyry and Julian," 1125–36; and J. Hargis, *Against the Christians: The Rise of Early Anti-Christian Polemic* (New York: Peter Lang, 1999), 63–90.

[44]For more on Porphyry's treatment of Daniel see Labriolle, *La Rèaction païenne*, 266– 68; A. Meredith, "Porphyry and Julian," *ANRW* 23.2, 1132–33; P. M. Casey, "Porphyry and the Origin of the Book of Daniel," *JTS* n.s. 27, 1976, 15–33.

[45]A. Meredith, "Porphyry and Julian,"1133.

Thus Porphyry's revised chronology threatened those Christian exegetes, such as Julius Africanus, who summoned Daniel to construct their tendentious timetables and to serve as an important prophetic witness to the messianic identity of Jesus.[46]

As an antagonist of Christianity, then, Porphyry directed his assault at the disciples of Jesus and their scriptural foundation. He pored over their books and underscored their mistakes. Errors and inconsistencies in the text were proof for him of the blatant and dangerous lie that constituted, in his mind, the foundation of the Christian cult. Under the perspicacious glare of Porphyry the sacred writings of believers fell susceptible to detailed scrutiny, and the vulnerable underbelly of Christians showed again, as it had similarly before under the criticism of Celsus. Where Origen could effectively answer his criticism with factual correction or allegorical exposition, Porphyry anticipated both responses. It was precisely their own data he was using against them, and he refused to accept allegory as an answer. Therefore, where the text was vulnerable to pagan critique so was the faith and so were the faithful. The text, therefore, *was* a battlefield.

Among those texts he singled out as erroneous was Mark 1:2.[47] Porphyry himself read the evangelist and reproached him specifically for attributing to Isaiah alone a citation that was his in part only, with the other part issuing from Malachi. In *Against the Christians*, then, Porphyry was wielding this verse like an epee, attempting to pierce the hearts of scriptural authority and the intellectual integrity of the evangelists. Mindful of this, it seems noteworthy that some fastidious scribes—whose efforts are represented by A W f^{13} vg^{ms} sy^h and the Latin rendering of Irenaeus—intentionally replaced the erroneous attribution to Isaiah with a general and incontestable reference to "the prophets." Although scholarship has generally recognized that the modified reading represents an attempt on the part of scribes to address the erroneous attribution of the quotation as it stands to Isaiah, far too many commentators have stopped short of offering sufficient explanation for what forces may have been at work prompting the correction.[48] The fact that this was, indeed, a text singled out by Porphyry to ridicule the sobriety and propriety of the Christian scriptures suggests that more than mere editorial felicity may have been at work here. It is difficult to restrain the notion that scribes might have been reacting in direct response to the attacks expressed by Porphyry; precisely the scribal activity reflected in the manuscript tradition of Mark 1:2 signals a correction to this verse that would have been what was necessary to deflect Porphyry's assault and to reclaim the text as another prophetic

---

[46]See B. Croke, "The Era of Porphyry's Anti-Christian Polemic," *JRH* 13/1 (1984), 6 for the suggestion that Porphyry with his chronology of Daniel may have taken direct aim at the timetable of Africanus.

[47]A. Harnack, *Frag.* 9. See P. Labriolle, *La Réaction païenne*, 252.

[48]Vincent Taylor states matter-of-factly that the reading "in the prophets" is an attempt to meet the difficulty that the first part of the quotation is not from Isaiah (Idem, *Gospel According to St. Mark*, 153). C. S. Mann similarly states the obvious (Idem, *Mark*, 195). C. E. B. Cranfield likewise asserts that the *v. l.* is no doubt an attempt to remove a difficulty (Idem, *The Gospel According to St. Mark*, 38).

proof for demonstrating the identity of Christ and the anticipated rise of the faith. This nimble but banal alteration would have hardly affected the meaning of the reading, yet it would have effectively safeguarded the verse from the truculent scrutiny of antagonists like the learned Neo-Platonist. In the words of M.-J. Lagrange, "On a donc voulu reparer l'erreur reprochee à l'évangéliste entre autres par Porphyre."[49] In this respect, the conspicuous repair of Mark 1:2 may well stand as a transparent instance of scribal activity being shaped by apologetic concerns.

Porphyry noticed also a similarly fallacious attribution in Matthew 13:35, and once more cited it as evidence for the ignorance of the evangelist.[50] This, too, is a text that—in a manner similar to the variant in Mark 1:2—shows evidence of editorial corruption. Due to certain complications inherent in this variant, however, the precise nature of that corruption is more difficult to determine. Hence, it is necessary to seek clarification with regards to the variant reading itself prior to considering whether its alteration was due to the influence of apologetic interests.

The verse occurs in the context of the evangelist offering a prophetic explanation for why Jesus taught the crowds exclusively in parables. It reads, "This was to fulfill what was spoken by the prophet (διὰ [v. l., insert or omit Ἡσαΐου] τοῦ προφήτου): "I will open my mouth in parables, I will utter what has been hidden since the foundation of the world." Clearly, the variant reading inventoried in this verse resulted from the activity of a scribe who either introduced into or excised from the text the name "Isaiah." Yet, the most glaring feature of the citation under review is that it does not issue from Isaiah at all; rather, the words stem from Psalm 78:2 (Psalm 77, LXX). In the Hebrew tradition, this psalm is identified as "A Maskil of Asaph"; and, in the Septuagint (LXX), Asaph is labeled by the Chronicler (2 Chr 29:30) as τοῦ προφήτου. Jerome indicates that all of the oldest codices ascribe the verse to Asaph, though Metzger points out that no known extant witness to this text reads Ἀσάφ.[51]

On the basis of the weighty external support against the inclusion of Ἡσαΐου —an omission sustained by ℵ[1] B C D L W 0233 0242[vid], the Majority text, some Old Latin, Syriac, and Coptic versions—commentators frequently dismiss the variant outright. Moreover, Metzger postulates that, in the instance that no name appeared in the exemplar, assorted scribes working independently might have been constrained to introduce into their copies the name of the best known prophet, a relatively common practice attested to by Matthew 1:22, 2:5, 21:4, and Acts 7:48.[52] This assertion reflects a notion developed by Metzger more fully elsewhere in which he reached the

---

[49]M.-J. LaGrange, *Évangile selon Saint Marc*, 3, where LaGrange goes on to quote Porphyry: *locum istum impius ille Porphyrius...disputat et dicit: Evangelistae tam imperiti fuerent homines non solum in saecularibus sed etiam in scripturis divinis ut testimonium quod alibi scriptum est, de alio ponerent propheta* (Ad Marcellam).

[50]A. Harnack, *Frag.* 10 (=Jerome, Tract. Ps. 77). See A. Meredith, "Porphyry and Julian," 1130.

[51]Metzger, *Textual Commentary*, 27.

[52]Metzger, *Textual Commentary*, 27–8.

conclusion that, as a general rule, early Christians felt a reluctance to leave unidentified in the New Testament narratives persons who were mentioned but not named.[53] Despite the deafening roar of this external testimony and transcriptional reasoning, though, the UBS[4] editorial committee awarded this omission only a {C} rating.[54] Their lack of conviction may have been warranted.

In reporting both sides of the argument, Metzger points out that in addition to the sources that support reading "through Isaiah the prophet" (among them, the first hand of Codex Sinaiticus, several important minuscules, one Ethiopic manuscript, and copies of the Gospel known to Eusebius, Jerome, and Porphyry), transcriptional probabilities weigh more heavily in favor of inclusion, since so obvious an error could be construed as the more difficult reading. It is easy, he proposes, to anticipate the correction of so obvious an error by copyists, and Metzger directs readers to the previously discussed Mark 1:2 along with Matthew 27:9 as examples to support his claim. He also reports that both Eusebius and Jerome knew of some manuscripts in which the oracle cited in Matthew 13:35 was attributed to Isaiah, though in his edition of the Vulgate, Jerome penned simply *per prophetam* ("through the prophet").[55] Metzger here omits any consideration of intrinsic probabilities.

This is unfortunate, since examination of Matthew's compositional style may well provide important additional reasons for supporting the contention that Ἡσαΐου issued from the author, and provide a reply to Metzger's thesis about "naming the nameless." It was precisely on this basis that F. J. A. Hort was led to favor inclusion as the "original" reading. "It is difficult not to think Ἡσαΐου genuine," he wrote, arguing that there was in antiquity a strong temptation to omit erroneous references, as evidenced again by Mt 27:9 and Mk 1:2. Thus he labeled the evidence in favor of the claim that scribes frequently inserted the name of the most familiar prophet "trifling." In support of this assertion, he pointed out that in the five other places where the "true text" has simply τοῦ προφήτου, the erroneous insertion of Ἡσαΐου is limited to two instances, in each case to a single Latin manuscript.[56]

---

[53]Bruce Metzger, "Names for the Nameless in the New Testament," in *Kyriakon: Festschrift Johannes Quasten*, Patrick Granfield and Josef A. Jungmann, eds. (Münster:1970), 79–99. Here Metzger explores ancient Christian traditions that provided names for the magi, the seventy (or was it seventy-two?) disciples, the rich man, the two thieves crucified with Jesus, and various other women and men who are mentioned but left unnamed in the canonical sources. In his description of sources that bear testimony to his thesis that tradition was reluctant "to respect the silence of the New Testament narratives" (98), he also cautions that "one must not imagine that the movement was always from less to more...."(99).

[54]Metzger, *Textual Commentary*, 33.

[55]Bruce Metzger, "St. Jerome's Explicit References to Variants Readings in Manuscripts of the New Testament," in *Text and Interpretation*, edited by Ernest Best and R. McL. Wilson. (Cambridge: Cambridge University Press, 1979), 181. This article features a brief but excellent survey of the specific references to variant readings in the works of Jerome.

[56]B. F. Westcott and F. J. A. Hort, *Introduction to the New Testament in the Original Greek*. (Peabody, MA: Hendrickson, 1988 [Originally published in 1882]), II, 12.

Hort's insights here prompt us to pursue a thorough examination of Matthew's use of this term, "prophet," toward the aim of discerning whether or not the author shows a tendency to employ that term with or without a proper name. Thirty-six times in his Gospel the author uses the term "prophet" (προφήτης). Of these, thirteen are plural grammatically and refer to the prophets in general, such as in the phrase, "the law and the prophets." Another five are generic in content, such as in the instance that "they took him [i.e., John] to be a prophet." Eighteen more times Matthew uses προφήτης, and two-thirds (12) of those instances occur in association with a proper name, such as "by Jeremiah the prophet" (2:17, 27:9), or "spoken by Isaiah the prophet" (3:3, 4:14, 8:17, 12:17), or the "sign of the prophet Jonah" (12:39, 16:4), or "Daniel the prophet" (24:15). John (11:9, 14:5, 21:26) and Jesus (21:11, 21:46) are also directly specified as prophets by the author.

Review of the six remaining uses of προφήτης, those in which it stands alone apart from the designation of a proper noun, educes several observations. One of these instances occurs in Matthew 27:35, a verse argued by some textual scholars to be an assimilation to John 19:24. If this judgment is correct, this verse would therefore not serve as a representative of Matthean literary style.[57] Another of these uses occurs in Matthew 2:5. Although in this text the name of the cited prophet is left unexpressed, the speakers here are Herod's consultants and are, therefore, adversaries and not proponents of Matthew's cause. One would not necessarily expect Matthew to place into the mouths of opponents the same level of knowledge one would or could expect from a Christian character or narrative voice. Still, it should be noted that the textual tradition does include witnesses, though they are admittedly unimpressive, that incorporate a proper name into the text at this point. The correct reference of Μιχαίου was added by 4 (a 13th century minuscule), sy[hmg (ms)], and cop[bo ms], while Old Latin Vercelliensis (a) attributes the prophecy to Isaiah, reading *per Esiam prophetam dicentem*. Yet another reference, Matthew 21:14, cites a text that is a composite quotation, specifically a conflation of Isaiah 62:11 and Zecharian 9:9. As we have seen previously in reviewing the variant reading of Mark 1:2, one way to avoid problems in attributing composite texts is simply not to specify any particular prophet by name. It is quite possible that Matthew followed that logic here.

That leaves three final instances, including the variant presently under consideration, in which Matthew appears to have used the term προφήτης in some form of citation without any further identification (Mt 1:22, 2:15, 13:35). In all three of these, however, it should be noted that there exists manuscript testimony that in part attributes the citation to Ἡσαίου. In Matthew 1:22, chiefly "Western" sources (D, 267, 954, 1582*[vid], it, vg[mss], sy[s.(c).h pal], arm, sa[ms], Ir[lat pt], Diatessaron) are responsible for the acknowledgment, while only Syriac Sinaiticus recognizes Ἡσαίου in Matthew 2:15. Still, in the former case, external evidence alone provides sufficient reason not to dismiss offhandedly Ἡσαίου as "original."

---

[57]Metzger, *Textual Commentary*, 69.

With regard to intrinsic probabilities, then, it seems evident that the general and fairly dominant pattern of Matthew's literary style is to incorporate a prophet's name into his oracle formulas. Of the fifteen unqualified instances that the term προφήτης is employed by Matthew in the singular and in reference to an individual prophet, only twice apart from our text under discussion—and, since one of those involves a disputed reading, maybe only once—does the writer in quoting an oracle fail to credit a prophet by name. In sum, Matthew's dominant proclivity is to qualify the term προφήτης with a proper noun. Intrinsic probabilities, it would seem, favor inclusion as the "original" reading.

Further support for this conclusion may derive from consideration of transcriptional probabilities with regard to the Syriac versional tradition.[58] The first six hundred years of Christianity witnessed the production of at least five separate versions of Syriac scriptures, among these the earliest translations of the Gospels.[59] Controversies rage among scholars who seek to understand this branch of New Testament transmission, due in part to the wide variety of translations and revisions that constitute the Syriac tradition, and in part to the unresolved question of their mutual relationship.

Despite these unresolved questions in identifying the *literary* relationships among these versional witnesses, however, their undisputed *geographical* relationship begs the question of how these manuscripts relate to one another in terms of the scribal transmission of the text. In particular, certain details that issue from the Syriac witnesses in regards to prophetic citations plead for consideration. In at least three instances (Mt 1:22, 2:15, 27:9) some portion at least of the Syriac tradition incorporates a proper name alongside τοῦ προφήτου, and, in those cases where apparent scribal

---

[58]For a thorough introduction of the Syriac versions of the New Testament see the classic study, Bruce Metzger, *The Early Versions of the New Testament* (Oxford: Clarendon Press, 1977), 3–98.

[59]Probably Tatian's Diatessaron (ca. 170 C.E.), but some scholars argue that Old Syriac translations of separate Gospels may have preceded Tatian's harmony. Those witnesses available to us today consist of the following: (1) Tatian's Diatessaron, available, except for fragments, only in secondary translations or in the commentary of Ephraem; (2) Two Old Syriac manuscripts, the Curetonian Syriac (sy^c), assigned a date to the mid-fifth century, and Sinaitic Syriac (sy^s), a palimpsest manuscript discovered by two Scottish sisters visiting the monastery of St. Catherine believed produced in the late fourth century; (3) The Peshitta (sy^p), sometimes referred to as the Syriac Vulgate, a carefully transcribed text believed to represent the New Testament in use in Antioch during the fourth and fifth centuries; (4) the Philoxenian (sy^ph), and/or Harclean (sy^h/hmg) versions; and (5) the Palestinian Syriac (sy^pal), a distant cousin of these other versions, preserved in transcripts marked by a dialect closer kin to Jewish Palestinian Aramaic than classical Syriac and by lectionary and liturgical embellishments. For more on this see Metzger, *Early Versions*, 3.

correction has been effected, theirs is usually the correct one.[60] Upon close examination, for example, one observes that the Syriac tradition appears divided over the citation of Matthew 27:9. Among Syriac witnesses, only the text of the Harclean Syriac (sy^h) incorrectly reports the firmly established reading, Ἰερεμίου; this same text, however, in its marginal notes (sy^{hmg}, as well as minuscule 22) correctly credits Ζαχαρίου. Taking the other fork, Tatian's *Diatessaron*, Sinaitic Syriac and the Peshitta (Diatessaron^{a,l}, sy^{s,p}, along with Φ 33 a b bo^{ms}) simply omit altogether reference to any particular prophet. The fragmentary Curetonian Syriac has a lacuna here. This brief examination suggests a pattern. In this particular instance (Mt 13:35) the bulk of the Syriac tradition makes the effort either to correct the citation or to eliminate the error. Elsewhere at least a portion of the Syriac witnesses testify to variants that emphasize or accent the prophetic tradition, such as Matthew 16:4, which designates Jonah as a prophet; or 21:4, in which the insertion of [Syriac], the Syriac equivalent to ὅλον, emphasizes how totally Jesus fulfills the prophets; or 27:35, where sy^h includes the apparent assimilation to John 19:24. Although these data constitute only the beginnings of a conclusive argument—a thoroughgoing study of the Syriac tradition's treatment of Matthew lies beyond the scope of this work—they direct us toward locating within this versional tradition a pattern for how the scribes responsible for the Syriac texts transmitted Matthean oracles. In their transcriptions of the Matthean text, these scribes appear to demonstrate an acute awareness of the prophetic tradition. When they are met with an erroneous citation, they almost always either correct the attribution or omit the error. When, however, they are met with an oracle assigned anonymously to τοῦ προφήτου, they usually insert a name, most often the correct one.

To the extent this description accurately represents a practiced tendency on the part of the Syriac scribal tradition, it provides information that may help us settle on the reading of Matthew 13:35. If Syriac scribes had encountered in their exemplar the phrase τοῦ προφήτου, the pattern would suggest that they would have made an effort to insert an acknowledgment, and likely the correct one. On the other hand, if they came across an error in attribution, it would be in keeping with the pattern if they simply omitted the improper name. Since the oracle stems from a psalmist (Asaph?) and not Isaiah, we would expect the Syriac tradition in this particular case to omit the name. According to the textual apparatus, this is exactly what happens. This may well serve as transcriptional support for reading Ἡσαΐου as "original."

While the foregoing data may not produce absolute conclusions, it offers reasonable if not strong evidence in favor of Ἡσαΐου as the "original" reading of Matthew 13:35. Though the external evidence remains inconclusive, it leans more heavily on the side of inclusion. Moreover, I have adduced intrinsic and tran-

---

[60]One exception to this is an erroneous attribution to the prophet Isaiah reported in Matthew 2:15 rendered in the Sinaitic Syriac. Here, though, it should be noted that this versional witness is unique as the only manuscript that inserts, albeit an incorrect one, any name at all. Even here, then, an apparent concern for prophetic citation remains consistent.

scriptional probabilities that offer additional reasons for favoring inclusion of the proper name as "original."

Presuming, then, that the "original" text of Matthew 13:35 included specific reference to Isaiah, we are faced with the text-critical question of why scribes intentionally altered the text. Of course, it is possible to attribute the omission to manual error, but evidence of deliberate correction in the margins of Codex Sinaiticus testifies that in at least some cases the omission was intentionally enforced. Perhaps for some it is enough to posit that some scribes were compulsive in their efforts to eliminate errors from the text, much in the way Metzger has already expressed. Yet, here it seems that something more can be inferred from their activity. Porphyry, a ferocious and formidable opponent of Christianity, had in his polemic writings against the new faith singled out this text, along with Mark 1:2, as evidence against the competence and integrity of the evangelists, and, by way of extension, the sacred authority of their New Testament writings. To claim that the scribe responsible for correcting the attribution did so out of compulsion implies that the scribe would have been knowledgeable enough about the Hebrew scriptures to recognize the error. It is equally tenable to reason that a scribe so knowledgeable could also have been similarly informed or aware of the content of Porphyry's attacks. Moreover, a less attentive scribe might have even been made aware of the error by such voiced criticism. In either case, it is reasonable to posit apologetic interests as the momentum behind this scribal alteration. Certainly the effect of the change served apologetic interests, as the correction buttressed a vulnerable spot in the text that had already been exploited by an antagonist.

Other variants additionally demonstrate a scribal interest in emphasizing and supporting the prophetic foundation of Christianity. Consider, for example, the text of Luke 9:54, which reads as follows:

ἰδόντες δὲ οἱ μαθηταὶ Ἰάκωβος καὶ Ἰωάννης εἶπαν· κύριε, θέλεις εἴπωμεν πῦρ καταβῆναι ἀπὸ τοῦ οὐρανοῦ καὶ ἀναλῶσαι αὐτούς [*v. l.* ὡς καὶ Ἡλίας ἐποίησεν].

And when the disciples James and John saw it, they said "Lord, do you want us to bid fire come down from heaven and consume them [*v. l.* as Elijah did]?"

Repeating the Septuagint nearly verbatim, the verse recalls 2 Kings 1:10, 12, where Elijah twice summons and receives a divine conflagration to consume a captain and his company. Most commentators, except for J. M. Ross, identify the variant phrase, ὡς καὶ Ἡλίας ἐποίησεν as a scribal gloss.[61] Although the quality of witnesses that testify to the phrase is high (A C D W Θ Ψ *f*.13 33 Maj it sy[p.h] bo[pt]), the early and impressive witnesses (P[45.75] ℵ B L Ξ 579 700* 1241 lat sy[s.c] sa bo[pt]) that attest to them not being part of the "original" text is even stronger. A. Plummer merely acknowledges

---

[61]J. M. Ross, "The Rejected Words in Luke 9:54–56," *ExpT* 84 (1972–73), 85–88.

insertion as the greater likelihood, while J. Fitzmyer explains the phrase as the product of scribes who recognized the allusion and could not resist the impulse to demonstrate their acumen.[62] J. R. Harris offers the unique view that the gloss found its way into the text under Marcionite influence. He argues that the added words fit precisely the concern Marcion and his followers would have had, namely, to distinguish Jesus and his Father from the God of the Old Testament who would have rained hostile fire in response to the petition of Elijah.[63] This argument suffers slightly, however, from the view that Marcion's prevailing pattern was to excise difficulties rather than refine them, as he is known to have done, for example, with Luke 4:16.[64]

Another option for explaining the origin of the gloss is the influence of apologetic interests. If, as it seems, the phrase is an embellishment, copyists by means of this insertion establish much more directly a connection between Jesus and one of the most charismatic of the Old Testament prophets. Now, to be sure, Elijah probably was not a household name among pagans, although some intellectuals such as Porphyry would have certainly known who he was. What the general populace *did* recognize, however—and certainly what the pagan elite respected—was antiquity, a commodity which for Christians could be obtained most affordably by borrowing from the Hebrew scriptures. Also, as I have noted earlier, apologetic writings were intended, at least in part, "to preach to the choir," i.e., to undergird the faith of believers who were in the minority, and whose trust in Jesus was either by hearsay, rhetoric, or accusation regularly challenged. To place into the mouths of his followers the straightforward declaration that Jesus could have done "just as Elijah did" would have both mollified the violent character of the question ("Shall we bid fire come down...?") and associated their near-contemporary Jesus with one of the most ancient prophets. The copyists who embossed Luke 9:54 with the phrase, "even as Elijah did," could understandably have been inspired by apologetic interests.

Let us consider another probable scribal embellishment to Luke's gospel. Codex Bezae and the Old Latin Vercelliensis (a) indicate that copyists interpolated the content of Matthew 2:23 into Luke 2:39. The revamped Lucan text, καθὼς ἐρρέθη διὰ τοῦ προφήτου ὅτι Ναζωραῖος κληθήσεται, varies only slightly from the verse in Matthew, ὅπως πληρωθῇ τὸ ῥηθεν διὰ τῶν προφητῶν ὅτι Ναζωραῖος κληθήσεται. One thing is conspicuous here, however, namely that there appears to be no antecedent in the Hebrew Bible with which this, the fifth of Matthew's formula quotations, corresponds. Many scholars suggest that "Nazorean" may be an allusion to the "righteous branch" (Hebrew נצר) spoken of in Isaiah 11:1, while others point

---

[62]A. Plummer, *Luke* (ICC 29; Edinburgh: T&T Clark, 1922), 264. J. Fitzmyer, *Luke I–IX* (AB 28; Garden City, NY: Doubleday, 1981), 830.

[63]J. R. Harris, *A Study of Codex Bezae* (TS II.1; Cambridge: Cambridge University Press, 1891), 232–33.

[64]Where Jesus arrives at the synagogue in Nazareth and is called upon to read the prophets; Harris himself makes note of this. Harris, *Codex Bezae*, 232.

to Judges 13:5–7 (LXX ὅτι ναζιρ θεοῦ ἔσται).[65] In either case, the connection appears forced. So, what we have in this scribal interpolation is an instance where scribes have followed Matthew, almost blindly it would seem, in the evangelist's claim that there was prophetic anticipation that the Messiah would at some point hail from Nazareth. The scribes responsible for this embellishment were clearly less concerned with tracking down source citations than with incorporating traditional evidence that explained the location of Jesus' boyhood home as yet another instance of prophetic fulfillment. In this sense, for those scribes responsible for this amendment to Luke's Gospel, this prophetic association may have also fulfilled an apologetic impulse.

Moreover, the similar pattern that occurs in these next two textual variants appears to reflect closely themes and language that appear in the apologists, in particular Justin Martyr. A number of witnesses (B C³ W $f^{1.13}$ 33 Maj q vg^{cl} sy^h sa mae bo^{ms}) add to the text of Matthew 21:4, ὅλον, thereby adding emphasis to the prophetic interpretation of Jesus' triumphal entry into Jerusalem: "*all* this happened in order that the word of the prophet might be fulfilled."[66] Similarly, into the text of Matthew 24:6 copyists inserted variously πάντα or ταῦτα or πάντα ταῦτα, so that emphasis was given in Jesus' visionary declaration about the end and the outbreak of violence that "all these things" must rightfully transpire prior to the arrival of the consummation. In both cases these scribal amendments accent the apologetic theme that everything associated with the Jesus narrative was anticipated and presaged by divinely-inspired prophets. This theme had been previously expressed with particular drama by Justin when he declared, "Now since we show that all those things (πάντα) that have happened had been foretold by the prophets (προκεκηρύχθαι διὰ τῶν προφητῶν) before they happened, it must of necessity also be believed that those things which were likewise foretold, but are yet to happen, shall with certainty come to pass."[67] The scribes who imported these terms of comprehensive scope into their texts echoed the theme and words of Justin. Here, apologetic motivation appears as ready an explanation for what drove these scribes to alter their exemplars as accident.

---

[65] For reference to this and a fuller discussion of this verse see W. D. Davies and Dale C. Allison, *Matthew*, Volume I (ICC 27; 3 vols.; Edinburgh: T&T Clark, 1988), 274–5.

[66] Commentators treating this verse devote more interest to the other variant reading in this verse, one that involves the inclusion of a proper name. A few witnesses, the earliest being a few of the Old Latin manuscripts, add before or after "the prophet" the name of either Isaiah or Zechariah. The external evidence suggests that the insertion is secondary. Once again, as seen earlier in our discussion of Mark 1:2, the oracle that follows in verse 5 is a conflate reading, consisting of material from Isaiah 62:11 and Zechariah 9:9. Other instances of scribes inserting a prophet's name can be located in Matthew 1:22 and 2:5, where in the latter instance Syriac and Coptic versions correctly attribute the text to Micah, while Old Latin Vercelliensis (a) erroneously credits Isaiah. See B. M. Metzger, *Textual Commentary*, 8–9.

[67] *Ap.* I.52. For the Greek critical edition see M. Marcovich, *Iustini Martyris Apologiae pro Christianis* (Berlin: Walter de Gruyter, 1994), 104. *Writings of Saint Justin Martyr* (FC 6; trans. Thomas Falls; Washington, DC: Catholic University of America Press, 1948), 88–9

At both Matthew 16:4 and Luke 11:29, a set of manuscripts and versions very similar to each other testify that scribes expanded the evangelists' reference to the sign of Jonah by identifying him as "the prophet." Where Matthew 5:18 recounts Jesus' pronouncement that until heaven and earth pass away neither will one jot or tittle "of the law," some mainly Caesarean witnesses testify to the scribal addition of "and the prophets." One plausible explanation for this is that scribes could have simply imposed the customary phrase "the law and the prophets" onto their exemplar.

This examination of these several textual modifications all concern the relationship between the Gospel narratives and the prophetic tradition of the Hebrew Bible. Interpreting the birth, life, teachings, death, and resurrection of Jesus as fulfillment of Jewish prophetic oracles emerged in early Christian writings as a central and crucial argument, a trump card of sorts in the apologetic games. The textual modifications recorded in these verses offer plausible evidence—and in places quite concrete testimony—that scribes, at points, changed the text of the New Testament intentionally, deliberately, and mindfully in tune with the dynamics of pagan polemic and apologetic response. Concerned copyists changed their exemplars, not to the extent that they composed a different tune, but in the sense that they transposed them into an apologetic key.

EXCURSUS: THE TEMPORAL PRIORITY OF JESUS TO JOHN THE BAPTIZER

Scholars have long noted the embarrassment the earliest Christians suffered as a result of Gospel accounts that Jesus submitted himself to the baptism of John, thereby giving the appearance that he was subordinate to John.[68] This problematic relationship of the Nazarene to the Baptist did not manufacture grounds for an internecine controversy only, however; pagan critics also seized upon this event to subjugate the prominence of Jesus to John. Celsus serves as the prime example.[69]

The evangelists themselves, in part, anticipated this scandal. The Fourth Gospel's account of this story directly addresses the problem of the temporal priority of John. Of course, this theme had already been developed quite thoroughly in the Prologue (Jn 1:1–18) by the time the testimony of John is deposed. To the question of how Jesus and John related, the answer of this evangelist was firm: Jesus was superior to John in every way, eternal in time as the pre-existent *logos* and unrivaled in identity as the holy Lamb of God destined to take away the sin of the world (Jn 1:29). The Baptizer

---

[68]See, e.g., the extremely lucid discussion of the criterion of embarrassment applied to the portions of the Gospel narrative that pertain to John the Baptist and his relationship to Jesus in John P. Meier, *A Marginal Jew: Rethinking the Historical Jesus—Volume Two: Mentor, Message, and Miracles* (ABRL; New York: Doubleday, 1994), 19–233, esp. 21–22 and 101–105. Meier's evaluation of the evidence results in his firm conviction, based in large measure on the criterion of embarrassment, that the baptism of John can be taken as "the firm historical starting point for any treatment of Jesus' public ministry" (105).

[69]*Cels.* II.4.

speaking in John 1:15 and again in 1:30 says, "This is he of whom I said, 'After me (ὀπίσω μου) comes a man who ranks before me (ὃς ἔμπροσθέν μου γέγονεν), for he was before me (ὅτι πρῶτός μου ἦν).'" The two words used here, ἔμπροσθέν and πρῶτος, frequently indicate primacy of origin in time and superiority in degree.[70]

It is interesting to note in this context the variant reading of John 1:27, in which a third occurrence of this phrase, ὃς ἔμπροσθέν μου γέγονεν, is crowded into the pericope. This insertion appears the product of scribal assimilation. The manuscript testimony of P[5.66.75] ℵ B C* L N* T W[s] Ψ *f* 33 579 as well as some Old Latin (b, l), Syriac (Sinaitic and Curetonian) and Coptic versional witnesses over against that of A C[3] (Θ) *f*[13] Maj lat sy[(p).h] bo[mss] strongly suggests that the phrase in this verse was absent in "original" John. While one could argue from the perspective of intrinsic probabilities that the phrase corresponds favorably with the author's language and themes, it becomes difficult to explain from the transcriptional point of view why a scribe would have accidentally or deliberately omitted it. No clear problem of homoeoarcton or other mechanical explanation for the omission is evident, although the close proximity in the verse of several words beginning with omicron (ὁ, ὃς, οὗ οὐκ) could be pressed as a plausible explanation. The proposal of any purposeful omission in 1:27 on the part of scribes becomes suspect since the exact phrase appears without modification in 1:15 and 1:30. On the other hand, the decisions of the scribes represented by these later Alexandrian, Caesarean, Western and Byzantine/Majority witnesses to insert the phrase would serve the apologetic cause by enhancing further the apologetic theme of the temporal priority of Jesus to John.

The textual tradition of the synoptic gospels also exhibits an effort on the part of some scribes to address this issue. In Matthew 3:11, for example, John the Baptizer in explaining himself and his baptism describes one that is coming after him (ὀπίσω μου) who is mightier than he, whose sandals he is not worthy to unlace, who will baptize with the Holy Spirit and with fire. In transmitting this account, however, a small number of copyists, those represented by a d sa[mss] and Cyprian, eliminated the phrase ὀπίσω μου. Certainly, one could account for this variant by positing the mechanical omission of so short a phrase; other than the presence of several omicrons in the verse, however, there is no obvious reason to suspect so. The influence of harmonization to Luke 3:16, which lacks ὀπίσω μου entirely, is even less likely. Other than the lacking phrase, the edited Matthean text does not otherwise follow Luke's wording. Where Luke 3:16 reads ...ἐγὼ μὲν ὕδατι βαπτίζω ὑμᾶς· ἔρχεται δὲ ὁ ἰσχυρότερός μου..., the text of Matthew 3:11 appears as Ἐγὼ μὲν ὑμᾶς βαπτίζω ἐν ὕδατι εἰς μετάνοιαν, ὁ δὲ ἐρχόμενος [*v. l.* ὀπίσω μου] ἰσχυρότερός μού ἐστιν.... The differences in word order, use of a participle rather than the finite verb, and other minor variations do not enhance the case that scribes harmonized Matthew to Luke. In fact, manuscript evidence exists to support the claim that just the opposite assimilation transpired. In rendering Luke 3:16, Codex Bezae (D) and one Old Latin manuscript (l) substituted the exact words of Matthew (except for the disputed phrase),

---

[70] J. Fitzmyer, *Luke*, 548, 1534–5.

ὁ δὲ ἐρχόμενος ἰσχυρότερός μου. Therefore, neither mechanical error nor harmonization offer a clear explanation behind the omission of ὀπίσω μου. Something more and something intentional appears to lie back of this change. Let us consider whether the influence of apologetic interests might prove a better explanation for the omission.

For scribes sensitive to the dispute regarding the relationship between John the baptizer and Jesus, the prepositional phrase, ὀπίσω μου, could have been construed as problematic on two counts. Temporally, the phrase "after me" refers to the future, in the sense of "hereafter" or "yet to come."[71] As seen in the critique of Celsus, the notion of Jesus entering history after John was an embarrassment to the Christian cause.

In addition, the phrase can also be used in reference to one's disciples, as it is in Matthew (4:19) when Jesus calls to Peter and Andrew, "Come follow me (δεῦτε ὀπίσω μου) and I will make you fishers of people." Scribes may have seen the potential for interpreting the phrase in 3:11 to mean that John was indicating that it would be one of his own disciples, albeit a more talented one, who would ultimately administer a more spiritually potent form of his redemptive washing. With either or both of these concerns in mind, scribes sensitive to the vulnerabilities of the text in these regards may have chosen to navigate the hazard by simply eliminating it. The omission of ὀπίσω μου would obviate the verbal cues that Jesus came "after" John, either temporally or as his follower. An interesting constellation of variants to be considered in this context is located at John 12:28 in the Johannine narrative that most closely emulates the content of the Gethsemane prayer of the Synoptics. The pericope begins with Jesus giving voice to his troubled soul, but abruptly changes. "And what shall I say, 'Father save me from this hour?' No for this purpose I have come to this hour. Father, glorify your name" (σου τὸ ὄνομα). At least, that is the text as rendered by the UBS[4]/N-A[27] Committee, earning from them a {B} rating.[72] Codex Vaticanus substitutes μου for σου, thus producing the petition, "Father, glorify *my* name." A number of later witnesses (L X *f*[.13] 33 1071 1241) appear, according to Metzger, to be influenced by the opening words of the High Priestly Prayer (Jn 17:1) and read, "glorify your *Son*." Codex Bezae also anticipates the High Priestly Prayer as it appears to assimilate to the reading in 17:5; Jesus according to D prays, "Father, glorify your name *with the glory that I had with you before the world came to be....* "

Such probing into this verse uncovers two relevant insights. One is the recognition that an evolving high(er) christology is sometimes discernible in the labor of the scribes. Of course, they were not responsible for introducing this doctrinal feature into the High Priestly Prayer. Already strokes from the brush borne by the Johannine artist had blotted out the synoptic image of a Jesus offering desperate petitions to God at the eleventh hour and colored in the profile of a nimble, nimbused

---

[71]See Henry George Liddell and Robert Scott, *A Greek-English Lexicon* (Revised by Sir Henry Stuart Jones, *et al.*; Oxford: Clarendon Press, 1968), 1239.

[72]B. M. Metzger, *Textual Commentary*, 237–38.

incarnate Lord in complete command of the unfolding events.[73] What Jesus was about to do he would do willingly and knowledgeably, informed by his intimate union with the divine author of this drama.

Apparently, the scribes built on this high christology as they blurred more and more the lines between the Father and the Son, just as some of the apologists had before them. Athenagoras, for example, compared the father-son relationship of Marcus Aurelius and Commodus, to both of whom his apology is addressed, with that of God the Father and his Son. He wrote:

> May you find it possible to examine by your own efforts also the heavenly kingdom; for as all things have been subjected to you, a father and a son, who have received your kingdom from above ('for the king's life is in God's hand,' as the prophetic spirit says), so all things are subordinated to the one God and the Word that issues from him whom we consider his inseparable Son.[74]

Both of the scribal changes, i.e., the shift of second and first person pronouns and the substitution of "Son" for "name,"effectually served to elevate the status of Jesus.

Second, and more directly relevant to the present discussion, is the fact that the expanded reading of Codex Bezae not only elevates the christological identity of Jesus but also accents his temporal pre-existence. Codex D speaks of Jesus sharing a glory with the Father prior to creation itself. Of course, once again, this notion is nothing new in the Fourth Gospel; it was propagated from the outset of John in the prologue. Here, though, in John 12:28, the declaration of high christology results from the labors of scribes rather than of the evangelist. With great conviction, scribes portray Jesus as glorifying his own name, being glorified as God's own Son, and returning to the experience of a glory divine and preexistent in character. Copyists issuing these embellishments to the Fourth Gospel imposed the feature of preexistence upon Jesus at a point in the narrative where the evangelist did not compose it. Clearly they are doing theology here, implanting and cultivating the high christology of the Johannine Gospel in beds the original gardener never sowed.

Yet, their theological embellishment also serves an apologetic purpose. More than any other, the Fourth Gospel diminishes the role of John the Baptist in relation to Jesus. In part, this is carried out by the proclamation of the preexistence of Jesus in the prologue. A preexistent Christ is prior to John both temporally and ontologically. The evangelist (or an early redactor) made him so in the prologue (1:1–8); later scribes have made him so here (12:28). Jesus as the preexistent Son of the Father is temporally prior

---

[73]The literature on the subject of John and the Synoptics is, of course, vast and steeped in nuances, but the basic distinctions are generally apparent and familiar. For a clear and terse treatment of what he calls in lieu of christology the "presentation of Jesus" in the Gospel of John see D. Moody Smith, *Johannine Christianity: Essays on Its Setting, Sources, and Theology* (Columbia, SC: University of South Carolina Press, 1984), especially 175–189.

[74] *Leg.* 18.2. The English translation is from William Schoedel, ed. *Athenagoras: Legatio and De Resurrectione* (Oxford: Clarendon Press, 1972), 36–7.

and ontologically superior to John the Baptist—and, for that matter, even Moses, Abraham, and Adam!

The variants I have adduced in this section served either to de-emphasize John in relationship to Jesus or to highlight the pre-existence and temporal priority of Jesus in such a way that claim of Christians to the sublime virtue of antiquity could be enhanced. Once again, these variants mirror apologetic strategies, particularly as they appeared, as indicated above, in Justin and Athenagoras. These variant readings point once again to the activity of scribes who showed an active interest in apologetic discourse by incorporating its strategies into their labors of transcription.

PAGAN CRITICISM OF INCONSISTENCY AND CHRISTIAN HARMONIZATION

Early Christians found their texts vulnerable to criticism. Attentive readers, particularly those with an axe to grind, noted within the gospels glaring factual errors, Old Testament citations wrongly attributed, and inconsistencies in the details reported by the separate evangelical accounts. Of course, the distinctions in the four Gospels had been observed by the church fathers, and, by some, even embraced. Irenaeus, for example, early in the second century, lauded the tetrarchy of sacred writings as reflective of a divine scheme, akin to that of the four corners of the earth or the four winds.[75] Short years later, however, Christian apologists were faced with challenges that demanded more than a sublime metaphor for an adequate response. The inconsistencies and lack of harmony readily apparent in a comparative reading of the four canonical Gospels drew the attention of critics, for whom such asymmetry in the particulars of the Jesus story represented a logical and factual inconsistency that aroused historical suspicion. Celsus, as a prime example, was wont to seize upon narrative infelicities and set them as stumbling blocks before the new religion. In scathing tone, he wrote:

> Some believers, as though from a drinking bout, go so far as to oppose themselves and alter the original text of the gospel three or four or several times over, and they change its character to enable them to deny difficulties in face of criticism.[76]

Whether Celsus here was referring to discrepancies among the separate Gospels or deliberate modifications imposed upon the text by scribes remains a puzzle to scholars,[77] but there is no mystery surrounding the conclusion that, for Celsus, the

---

[75]Irenaeus, *Ad. Haer.* III.11.8, *ANF*, Vol. I, 428. For a brief discussion of Irenaeus on scripture see J. Quasten, *Patrology*, Vol. I (Utrecht-Antwerp: Spectrum, 1950), 306–308.

[76]Origen, *Cels.* II.27. Cited here from Henry Chadwick, *Origen: Contra Celsum* (Cambridge: Cambridge University Press, 1953), 90.

[77]For discussion of this scholarly conundrum see H. Chadwick, *Origen: Contra Celsum*, 90, n. 2, and Tjitze Baarda, "ΔΙΑΦΩΝΙΑ-ΣΥΜΦΩΝΙΑ: Factors in the Harmonization of the Gospels, Especially in the Diatesseron of Tatian," *Gospel Traditions in the Second Century* (ed. William L. Petersen; Notre Dame: University of Notre Dame Press, 1989), 133–154. In contrast

5555555555555555

gospel accounts enjoyed no privileged status under his unyielding investigation. Celsus was ever ready to bring low the faith by highlighting its faults, an inconsistent text being one of them.

Even more intimidating in this regard was Porphyry, labeled by Robert Wilken the "most learned critic of all."[78] Porphyry routinely tried to discredit the Gospels by searching out and reporting discrepancies and apparent contradictions in the text.[79] In addition, a host of the extracts attributed to Porphyry in the *Apocriticus* of Macarius Magnes focus on this issue. We read, for example:

> The evangelists were fiction writers—not observers or eyewitnesses to the life of Jesus. Each of the four contradicts the other in writing his account of the events of his suffering and crucifixion.[80]

Nor could Christian intellectuals like Origen ignore the facts. He framed it as a critical problem to be resolved:

> The truth of these matters must lie in that which is seen with the mind. If the discrepancy between the Gospels is not solved, we must give up our trust in the Gospels as being true and written by a divine spirit, or as records worthy of credence, for both these characters are held to belong to these works.[81]

---

to those who argue that gospels harmonies were produced for reasons of cost or reduced size, Baarda postulates that "textual harmonization was most probably one of the attempts to remove or neutralize the disagreements among the Gospels."

[78]Robert L. Wilken, *The Christians As the Romans Saw Them* (New Haven: Yale University Press, 1984), 126–163.

[79]A. Meredith, "Porphyry and Julian," 1119–1149.

[80]*Apocrit.* II.12–15, translated by R. Joseph Hoffmann, *Porphyry's Against the Christians: The Literary Remains* (Amherst, NY: Prometheus Books, 1994), 32. Although in my judgment Hoffmann dismisses too readily the challenges of T. D. Barnes ("Porphyry Against the Christians: Date and Attribution of Fragments," *JTS n. s.* 24 (1973), 424–42) and too easily follows Harnack in ascribing the objections cited and addressed by Macarius Magnes to Porphyry himself, the content of the fragments, at least in part, does bear resemblance to protests that can be traced to Porphyry. So, although I am not, with Hoffmann, content to reference these as Porphyry's own, I do believe it is reasonable to consider that his influence may be seen here, and, more importantly for this present work, to recognize these protests as ones that were probably circulating in the era of the apologetic wars and scribal transmission that constitutes the chronological and historical framework of this study. It is within the parameters of this caveat, then, that I cite the work of Macarius Magnes.

[81]Origen, *Commentary on John* X.2. Cited here from *ANF*, Volume X (ed. Alan Menzies; Grand Rapids, MI: Eerdmans, 1951), 382.

Since so much was at stake, then, it is no wonder that this issue of inconsistency was addressed frequently, if variously, by apologetic writers, including Justin Martyr,[82] Tatian,[83] Aristides,[84] Theophilus of Antioch,[85] and Origen.[86]

There can be no doubt that the text itself was a battlefield in the apologetic scrimmages. Scrutinizing opponents highlighted variations in narrative detail as evidence of either factual error, which brought suspicion upon the historical reliability of the gospel accounts, or composed fiction, a charge that rendered the gospels void of significance for enlightened thinking persons. Apologists responded to these threats by either, like Origen, offering allegorical or clarifying explanation, or, in the manner of Tatian, harmonizing accounts.[87] The detectable volume of energy expended by the apologists in executing these strategic responses demonstrates how seriously they viewed these assaults on the text.

This concern, though, extended back even earlier. Even in the labors of Matthew and Luke there can be recognized an obvious need for the sacred writings of their faith to bear the marks of consistency, harmony, and factual felicity. In the prologue to his Gospel, for example, Luke identified his composition as "an orderly account" constructed out of transmitted eye witness accounts that Luke himself has traced from the beginning and arranged systematically in writing for his excellency, Theophilus. In so prefacing his narrative, Luke adopted, much as Josephus did before him, a standard Hellenistic literary formula and exhibited his own free-flowing prose apart from any source material.[88]

Use of these Hellenistic conventions strongly suggests that Luke intended his composition for a predominantly Gentile audience, and one composed, at least in part, of persons owning some degree of literary sophistication.[89] H. J. Cadbury detected in his reading of this prologue evidence of this apologetic concern for order and

---

[82]Justin throughout his apologetic works is concerned with interpreting Christian doctrines and scriptures in a way palatable to the philosophical mind, but for a direct instance of this see, e.g., *Dial.* VI–IX.

[83]Tatian, *Or.* 25.2, who characterizes followers of Greek philosophy and mythology as persons who have inherited contradictory (ἀσύμφωνοι) teachings. See Mk. Whittaker, ed., *Oratio*, 48–49.

[84]Aristides, *Ap.* 16. See J. Rendel Harris, *The Apology of Aristides.* (TS I, edited by J. A. Robinson; 2d ed.; Cambridge: Cambridge University Press, 1893; repr., 1967), 50–51 and 111.

[85]*Ad Auto.* III.1. See in Grant, ed. *Theophilus*, 100–101.

[86]Throughout his reply to Celsus Origen is concerned with clarifying, elucidating, interpreting, or otherwise defending Christian sacred writings. For especially bold instances see Origen, *Cels.* II.23–24, II.26–27, III.1–2, V.52–56.

[87]Cf. Tjitze Baarda, "ΔΙΑΦΩΝΙΑ," 133–35.

[88]For a thorough treatment of the Lucan prologue see J. Fitzmyer, *Luke (I–IX)*, 287–302.

[89]For more on the intended readers for Luke's gospel see J. Fitzmyer, *Luke (I–IX)*, 57–59, and Jacob Jervell, *Luke and the People of God: A New Look at Luke–Acts* (Minneapolis: Augsburg, 1972), esp. 41–74.

accuracy.[90] Not convinced, however, J. Fitzmyer finds this interpretation of the prologue too confining, and argues that the assurance that Luke wishes to extend to Theophilus is not in character apologetic but catechetical. "In seeking to trace matters to their beginning, Luke discloses the solidity of the early church's catechetical instruction."[91] Fitzmyer goes on to explain the author's concern to craft his tale "systematically," including (unlike Mark) both an infancy story and a sequel to the Jesus saga.

Whether or not he is correct, Fitzmyer's reading of the prologue fails to dismiss the possibility of an apologetic ambition on the part of the writer. As noted earlier, the effort to clarify Christian teachings and systematize Christian narratives was itself a concern of Christian apologists. Theophilus, in particular, took the offensive on this point, ridiculing the pagan myths as inconsistent (ἀσύμφονα).[92] Therefore, that Fitzmyer wishes to call attention to the care of composition and depth of meaning inherent in the prologue is to his credit; but there is no need to dispute Cadbury's judgment that apologetic interests are reflected therein.

Matthew's edition of the gospel narrative, though addressed to a different audience, also bears the marks of careful organization, structure, and clarification.[93] Milton Brown describes the author of Matthew as a scribe (γραμματεύς) with the heart of a peacemaker (ειρηνηποιός). By this he means, "he goes about his scribal duties, not as a mere collector of traditions or impartial redactor of ecclesiastical law, but as a churchman sensitive to the varying winds of doctrine blowing among his fellows and as one eager to reconcile the factious and to preserve the unity of the church."[94] Davies and Allison concur with the notion that the author of Matthew sought a compromise of sorts, one that would uphold the traditional roots of his

---

[90]H. J. Cadbury. *The Making of Luke–Acts* (London: SPCK, 1961), 344 f. Cadbury asserts that Luke is addressing himself not so much to scientific scepticism, but to ignorance and prejudice. Regarding specific terms in the preface, he explains that ἀκριβῶς implies exact detail; its opposite is not falsehood but insufficient information. Also, ἀσφάλεια for the author has to do with "meeting unfavorable judgments of Christianity. It appeals to 'the facts.' Its opposite is rumor and prejudice." (346)

[91]Fitzmyer, *Luke (I–IX)*, 289–290.

[92]*Ad Auto.* III.3. See Grant, ed. *Theophilus*, 102–103.

[93]For a comprehensive survey of the various theories regarding the structure of Matthew see Davies and Allison, *Matthew*, Vol. I, 58–72. The proposals include that Matthew structured his narrative (a) in five parts after the pattern of the Pentateuch (B. W. Bacon), (b) based on a chiastic outline involving narrative and discourse (C. H. Lohr), (c) a three-fold structure around the themes of person, proclamation and passion of Jesus (J. D. Kingsbury), and (d) in accordance with the Jewish lectionary (M. D. Goulder). A minority of scholars urge to the contrary that no fixed arrangement is to be inferred from Matthew (R. H. Gundry). Davies and Allison express support for the theories of Bacon and Gundry.

[94]Milton Brown, "Matthew as ΕΙΡΗΝΟΠΟΙΟΣ," in *Studies in the History and Text of the New Testament in honor of Kenneth Willis Clark, Ph. D*, edited by Boyd Daniels and Jack Suggs (SD, Volume XXIX; Salt Lake City: University of Utah Press, 1967), 39–50.

religious heritage even as it embraced the tide of Greco-Roman influence that appeared inevitable.[95]

Long before Davies and Allison, or Brown, Origen himself, in his exegesis of this very term, described "peacemakers" as persons who "demonstrate that that which appears to others to be a conflict in the Scriptures is no conflict, and exhibits their concord and peace...."[96] Origen sought to explain the seeming occurrence of incongruence by drawing an analogy from music. To one ignorant in music, Origen tutored, the dissimilar notes of a chord, because they do not each effect the same sound, might appear inharmonious; similarly, those untrained in hearing the harmony of God in the counterpoints of the Old and New Testaments or in the comparisons of the Gospels with one another might puzzle over their seeming discord. The one who would become instructed in the music of God, however, would come to know that "all the Scripture is the one perfect and harmonized instrument of God, which from different sounds gives forth one saving voice to those willing to learn." [97]

According to Eusebius (*Hist. eccl.* VI:36), Origen wrote this in his *Commentary on Matthew* close to the time he penned *Contra Celsum*. Both Crouzel and Trigg emphasize that these works both belong to Caesarea and were products of his mature old age.[98] This suggests that between the time Celsus published *True Doctrine* and Origen wrote his rebuttal and Matthean commentary that there had developed a growing consciousness of the discrepancies between the Gospels.[99] In any event, it is clear from his thoughtfully composed music analogy that Origen recognized the extent to which even minor discrepancies could prove injurious to the Christian cause of survival and propagation, especially when they were adduced by minds so perspicacious and uncompromising as those of the pagan despisers of Christianity.

HARMONIZATION

Before proceeding to an examination of relevant variants, some additional discussion of harmonization is in order. Scholars generally agree that the practices of harmonization, assimilation, and conflation of readings were frequently practiced by ancient copyists of the Gospels.[100] Willem Wisselink identifies four kinds of

---

[95] In their eyes, however, he failed. They argue that the Gentile form of Christianity became dominant by the time of Ignatius of Antioch. See Davies and Allison, *Matthew*, Vol. III, 722–23.

[96] Origen, *Commentary on Matthew*, II.1, cited from *ANF*, Vol. X, 413.

[97] Origen, *Comm. Matt* II.1, cited from *ANF*, Vol. X, 413.

[98] H. Crouzel, *Origen* (trans. by A. S. Worrall; San Francisco: Harper & Row, 1989), 40, 43; J. W. Trigg, *Origen* (London/New York: Routledge, 1998), 52–61.

[99] W. R. Farmer, *The Last Twelve Verses of Mark* (Cambridge: Cambridge University Press, 1974), 28–29.

[100] For example, see Bruce Metzger, *The Text of the New Testament* (3d ed.; New York: Oxford University Press, 1992), 197–98; Kurt Aland, *The Text of the New Testament* (2d ed.; Grand Rapids, Michigan: Eerdmans, 1995), 290–91, 293. For a synopsis of the nuanced views of seventeen scholars on the subject of assimilation see Willem F. Wisselink, *Assimilation as a Criterion for*

assimilation that occur in the Gospels: (1) mutually among the Gospels, (2) within a single Gospel, (3) to the Septuagint, and (4) to an otherwise known wording.[101] Scholars have frequently asserted that this tendency was inevitable, in part due to the bent of the human mind for unity and the belief that scripture cannot contradict itself.[102] Unconscious familiarity with a favorite or dominant Gospel, usually Matthew, is widely mentioned as another reason copyists assimilated a verse in one Gospel to that of another. Substitution of the Matthean version of the Lord's Prayer for the shorter, more abrupt Lucan rendering serves many as an example.[103] In the opinion of C. S. C. Williams, "The scribes familiar with parallel passages to the one that they were copying were tempted, sometimes unconsciously but more often quite consciously, to assimilate their text to its parallel."[104]

Several scholars, though, have cautioned appraisers of scribal activities to be wary of such absolute statements. Nowhere have reasons for these reservations been better demonstrated than in the search for possible tendencies in the Synoptic tradition undertaken by E. P. Sanders.[105] In his study, performed with an eye toward resolving issues of priority related to the Synoptic problem, Sanders examined several possible tendencies that were generally asserted to be commonly operative among scribes. He tested these presumed categories in light of a cross section of Synoptic material and its transmission in church fathers and apocryphal gospels. After an extensive collation and evaluation of the data located in these sources, Sanders came to the conclusion that few of these formerly functional tenets held water. Among the sacred cows he slew were two that had become virtual axioms: the evidence failed to indicate that the tradition either grew in length or became less Semitic. Although certain tendencies surfaced as "fairly common," such as the penchant for adding detail and for changing indirect discourse into direct discourse, Sanders indicated that in large measure his findings were negative. Hence, he summarized:

> There are no hard and fast laws of the development of the Synoptic tradition. On all counts the tradition developed in opposite directions. It became both longer and shorter, both more and less detailed, and both more and less Semitic. Even the

---

Establishing the Text (Kampen: Uitgeversmaatschappij J. H. Kok, 1989), 43–61.

[101]W. Wisselink, 54. Wisselink in this report builds on the work of Gordon Fee, "Modern Textual Criticism and the Synoptic Problem," in B. Orchard and T. Longstaff, eds., *J. J. Griesbach: Synoptic and Text-Critical Studies 1776–1976* (Cambridge: Cambridge University Press, 1978), 161–62.

[102]E. L. Titus, *The Motivation of Changes Made in the New Testament Text by Justin Martyr and Clement of Alexandria: A Study in the Origin of New Testament Variation* (Ph.D. diss., University of Chicago, 1942), 18.

[103]B. M. Metzger, *Text of the New Testament*, 197.

[104]C. S. C. Williams, *Alterations to the Text of the Synoptic Gospels and Acts* (Oxford: Basil Blackwell, 1951), 1.

[105]E. P. Sanders, *The Tendencies of the Synoptic Tradition* (Cambridge: Cambridge University Press, 1969).

tendency to use direct discourse for indirect, which was uniform in the post-canonical material which we studied, was not uniform in the Synoptics themselves. For this reason, *dogmatic statements that a certain characteristic proves a certain passage to be earlier than another are never justified.*[106]

Such a cognizance of the complexities involved in discerning the tendencies of transmissional activity, with particular attention to harmonization, is also reflected in the keen musings of E. C. Colwell. The most obvious improvement from a viewpoint of a scribe, he explains, was to make the reading fit the context. Harmonization within a book, or to the immediate context, was commonplace.[107] Even when to do so led to an error, scribes often made the reading fit into its context. Thus, he cautions, textual scholars who choose the reading that best fits the context may well be choosing the wrong reading. On the other hand, Colwell qualifies, to disregard the dominant pattern of an author's style may also lead to error. Hence, intrinsic inclinations and transcriptional probabilities may cancel each other out.[108]

James Royse on this topic offers his own caveat: "Instead of saying that scribes tend to do something, one should rather say that some scribes tend to do one thing, and other scribes tend to do something else."[109] Assimilations and harmonized readings, then, must be evaluated as to their "originality," like all other variant readings—individually, case by case and not in groups.

With those warnings duly noted, scholars do recognize that scribes did, on occasion, consciously impose harmony on otherwise discordant passages. In this regard the words of Tjitze Baarda are instructive.

> Apart from an amount of unconscious assimilation by scribes who inadvertently reproduced the text of the Gospel with which they were most familiar, and not the text of the exemplar being copied, there are certainly deliberate alterations, omissions or additions. Scribes consciously altered their manuscript, and made it conform to that of the other Gospels, especially when these latter texts stood in high esteem in their community because of their archaic character or supposed apostolic origin.[110]

---

[106]E. P. Sanders, *Tendencies*, 272. His italics.

[107]E. C. Colwell, "Method in Evaluating Scribal Habits: A Study of P[45], P[46], P[75],"106–124.

[108]Colwell, E. C. "External Evidence and NT Textual Criticism," in Boyd L. Daniels and M. Jack Suggs, eds. *Studies in the History and Text of the New Testament in honor of Kenneth Willis Clark, Ph.D.* (SD XXIX; Salt Lake City: University of Utah Press, 1967), 4.

[109]James R Royse, "Scribal Tendencies in the Transmission of the Text," 239–52. Royse, e.g., cites his own studies of scribal habits in particular manuscripts—as well as work done by E. C. Colwell, E. W. Tune, and Günther Zuntz, among others—all of which challenge the sweeping application of the canons of criticism regarding transcriptional probabilities. Although the general sentiment among scholars is that the text expanded in transmission, analysis of specific early mss (P[45.46.47.66.72.75]) suggests that the tendency of these copyists was to lose rather than gain words and to harmonize to the immediate context more often than to parallel accounts.

[110]T. Baarda, "ΔΙΑΦΩΝΙΑ," 138.

This process, he surmises, most likely began in the middle of the second century when awareness of these discrepancies became a problem, though, he reminds us, the impulse toward harmonization existed from the beginning of the process. The Gospels themselves may rightly be described as products resulting from the labor of combining sources: Mark of various oral traditions (at the very least), Matthew and Luke of Mark, Q, M, and L, and the Fourth Gospel, apart from the sources we do not know, of the "signs" source among others.[111] Apocryphal gospels, too, it has been conjectured, were the result of "popular" (in contrast to a carefully produced scholarly work) harmonizations which served a devotional or evangelical purpose.[112] William Petersen points out that recent studies have disclosed that the Gospel according to the Ebionites, the Gospel according to the Nazoraeans, and the Gospel according to the Hebrews all feature textual affinity with Tatian's Diatessaron.[113] He also discusses the limited but provocative evidence that the second-century apologists Justin and Theophilus of Antioch may have used or been responsible for constructing gospel harmonies.[114]

To be sure, many factors undoubtedly inspired scribes to engage in the process of harmonization. One was geographical location. Studies have shown that the distinctive scribal habits and purposes associated with certain geographical regions shaped the contours of assimilation. Seemingly, e.g., Alexandrian scribes occupied themselves differently than their counterparts in other regions. As Wisselink generalizes:

> Outside Egypt it was not philology that ruled, but the ecclesiastical or theological interest. Outside Egypt, the issue was not the original text, but the text regarded by the editor as the "best" text.[115]

Two other factors frequently postulated as reasons behind the design and composition of full-scale Gospel harmonies are economics and practicality. One smaller book, it is construed, rather than four larger ones would have cost less to produce and been easier to transport. Baarda, though, questions the real relevance of these practical matters. He argues that the standard harmony would have consisted of roughly three-fourths of the four gospels, and that Tatian's Diatessaron, he estimates,

---

[111]T. Baarda, "ΔΙΑΦΩΝΙΑ," 140–41. On the sources of the Fourth Gospel see D. Moody Smith, Johannine Christianity, 39–93.

[112]T. Baarda, "ΔΙΑΦΩΝΙΑ,"141. See also Raymond Brown, "The Gospel of Peter and Canonical Gospel Priority," NTS 33 (1986/1987), 321–343.

[113]William L. Petersen, Tatian's Diatessaron: Its Creation, Dissemination, Significance, and History in Scholarship (Leiden: E. J. Brill, 1994), 29–31.

[114]W. Petersen, Tatian's Diatessaron, 27–9, 32–4.

[115]W. Wisselink, 45.

would have contained an even greater measure of them. Therefore, he points out, not a great deal would have been saved either in cost of production or convenience.[116]

Tendentious motivation undoubtedly constituted yet another factor. W. Petersen, for example, points out that in comparison with the canonical Gospels, the *Diatessaron* appears "to have been redacted by a hand sympathetic to Encratism."[117] T. Baarda argues, though, that the most compelling motive that led Tatian to produce his *Diatessaron* consisted of Tatian's apologetic dedication to truth, unity, and historical reliability. The arguments of Tatian, as well as those of Theophilus of Antioch, reflect the principle that people whose chronological records were inconsistent (ἀσυνάρτητος) could not be deemed reliable in reporting history. Descriptive error, it was widely maintained by both sides, resulted from composing stories that were not true (τὰ μὴ ἀληθῆ). Christian writings to be reliable had to be void of factual error and narrative inconsistency. Tatian, himself a Christian apologist, took on as a personal crusade the challenge of reconciling the Gospels. His publication of the *Diatessaron*, therefore, was motivated out of and was intended, at least in part, to serve an apologetic purpose.

VARIANT READINGS RELATED TO ISSUES OF
TEXTUAL HARMONY AND CONSISTENCY

Examination of several variant readings in the canonical Gospels suggests that some scribes may have enlisted in this cause. Evidence is indisputable that the text of the New Testament was modified in transmission by scribes concerned with internal consistency, factual agreement, and consonance among the gospels. An untold number of variant readings bear the stamp of deliberate harmonization and factual correction. Yet, textual scholars have been content generally to attribute these changes to transcribers whose sole preoccupation was with the correction of a writer's errors, and not with the deflection of pundit's arrows. Following are a representative sample of scribal alterations that with some justification can be attributed to the apologetic motives of textual agreement, factual accuracy, and logical consistency.

We begin with an appraisal of the particularly vexing textual variant reported in the transmission of John 7:8. UBS[4]/NA[27] reconstructs John 7:8–10 as follows:

⁸ὑμεῖς ἀνάβητε εἰς τὴν ἑορτήν· ἐγὼ οὐκ [*v.l.*, οὔπω] ἀναβαίνω εἰς τὴν ἑορτὴν ταύτην ὅτι ἐμὸς καιρὸς οὔπω πεπλήρωται. ⁹ταῦτα δὲ εἰπὼν αὐτὸς ἔμεινεν ἐν τῇ Γαλιλαίᾳ. ¹⁰ Ὡς δὲ ἀνέβησαν οἱ ἀδελφοὶ αὐτοῦ εἰς τὴν ἑορτήν, τότε καὶ αὐτὸς ἀνέβη οὐ φανερῶς ἀλλὰ [ὡς] ἐν κρυπτῷ.[118]

---

[116]W. Wisselink, 144.
[117]W. Petersen, *Tatian's Diatessaron*, 79.
[118]N-A[27], 269–70.

Go to the feast yourselves; I am not [*v.l.,* not yet] going up to this feast, for my time has not yet fully come. So saying, he remained in Galilee. But after his brothers had gone up to the feast, then he also went up, not publicly but in private.

"*Not* to go" or "*Not yet* to go"? That is the question broached by the variant reading located at John 7:8. Does Jesus flatly deny that he is going to Jerusalem, or does he merely indicate a delay in his travels? Response to this question assumes some urgency when the reader notices in verse 10 that Jesus does, in fact, travel "in secret" to Jerusalem and arrives there shortly after his brothers. Of course, no problem exists if the reading οὔπω is regarded as "original," as is indicated by several of our most reliable manuscripts; but if οὐκ issued from the writer's pen, the inconsistency between his words and deeds in verses 8 and 10 makes Jesus vulnerable to accusations of deceit, duplicity, or indecisiveness. Substituting οὔπω in place of οὐκ in verse 8, of course, resolves this problem, which is why the majority of scholars believe this to be the product of a concerned scribe. Yet, not everyone concurs. The UBSGNT Committee, in spite of Metzger's confident assertion that οὔπω was early on introduced by a scribe seeking to ameliorate the conflict between verse 8 and 10, still assigns it only a {C} rating.[119] For the purposes of this study, a more thorough investigation into this textual problem is called for. Let us begin with a review of the external evidence.

With regard to external evidence, Ernst Haenchen points out that οὔπω boasts an impressive set of credentials, among them P[66] P[75] B L T W.[120] Other apparatus in addition marshal Θ Ψ 070 0105 0250 $f^{1.13}$ Maj f g q sy[p.h]sa ac pbo in support of οὔπω as "original."[121] Clearly, οὔπω comes to dominate the tradition, but that does not make it "original." Supporting οὐκ in its claim to priority are some similarly reliable witnesses: ℵ D K 1241 lat sy[s.c] bo. Here, as is so often the case, mainly "Western" witnesses (reading οὐκ) oppose the remaining lines of transmission. Still, the most striking sources in support of οὔπω are the two ancient papyri, P[66] and P[75]. The weight of their testimony requires closer scrutiny.

P[66] is generally ascribed a date around 200 C.E.; the editors of P[75] place it between 175–225 C.E.[122] Both stand as ancient and important witnesses to the textual tradition. Scholars some time ago became mindful of the unparalleled excellence of the

---

[119]B. M. Metzger, *Textual Commentary*, 216.

[120]Ernst Haenchen, *John 2: A Commentary on the Gospel of John Chapters 7–21* (Translated by Robert Funk; Hermeneia Series; Philadelphia: Fortress, 1984), 7.

[121]See N-A[27], 269; also Rudolf Schnackenburg, *The Gospel According to John*, Volume 2. (New York: Seabury Press, 1980), 185.

[122]B. M. Metzger, *Text of the New Testament*, 40–41. Metzger notes that at least one scholar argues for an earlier dating of P[66], placing it in the middle or even first half of the second century. The reference is Herbert Hunger, "Zur Datierung des Papyrus Bodmer II (P 66)," *Anzieger der österreichischen Akademie der Wissenschaften*, phil.-hist. Kl., 1960, Nr. 4, 12–33. Even an earlier dating of this papyrus, however, would not exempt it from the criticism applied herein and elsewhere.

testimony shared by the pair of manuscripts, P[75] and Codex Vaticanus (B), and frequently view it as representing the best type of third-century texts.[123] Some scholars even regard P[75] as the *de facto* exemplar of Vaticanus.[124] Perhaps, though, the P[75]--Vaticanus line of tradition is best understood as the quintessential representative of the "Alexandrian" text, which, it should be recalled, bears characteristics of a highly polished, skillfully edited text.[125] P[66], similarly, has been described as the product of a scriptorium, a composite recension manufactured by a "careless" scribe who was evidently correcting his own work against at least two other manuscripts. This copyist frequently abandoned Johannine style in an effort to impose on the text a more vernacular Greek, "thereby revealing at a very early period a scribal attitude that removes difficulties and seeks the best sense of the text rather than showing a rigid concern for the preservation of the 'original text.'"[126] Therefore, both P[66] and P[75] report a text that is both very old, on the one hand, but that bears marks of intentional shaping or polishing, on the other. Both papyri reflect the concern of their scribes to produce an improved (in their view) text, not just preserve an "original" one. This statement is not intended to diminish the importance of these papyri as witnesses. I simply mean to specify that no pair of manuscripts, even ones as old and reliable as these papyri, can be assumed to harbor the "original" text.

So we are left, as stated earlier, with a familiar plight: a "Western" reading standing virtually alone against the rest of the corpus. Textual criticism, though, is not a numbers game; variants must be evaluated on the basis of the quality of witnesses and not their quantity. A Johannine reading that locates its lineage in Sinaiticus, Bezae, and the Old Latin tradition bears a reasonable claim to antiquity, and a "Western" reading that does not reflect expansion or embellishment must be taken particularly seriously. In short, external evidence will not decide this case.

Let us now turn our attention to the internal evidence. In terms of transcriptional probabilities, one obvious possibility is scribal error. Since the variation consists of only two letters and the meaning of the words is so similar, a fallacious slip on the part

---

[123]See, for example, C. L. Porter, "Papyrus Bodmer XV (P 75) and the text of Codex Vaticanus," *JBL* 81(1962), 363–76; K. W. Clark, "The Text of the Gospel of John in Third Century Egypt," *NovT* 5 (1962) 17–24; and Eldon J. Epp, "The Papyrus Manuscripts of the New Testament," in *The Text of the New Testament in Contemporary Research: Essays on the Status Quaestionis*, (ed. Bart D. Ehrman and Michael W. Holmes; Grand Rapids, Michigan: William B. Eermans, 1995), 3–21.

[124]Again, see C. L. Porter, "Papyrus Bodmer XV (P 75) and the text of Codex Vaticanus," 374, where he notes that collation produces only the slightest and most insignificant variations between P[75] and Vaticanus. For him, the correlation between them proves sufficient to demonstrate a strong affinity between the two manuscripts.

[125]B. M. Metzger, *Text of the New Testament*, 215. But see also Carlo M. Martini, "Is There a Late Alexandrian Text of the Gospels?" *NTS* 24 (1978), 285–96, where he suggests that the papyri of Didymus the Blind discovered at Toura in 1941 imply the existence of an early Alexandrian text even older than the refined P[75]-Vaticanus type.

[126]E. J. Epp, "The Papyrus Manuscripts of the New Testament," 15–16.

of the copyist could have produced either reading. To pursue this line of thought one more step, however, since οὔπω appears in the second half of the verse, homoeoarchton could easily account for the alteration of οὐκ to οὔπω; the scribe's eye could have momentarily picked up the word in the next line—both of which began with OY—and inserted it. Considering this variation in light of mechanical error, then, suggests that modification in the opposite direction, οὔπω to οὐκ, is the more difficult accident to account for.

For many scholars, the argument hinges on the question of intrinsic probabilities. Contrary to the judgment of the editors of UBSGNT, for example, R. H. Lightfoot ascribes οὔπω to the hand of the evangelist, believing that this term conforms more nearly to the author's clear statement that Jesus' time has not yet come. Lightfoot, though, realizes the necessity of defending his claim, since οὐκ in his mind represents the more difficult reading (*lectio difficilior*). In favor of his judgment he offers two reasons. First, he explains that the reader should understand that Jesus in the text is refusing to defer to the "brothers" who want him to go up to the feast. That is, John's portrayal of Jesus is that he will not acquiesce to public pressure. Only later, in response to the will of his Father and not the wishes of his "brothers" will he "go up" to Jerusalem. Secondly, Lightfoot argues that the writer of the Fourth Gospel employs this verb ἀναβαίνω not only to describe Jesus visiting Jerusalem but also ascending and returning to the Father (cf. 3:13, 6:62, 20:17), an action associated in John directly with the "elevation" of Jesus on the cross.[127] Lightfoot concludes:

> Possibly therefore, although using the word in this passage in its natural sense so far as the Lord and his brethren at 7:8, 10 are concerned, at 7:8 St. John uses it, in reference to the Lord, of his ascent to the Father through the cross: 'I go not up at this feast.' However strange this meaning of the word in the present context may seem to us, it is probably not impossible for a writer like John.[128]

Expressing dissension, Rudolf Schnackenburg finds this approach untenable because he locates elsewhere in the Fourth Gospel (2:13, 5:1, 7:14) examples where the evangelist uses ἀναβαίνω to convey matter-of-factly the act of "going up to Jerusalem." Instead he insists, "There is no room for a double meaning in this instance."[129]

Haenchen in contrast to Schnackenburg joins Lightfoot in his view, but offers his own reasons. He points out that the reading οὐκ is plagued by an internal difficulty, namely, that, since Jesus does not yet know the time when his Father will call upon him to die, such a definitive pronouncement about his travel plans would oppose the logic of his situation. Therefore, for Haenchen, just as John 7:6 reads, "My hour has

---

[127]R. H. Lightfoot. *St. John's Gospel: A Commentary* (ed. C. F. Evans; Oxford: Clarendon Press, 1956), 175–176.

[128]R. H. Lightfoot, *St. John's Gospel*, 176.

[129]R. Schnackenburg, *John*, 143.

not yet (οὔπω) come," so must verse 8 have read "originally," "I am *not yet* (οὔπω) going to the feast."[130]

Returning to the other side of this debate, C. K. Barrett on the basis of transcriptional probabilities expresses certainty that οὔπω represents the modification, one grounded in the efforts of early copyists to reconcile the "superficial contradiction" between verse 8 and 10. Barrett believes the "original" reading οὐκ merely negates the request of his brothers that he go up to Jerusalem, since their request is based on the desire that he manifest his works "openly" (ἐν παρρησίᾳ) and "show himself to the world" (φανέρωσον σεαυτὸν τῷ κόσμῳ). The evangelist, to Barrett's mind, portrays a Jesus who "refuses in the plainest terms to comply with human—and unbelieving—advice, acting with complete freedom and independence with regard to men, but in complete obedience to his Father."[131] Alan Culpepper sharpens this contrast, arguing that, as characters in the Fourth Gospel, the "brothers" of Jesus are viewed contemptuously as unbelievers who will, in time, be rejected and replaced by Jesus' disciples.[132] Several commentators suggest that "not" (οὐκ) should *not* have been taken as a problem in that there stands a well-defined distinction between verses 8 and 10, namely that of performing publicly and doing things privately. An advocate of this position, Charles Talbert outlines how the themes of private (ἐν κρυπτῷ) and public (φανερῶς) provide concentric and chiastic structure patterns for John 7:1–14.[133]

In the mind of Raymond Brown, though, it is precisely the conspicuous problem caused by the appearance of οὐκ in verse 8 that serves the writer's purpose. The fact that Jesus later does precisely what he tells his brothers he is not going to do glares as too blatant a contradiction to be anything but intentional. In his judgment, the evangelist employs this literary inconsistency to call attention to the double-entendre of his statement, what Brown terms a "classic instance of the two levels of meaning found in John." It is true that Jesus' time has not come at this festival of Tabernacles; his time (καιρός) is reserved for a subsequent Passover.[134] Similarly, Schnackenburg locates a resolution to the intrinsic textual problem by shifting the focus of the discussion away from the troublesome adverb and calling attention to a revealing pronoun. "His saying 'to *this* feast' carries the underlying thought that he will be going to Jerusalem to another feast: the next Passover, the Passover of his death." Informed by this point of view, Schnackenburg declares that it does not really matter whether

---

[130]E. Haenchen, *John*, 7.

[131]C. K. Barrett. *The Gospel According to St. John* (2d ed.; Philadelphia: Westminster, 1978), 312–313.

[132]R. Alan Culpepper. *Anatomy of the Fourth Gospel: A Study in Literary Design* (Philadelphia: Fortress, 1983), 138–139.

[133]Charles H. Talbert. *Reading John: A Literary and Theological Commentary on the Fourth Gospel and the Johannine Epistles* (New York: Crossroad, 1994), 143–145.

[134]Raymond Brown. *The Gospel According to John (I–XII)* (AB 29; New York: Doubleday, 1964), 308.

one regards "not" or "not yet" as "original." The emphasis of the verse is on Jesus not (or not yet) going up to *this* particular feast.[135]

This survey of the various opinions held by different commentators demonstrates a wide range of opinions and suggestions in attempting to resolve this vexing text-critical question, but in many respects they may be reduced to two basic arguments—one concerned with external evidence, and the other with internal probabilities. For the reasons noted above, the case can hardly be decided on the sole basis of external evidence. Since for many the question hinges on intrinsic probabilities, let us pursue this line of thought. In particular, let us examine how οὔπω is generally employed by the writer of the Fourth Gospel.[136]

Apart from the *v. l.* under dispute, οὔπω is employed in the Fourth Gospel ten times.[137] Of those instances, a full half of them are associated with prophetic allusion to the hour/time of Jesus, and two others are related to things that occur when his hour does come (the giving of the Spirit and his ascension). Moreover, three of the four times the evangelist places the term on the lips of Jesus it is in the declaration, "My hour/time has *not yet* come." Thus, the majority of the occurrences of οὔπω in the Fourth Gospel refer to the hour of Jesus.

In terms of informing intrinsic probabilities, these data seem compelling. The writer-editor of the Fourth Gospel appears to have been very deliberate in his use of the term, οὔπω, incorporating it into his pronouncements about the hour of Jesus almost as a formula. This much seems evident: the author of the Fourth Gospel

---

[135]R. Schnackenburg, *John*, 141.

[136]Attempting to locate characteristics of the "author" of the Fourth Gospel is akin to chasing a phantom. Scholars have long noted that the Gospel is the product of a community and a document that has evolved over time and experienced redaction. To speak, then, of an "author" of the Fourth Gospel can appear either misleading or naive. I do not wish to be either, though to do justice to these questions lies beyond the focus and scope of this present work. For discussion of these issues see, for example, D. M. Smith, *The Composition and Order of the Fourth Gospel*. New Haven: Yale University Press, 1965, esp. 1–56 and 116–249, and Alan Culpepper, *Anatomy of the Fourth Gospel*, 3–11. For the purposes of this project, in speaking here of the "author" I am thinking mainly of the entity (described in Smith as the ecclesiastical redactor) responsible for "editing" John into the form that came to be published and transcribed.

[137]They are as follows: 2:4, 3:24, 7:6, 7:8 (twice here; only the first instance is currently under dispute), 7:30, 7:39, 8:20, 8:57, 11:30, 20:17. Four times it is placed directly on the lips of Jesus. In three of those four instances he makes direct reference to his hour having *not yet* come (2:4, 7:6, 7:8 [second occurrence in the verse]), and in the fourth instance (20.17) he tells Mary he has *not yet* ascended to his Father, a statement also related to his divine timetable. Two other times the term is used by the narrator to refer to the hour/time of Jesus (7:30, 8:20) and in yet another instance, again assigned to the voice of the narrator, it reports that the Holy Spirit has *not yet* been given (7:39), once again a use related to the divine timetable. The other applications of this term are as follows: the report that John had *not yet* been cast into prison (3:24); someone murmuring that Jesus was *not yet* fifty years old (8:57); and the narrative detail that Jesus had *not yet* come into the village (11:30).

consistently used οὔπω whenever he wished to signal that the arrival of the καιρός was still pending; and, when the writer placed it on the lips of Jesus, the term is used exclusively in the sense of a prophetic formula.

Unless, of course, the occurrence in John 7:8 (first occurrence) is taken to be "original." If this is so, ἐγὼ οὔπω [rather than οὐκ] ἀναβαίνω εἰς τὴν ἑορτὴν ταύτην ὅτι ἐμὸς καιρός οὔπω πεπλήρωται stands as the singular exception to John's otherwise careful and reserved use of this term. Presumably, one could argue that it is the entire sentence that constitutes the prophetic formula, so that the Johannine pattern actually consists of a doublet form of οὔπω. No such doublet appears, however, in John 2:4 or John 20:17, to cite just two examples. John's pattern is that the prophetic formula punctuates the second half of a sentence; nowhere else does οὔπω invade the prefacing remarks of Jesus.

So the question remains. Is this the only instance in John's narrative where he violates an otherwise carefully prescribed and consistent use of the term οὔπω? Is this the conclusion that is best drawn from the data that has been presented? Or is it more likely that οὔπω is not "original" in the first instance of 7:8, and that its entry into this verse is the result of a scribe's perspicacity rather than the author's lassitude? In my judgment, the latter appears more likely. It is commonly acknowledged among scholars that the writer of the Fourth Gospel narrates his version of the Jesus story according to a chronology distinct from that of the Synoptics, often with a theological purpose in mind. Multiple meanings are also standard literary devices employed by the evangelist. Such observations indicate that the writer-redactor of the Fourth Gospel is a narrative artist of no mean skill. With finesse and attention to detail, particularly chronological detail, he imposes nuance, irony, and interpretive substance upon his story. The data compiled for this discussion show the care with which the writer has crafted the prophetic pronouncements about his hour/time that he attributes to Jesus. There is no obvious reason to suggest that his literary skills suddenly and mysteriously lapsed in 7:8.

On the other hand, ample reason to motivate an informed scribe to effect this particular change in the text did exist in the form of a pagan intellectual who drew attention to this verse to the detriment of the Jesus movement. Among the extant fragments of his work that are most clearly attributable to Porphyry is one that called attention to this very verse, and called into question the Jesus described there. Here Porphyry noted that Jesus first denied that he would visit Jerusalem, but then proceeded to arrive there (John 7:8–10).[138] His words have survived in Jerome's *Adv. Pelag.* (II.17), and read as follows:

---

[138] A. Meredith, "Porphyry and Julian," 1134. Meredith explains that of the twenty-five fragments (nos. 48–72) collected by Harnack few can be attributed with certainty to Porphyry, but are derived in actuality from the writings of Macarius Magnes. Thus, he explains, much of the New Testament criticism attributed to Porphyry by P. Labriolle should not be considered. The fragment regarding John 7:8–10 is a notable exception.

Jesus iturum se negavit, et fecit quod prius negaverat. Latrat Porphyrius; inconstantiae ac mutationis accusat, nescius omnia scandala ad carnem esse referenda.[139]

Judging from these remarks, it is easily ascertained that Porphyry's text read οὐκ in verse 8. Moreover, he perceived between verses 8 and 10 either a breech of etiquette or an act of erratic vacillation (*inconstantiae ac mutationis*). In either case, Jesus' behavior as recorded in this rendering of John's narrative hardly reflected that of a holy figure boldly and decisively executing a foreordained, divine plan. This passage, then, is a text that was specifically enlisted by a pagan critic to denounce either the wavering disposition of Jesus or the historical infelicities of the gospel accounts. In any event, Porphyry adduced this text to the detriment of Christians.

The simple change of οὐκ (not) to οὔπω (not yet), however, effectively quelled any impression of inconsistent action on the part of Jesus as seen in the comparison of verses 8 and 10. No longer, then, did the text present Jesus one moment asserting his decision *not* to journey to Jerusalem, only to change his mind and go there; rather, through the technology of scribal revision, John's narrative stated without equivocation that Jesus would *not yet* go up to Jerusalem along with his disciples, suggesting that he would, as he did, find his way there later. That move would have rendered impotent efforts on the part of pagan critics like Porphyry to adduce this text for antagonistic purposes.

Certain logical inconsistencies were similarly assuaged. In response to Celsus' Origen himself voiced text-critical concern with the reading of Luke 23:45, in which it is reported that when Jesus was crucified the sun became "eclipsed" (ἐκλιπόντος).[140] He recognized both the lack of historical record for this happening and the astronomical impossibility of such an event, since Passovers occur at full moon and solar eclipses occur only at new moon. To connect the Passover death of Jesus with a solar eclipse, then, fomented doubt. By way of defense, Origen insisted that secret enemies of the church had introduced the notion of an eclipse into the text to make it vulnerable to a show of reason.[141] In other words, Origen himself offered a text-critical explanation as an apologetic response to Celsus.

To whatever extent that defense proved effective, however, external evidence weighs in favor of modification moving in the opposite direction. Where P[75*] ℵ C[*vid] L 070 579 2542 sy[hmg] testify to the primary reading (with P[75c] and B reporting the variant spelling ἐκλειπόντος), A C[3] (D) W Θ Ψ *f*[1.13] Maj lat sy along with Marcion bear witness to the secondary reading in which the neutral verb "grew dark"

---

[139]"Jesus said he would not go up, and he did what he had previously denied. Porphyry rants and accuses him of inconstancy and fickleness, not knowing that all scandals must be imputed to the flesh."

[140]*Cels.* II.33.

[141]For several insightful discussions of this text and Origen's treatment of it see P. Labriolle, *La Réaction païenne*, 205–207; E. L. Titus, *The Motivation of Changes Made in the New Testament Text by Justin Martyr and Clement of Alexandria: A Study in the Origins of New Testament Variation*; and F. J. A. Hort, *Introduction*, II, 70.

(ἐσκοτίσθη) was substituted for its problematic synonym. Still other scribes, as seen in 33 and vg[ms], omitted the troublesome phrase altogether. So, although Origen appears to have been incorrect as to which reading was "original," it appears that his argument caught the attention of some scribes who subsequently customized their exemplars to complement his case.

It should be noted that the chronological and geographical spread of witnesses provides us with a rare opportunity to venture a fairly precise provenance for this reading. P[75], generally regarded to have been produced between 175–225 C.E., constitutes the earliest known copy of Luke's Gospel.[142] It transmits the apologetically troublesome reading, and serves as the only witness on either side of the textual question that can with certainty be dated prior to Origen's *Contra Celsum*. Also, of those later witnesses that modify the reference to an eclipse, i.e., that bear witness to an intentional alteration modification, some of the strongest among them (Θ *f*[.13]) represent the so-called "Caesarean" text-type, the sort of text widely associated with Origen's move from Alexandria to Caesarea. Notice, too, that the modification follows precisely the contours of Origen's own text-critical arguments. Where he insisted that his preferred reading was "original," and that enemies had maliciously and with forethought inserted "eclipsed," the scribes attested here appear to have followed Origen's lead in replacing ἐκλιπόντος with ἐσκοτίσθη. Therefore, not only do apologetic interests seem to lie at the foundation of this textual alteration, but Origen himself appears to rest at the heart of the matter. The evidence presented here invites the conclusion that this variant reading found its way into the textual tradition after 175 C.E. (the earliest date for P[75]), and very likely in near approximation and close association with the publication of *Contra Celsum* (ca. 244–249 C.E.).

Several other variants betray the measure of discomfort some scribes felt when they came upon similarly problematic or disparate details in the separate gospel traditions. Routinely, though not systematically, some copyists assimilated or conflated the details of one Gospel to another in order to ameliorate problems of factual inconsistency or error. Pursuant to the question of whether Jesus was crucified beginning at the sixth hour, as John reports, or the third hour, as per Mark's account, certain punctilious scribes eliminated the conflict by merely imposing agreement of one gospel with the other. Editors of Codices Sinaiticus and Bezae, among others, acted to assimilate the chronology of John 19:14 with that of Mark 15:25, while Codex Koridethi (Θ) and some of the Syriac tradition worked in reverse and revised Mark 15:25 to agree with John 19:14.

Another factual error appears in Mark 2:26 where Jesus is said to have recounted David's act of commandeering the bread of presence as occurring during the high priesthood of Abiathar, despite the fact that 1 Sam 21:1–7 clearly states that Ahimelech was high priest when this happened. The scribal tradition shows an awareness of and an apparent concern for this factual error. Craig Evans, assuming Marcan priority, adduces Matthew and Luke as the first Christian interpreters who worked to resolve

---

[142]B. M. Metzger, *Text of the New Testament*, 41.

this problem. In their parallel accounts, Matt 12:4 and Lk 6:4, both evangelists manage the error by simply removing the troublesome phrase altogether.[143] Conforming to the precedent established by the synoptic redactors of Mark, Codex Bezae, the Freer manuscript, 1009, 1546ʹ, and several of the Old Latin and Syriac versional witnesses similarly omit the temporal phrase ἐπὶ Ἀβιαθὰρ ἀρχιερέως, and with it the problem. Others, as Metzger explains, place an article into the verse in such a way that allows one to understand that the event occurred in the time of Abiathar, but not necessarily while he was high priest.[144] Evans recalls that a few witnesses (Δ f goth) read "priest" (ἱερέως) instead of "high priest" (ἀρχιερέως), thereby bringing the Marcan text into factual agreement with the Samuel narrative, since Abiathar, though having not yet succeeded his father as "high priest" was already a "priest." He further reports that Chrysostom (c. 347–407) would later deal with this inconsistency by suggesting that the confusion of Ahimelech with Abiathar arose from the latter having two names, while Jerome (c. 342–420) would dismiss all such minor infelicities with the pronouncement that apostles and evangelists frequently paraphrased scripture, concerned with its meaning rather than its words.[145]

Two other instances of buttressing the text by way of correction or precision may be seen in the textual tradition of Luke's Gospel. Codex Bezae at Luke 3:1 substitutes "procurator" (ἐπιτροπεύοντος) for "governor" (ἡγεμονεύοντος), thereby substituting the term that was in vogue during the second century,[146] precisely the time when many textual scholars believe the D-text was composed. This is an instance in which accuracy appears to have given way to vernacular currency.

Since the verse begins with καί, as do several others around it, the omission of Luke 21:18 by syᶜ and Mcionᴱ can conceivably be attributed to homoeoarcton. It is also possible to reason, however, especially in the case of the Curetonian Syriac, that a meticulous scribe could not reconcile the promise that "not one hair of your head shall perish" with the historical reality of martyrdom, and therefore deliberately omitted the verse.

CONCLUSION

Examples of textual harmonization and assimilation dominate the scribal tradition. An exhaustive catalogue and analysis of each such variant is beyond the scope and

---

[143]Craig A. Evans, "Patristic Interpretation of Mark 2:26 'When Abiathar Was High Priest'," *VC* 40 (1986), 183–86. This article is a concise but highly informative treatment of this variant reading.

[144]B. M. Metzger, *Textual Commentary*, 79.

[145]C. Evans, 184–85.

[146]According to Raymond Brown, the term used for Pilate by Tacitus in his Annals (15.44), *procurator* (approximate Greek equivalent, ἐπίτροπος), was in vogue during the second century. Josephus also referred to Pilate as an ἐπίτροπος. Brown argues that both Josephus and Tacitus are using popular designations rather than technical terms. For his full discussion see R. Brown, *The Death of the Messiah*, I (New York: Doubleday, 1994), 336–338.

100 APOLOGETIC DISCOURSE AND THE SCRIBAL TRADITION

purpose of this volume. Nor is it necessary. There is no dispute among scholars that the manual transmitters of the text of the canonical gospels imposed consensus on their disparate voices through the medium of harmonization. It has not been the purpose of this section to belabor the obvious.

What has not been broached in scholarly discussions with due frequency, though, has been a deliberate and focused effort to establish or characterize precisely what sorts of impetuses lay behind this scribal impulse. It *has* been, therefore, the purpose of this chapter to demonstrate that such apparently simple editorial "corrections" may reflect, at least in part, the motivation of apologetic interests. The subtle actions of substituting or inserting the correct antecedent of a prophetic oracle or emphasizing the preexistence of Jesus by deleting a prepositional phrase aided the apologetic stratagem of alleging for Christianity a primeval origin. Moreover, assimilating one gospel to another by incorporating phrases or verses and harmonizing inconsistencies through the omission or alteration of details smoothed the way for apologetic arguments by removing potential stumbling blocks from Christian sacred writings in the process of copying them. In many cases these changes were brought to bear on the very texts that pagan despisers initially cited in their polemic assaults against Christians. It is not my contention that this was necessarily a systematic or even extensive effort. The evidence appears too random and geographically scattered to support such a thesis. What does appear quite reasonable, though, is to count among the conscious and unconscious forces that motivated scribes to correct and harmonize their exemplars a sensitivity to and concern for apologetic interests.

3

JESUS:
ACCORDING TO THE SCRIBES

Perceived through the eyes of a typical pagan, the Jesus portrayed in the canonical Gospels deserved his fate. Pagans had recognized early on in their disputes with devotees of the Jesus movement that the surest way to castigate Christianity was to discredit its founder. Indeed, there could have hardly been a more compelling testimony against Christianity than dissemination of the pagan portrayal of Jesus. The stories repeated about him and the words placed on his lips represented him as the misbegotten son of a harlot who grew up to become a political revolutionary, a wonder-working magician, an apostate from a respected ancient religion who founded a novel superstition, and a social miscreant who spread dissension and false hopes wherever he went.

A variety of sources record this hostility expressed toward Jesus. "Dishonorable and inglorious" was the assessment Justin projected onto his representative Jewish antagonist, Trypho.[1] Caecilius, the constructed voice of opposition in the *Octavius* of Minucius Felix, objected to Christians for venerating an executed criminal and his cross.[2] Lucian, the famed satirist of the second century, described Jesus as a "crucified sophist" who was executed for spawning a new religious movement that adjured denial of the Greek gods.[3]

Among the extant writings of pagan critics of Christianity, however, distinction for the first sustained literary assault upon the character of Jesus belongs to Celsus.[4] Indeed, much of his polemic that Origen recalled in *Contra Celsum* was directed

---

[1]*Dial.* XXXIII.

[2]*Oct.* IX.3–4.

[3]Lionel Casson, editor and translator. *Selected Satires of Lucian.* (New York: W. W. Norton, 1962), 369.

[4]The volume of literature on the polemic of Celsus in *True Doctrine* and the reply of Origen in *Contra Celsum* is immense. The classic introduction is located in Carl Andresen, *Logos und Nomos: Die Polemik des Kelsos wider das Christentum.* (Berlin: Walter de Gruyter, 1955). Other essential volumes are Henry Chadwick, *Origen: Contra Celsum* (Cambridge: Cambridge University Press, 1953); Pierre de Labriolle, *La Réaction païenne: Étude sur la polémique antichrétienne du Iᵉʳ au VIᵉ Siècle* (Paris: L'Artisan du Livre, 1948), esp. 111–169; and Eugene Gallagher, *Divine Man or Magician? Celsus and Origen on Jesus* (Chico, CA: Scholars Press, 1982). For an overview of the life and work of Origen see Henri Crouzel, *Origen* (Translated by A. S. Worrall; San Francisco: Harper & Row, 1989) and Joseph W. Trigg, *Origen* (London/New York: Routledge, 1998).

specifically at the Nazarene himself. Discharging salvoes of *ad hominem* arguments with the fury of an artillery barrage, Celsus challenged the integrity of Jesus' birth (I.28), accused him of beguiling followers through sorcery and command of demons (I.6, 68), and castigated him as an itinerant beggar (I.61) who collected round him ruffians of the most sordid dispositions (I.62). Celsus further contended that Jesus was full of conceit (I.28), an arrogant liar (II.7), profane and self-aggrandizing (II.7), the head of a movement founded upon vulgarity and illiteracy (I.27), and a common carouser who by example led astray his compatriots into impiety and wickedness (II.20). Jesus was further portrayed as the "author of sedition" (VIII.14) and a wicked man possessed by a demon (I.68). In his survey of the crucifixion, Celsus framed Jesus as one who was arrested disgracefully and crucified as a criminal (II.31), who from the cross greedily slurped a disgusting potion (II.37), and whose failure to laugh at his fate distanced him from persons of genuine heroic virtue and disclosed his lack of character (II.33). In the final analysis, the carpenter from Nazareth was merely a wicked sorcerer despised by God (I.71). Christians worshiped a man who was wretched (VII.36).

Some seventy years after the publication of *True Doctrine* Ambrose petitioned his champion, Origen, to author a response to the reproach of Celsus, the work we now know as *Contra Celsum*. Over the years, some scholars have educed from this observation the belief that *True Doctrine* had a long run of success as a major polemical work against Christianity and proved a thorn in the flesh to the new movement. If, for example, Joseph Trigg is correct that a renewed interest in *True Doctrine* "presaged a new hostility toward Christianity in Roman ruling circles," it would explain both the urgency of Ambrose's petition and the acerbic tone of Origen's rhetoric.[5]

More recently, however, researchers have seriously questioned this view. A recent article by Michael Frede serves to illustrate this avenue of thought.[6] He doubts the lingering impact of *True Doctrine*, as well as whether it ever enjoyed wide circulation or represented a well-known challenge to Christianity. He points out that Origen had apparently never even heard of Celsus before being approached by Ambrose, and almost certainly did not possess a copy of his work until his patron presented it to him. Moreover, he contends that *True Doctrine* most certainly would have been a dated and inadequate work by the time Origen was commissioned to answer it. For Frede, instead, the fact that an apology of this sort could be commissioned by a Christian serves as a central clue to uncovering the mystery of the intended audience of *Contra Celsum*. He maintains that Christian apologetic was generally written for Christians, just as pagan criticism was penned by pagans for other pagans. Frede, therefore, incisively characterizes *Contra Celsum* as "responses not given in court to accusations not raised in court."[7]

---

[5] J. Trigg, *Origen*, 61.
[6] Michael Frede, "Origen's Treatise *Against Celsus*," in M. Edwards, M. Goodman, and S. Price, eds. *Apologetics in the Roman Empire: Pagans, Jews, and Christians* (Oxford: Oxford University Press, 1999), 131–55.
[7] M. Frede, "Origen's Treatise," 137.

Perhaps it is enough for our purposes to say this: what appears evident is that something about work penned by Celsus—either its content or rhetorical persuasiveness—fomented for Ambrose the need or desire for a level of response that was beyond his own talents to produce. Frede reasons that Ambrose's petition may have been born out of his concern that Christians might want to know how to answer the objections to Christianity found in Celsus, and therefore concludes that *Contra Celsum* was directed to Christians weak in faith.[8] In this regard, also, it is natural to wonder if it was Ambrose himself who was found stymied by Celsus' arguments. At any rate, that he required the genius of Origen on this matter intimates that *True Doctrine*, dated and inadequate as it may have been, continued to have an impact of some consequence those many decades later, even if that impact was only on Ambrose or sibling believers who were found fragile in their faith.

As part of his apologetic refutation of *True Doctrine*, Origen naturally sought to redeem Jesus from the character assassination portrayed there.[9] In place of the wicked, base, vain villain represented by Celsus, Origen described Jesus as a person of humble and heroic character (I.29–31). Jesus did not lead astray, but "cured, converted, and improved the souls of many" (I.9). Origen contrasted him with the gods and heroes who, as depicted by the Greek poets, indulged their wanton appetites in cavalier fashion (I.17), and left no lasting positive influence on humankind (I.67). Jesus was not the author of sedition, but the author of all peace (VIII.14) and the heir of a divine kingdom (I.60). The execution of Jesus was not the inevitable consequence of criminal behavior, but occurred to fulfill prophecy (II.37) and for the advantage of others (II.68–69). His death did indeed reflect his heroic nature, for there is no record of him at his condemnation lamenting or uttering anything ignoble (II.34). The exemplary character of Jesus, Origen maintained, could be demonstrated in how his name continued to remove effectively mental distractions, drive out demons, and implant "a wonderful meekness and tranquility of character, and a love to mankind and a gentleness" in those who have accepted the gospel (I.67).

Origen thus serves to illustrate with what urgency and vigor apologists labored to offer a portrait of Jesus contrary to that which was painted by most pagan critics.[10] Peering across the apologetic corpus, one cannot fail to notice how much energy these writers expended seeking to defend their founder and Lord. Often framed in the

---

[8]M. Frede, "Origen's Treatise,"154–55.

[9]Reference is made here to the divisions and phrases that appear in Henry Chadwick's annotated translation of *Origen: Contra Celsum* (Cambridge: Cambridge University Press, 1953).

[10]Porphyry became in his later years a notable exception. By the time he wrote *Philosophy from Oracles*, some twenty years after *Against the Christians*, he came to praise the noble character of Jesus and even compared him with other divine men. Porphyry's ire against the Christians was redirected at his followers, especially Peter and Paul, who he believed radically altered the teachings of Jesus and spawned a movement of their own making built on a foundation of deceit. See P. Labriolle, *La Réaction païenne*, 251–81; A. Meredith, "Porphyry and Julian Against the Christians," *ANRW* II.23.2, 1119–49; and W. H. C. Frend, "Prelude to the Great Persecution," *JEH* 38/1 (1987), 1–18, esp. 10–12, 15.

reactionary rhetoric of *via negativa*, his proponents maintained that Jesus was neither a common laborer nor a criminal malefactor. He was not a bastard, they insisted, but the Son of God born of a virgin. He was neither a charlatan nor a sorcerer; clearly the generous and good nature of his acts of power demonstrated their divine provenance. To the charge of treason, they countered that Jesus was not a revolutionary nor did his followers pose a threat to the empire; rather, in fact, the effectiveness of the persistent prayers offered by believers on behalf of Rome and the emperor were in no small measure responsible for their welfare and prosperity. Christian writers explained the ridicule and shame of the cross in light of prophetic anticipation.[11] Moreover, in the words of Justin, Christians gathered for the purpose of fostering piety toward the end of being found "good citizens" and keepers of the commandments.[12] By distinguishing Jesus from such stock components of rhetorically imposed ignominy, then, Christian apologists sought to deliver Jesus from the disenfranchised margins of society and establish him within the mainstream of Roman society as a man of peace. Their efforts were designed to make Jesus appear respectable, moral, and loyal to the welfare of the state.

This was not always an easy case to make. After all, the New Testament supplied opponents plenty of pellets for their potshots. In some cases no manipulation of the tradition was required to compile evidence for the prosecution; unexaggerated features of the gospels reported Jesus as the subject of numerous statements befitting an insurrectionist. In several of these instances, however, it is noteworthy that within the transmissional history of the text there appears among some scribes a discernible concern or tendency to ameliorate the bellicose character of these actions or pronouncements. Many of the features that fueled these dueling portraits of Jesus can be seen in what follows to have gained the attention of certain copyists and to have been subjected to the strokes of scribal activity. In short, one can trace in the variant tradition an effort on the part of scribes to depict a Christ less vulnerable to stock criticism and more palatable to the pagan populace.

VARIANT READINGS

Guardianship of this apologetic thrust and parry was taken up frequently by transmitters of the textual tradition of the New Testament. Finding their way into various copies of the scriptures were numerous variant readings that appear to reflect this paradigmatic concern with the person and character of Jesus. Modifications of the text occur that mirror the precise issues specifically raised in and tangentially related

---

[11] As is so succinctly stated in the words of André Thayse: "Les théologiens chrétiens ont pensé que le serviteur souffrant représentait prophétiquement le Christ. La réflexion du prophète Isaïe sur la souffranace du juste est universelle. Elle inclut donc bien la souffrance du Christ mais elle ne s'y réduit pas." Idem, *Matthieu: L'Évangile Revisité* (Brussells: Éditions Racine, 1998), 228.

[12] *Ap.* I.65.

to these disputations. Readings produced by scribes may be observed that ameliorate perceptions of a Jesus who was angry or beside himself, who engaged in pedestrian labor or the magical arts, whose legitimacy was questioned, and who was executed as a radical revolutionary and criminal malefactor. It will be argued via the compilation and analysis of the textual variants reported in the following pages that scribes consciously modified texts related to the person and character of Jesus in a way that mirrors apologetic efforts to defend Jesus against antagonistic character assassination, on the one hand, and, on the other, to foster the cause of making him more tenable to a pagan audience. For the sake of order, the variants in this unit will be classified under the following headings, all of which represent pagan accusations directed toward Jesus: The Folly of the Cross, The Author of This Sedition, A Carpenter by Trade, A Magician and Deceiver of the People, and A Man of Profane Temperament.

THE FOLLY OF THE CROSS

Long before the earliest apologists began to craft defenses of the faith, Paul wrote the Corinthians, "We preach Christ crucified, a stumbling block to the Jews and folly to the Gentiles..." (1 Cor 1:23). More than a century later, Christian apologists grappled even more fiercely with their opponents over the offensive character of the untimely, unseemly death of its founder. Jesus' execution under Roman authority by means of crucifixion, the torturous death reserved for only the most despicable of plaintiffs, appeared to outsiders as proof of the treasonous and seditious character of this new religion, and pagan critics seized on the scandal of the cross to denigrate the movement. Lucian denigrated Christians for worshiping "the man who was crucified in Palestine."[13] For Caecilius, Christianity consisted of the adoration of an executed criminal and his cross.[14] Keenly recognizing a rhetorical obligation to do so, Justin provided in his *First Apology* a rationale for believing a crucified man to be the unbegotten God (1.53), and, in *Dialogue with Trypho*, framed a response to the typical Jewish expression of offense at the cross (59).[15] Moreover, Justin argued that the symbolic importance of the cross could be seen in the fact that it permeated creation, from the mast of a ship to the human frame and even to the Roman standards.[16] Paul had been right. The cross was a folly and a stumbling block, a scandal, one that had to be faced and dealt with—somehow.

In the previous chapter we noted the primary role prophecy played in the apologetic tradition. By describing their religious movement as the current fulfillment

---

[13]Lucian, *Peregrinus*, 11.

[14]*Oct.* 8.

[15]Here Trypho gives voice to what was clearly one of the most frequently adduced citations underlying Jewish offense at the cross, namely reference to Deuteronomy 21:23, "he who hangs on a tree is accursed." Justin responds by arguing that prophetic predictions regarding the sufferings of Jesus take precedence and thus override the "curse" associated with crucifixion.

[16]*Ap.* I.55, 60.

of ancient prophecy, apologists claimed for their nascent movement the instant credibility associated with antiquity. Attention to the subject of this chapter points us to another reason apologists appealed to prophecy, namely, to redeem the character of Jesus. Since their founder was viewed by outsiders as an executed troublemaker, and since their celebration of the cross was central to their faith, Christians were obligated to explain the cross and the execution of Jesus in a way that abated criticism. Their stratagem for doing so, in large measure, was to pronounce the heinous and dishonorable death of Jesus as a fulfillment of prophetic oracles. Featuring prominently, therefore, in the writings of the apologists were Old Testament citations such as Psalm 22 and the Suffering Servant songs of Isaiah. Defenders of the faith interpreted such texts as anticipating the particular events that surrounded the Nazarene's crucifixion. The fate that befell Jesus, then, did not consist of Romans meting out due justice, but of the erroneous execution—or, for some like Melito of Sardis, the manipulated murder—of a holy innocent. In short, the crucifixion constituted a travesty of justice. His death, however, though it was portrayed as the product of false charges, deceit, and evil, did not come as a surprise. Indeed, part of what legitimized the suffering death of Jesus was the belief that it was anticipated by ancient and divinely inspired seers.

This defensive strategy may also be discerned in the textual tradition. A case in point is located in Matthew 27:35, the central verse in Matthew's passion narrative that reports the actual crucifixion of Jesus. The undisputed text reads, Σταυρώσαντες δὲ αὐτὸν διεμερίσαντο τὰ ἱμάτια αὐτοῦ βάλλοντες κλῆρον, "And having crucified him, they divided his garments by casting lots." The vast number and most highly regarded of textual witnesses end the verse there. Some manuscripts (the predominantly "Western" and Caesarean witnesses Δ Θ 0250 $f^{.13}$ 1424 it vg^{cl} sy^h Eus), though, associate this moment of the crucifixion with the Psalmist (22:8) by adding these words, ἵνα πληρωθῇ τὸ ῥηθὲν ὑπὸ τοῦ προφήτου· Διεμερίσαντο τὰ ἱμάτιά μου ἑαυτοῖς καὶ ἐπὶ τὸν ἱματισμόν μου ἔβαλον κλῆρον, "in order that which was spoken by the prophet might be fulfilled, 'They divided my garments among themselves and for my clothing they cast lots.'"

With a high degree of certainty the UBSGNT Committee determined the longer text to be secondary. Although, as Metzger points out, the passage could have fallen out as a result of homoeoteuleton (κλῆρον...κλῆρον), due to the impressive array of external witnesses (among them ℵ A B D L W Γ Π 33 71 157 565 700 892 ff² l vg^{mss} the Ethiopic and most of the Syriac mss) and the likelihood of scribal assimilation to John 19:24 the committee felt their judgment merited an {A} rating.

Still, we are left with a deeper question, albeit one that poses no interest for most commentators: Why did scribes choose to interject Johannine material at this point? The prospect of apologetic motivation offers a plausible explanation for this. We have already discussed how pagan writers adduced the crucifixion as evidence that Jesus deserved to die. Where Jewish antagonists quoted "Cursed is everyone who hangs on a tree" (Deut 21:23), it was widely known that Romans reserved crucifixion for only the most heinous of crimes. Both Jews and Romans, then, viewed this form of death as merited by the one who suffered it.

One of the most frequent means of response crafted by Christian apologists was to identify passages from the Hebrew scriptures that appeared to coincide with events from Jesus' life (and death) story, and use them to argue that these writings demonstrated a divinely inspired anticipation of Jesus and all that occurred during his life. Jesus, as apologists interpreted events, was not the recipient of Roman justice; he was a holy innocent whose very existence was foretold and whose symbolic death was presaged. This point can be seen most clearly in Justin Martyr. Justin, in fact, recited these very verses from and then the whole of Psalm 22 in his *Dialogue with Trypho* in order to orient his disputant to a Christian understanding of the fate of Jesus and the desire of his disciples to follow after him. The Martyr wrote:

> The words of the Law, 'Cursed is everyone who hangeth on a tree,' strengthen our hope which is sustained by the Crucified Christ, not because God predicted what would be done by all of you Jews, and others like you, who are not aware that was He who was before all things....Now, you can clearly see that this has actually happened. For in your synagogues you curse all those who through Him have become Christians, and the Gentiles put into effect your curse by killing all those who merely admit that they are Christians....[17]

Justin then continued with a series of "proof-texts" from the Hebrew Bible to support his claims. He referenced Moses, Isaiah, and David as witnesses for his case, at which point he stated:

> And again, David, in his twenty-first Psalm, refers to His passion on the cross in mystical parable: 'They have pierced my bones and feet. They have numbered all My bones. And they have looked and stared upon Me. They parted my garments amongst them, and upon my vesture they cast lots.' For when they nailed Him to the cross they did indeed pierce His hands and feet, and they who crucified Him divided His garments among themselves, each casting lots for the garment he chose. You are indeed blind when you deny that the above-quoted Psalm was spoken of Christ, for you fail to see that no one among your people who was ever called King ever had his hands and feet pierced while alive, and died by this mystery (that is, of the cross), except this Jesus only.[18]

These lines demonstrate both the general strategy Justin employed in crafting his defense as well as the specific attention he gave this verse (Ps 22:18–19). The variant

---

[17]Justin, *Dial.* 96 (selections). The translation is from Thomas B. Falls, *Saint Justin Martyr* (FC 6; Washington, DC: Catholic University of America Press), 299.

[18]Justin, *Dial.* 97. Again, the translation belongs to T. Falls, *Saint Justin Martyr*, 300–301. Justin quotes Psalm 22 in its entirety in *Dial.* 98. Justin's identification of Psalm 22 as Psalm 21 is due to the dissonance of numbering that occurs, beginning with Psalm 10, between the Hebrew Bible and the text of the Septuagint. See the edition of the Septuagint by L. C. L. Breton, *The Septuagint with Apocrypha* (Peabody, MA: Hendrickson, 1992 [originally published in 1851]), 703, n. β. and 709.

reading under consideration mirrors precisely this apologetic stratagem and the use of this verse. Of course, it can be stated that the evangelists themselves crafted their narratives with attention to the prophetic character of Hebrew writings, and that the scribes might have merely been imitating them.[19] Thus they inserted John 19:24 into the Matthean narrative they were transcribing. Still, in this instance we have a case in which the coincidence with Justin's line of thought is virtually exact. Moreover, this is arguably the most shameful moment in the narrative. As Davies and Allison point out, the fact that his executioners, as was customary, are gambling over his garments means that he is no longer wearing them; Jesus has been stripped naked.[20] Therefore, it would make sense that, of all the moments an apologetically-sensitive scribe might wish to underscore the prophetic anticipation of the events being narrated, he would choose the most embarrassing. There is reason to suspect that the scribes who interpolated the words of Psalm 22:18–19/John 19:24 into the text of Matthew 27:35 did so under the influence of apologetic interests. It is even conceivable that they were familiar with this very argument from Justin himself.

The following pair of variant readings also appear to be derived from a concern commonly associated with apologetic writers. These modifications lead to the effect of mollifying the perception of Jesus as a criminal revolutionary. The diametrically opposite pattern of alteration, however, supports the contention that scribes more likely acted spontaneously and pragmatically rather than with an overarching strategy or anticipated pattern of modification.[21]

In its "original" phrasing, Luke 23:32 resounded as a potentially devastating text for the reputation of Jesus and his followers. Scholars generally agree that, in this instance, certain Alexandrian witnesses (P[75], ℵ, B) harbor the "original" rendering of the verse: "Ἤγοντο δὲ καὶ ἕτεροι κακοῦργοι δύο σὺν αὐτῷ ἀναιρθῆναι, "And with him they also led away *two other evildoers* to be crucified (my italics)." So written, the verse implied that Jesus was one of three evildoers (κακοῦργοι) summarily executed on the occasion. At first glance, it may seem difficult to imagine that the evangelist could have missed the derisive insinuation of what he wrote. Fred Craddock is probably correct, though, in his suggestion that the writer of Luke penned these words

[19]For example, Warren Carter in his commentary offers a chart that outlines the parallels between this section of Matthew and Psalm 22. Clearly, the evangelist has drawn on his knowledge of the psalm in crafting his story. See idem, *Matthew: Storyteller, Interpreter, Evangelist* (Peabody, MA: Hendrickson, 1996), 213.

[20]W. D. Davies and D. Allison, *Matthew III*, 614.

[21]For a thoroughgoing study on the identity and practices of ancient scribes see Kim Haines-Eitzen, *Guardian of Letters*.

with Isaiah 53:12²²² in mind.²³ The Gospel writers did craft their narratives with attention to the prophetic tradition, especially the late Isaian writings. It requires no stretch of reason to imagine the author subtly but carefully intending to reckon Jesus among the transgressors and thus fulfill the oracle.

Prophecy and politics are, however, seldom compatible bedfellows. Where to one schooled in the poetry of the Hebrew prophets, reckoning Jesus among transgressors sounded sublime, to one grounded in vernacular of pagan politics it sounded subversive. As noted earlier, among the most serious and dangerous charges directed at Jesus and early Christians were those that described them as workers of iniquity, immorality, crime, and treason.

Some later scribes appear to have determined that the practical cost of this prophetic fulfillment was more than the cause could bear. As a result of their efforts, two forms of major variation found their way into the text, both of which effectively subordinate the term κακοῦργοι. Most Greek manuscripts record a simple modification in the sequence of critical terms, so that the text reads ...ἕτεροι δύο κακοῦργοι... ("And with him they led away others, two evildoers, to be crucified.").²⁴ Commentators widely agree that this variance in word order issues directly from an apologetic impulse to nullify the implied identification of Jesus as an evildoer.²⁵ The other form of variation detected in the manuscripts resides in two Old Latin manuscripts (*c* and *e*), Sinaitic Syriac and the Sahidic version; they resolve the issue by simply eliminating the word ἕτεροι.²⁶ In effect, this elimination transformed a potentially controversial text into the bland report that, along with Jesus, two criminals were also led away to be crucified. Here then, it appears, assimilation to the prophetic tradition proved too costly to bear, and so Luke's fulfillment motif of being counted among the transgressors was sacrificed in order to do away with the implication of treason.

On the other hand, consider Mark 15:28. The text reads, καὶ ἐπληρώθη ἡ γράφη ἡ λεγοῦσα· καὶ μετὰ ἀνόμων ἐλογίσθη, "And so was fulfilled the scripture which says, 'And he was counted among the lawless.'" These words echo the content of Luke 22:37 and cite specifically the Septuagint reading of Isaiah 53:12, the same text discussed immediately above. The entire verse is lacking in many of the best

---

²²Isaiah 53:12 in the RSV reads, "Therefore I will divide him a portion with the great, and he shall divide the spoil with the strong; because he poured out his soul to death, and *was numbered with the transgressors*; yet he bore the sin of many, and made intercession for the transgressors" (my italics).

²³Fred Craddock, *Luke*. (Interpretation Series; Louisville, KY: John Knox, 1990), 271. For specific reference to Isaiah 53:12 in the text of the Gospels see Luke 22:37 and the textual variant at Mark 15:28. This variant will be discussed presently.

²⁴These witnesses include A C D L W Θ Ψ 070 0250 *f*.¹³ Maj syʰ.

²⁵See for example B. Metzger, *Text of the New Testament*, 202; J. Fitzmyer, *The Gospel According to Luke*, 2, 1499; A. Plummer, *The Gospel According to Luke*, 5th edition. (ICC; Edinburgh: T&T Clark, 1922), 530.

²⁶B. Metzger, *Text of the New Testament*, 202.

manuscripts (including א A B C D) and parts of the Old Latin, Syriac, and other versional witnesses. Commentators recognize on the basis of both external witnesses and intrinsic probabilities that this reading probably did not originate with Mark, but rather that this entire verse represents a scribal interpolation.[27]

This appears to be another instance where labeling this a product of assimilation seems incomplete. The scribe has imposed the content of Luke 22:37/Isaiah 53:12, but he did not employ Luke's exact words, which read as follows:

λένω γὰρ ὑμῖν ὅτι τοῦτο τὸ γεγραμμένον δεῖ τελεσθῆναι ἐμοί τό· καὶ μετὰ ἀνόμων ἐλογίσθη· καὶ γὰρ τὸ περὶ ἐμοῦ τέλος ἔχει.

> For I tell you that this scripture must be fulfilled in me, 'And he was reckoned with transgressors'; for what is written about me has its fulfilment.

In fact, except for the quotation of Isaiah 53:12 (LXX), the vocabulary is quite different. It is possible, therefore, that he is drawing from another source (an apologist?) or from his own memory and independent logic. Moreover, the modified reading serves, in essence, serves to explain the previous verse (15:27), "And with him they crucified two robbers, one on his right and one on his left." Although, in contrast with the Lukan Christ, Mark's Jesus is not depicted as one of three κακοῦργοι, the soldiers do crucify him (σταυροῦσιν) flanked by two robbers (δύο λῃστάς). Thus, the scene itself implies guilt by association. As noted earlier, crucifixion was a brutal form of punishment, reserved for the most heinous of criminals, usually runaway slaves, violent criminals, and political revolutionaries. For Jesus to be slain in such a manner and in such company suggested that he deserved his fate.

Pagan critics frequently underscored this point. Celsus, for example, chided Christians for submitting as the divine Logos not a person pure and holy but "a man who was arrested most disgracefully and crucified"[28] and, even more directly, where Celsus claimed a correspondence between Jesus' demise and his designation as a robber.[29] To add substance and credibility to his rebuttal of such claims, Origen frequently summoned the prophetic tradition. Where Celsus mocked Jesus for slurping greedily from the vinegar and gall offered him, for example, Origen retorted that he did so in fulfillment of Psalm 68:22.[30] Where Celsus depicted Jesus as "a robber not a god," Origen, employing the language of Isaiah 53:12, asserted that God's being "numbered among the transgressors" was somehow foretold.

It appears, then, that the scribe responsible for the interpolation of Mark 15:28 is imitating the apologetic strategy of defending Jesus by arguing from prophecy.

---

[27]See, e.g., V. Taylor, *Gospel According to St. Mark*, 591, and C. S. Mann, *Mark*, 647, and Joachim Gnilka, *Das Evangelium nach Markus*, 2 vols. (Zürich: Benziger Verlag, 1979), II.318, n. 58.

[28]*Cels.* II.31.

[29]*Cels.* II.44.

[30]*Cels.* II.37. See Chadwick, *Origen: Contra Celsum*, 96.

Whether he has modeled his technique after evangelists like Luke or apologists like Origen is difficult to know. What the evidence does sufficiently demonstrate, however, is that "this scribe," in the act of transcribing the report of the crucifixion, halted at Mark's straightforward account of Jesus' death. Something more for him was required here, some form of explanation; and so he inserted the standard prophetic explanation for why Jesus was slain among transgressors. Events could have unfolded no other way, he thereby explained, for only so could it fulfill Isaiah's oracle (53:12). That is why he was reckoned among the lawless, numbered among the transgressors, καὶ μετὰ ἀνόμων ἐλογίσθη.

Let us briefly summarize our findings. Each of these three texts shows evidence of scribal tampering. Moreover, each of the modifications is bound by a common motif: at a critical moment in the climax of the crucifixion narrative, scribes inserted a prophetic explanation for the execution that was being related. Mark 15:28 consists of a verse composed by scribal activity, framed precisely in accord with the common apologetic counterpunch that strange events are sometimes best explained as prophetic fulfillment. But not always. For the scribal modification of Luke 23:32 indicates that, at least in the minds of some wary scribes, where the writer of Luke drafted a detail of his tale in accord with this very same text (Isaiah 53:12), the implication that Jesus was literally and not merely figuratively numbered among those evildoers posed too great a threat to leave unattended. Here, discretion was the better part of valor. Jesus' death alongside two ruffians was mere coincidence, nothing more. Finally, in Matthew 27:35 scribes explained a different element of the story—the division of his garments among the soldiers—but did so on the basis of prophetic fulfillment. Scribes in effecting these alterations to the texts put an apologetic spin on these synoptic yarns.

THE AUTHOR OF THIS SEDITION

Celsus once labeled Jesus "the author of this sedition."[31] Elsewhere in *Contra Celsum*, we find evidence of Celsus further characterizing him as wicked (I.71), a liar (II.7), pestilent (II.29), and one who shouted threats (II.24, 76) and gathered round himself the most sordid collection of sailors, tax collectors, and other wicked men (I.62, II.46). Even earlier, Tacitus in his *Annals* had reported that Christians owed their name to one who has been executed as a criminal.[32] This reflected an attitude that was common among some pagans that Jesus was a dangerous man who represented a

---

[31] *Cels.* VIII.14. Tacitus similarly refers to Jesus as *auctor nominus eius Christus* in his *Annals* (15.44). See the footnote immediately below.

[32] Tacitus. *Ann.* 15.44, where he writes, "Christus, the founder of the name had undergone the death penalty in the reign of Tiberius, by sentence of the procurator Pontius Pilate, and the pernicious superstition (*exitabilis superstitio*) was held in check for a moment only to break out once more, not merely in Judaea, the home of the disease (*mali*), but in the capital itself, where all things horrible or shameful in the world collect and find a vogue." The text and translation are located in John Jackson, trans. *Tacitus: The Annals, Books XIII-XVI* (LCL: Cambridge, MA: Harvard University Press, 1969), 282–3.

threat to society. Apologists were keen therefore to show Jesus' good side. Justin, Clement of Alexandria, Theophilus of Antioch, and Tertullian all made clever use of a standard "homiletic device" that developed among early Christians, playing off of the pun between the Greek word χρηστός, "good," and χριστός, "Christ."[33] The texts that follow suggest that scribes also reflected this concern, and refined their texts in such a way as to enhance Jesus's reputation as a sober peacemaker, and not a threatening figure of violence.

Such is the case in Matthew 10:34. Where the author repeated the apocalyptic announcement of Jesus, "I have not come to bring (βαλεῖν) peace but rather *a sword*" (μάχαιρα), the scribe responsible for the Curetonian Syriac substituted, "I have come to bring *division of mind*" (διαμερισμὸν τῶν διάνοιων). In the first place, it seems likely that the scribe responsible for this change borrowed those of Luke 12:51, ἀλλ' ἢ διαμερισμόν, and assimilated them into his copy of Matthew. Still, that does not completely explain the change. Commentators waffle on this verse. Albright and Mann declare that Luke's version of the saying cannot be derived from any written source shared with Matthew, and are driven to explain the origin of Matthew on the basis of conjecture. "Our suggestion is that originally the text ran: 'Do not think I have come to impose peace on earth by force; I have come neither to impose peace, nor yet to make war. But I have come to divide the just from the unjust...a man against his father....'"[34] Davies and Allison also voice difficulty with regard to this verse. They reflect, "Although one can hardly decide whether Matthew has increased the parallelism (cf. 5.17) or whether Luke has changed the sentence structure, Luke's 'division' for 'sword' does appear to be secondary."[35] These remarks, however, fail to deal with all the elements of textual variation. Not only did the scribe transpose Luke into Matthew, he also introduced two new words into the text, thereby qualifying διαμερισμὸν with τῶν διάνοιων. This modification is unequivocally the product of a thinking scribe. He is like a smith with a hammer who has beaten a sword into a plowshare. He has first exchanged "division" for "sword," but then has gone on to define division as a thing "of mind." To hear this scribe tell the story, while Jesus may have announced that he did not come to bring "peace," neither did he come to bring either a "sword" or even "division." He came to bring a "division of mind," a difference of opinion, a distinction in thought. Such things are not cause for persecution or execution; they are the raw materials of philosophers. Much more than assimilation is involved in this reading. The responsible scribe sought to transform Jesus from a figure whose arrival bred contention to one whose presence induced followers to pursue a deeper, more precise way of thinking. The copyist who

---

[33]For the references and further discussion of use of the pun in Christian circles see S. Benko, "Pagan Criticism," 1057–58, where he states that this "homiletic device" (his phrase) had been used among Christians from earliest times.

[34]W. F. Albright and C. S. Mann, *Matthew*, 130–31.

[35]W. D. Davies and D. Allison, *Matthew II*, 218.

manufactured this reading appears to have done so under the influence of apologetic interests.

Jesus' announcement in Matthew 9:13 might have sounded like music to the ears of some, but to pagan despisers of the faith his declaration that he had come to call "not the righteous but sinners" could have confirmed their suspicions that he was mustering brigands for some unseemly purpose. Ancient sources reveal that such rumors circulated among some outside the movement. S. Benko summarizes it well:

> At the first trial of the Christians Pliny suspected in the movement conspiracy; it was not superstition that made it punishable but the belief that it was a secret gathering, dangerous for the peace and tranquility of society and not serving the interests of the state, the *utilitas publica*.[36]

Indeed, Celsus propagated these rumors to drive a wedge of distinction between Christians and other more palatable religious sects. Where "the other mysteries" summoned to their ranks persons marked by purity and wisdom, he alleged, Christians welcomed to their fold "sinners."[37] Compelled to reply to this point, Origen did not deny that sinners were made privy to the Christian message, but what he vigorously insisted was that the purpose that lay behind this invitation was to effect their healing. Robbers assemble other robbers for the purpose of robbery; but Christians gather thieves, bandits, and other despicables for the purpose of spiritual transformation. The make-up of the assembly may appear the same, but the groups are distinguished by their purpose. Thus Origen defended his cause.[38]

It is particularly interesting to compare the rhetorical strategies reflected here in *Contra Celsum* with the textual variant located at Matthew 9:13. Major Caesarean and Byzantine witnesses along with others report a clearly secondary reading that elaborates and qualifies Jesus' purpose statement. To the end of his mission statement that Jesus had come to call not the righteous but sinners these witnesses add "into repentance" (εἰς μετάνοιαν). The change can easily be attributed to assimilation to Luke 5:32.[39] Although comparison of the verses shows a great deal of difference in vocabulary and verb tenses, the words of the interpolation correspond exactly to those of Luke.

Once again, however, we are met with what could be an incomplete explanation. The significant change in meaning wrought by this modification should not be ignored. Brief as this addendum is, it transforms the sentence and, in essence, defends the actions of Jesus. It introduces onto an otherwise suspicious behavior a new and noble motive. This ploy mirrors the methods we just outlined in the writings of the apologist, Origen. Also in Justin, we see a preference in his *First Apology* for using the form of

---

[36] S. Benko, "Pagan Criticism," 1075–76. Cf. Pliny, *Letters*, 10.96.

[37] *Cels.* III.59.

[38] *Cels.* III.60–61.

[39] As it in fact is by W. D. Davies and D. Allison, *Matthew II*, 105, n. 108.

this logion that includes the phrase "into repentance."[40] Of course, there is no way to know if Justin is citing Luke 5:32 or an amended Matthew 9:13 (or is adapting the text himself); but we can discern that Justin favored the form of the saying that offered a palatable explanation for why Jesus called sinners. So it would seem did some scribes. It appears that some apologetically-minded copyists of this Matthean verse detected its troublesome ambiguity and sought to clarify its meaning by means of embellishment. These scribes chose in this instance to vary from their exemplar, and—by merely adding to the end of the pronouncement Luke's qualifying phrase εἰς μετανοίαν—to deflect any implication that Jesus was in the business of marshaling miscreants. No longer would a reader misunderstand him to be rallying the rabble rousers; he was summoning sinners *into repentance*. Ministry not mayhem was his mission; piety not politics was his purpose. Such was the way these scribes recast Matthew's story—apologetically.

Perhaps driven by similar concern, scribes inscribed into the text of Mark 13:33 another subtle expansion. Near the conclusion of the so-called little apocalypse, attributed to Jesus is the abrupt apocalyptic command to his disciples to "*Watch, be alert in the night*, for you do not know the appointed time" (my italics). It is easy to see how outsiders could have understood these words militarily as Jesus ordering nocturnal guard duty, and read into them a rebellious tone.[41]

By inserting just one more imperative (καὶ προσεύχεσθε), however, copyists replaced contentious discord with pious harmony. So in the manuscripts of א, A, C, L, W, Θ, Ψ, *f*[1.13], Maj., lat, sy, and co, we encounter the reading, "Watch, be vigilant, *and pray*...." While most commentators, sadly, are silent on this verse, except for identifying the phrase as secondary, a few venture to explain this modification as an adjustment related to Mark 14:38, "Watch and pray, lest you come into temptation."[42] Credible as this may appear on the surface, differences in vocabulary call this conclusion into question. Although καὶ προσεύχεσθε appears the same in both verses, the words for "Watch" are different: γρηγορεῖτε in 14:38, ἀγρυπνεῖτε in 13:33. If this is assimilation, it is not very precise. Besides, the difference in context of these two pericopes bears different implications for what the term "Watch" means. In the Markan apocalypse (13:1–37), ἀγρυπνεῖτε is a command to battle sleep and stand vigil in the midst what Jesus has just described as tribulations, persecutions, and the near advent of the Son of man. On the other hand, the term γρηγορεῖτε occurs in the setting of Jesus at prayer in Gethsemane (14:32–42), and is spoken with specific

---

[40]*Ap.* I.15.8.

[41]Albrecht Oepke reports that the synonymous terms γρηγορεῖτε and ἀγρυπνεῖτε can refer to watching over a city or keeping zealous watch over men or beasts. Idem, "ἐγείρω," in G. Kittel, ed., *TWNT*, 338.

[42]See, e.g., A. Oepke, "ἐγείρω," 338; B. Metzger, *Textual Commentary*, 112. Among those who offer nothing more than declaration that "and pray" is secondary (and some do not offer even that) are E. Gould, V. Taylor, E. Schweizer, J. Gnilka, and B. Witherington. See the bibliography for the references to their commentaries.

reference to guarding against temptation. Jesus tells his heavy-eyed followers to "watch and pray that you may not enter into temptation; the spirit indeed is willing, but the flesh is weak." My point is that these two commands to "watch" sound very different when read in context. One reads as a call to arms in the midst of physical tribulation, while the other is a call to prayerful vigil in the face of spiritual temptation. I am not arguing against any possible influence from Mark 14:38, though I am not convinced of its direct bearing on Mark 13:33. What I am arguing is that there is sufficient reason on the basis of content to locate the origin of this expansion in apologetic interests. That is, how this modification alters the perception of this text fits the contours of apologetic themes and patterns. We have seen already how important the motif of prayer and piety was for the Christian apologists. They argued that the prayers of Christians sustained the emperor and blessed the empire. So whether it was to soften the harsh apocalyptic tone of the passage or to interject the motif of prayer so prevalent in apologetic writings, certain copyists of Mark 13:33 added two words that significantly altered the configuration of this verse. "And pray," these scribes added, thereby using the stylus—the way a carpenter applies sandpaper to uneven wood—to smooth the pugnacious edge from an ambiguous apocalyptic saying of Jesus and transform it into a phrase that was an unambiguous plea for piety.

The rhetoric of prayer also found its way into yet another passage by means of the deliberate strokes of copyists. The text of John 6:15 reads as follows:

Ἰησοῦς οὖν γνοὺς ὅτι μέλλουσιν ἔρχεσθαι καὶ ἁρπάζειν αὐτὸν ἵνα ποιήσωσιν βασιλέα ἀνεχώρησεν [v.l. φεύγει] πάλιν εἰς τὸ ὄρος αὐτὸς μόνος [v.l. κἀκεῖ προσηύχετο].

Perceiving then that they were about to come and take him by force to make him king, Jesus withdrew [fled] again to the mountain by himself [and he prayed].

Two interesting variant readings surface in this verse. The first requires some care in determining the "original" text. This verse punctuates the Johannine version of the feeding of the five thousand, the only miracle story reported by all four evangelists. Having received their fill, the sated multitude determines that have witnessed a sign (σημεῖον, Jn 6:14) and give every indication that they are about to coronate Jesus. He demurs, however, by retiring to the mountain to be alone. The textual tradition presents us with two different verbs to describe his departure: ἀνεχώρησεν and φεύγει. Reporting for the UBSGNT committee, Metzger argues that the former is the "original" reading.[43] Their judgment, which elicited from the committee a {B} rating, is based largely on the impressive external evidence, though the support for φεύγει—the first hand of Sinaiticus, much of the Old Latin tradition, and the Curetonian Syriac (which is a conflated reading)—is sound enough not to be summarily dismissed. Metzger goes on to disclose, however, that the term

---

[43]Metzger, *Textual Commentary*, 211–12.

ἀναχωρέω, although frequent in Matthew, occurs nowhere else in the Fourth Gospel. Thus, based on this analysis of word usage, intrinsic probability would favor φεύγει. Metzger also acknowledges that from the perspective of transcriptional probabilities, scribes might have found "flight" unbecoming to Jesus, and changed it accordingly. This thought gains credibility when one observes that Celsus questioned the divine status of Jesus, in part, on the basis that no divine being would be driven to "flee" capture.[44] Jesus, scribes would have readers of the text understand unequivocally, is no coward.

The second variant consists of the addition of two words at the end of the verse and can easily be recognized as secondary. Whether Jesus departed or fled, the parties responsible for Codex Bezae (and sa[ms]) pressed upon their exemplars a further motive for his disappearance. He went away *to pray* (κἀκεῖ προσηύχετο). This modification, too, transforms the report of Jesus' departure. His withdrawal both punctuates an attempt to make him king, demonstrating that Jesus is not in the business to acquire earthly power, and is configured as a devotional exercise. He does not seek an earthly throne but a divine audience. He is a man of prayer. So the scribes responsible for these changes portrayed Jesus.

In summary, random rumors and careful arguments crafted by opponents like Celsus convinced many that Jesus rightly bore the mantle of "the author of this sedition." Apologists were driven to defend him against this charge. Whenever possible, they sought to accent features of his story that resembled those of a man of peace, and distance Jesus from words, gestures, or behaviors generally associated with social miscreants, political revolutionaries, or even persons of the pedestrian classes.

It seems apparent from this group of readings we have just surveyed that some of those scribes engaged in the work of transmitting the Gospels were shaped by the rhetoric of the apologetic wars. For the most part, their efforts were anonymous and subtle, much like an underground movement clandestinely assisting one side in a cause; but in specific cases they boldly followed the footsteps of apologists in shaping the text to the advantage of those defending Christ from criticism. For them, he was clearly no "author of sedition," but a man of piety and peace. The composite Jesus drawn by the strokes of these scribes portrayed a man who did not seek earthly power for himself or to undermine the mainstream culture. Those who appraised his work as that of a brigand gathering confederates for mischief and mayhem needed to reexamine the motives for why he gathered sinners into his presence. It was, they emphasized, for the sole purpose of their repentance and moral transformation. Many of his sayings and deeds these scribes qualified as acts of piety and devotional prayer. In each of these instances scribal activity imposed on the text, usually with great finesse, a feature or

[44]*Cels.* II.9–10. See the text of M. Borret, *Contra Celse*, 300, 308. In II.9–10, Celsus ridicules Jesus for "hiding himself" (κρυπτόμενος) and "running away" (διαδιδράσκων), while at the same time mocking his inability to flee (φεύγειν) from capture. Tatian (*Or.* 8.2) also ridicules so-called deities who "flee" (φεύγων) the battlefield. See the text of M. Whittaker, *Oratio*, 14–15.

qualification that moved the Jesus presented in the pericope out of the firing range of his assailants. The labors observed here reflect apologetic concerns, or, perhaps more accurately, the activity of concerned scribal apologists.

A CARPENTER BY TRADE

The perception that Christianity consisted of a sect constituted mainly by the lower laboring classes greatly contributed to the sense of disdain felt for the Jesus movement by its literate pagan critics. Caecilius, the characterized voice of paganism in the *Octavius* of Minucius Felix, for example, described the adherents of this sect as "dregs of the populace."[45] Fueling this perception in part may have been the report that the founder of the movement had earned his living as a common woodworker. While generations earlier the apostle Paul had taken pride in declaring that he had chosen to earn his own living and thus forego his deserved right to live off the alms of his congregations, by the time the apologists were interfacing with the prevailing culture, the image of Jesus as a working carpenter had become for them something of an embarrassment. Typical of the derision held in this regard by outsiders is the well-known ridicule of Celsus:

> And everywhere they speak in their writings of the tree of life and of resurrection of the flesh by the tree—I imagine because their master was nailed to a cross and was a carpenter by trade. So that if he happened to be thrown off a cliff, or pushed into a pit, or suffocated by strangling, or if he had been a cobbler or stonemason or blacksmith, there would have been a cliff of life above the heavens, or a pit of resurrection, or a rope of immortality, or a blessed stone, or an iron of love, or a holy hide of leather. Would not an old woman who sings a story to lull a little child to sleep have been ashamed to whisper tales such as these?[46]

From their creative efforts to downplay or dismiss it altogether, it is evident that some apologetic writers encountered the perception that Jesus was a carpenter as degrading and problematic. Justin dismissed the issue in his *Dialogue with Trypho* by explaining that people presumed him to be a carpenter because Jesus customarily fashioned ploughs and yokes as symbols to teach righteousness and active living.[47] More pointedly, Origen's direct reply to Celsus implied that his opponent had misread the text. "Furthermore," Origen wrote, "he did not observe that Jesus himself is not described as a carpenter anywhere in the gospels accepted in the churches."[48]

---

[45]Minucius Felix, *Oct.* VIII, cited from LCL, 334–5.

[46]*Cels.* VI.34, cited from Chadwick, 350.

[47]*Dial.* 88, cited in ANCL, II, 212.

[48]*Cels.* VI.36, cited from Chadwick, 352. The complete sentence in Greek reads, οὐδαμοῦ τῶν ἐν ταῖς ἐκκλησίαις φερομένων εὐαγγελίων τέκτων αὐτὸς ὁ Ἰησοῦς ἀναγέραπται.

Origen's rejoinder begs the question of how he understood Mark 6:3, a citation which seems to contradict him. Bruce Metzger considers that either Origen did not recall Mark 6:3 or that he was acquainted with this verse through copies that had already been assimilated to Matthew.[49] The clearly "original" text reported by all the uncials and most other minuscules and versions reads, οὐχ οὗτός ἐστιν ὁ τέκτων ὁ υἱός τῆς Μαρίας..., "Is this not the carpenter, the son of Mary...?" It is unlikely that Origen would have been unacquainted with the principal reading, particularly in light of how Origen so carefully qualified his rebuttal. Jesus, he said, was not depicted as a carpenter "anywhere in the *gospels accepted in the churches*."[50] The care with which he qualified his statement implies that Origen knew of gospels or readings that did in fact describe Jesus as a carpenter. Whether he had in mind apocryphal gospels not read liturgically by the wider church, or whether this reference is to specific manuscripts or textual traditions not preferred by Origen or his local church is difficult to know. What is manifest here is that Origen knew of such readings that portrayed Jesus as a carpenter by trade, but in the throes of Celsus' assault he rhetorically dismissed them.

In light of Origen's rebuttal, it is striking to examine the variant reading reported by a few Caesarean witnesses, namely *f*[13],(565), 700), along with P[45], 33[vid], (579, 2542), it, vg[mss], and bo[mss]. These manuscripts modify the verse by inserting the phrase τοῦ τέκτονος υἱός καὶ so that it reads, "Is this not the son *of the carpenter and* Mary...?" Some scholars attribute this modification to the scribal practice of assimilation, since the alteration emulates Matthew 13:55.[51]

Mere assimilation, though, does not seem to account adequately for the energies shaping this change. Kim Haines-Eitzen keenly observes that harmonization does not account for why Matthew and Luke changed their source nor for why some transcribers of Mark 6:3 opted for the longer reading.[52] Moreover, there is the fact that the Palestinian Syriac alters the verse not by assimilation but by deletion, omitting ὁ τέκτων.[53] This scribal change reflects no concern for harmonizing the verse to its Matthean parallel. The alteration does, however, effectively assuage the tensions

---

[49]B. Metzger, *Textual Commentary*, 88–89, n. 1.

[50]*Cels.* VI.36.

[51]See, e.g., the discussions in M.-J. Lagrange, *Évangile selon Saint Marc*, 148–9; V. Taylor, *Mark*, 299–300; and J. Gnilka, *Das Evangelium nach Markus*, 231–32. Gnilka's assessment is that the reading "the carpenter, the Son of Mary" represents the "original" reading; "the son of the carpenter" shows the influence of Matthew 13:55, and the reading "the son of the carpenter and of Mary" is a conflate reading.

[52]Kim Haines-Eitzen, *Guardians of Letters*, 117. See the rest of her careful treatment of this variant reading, 117–18, in which she, too, concludes that this text has been modified for apologetic purposes. See also his treatment of Mark 6:3 as reflective of apologetic interests in Bart D. Ehrman, "The Text of the Gospels at the End of the Second Century," in *Codex Bezae: Studies from the Lunel Colloquium, June 1994*, ed. D. C. Parker and C.-B. Amphoux. Leiden: E. J. Brill, 1996, 118.

[53]B. Metzger, *Textual Commentary*, 89. Cf. M.-J. Lagrange, *Évangile*, 148, who identifies the source of this change as the Harclean Syriac.

associated with Jesus being a carpenter. The question now posed by the text has merely to do with his lineage, not his livelihood. "Is this not the son of Mary...?" Noteworthy also is the fact that many of the witnesses attesting to the earlier modification reside in the so-called Caesarean tradition, described by scholars as the text brought to Caesarea from Egypt by Origen.[54] Therefore, whether by coincidence or design, the textual tradition most closely linked to Origen transmits an intentional modification that effectively undermines Celsus and validates Origen's apologetic argument against him. The impetus behind the scribal modification of Mark 6:3, then, may be traced beyond the generic tendency among copyists to assimilate the gospels to one another; but it is highly likely that apologetic motivation directed the hands responsible for altering this text.

A MAGICIAN AND A DECEIVER OF THE PEOPLE

Justin interpreted Isaiah 35:1–7 as a messianic prophecy fulfilled by Jesus. It was Christ, he asserted, who was the spring of living water springing forth in a thirsty land, which he explained to be the land void of the knowledge of God, i.e., the land of the Gentiles. Moreover, he explained that Jesus fulfilled the oracles of healing by restoring those who were maimed, lame, deaf, and blind, causing them to leap and hear and see, and even raising the dead. "But," Justin declared regarding those who witnessed these wonders, "though they saw such works they asserted it was a magical art. For they dared to call him a magician, and a deceiver of the people."[55]

Among the personalities of antiquity, Jesus of Nazareth did not stand alone in needing a defense against the calumny of being identified as a "magician." Indeed, it was a trump card frequently played by jilted lovers and losers in shrewd business dealings. Apuleius, for one, was forced to acquit himself against some who believed he had bewitched his wife and married her for her money.[56] More than defamation, however, such charges constituted damnation, for in the Roman Empire the practice of magic fell under the rubric of a capital offense.[57] The severity of the crime was

---

[54]See B. Metzger, *Textual Commentary*, xix. For a more thorough treatment of the Caesarean text see idem, "The Caesarean Text of the Gospels," *JBL* 64 (1945), 457–489.

[55]*Dial.* 69.

[56]For the text in English, see Apuleius, "The Defence of Apuleius: A Discourse on Magic," in *The Works of Apuleius* (London: G. Bell and Sons, 1914), 247–349; and for additional details and further discussion, see the introduction to Apuleius, *The Golden Ass* (Translated by Jack Lindsay; Bloomington, Indiana: Indiana University Press, 1962), especially pp. 8–11, and also S. Benko, *Pagan Rome and the Early Christians* (Bloomington, Indiana: Indiana University Press, 1984), 104–108.

[57]The seriousness of the charge and the possible capital consequences attached to it may be seen in Suetonius (*Augustus* 31.1), who reports that Augustus ordered two thousand magical scrolls burned in the year 13 B.C.E. In a line from his defense in Sabratha, where Apuleius was accused and tried as a magician, the accused speaks of defending himself against a capital charge: "But here, on the other hand, he who *puts a magician*, such as they speak of, *on trial for his life*, by

based not so much in contempt of fraud but in concern for social subversion.[58] This was, in part, because it was at the same time believed that magical practice was potent and effective. Therefore, although it was among the more serious charges leveled against Jesus, it was perhaps the one some of his followers were most reluctant to deny. To be sure, then, this rhetoric comprised in the Greco-Roman world no small slander. The label "magician" had the potential of being much more than a term of abuse; it constituted a charge that, if confirmed, could earn the accused a painful execution.

Many social scientists contend that the magic/miracle dichotomy is artificial, erroneously based on the false presumption that there is an unequivocal difference between magic and religion.[59] They emphasize that the distinction between them is based on perception rather than reality. Drawing on this social theory, David Aune summarizes the relationship of magic and religion in this way:

> (1) Magic and religion are so closely intertwined that it is virtually impossible to regard them as discreet socio-cultural categories; (2) The structural-functional analysis of magico-religious phenomena forbids a negative attitude toward magic; (3) Magic is a phenomenon which exists only within the matrix of particular religious traditions; magic is not a religion only in the sense that the species is not the genus. A particular magical system coheres with a religious structure in the sense that it shares the fundamental religious reality construction of the contextual religion; (4) Magic appears to be as universal a feature of religion as deviant behavior is of human societies.[60]

Any claim to an ancient distinction between "manipulative" magic and "supplicative" religion, therefore, is contrived and erroneous. The label "magic" or "magician" was grounded in perception more than substance. In the words of Susan Garrett, the meaning of magician "depends on culturally governed behavioral norms of the persons involved, on their relative social locations, and on the complex particularities of the given situation."[61]

This anthropologically informed understanding of magic guides Garrett's analysis of this topic with relation to the Gospels. She describes how highly vulnerable Jesus and his followers were to charges of practicing magic. All four evangelists, she points

---

means of what attendants, what precautions, what guards, is he to ward off a destruction that is as unforeseen as it is inevitable?" See Apuleius, *The Works of Apuleius*, 273. H. D. Betz adds the comment, "Indeed, the first centuries of the Christian era saw many burnings of books, often of magical books, and *not a few burnings that included the magicians themselves*." (Idem, *Greek Magical Papyri*, xli). In both cases, my emphasis.

[58] M. Smith, *Clement of Alexandria and a Secret Gospel of Mark*, 220.

[59] See D. Aune's wonderfully thorough and lucid summary of the social theories underlying this discussion, including the work of E. E. Evans-Pritchard, A. D. Nock, E. Durkheim, M. Mauss, M. Douglas, and J. Z. Smith, in idem, "Magic in Early Christianity," 1510–1516.

[60] D. Aune, "Magic in Early Christianity," 1516.

[61] S. Garrett, *Demise of the Devil*, 4.

out, record Jesus' self-defense against accusations that he was in league with the devil. "It was urgent," she writes,

> that the Gospel writers and early Christian apologists show that Jesus' and the church leaders' activities were not magical in character, especially since Christians' practice of casting out demons and healing the sick 'in the name of Jesus'—who had been crucified as a criminal—looked very much like the feats of conventional magicians.[62]

Even the Gospels, as expressed in the views of P. Samain, D. Aune, and S. Garrett, report polemic by his opponents that reflects a belief on their part that Jesus was a magician.[63] It should be noted as P. Samain has observed, however, that within the Gospels, Jesus is never *expressly* accused of being a magician.[64] He goes on to say, though, that several features of the canonical miracle stories match details closely associated with magical papyri and practice. For example, he argues that the charge of being an imposter, such as one finds in Matthew 27:63, is in essence an accusation that Jesus accomplished miracles by means of trickery or magic. He also adduces Mark 3:22–30, a pericope in which Jesus' opponents avow that he casts out demons by the power of Beelzebul, as a text that implies that Jesus was a magician.[65] S. Benko observes that even reports of Christians singing hymns could have been perceived by Roman ears as reciting a spell.[66]

To be labeled as a magician, then, was both to be marked with disgrace and recognized as an outlaw. Yet, where his critics accused Jesus of being a magician, many of his supporters admired him as one.[67] Thus is the scholarly reflection upon magic in antiquity marked with ironies.[68] On the one hand, magic was deemed a crime against society and frequently viewed with disdain by the educated population. The irregularity of its practices stood in sharp contrast to the fastidiously structured and precisely regular observance of religious rituals, as did its popularity among the lower classes stand in relief to its disdain by the upper classes. On the other hand, magic pervaded first century Greco-Roman cults, Judaism, and Christianity, and only increased in

---

[62]S. Garrett, *Demise of the Devil*, 3.

[63]P. Samain, "L'Accusation de magie contre le Christ dans les Évangiles," Ephemerides Theologicae Lovianienses, 15 (1938), 449–90; and David E. Aune, "Magic in Early Christianity," 1507–1557, esp. 1540–42.

[64]Yet, as pointed out in conversation by Moody Smith, Jesus is openly accused of having a demon (Jn 8:48ff.).

[65]P. Samain, "L'Accusation de magie," 456–64 and 466–69.

[66]S. Benko, "Pagan Criticism,"1076; cf. *Twelve Tables* 8.1.

[67]M. Smith, *Jesus the Magician*, 94.

[68]Scholars have focused great attention upon this matter of the relationship of magic in Greco-Roman antiquity to early Christianity. Among the featured literature informing this project are the following sources: Hans Dieter Betz, *The Greek Magical Papyri*; David E. Aune, "Magic in Early Christianity,"; Eugene Gallagher, *Divine Man or Magician?: Celsus and Origen on Jesus* (Chico, CA: Scholars Press, 1984); and S. Benko, *Pagan Rome and the Early Christians*.

popularity during the second through the fifth centuries. Moreover, magic intrigued many among the elite—Apuleius dabbled in sorcery and Nero was tutored in magical arts. Most significant for our purposes, though, is the fact that the line between miracle and magical feat remained blurry, at best, and yet miracles were an essential element in the testimonies about and aretalogies of "divine men," certainly no one more than Jesus.

Accusations that Jesus was a "magician" figured prominently in both ancient Jewish and pagan polemic against the founder and his followers.[69] Morton Smith's familiar but controversial claim that, by those who did not accept or follow him, Jesus would have been described as a magician is well-known and his adduced evidence—in spite of being pressed beyond its limits at times—begets abundant insights.[70] M. Smith observes that the evangelists could not eliminate the miracle stories from their narratives because they were essential features of their stories. What they could do, however, was tailor the telling of the tale. Matthew and Luke excised Mark's impetuous recollections of the physical means Jesus used to effect miracles (cf. parallels to Mk 7.33; 8.23), and John reduced the number to seven, and described them as "signs" not "miracles." Jesus' claim to divinity as Son of God Mark posed in the rhetoric of a "messianic secret," the testimony to which issued only from the lips of heaven, demons, disciples, and crowds until the high priest finally forced him to admit it.[71]

Informed by this discussion, let us turn our attention to the textual tradition. There appear in the Gospels several variant readings bearing the marks of intentional modification that, when considered in light of this accusation of magic, seem to function apologetically. A prime example is located in Mark 6:2, a text that reads as follows:

καὶ γενομένου σαββάτου ἤρξατο διδάσκειν ἐν τῇ συναγωγῇ καὶ πολλοὶ ἀκούοντες ἐξεπλήσσοντο λέγοντες· πόθεν τούτῳ ταῦτα καὶ τίς ἡ σοφία ἡ δοθεῖσα τούτῳ καὶ αἱ δυνάμεις τοιαῦται διὰ τῶν χειρῶν αὐτοῦ γινόμεναι [v. l. ἵνα καὶ δυν...γίνωνται];

And on the sabbath he began to teach in the synagogue; and many who heard him were astonished, saying, "Where did this man get all this? What is the wisdom given to him? What mighty works are wrought by his hands?"[72]

---

[69]M. Smith, *Clement of Alexandria*, 224–5, 229–30. M. Smith points to a number of ancient works that discuss or portray Jesus in terms consonant with those of an ancient magician or thaumaturge (wonder worker), including, along with the Gospels (e.g., Jn 20:19, Mk 16:18) and apocryphal texts (*Infancy Gospel of Thomas*), Justin (*Ap.* I. 30), Tertullian (*Ap.* XXI.17), Origen (*Cels.* II.49ff.) and Irenaeus (*Haer.* I.23–25).

[70]M. Smith, *Jesus the Magician*, 229.

[71]M. Smith, *Jesus the Magician*, 92.

[72]Actually, the textual traditions include several variations of this verse, but I am considering here only the form relevant to this discussion of alterations affected by apologetic interests with regard to perceptions of Jesus as a magician. See the critical apparatus of N-A[27]

This verse occurs in Mark's pericope reporting Jesus' rejection at Nazareth. The "original" text read, "Where did this man get these things? And what is this wisdom (σοφία) given him? And (καί) what mighty works (δυνάμεις) come to pass (γινόμεναι) by his hands!" Certain copyists, attested by C* D K (Θ 700) it sy[h] sa[ms] , produced the variant reading, "Where did this man get all these things? And what is this wisdom that has been given to him that enables him to do (or, more literally, 'in order that he might do even...') such mighty works by his hands?" Although, in fact, several minor variations occur here, the reading relevant to this present discussion involves the transformation of two distinct questions into a single sentence with a purpose clause. There is no reason here to dispute the generally held opinion among textual scholars that modification of the participle into a finite verb and the introduction of ἵνα represents a secondary reading.[73] Granted, at first glance the changes appear to be little more than grammatical or stylistic; but notice what implications are introduced and how the meaning of the verse is altered.

The salient point is that the secondary reading effectively mollifies the hint of magic left unattended in the primary reading.[74] The "original" reading, by reporting that the crowd asked two explicit questions, implies a distinction (or at least in its ambiguity leaves open the possibility of a distinction) in the gift of wisdom (σοφία) belonging to Jesus and his ability to perform acts generally regarded as miraculous. This implied separation of wisdom and wonder-working could have invited speculation on the part of the reader or hearer that Jesus effected cures and exorcisms by means of magic. As we have seen, for citizens of Greco-Roman antiquity, the distinction between magic and miracle—and therefore magician and divine man—often rested in the what source of power the observer perceived or conceived that the practitioner was using to effect the change. If it was perceived that the power was borrowed from outside, either by manipulation of elements, the summons of demons, or the casting of spells, it was labeled magic; but if the onlooker believed that the power issued from within the person, was a product of his innate being, he could well be perceived as a divine man.[75] It is striking, then, that the secondary reading serves to connect Jesus' miraculous power with his wisdom in such a way that *sophia* is named as the specific and direct means by which Jesus is able to perform mighty works. Subtle as this shift is, the effect of this scribal interpolation corresponds precisely to apologetic strategies and pagan perceptions. One of the fundamental principles of Justin's apologetic theology was that Jesus was the incarnate *Logos* of

---

for a fuller display of variants within the reading.

[73]For a fuller discussion of this and the other variant readings connected to Mark 6:2 see B. Metzger, *Textual Commentary*, 88, and V. Taylor, *Mark*, 299.

[74]J. Marcus makes note of the implications of this text related to magic, but does not deal with the textual variant in this regard. See idem, *Mark 1–8*, 374–79.

[75]About these distinctions, see Eugene Gallagher's discussion of the distinction between articulate and inarticulate channels of power in idem, *Divine Man or Magician?*, 55–57; and M. Smith, *Jesus the Magician*, 91–93.

God. Justin believed that Jesus' power neither was derived from demonic manipulation nor issued from any source other than himself; it simply was an extension of his own divinely-endowed wisdom.

This understanding of what motivated certain scribes to so alter this text is supported by evidence located in several ancient writers. First of all, the basic strategy can be observed even in opponents of Christianity. Hierocles (c. 304 C.E.), for example, who crafted a comparison of Apollonius of Tyana and Jesus much to the detriment of the latter, argued that, where Jesus was clearly to be identified as a sorcerer, Apollonius bore the classic traits of a true philosopher and man of wisdom (*Hierocl.* 1–2).

Eusebius, of course, answered to the contrary, arguing in *Against Hierocles* that it was indeed Jesus who bore the character of a wise man, and Apollonius who resembled a magician.[76] He dedicated a portion of his *Demonstratio evangelica* (III.6–7) to defend Jesus against those who held him to be a magician. Taking a different approach, Justin,[77] Origen,[78] and Lactanius[79] also defended Jesus against the charge of magic by appealing to prophecy, interpreting Jesus' healing activity as fulfillment of ancient oracles, particularly those of Isaiah. Origen bolstered his position even further by emphasizing the moral reform and enduring beneficial effect brought about in association with Jesus' miracles.[80] Also, further support against the accusation of magic could be found in the most unlikely of places, Porphyry. It is noteworthy that, unlike most other pagan critics of Jesus and his movement, Porphyry did not accuse Jesus of being a magician. Rather, he diminished his status with faint praise, substituting for notions of his divine status credit for being a man of piety. According to Eusebius, Porphyry in his book *Philosophy from Oracles* declared that the oracles announced that the gods themselves affirmed the piety of Jesus and bestowed an immortal nature upon him. For Porphyry, Jesus did not live up to the billing of the Christians, but neither did he bear the disrepute heaped on him by Celsus and others; he was neither god nor sorcerer.

Clearly grounded in the apologetic corpus, therefore, is abundant evidence of concern for this matter of magic on the part of the defenders of the faith. In view of this, and in light of the corresponding effect observed in the scribal reading, evidence of apologetic interests appears a likely motivation lying behind the modification of this text.

Concern with charges of magic also may have prompted scribes to produce the variant reading located in Mark 1:34. This pericope occurs early in Mark's gospel, in the context of the first of the synoptic miracles—Jesus healing Simon's mother- in-law. Word of the healing spreads quickly through Capernaum, the evangelist narrates, so

---

[76]See M. Smith's treatment of Eusebius response to Hierocles in idem, *Jesus the Magician*, 90.

[77]*Ap.* I.30.

[78]*Cels.* II.48.

[79]*Div. Inst.* V.3.9.

[80]*Cels.* V.62, VI.39.

that by sundown townspeople have brought to him those known to them who are sick and possessed with demons. Jesus heals many of them with various ailments. He also exorcizes many demons, but in the act of doing so, we are informed, he does not permit them to speak "because they knew him" (ὅτι ᾔδεισαν αὐτόν).

For Mark, of course, this prohibition is undoubtedly related to his messianic secret motif.[81] Outsiders, however, could have easily understood this text as evidence that Jesus was a magician. Although educated persons generally detested sorcerers, everyone who believed in the existence and power of the *daimonia* to effect daily life usually took seriously the possibility that a γόης or μάγος could manipulate them.[82] We have already noted that Jesus' adversaries were quick to ascribe his ability to perform exorcisms to his familiarity with the prince of demons, Beelzebub (Mark 3:19–27). Moreover, use of the imperative mood to cast out demons in the Gospels imitates a form of adjuration quite common in the magical literature. In the words of D. Aune, "the short authoritative commands of Jesus to demons in the gospel narratives are formulas of magical adjuration."[83] Moreover, Morton Smith adds the point that observers generally believed that a person was able to perform exorcisms by either gaining power over demons or by conjuring greater spirits to do their bidding, or, in some cases, by becoming possessed by such a powerful spirit. Smith argues that those who thought Jesus was John the Baptist *redivivus* would have understood their belief in terms of magic.[84] All this was based on the proposition that the wonder-worker could contact and engage the spirit world. They knew spirits, demons, and their names, and were recognized by those spirits when summoned. The open-ended declaration, then, that "demons knew Jesus" appears to report an intimate association between residents of the spirit realm and Jesus; this, no doubt, would have sounded to many first-century Hellenists like the rhetoric of Greco-Roman magic.

In this regard, it is striking to recognize that the variant reading that currently occupies our attention has the effect of qualifying this specific acquaintance. As reported by ℵ² B C L W Θ *f*.¹³ 22 28 33 349 565 700 1424 vg^mss sy^h** sa^ms bo, certain scribes completed the verse by adding (τὸν) αὐτὸν χριστὸν εἶναι, so that the complete thought read, "he would not permit the demons to speak because they knew him *to be the Christ*" (my italics).

---

[81] As first detected by William Wrede, *Das Messiasgeheimnis in den Evangelien* (Göttingen, 1901). For more a recent treatment related to this text and a cogent summary of the matter in general see J. Marcus, *Mark 1–8*, 195–201, 525–27. It is interesting in this context, too, that G. Theissen argues that, while indications of the secrecy motif outside of the miracle stories are editorial in origin, those attached to the miracle stories are traditional and associated with magic. See idem, *The Miracle Stories of the Early Christian Tradition* (SNTW; Edinburgh: T&T Clark, 1983), 140–52.

[82] For definitions of these terms as they were used in antiquity, see Gerhard Delling, "γόης," I.737–8, and idem, "μάγος," IV.356–9, in G. Kittel, ed., *TWNT*; and G. W. H. Lampe, *Patristic Greek Lexicon*, 321; and Liddell-Scott, *Lexicon*, 856, 1071.

[83] D. Aune, "Magic in Early Christianity,"1532.

[84] M. Smith, *Jesus the Magician*, 34.

It should be noted that B. Metzger, V. Taylor, and others readily attribute the cause of this modification to synoptic assimilation; the altered reading imitates Luke 4:41.[85] One need not contend with so obvious a fact, but neither should it be presumed that upon recourse to assimilation the matter is settled.[86] It may prove useful if we press on and compare briefly the parallel accounts of this pericope across the triple tradition.

The parallels are located in Mark 1:32–34, Luke 4:40–41, and Matthew 8:16–17. Assuming Markan priority, let us begin our review with the Matthean revision of the story. Where Matthew follows Mark, he for the most part copies him verbatim. It is interesting, however, that Matthew focuses on the demon-possessed, omitting Mark's first reference to the sick and adding mention of them only as an afterthought. Also, where Mark reports that Jesus healed *many* who were sick with various diseases, Matthew says that Christ healed *all* who were sick. Matthew's major modification of Mark, though, is his conclusion that Jesus' healing activity is to be understood in light of Isaiah 53:4. Compared across the triple tradition, this theme of prophetic fulfillment is unique to Matthew's treatment of this story. It is noteworthy, then, that Matthew's assertion that Jesus' ability to work miracles was anticipated by the prophets reflects one of the major distinctions apologists found to emphasize between Jesus and Apollonius of Tyana.

Turning to Luke, one initially observes several features one would expect from the author's style. His prose is more fluid and lyrical than Mark's, and he underscores a relational element behind those who brought the sick to Jesus. "All those who had any who were sick," rather than simply "they," are the subjects who usher the ill to Jesus. Also, where Matthew informed that Jesus drove out the demons with a word, Luke, in keeping with his theme of compassion, narrates that Jesus healed by laying his hands on every one of them. Luke reverses Matthew's emphasis on exorcism, first reporting how Jesus healed the sick (again, like Matthew, *all* of them), and only secondarily mentions the demon-possessed. At the conclusion of the text, though, Luke follows Mark much more closely than Matthew does, though he embellishes the story in two ways. Where Mark simply reports that Jesus did not allow the demons to speak

---

[85]B. Metzger, *Textual Commentary*, 75; V. Taylor, *Mark*, 181–82; C. E. B. Cranfield, *The Gospel According to St. Mark*, 88; C. S. Mann, *Mark*, 216.

[86]Two questions remain. First, "Why, then, did Luke modify his source?" Secondly, "Why did some scribes choose to assimilate their texts here but not elsewhere?" As noted in the previous chapter, assimilation was not a rigid practice among scribes. If it had been, the Synoptics would in at least some manuscripts bear much closer resemblance to one another than they do. Many examples of scribal assimilation demonstrate that copyists *were* aware of synoptic relationships and *could be* informed by parallel texts; but the lack of systematic effort suggests that, at least in some cases, some other motivation or factor may have been active in calling attention to harmonize the dissonance between parallel texts. It was in this regard that I suggested earlier (in the previous chapter) that in certain instances some scribes, in order to reconcile disputed facts or events among evangelists, appear to have acted under the influence of apologetic concerns.

because they knew him, Luke places words in the mouths of the *daimonia*; they exclaim, "You are the Son of God!" Some later scribes further garnished this declaration, inserting, "You are *the Christ*, the Son of God!" Finally, Luke supplements his exemplar's epilogue, changing Mark's ὅτι ᾔδεισαν αὐτόν ("because they knew *him*") by substituting for the objective pronoun the phrase, τὸν χριστὸν αὐτὸν εἶναι ("because they knew *him to be the Christ*"). Therefore, Luke clearly created from Mark the reading that eventually found its way back into some versions of Mark by way of scribal assimilation. Moreover, it seems obvious that his embellishment is designed to clarify precisely what it is these demons knew about Jesus. They knew him, not as one of them, but as the holy one sent from God.

To summarize this point, both Matthew and Luke were led to ornament this miracle story with an explanation, albeit a different one for each, related to Jesus performing acts of power. Matthew explained this activity in terms of prophetic fulfillment, while Luke defended his work on the basis of messianic identity. What each accomplished, though, was the displacement of the dangling demonic recognition of Jesus that could have been understood by outsiders or critics as tantamount to magic. The scribes who chose to assimilate Mark's ending to that of Luke produced a reading that reflected issues and strategies that run throughout the apologetic corpus. Of course, we cannot enter the minds of scribes; we know them only from their manuscripts. Whether these scribes simply parroted Luke or acted with an awareness of the calumnies of "magician" directed at Jesus is hard to know. What we can know is that the amended reading functions apologetically.

Another textual variant that reflects this concern with associating Jesus and demons occurs in Matthew 9:34. The variant reading consists of whether or not the entire verse, οἱ δὲ Φαρισαῖοι ἔλεγον· ἐν τῷ ἄρχοντι τῶν δαιμονίων ἐκβάλλει τὰ δαιμόνια, belonged to the "original" or was added later by a scribe. This verse concludes the Matthean version of a brief pericope belonging to the triple tradition in which Jesus heals a deaf mute by driving out the demon ostensibly responsible for the affliction. When Jesus effects the cure, almost without breaking stride, the "crowds" marvel, acclaiming, "Nothing like this has ever been seen in Israel." The verse in question, though, appears as a counterpoint to the crowds and reports that "the Pharisees" disputed Jesus' action by growling, "He casts out demons by the prince of demons."

Some few manuscripts (only D a k sy^s and Hilary of Poitiers [c. 315–367]) bear witness to this verse, while others either omit it or reflect its absence to be "original." Unfortunately, the matter is not clear-cut. Acknowledging their own difficulty with the verse and rating their decision with only a {C}, Metzger on behalf of the UBS^4 Committee reports their tenuous conclusion that the verse was more likely "original."[87] Along transcriptional lines, he joins several commentators in noting that the verse could have been added by scribes under the influence of assimilation to Matthew 12:24 or Luke 11:15. Intrinsically, though, he points out that the passage seems to be

---

[87] B. Metzger, *Textual Commentary*, 25–26.

required to prepare the reader for Matthew 10:25,[88] and in this estimation Davies and Allison concur.[89] Albright and Mann support the "originality" of the verse on the basis that it recapitulates a frequent Matthean theme: the sharp contrast in response to Jesus as seen in the welcome of the crowds over against the hostility of some corners of Judaism.[90] In addition, the slim external evidence that testifies to its exclusion heavily favors the longer reading.

If on this collective basis we may determine the verse to be "original," then the choice on the part of scribes to omit the verse may well be explained by apologetic interests. The substance of what they excised from their exemplar consists of material that was cited by pagan critics against Christians.

More evidence related to the charge of magic may be discerned in light of Samain's contention that identification of "imposter" was often related to that of a magician. Twice variant readings located in Luke serve to buttress the claim that Jesus was no charlatan and his resurrection was no sham. In its transmission of Luke 23:52, one Old Latin manuscript (c) carefully reports that Pilate received clear word that Jesus had expired, and that he even praised the Lord upon hearing the news.[91] Moreover, the offhand insinuation that the stone might have been easily discarded and Jesus' body stolen by his followers (an allegation anticipated by Matthew in his report of a Roman garrison stationed to prevent any tampering with the tomb) was thwarted to some extent by various scribal embellishments attached to Luke 23:53. Several witnesses (among them U f^{13} 700 bo) give testimony that scribes assimilated from the parallel texts in Matthew 27:60 and Mark 15:46 the report that a great stone was rolled in front of the door of the tomb.[92] In Codices Bezae (D) and Colbertinus (c), along with the Sahidic version, we peruse the additional detail that the stone was so large that twenty men could scarcely move it.[93] Remembering that Jesus' confederates are generally numbered at "twelve," this statement would have implied that even the full complement of his detachment would have fallen short of the number necessary to budge the boulder. Something else, something supernatural perhaps, would be required to move that stone.

In both of these cases, the scribal modifications serve apologetic interests. According to the scribes, when he was taken to the tomb Jesus was really dead; this was verified by Pilate himself. Also, when he was laid in the tomb, his final fate was

---

[88]Which reads, "It is enough for the disciple to be like his teacher, and the servant like his master. If they have called the master of the house Beelzebul, how much more will they malign those of his household."

[89]W. D. Davies and D. Allison, *Matthew II*, 139.

[90]W. F. Albright and C. S. Mann, *Matthew*, 112–113.

[91]The Latin of the 12th/13th century Codex Colbertinus (c) reads, "Pilatus autem cum audisset, quia expiravit, clarificavit dominium et donavit corpus Joseph." Though it is difficult to know, it is possible that the reading located in this manuscript reflects scribal input from a much earlier era.

[92]See IGNTP, *Luke*, Vol. II, 228–29, and B. Metzger, *Textual Commentary*, 182–3.

[93]B. Metzger, Textual Commentary, 182–3.

sealed with a stone so heavy it would require a score of able bodies to contend with it. Both of these reports stand in bold opposition to any possibility of deception or fraud, both of which Jesus was accused of and both of which were frequently associated with magic.

A MAN OF PROFANE TEMPERAMENT

For Greco-Roman ancients enamored with the four cardinal virtues (prudence, temperance, fortitude, and justice), anger scarcely befitted a god.[94] Such crude emotion was in the eyes of both critics and advocates of Christianity viewed as an unseemly and unsuitable characteristic to be associated with divinity. The Christian apologist Aristides described God as being void of ire, saying, "anger and wrath he possesses not...,"[95] and contrasted the Christian god with those of the Greeks, some of whom he characterized as "adulterers and murders, jealous and envious, and angry (ὀργίλους) and passionate, and murderers of fathers, and thieves and plunderers."[96] So Athenagoras, who, contrasting his God with that of the carnal lascivious deities portrayed in Greek myths, avowed, "...for in God there is neither anger (ὀργή) nor lust and desire...."[97] Tatian, too, assumed this posture, ridiculing those who would ascribe immortality to beings subject to base desires, laughter, and anger (ὀργιζόμενος), and challenging, "Why should I demonstrate piety toward gods who take bribes and grow angry (ὀργιζομένους) when they do not receive them?" In concert with these predecessors, Arnobius of Sicca, a Christian apologist writing in Latin in the late third century and prior to the Constantinian elevation of Christianity, found all base passions incompatible with the nature of divinity.[98] Celsus declared that God lacked the capacity of doing anything ignoble and that his right and just nature transcended base appetites and irregularities,[99] and he ridiculed the Christian scriptures for their incompatible depiction of a god boorish in his susceptibility to human passions and his proclivity for angry utterances.[100] Similarly, Celsus ridiculed Jesus for

---

[94]"Cardinal Virtues," in F. L. Cross and E. A. Livingstone, eds., *The Oxford Dictionary of the Christian Church* (London: Oxford University Press, 1974), 239. These cardinal virtues were first espoused by Plato and Aristotle, and later adopted and adapted by Christian theologians, especially Augustine and Aquinas. In contrast to these cardinal or moral virtues, they placed the theological virtues of faith, hope, and love.

[95]J. R. Harris, *The Apology of Aristides* (TS I, J. A. Robinson, ed.; Cambridge: Cambridge University Press, 1893), 36. Cf. Greek text, 100.

[96]J. R. Harris, *Apology of Aristides*, 40. Cf. Greek text, 104.

[97]*Leg.* 21.1.

[98]Arnobius of Sicca, *Adversus Nationes*, Book III. For a brief discussion of Arnobius see J. Quasten, *Patrology* (Vol 2; Utrecht-Antwerp and Westminster, Maryland: Spectrum and Newman Press, 1950), 383–392.

[99]*Cels.* V.14.

[100]*Cels.* IV.71.

what he termed his threats and empty abuse.[101] These charges were of sufficient concern to Origen that he devoted an entire chapter to explain that "the so-called wrath (ὀργή) of God and what is called His anger (θυμός) has a corrective purpose...."[102]

In sum, anger was, in the attitudes of genteel intellectuals of the second and third centuries, unsuited to the divine character. These sources testify that for many of the participants in the apologetic dialogues of the second and third centuries the association of base human emotions with the divine character—particularly negative ones such as lust and anger—struck a strident chord. A profane temperament was, at best, uncharacteristic of a deity or a holy man.

Evidence located in the scribal tradition reveals that certain copyists of the New Testament apparently found this collision of hot-headedness with holiness equally shrill. A quintessential example of this occurs in Mark 1:41, a text familiar to all textual scholars. Because the context is so critical for evaluating this reading, I reproduce here the entire pericope. The story of Jesus healing a leper in Mark 1:40–45 reads as follows:

40 Καὶ ἔρχεται πρὸς αὐτὸν λεπρὸς παρακαλῶν αὐτὸν [καὶ γονυπετῶν] καὶ λέγων αὐτῷ ὅτι ἐὰν θέλῃς δύνασαί με καθαρίσαι. 41 καὶ σπλαγχνισθεὶς [v.l. ὀργισθείς] ἐκτείνας τὴν χεῖρα αὐτοῦ ἥψατο καὶ λέγει αὐτῷ· θέλω καθαρίσθητι· 42 καὶ [εἴποντος αὐτοῦ] εὐθὺς ἀπῆλθεν ἀπ' αὐτοῦ ἡ λέπρα καὶ ἐκαθαρίσθη. 43 καὶ ἐμβριμησάμενος αὐτῷ εὐθὺς ἐξέβαλεν αὐτὸν] 44 καὶ λέγει αὐτῷ· ὅρα μηδενὶ μηδὲν εἴπῃς ἀλλὰ ὕπαγε σεαυτὸν δεῖξον τῷ ἱερεῖ καὶ προσένεγκε περὶ τοῦ καθαρισμοῦ σου ἃ προσέταξεν Μωϋσῆς εἰς μαρτύριον αὐτοῖς. 45 ὁ δὲ ἐξελθὼν ἤρξατο κηρύσσειν πολλὰ καὶ διαφημίζειν τὸν λόγον ὥστε μηκέτι αὐτὸν δύνασθαι φανερῶς εἰς πόλιν εἰσελθεῖν ἀλλ' ἔξω ἐπ' ἐρήμοις τόποις ἦν· καὶ ἤρχοντο πρὸς αὐτὸν πάντοθεν.

40 And a leper came to him beseeching him, and kneeling said to him, "If you will, you can make me clean." 41 Moved with pity, he stretched out his hand and touched him, and said to him, "I will; be clean." 42 And immediately the leprosy left him, and he was made clean. 43 And he sternly charged him, and sent him away at once, 44 and said to him, "See that you say nothing to any one; but go, show yourself to the priest, and offer for your cleansing what Moses commanded, for a proof to the people. 45 But he went out and began to talk freely about it, and to spread the news, so that Jesus could no longer openly enter a town, but was out in the country; and people came to him from every quarter.[103]

Although several noteworthy variants reside in this pericope, our present interest lies in the disparate traditions regarding the participles that describe Jesus' emotional

---

[101] *Cels.* II.76.

[102] *Cels.* IV.72.

[103] The Greek text and English translation are derived from N-A[27]. B. and K. Aland, et al., eds., *Greek-English New Testament* (Stuttgart: Deutsche Bibelgesellschaft, 1994), 91–92.

condition when he healed this desperate petitioner. Jesus is portrayed at seemingly polar extremes on the emotional continuum. The vast majority of manuscripts, among them the strongest representatives of the Alexandrian, Caesarean, and Majority text-types, report innocuously enough that, when he was encountered by the pleading leper, Jesus was "moved with pity" (σπλαγχνισθείς), and so reached out, touched, and cleansed him. Against these witnesses, however, the best regarded witnesses of the "Western" tradition—among them Codex Bezae (D) and several Old Latin manuscripts—enigmatically attest that Jesus reacted to the leper's approach with anger (ὀργισθείς).

Scholars have remained divided in their evaluation of this variant reading in Mark 1:41. Mainly on the grounds of the preponderance of corroborating external evidence, the UBS[4] Committee determined the former reading to be "original," although they attached to their verdict only a {D} rating. An increasing number of scholars, though, favor ὀργισθείς as the product of the author. Some do so on the belief that ὀργισθείς is the more difficult reading (*difficilior lectio potior*), though even this opinion is not universally held. Exegetes have noted that the verbs that follow in Mark 1:43 more nearly correspond to anger than compassion.[104] In view of verse 43, then, σπλαγχνισθείς can be construed as the more difficult reading. Holders of this position offer the transcriptional argument that scribes substituted ὀργισθείς for σπλαγχνισθείς in order to lend stylistic consistency to the tone of the story.

Recent appeal to insights gleaned from synoptic comparison, however, have suggested a shift in the weight of external evidence.[105] While it is widely acknowledged that the particular confluence of sources represented by this specific constellation of "Western" witnesses represents text traceable to the second century, a further pair of witnesses offers testimony that enables this reading to trace its lineage back even a century earlier![106] It is almost universally recognized that Matthew and Luke used Mark as a source. Thus, pericopes of the triple tradition may be evaluated in such a way as to shed light on the original text of Mark's gospel. Illustrating this principle in his evaluation of this text, J. K. Elliott calls attention to the synoptic parallels of the healing of the leper, and notes with accuracy that the writers of both Matthew and

---

[104]The verbs are ἐμβριμησάμενος, meaning literally "to snort," and usually translated "rebuking" or "sternly warning," and ἐξέβαλεν, a term usually associated with casting out demons, but here generally read "sent away."

[105]For the substance of the following argument I am indebted chiefly to Bart D. Ehrman, "The Text of the Gospels at the End of the Second Century," in *Codex Bezae: Studies from the Lunel Colloquium, June 1994*, edited by D. C. Parker and C.-B. Amphoux (Leiden: E. J. Brill, 1996), 118–120.

[106]The recognition that Matthew and Luke as redactors of Mark inform the textual problems of Mark 1:41 has been observed at least as early as V. Taylor, 187, and, more recently, in Bart Ehrman, "The Text of the Gospels at the End of the Second Century," 119, and J. K. Elliott, "An Eclectic Textual Commentary on the Greek Text of Mark's Gospel," *New Testament Textual Criticism: Its Significance for Exegesis*, edited by Eldon J. Epp and Gordon D. Fee (Oxford: Clarendon Press, 1981), 52–3.

Luke omit the adverbial participle altogether, so that any remnant of emotion on the part of Mark's Jesus, whether anger or compassion, is omitted.[107]

Moreover, as we extend this approach across the entire triple tradition, we discover an informing pattern in how the synoptic redactors of Mark transmit episodes of Jesus exhibiting "anger" or "compassion." Like the number of apologists cited above, they betray a reluctance to ascribe anger to Jesus. As reported by Metzger himself, Mark portrays Jesus being angry or indignant two other times in his gospel, at 3:5 in the account of healing the man with the withered hand, and 10:14, the narrative of the blessing of the children. In the healing narrative, Jesus peers at the Pharisees and Herodians with anger for their hardness of heart, and in the incident involving the children, he grows indignant with his disciples when they attempt to deter children who seek to draw near to him. Comparison of the synoptic parallels (Mk 3:5=Mt 12:13, Lk 6:10; Mk 10:14=Mt 19:14, Lk 18:15) to these two episodes, however, reveals that in each instance Matthew and Luke delete any indication that negative emotion was displayed by Jesus.

On the other hand, apart from the text currently under consideration, Mark employs some form of the verb σπλαγχνίζομαι three times (Mark 6:34=Mt 14:14, Lk 9:11; Mk 8:2=Mt 15:32, no Lucan parallel; and Mk 9:22). The first use occurs in an episode of the triple tradition, the feeding of the five thousand. Matthew follows Mark verbatim in reporting that Jesus, upon seeing the crowd, "had compassion" (ἐσπλαγχνίσθη) on them. Luke, as is often the case, is more liberal in his use of Mark, and does not employ the term, but he does substitute for it a word that conveys a positive emotional state: ἐποδεξάμενος, "he welcomed them." The second use of the term σπλαγχνίζομαι occurs in the narrative of the feeding of the four thousand, which Matthew copies from Mark but Luke omits. As he did in reporting the previous feeding miracle, Matthew follows Mark word for word, repeating his use of σπλαγχνίζομαι. Mark's third use of the verb occurs in his report of Jesus healing the epileptic, and although neither Matthew nor Luke employ the term in their accounts, it should be noted that they so abbreviate this story that there is no verse that could rightly be considered a parallel to the one in which σπλαγχνισθείς occurs. Other examples do occur in Matthew and Luke, however, where Jesus displays compassion in the context of a healing incident (Mt 20:34, Lk 7:13).

From this survey of the synoptic parallels to Markan depictions of Jesus as either "angry" or "compassionate" there emerges a generally consistent pattern. On the one hand, at no time does either Matthew or Luke hesitate to describe Jesus as "compassionate," and Matthew, moreover, in two instances follows verbatim Mark's use of σπλαγχνίζομαι. On the other hand, never does either Matthew or Luke carry over into their texts from Mark the vocabulary of Jesus exhibiting anger or indignation. This demonstrates that these earliest "copyists" of Mark's Gospel willingly reproduced his characterizations of Jesus as compassionate, but intentionally stifled any report of him as angry.

---

[107]J. K. Elliott, "An Eclectic Textual Commentary," 52–3.

The implications of these results for determining the "original" reading of Mark 1:1 are clear. If, as seems likely, the evangelists had remained consistent to their pattern in treating this verse, if Matthew and Luke had found σπλαγχνισθείς in their exemplar at this point, they would have simply copied it. Yet, if they had come upon the reading ὀργισθείς they almost certainly would have deleted it. The synoptic parallels to Mark 1:41 omit the participle in question. It seems reasonable to conclude, then, that the first century text of Mark to which the authors of Matthew and Luke had access included the reading ὀργισθείς.

These fresh observations demand a radical reappraisal of the relative merits of the external evidence pertaining to Mark 1:41. Although the quality and quantity of the manuscript support for reading σπλαγχνισθείς remains formidable, the testimony of the significant combination of "Western" witnesses in concert with the augmenting evidence unearthed from synoptic investigation offers documentation that ὀργισθείς bears a literary legacy of great antiquity, and may well have issued from the stylus of Mark. Some will undoubtedly find this treatment of the external evidence compelling enough on its own merits to support ὀργισθείς as the preferred reading. Even those who remain unconvinced, however, must recognize that a final verdict on this text should not be rendered on the basis of external evidence alone.

Transcriptional consideration of this reading confirms this conclusion. Metzger himself concedes that it is easier to see why scribes would have moved from anger to compassion than to account for a change in the opposite direction.[108] It is this very concession, however, that a number of scholars find to be compelling reason for adopting ὀργισθείς as the variant which best represents the autograph. Vincent Taylor summarizes the sentiments of this contingent when he says, "It is easy to see why 'being angry' was changed to 'being filled with compassion,' but not easy to account for the alteration *vice versa.*"[109] Although I agree with this conclusion, it should be noted that seldom has any hard evidence been adduced to support it.

One notable exception to this appears in the previously referenced essay by Bart Ehrman, in which he examines the correspondence between textual variants located in Codex Bezae and second century scribal concerns related to the proto-orthodox cause: christological controversies, an evolving Christian anti-semitism, the ecclesiastical suppression of women, the impulse toward asceticism, and Christian apologetics. Ehrman reviews the textual problems of Mark 1:41 informed by this last category, reporting how the proposed mollification of the reading from "anger" to "compassion" corresponds to the apologetic impulse represented by the literary defenders of the faith.[110]

---

[108]B. M. Metzger, *Textual Commentary,* 76.
[109]V. Taylor, 187. For a sampler of other scholars favoring this reading see footnote 3.
[110]B. Ehrman, "Text of the Gospels," 120.

Although recently scholars have begun to adopt the stance represented here by V. Taylor and B. Ehrman, the argument has continued to lack the compelling force of being sufficiently grounded in the apologetic tradition. As stated earlier, too often transcriptional judgments have been rendered on the convictions of common sense rather than on the basis of hard evidence from the primary literature. Yet, as is noted above, this lacuna is unnecessary. The pagan critic Celsus as well as the defenders of the faith, Aristides, Athenagoras, and Arnobius articulate in their writings an evident reluctance to characterize deities or divine persons as angry. Thus, at least some second and third intellectuals were unwilling to let stand the juxtaposition of hostility and holiness. It is on this foundation, then, that textual critics can confidently erect the transcriptional argument that scribes conscientiously attuned to apologetic interests supplanted "anger" with "compassion." In this subtle but bold alteration of Mark 1:41, scribes produced a text that proclaimed a "kinder, gentler Jesus."

In summary, the aforementioned sketch of the censures of Celsus and Origen's pious replies embodies the dynamics of the Pagan-Christian polemic as it played out in the second and third centuries of the common era.[111] This, of course, was both the heyday of Christian apologetic and the period in which the consensus of New Testament textual scholars maintain that the majority of textual variants found their way into the tradition. Clearly the character of Jesus was at stake, and persons interested in defending the faith from frontal assault were becoming increasingly aware that pagans were searching out their own scriptures for ammunition to use against them. Despite the generally conservative practice of the manual duplication of sacred texts, it does not stress reason to conceive of an apologetically-sensitive scribe imbuing his manuscript with an occasional subtle modification, or mollification, which thus buttressed the sacred writings from being exploited by the opposition. The evidence for reading ὀργισθείς as "original" has been reported, and is in my judgment compelling. Moreover, this conception of apologetic motivation offers a plausible, historically-rooted transcriptional rationale for why a scribe might have—indeed, likely would have—altered ὀργισθείς to σπλαγχνισθείς.

This interest in portraying Jesus as benevolent rather than uncharitable, responsive rather than abrupt, and peaceful rather than violent appears to have been at work in several other variants, as well. The question of whether or not Matthew 21:44 should be numbered among them depends mainly on whether one determines the verse to be a product of the author or the interpolation of a copyist. The textual dispute involves the entire verse, which reads:

---

[111]For a more thoroughgoing treatment of the pagan critique of Christianity during this period, see Stephen Benko, "Pagan Criticism of Christianity During the First Two Centuries A.D.," *ANRW* II.23.2, 1055–1118. A useful summary addressed to wider audiences may be found in Robert L. Wilken, *The Christians as the Romans Saw Them* (New Haven: Yale University Press, 1984).

καὶ ὁ πεσὼν ἐπὶ τὸν λίθον τοῦτον συνθλασθήσεται· ἐφ᾽ ὃν δ᾽ ἂν πέσῃ λικμήσει αὐτόν.

And he who trips over this stone will be broken to pieces; and upon whomever it might fall, it will crush him.

Grading their judgment with only a {C} rating, the UBS[4] committee determined that the reading did not represent the author's handiwork but found its way into the Matthean narrative by way of assimilation to Luke 20:18. B. Metzger on behalf of the committee reports, on the other hand, that the words of this verse are not identical with those of Luke, and he surmises that, if inserted, they would have been better placed after the quote of Psalm 118 in 21:42 (as the Lukan text does). He also grants that mechanical error could easily explain the omission.[112] Taking the other side of the debate, Albright and Mann attribute the verse to Matthean authorship, treating it as an emphatic extension of the theme of this section—Israel's rejection of Jesus. Most manuscripts, in fact, do report the verse (א B C L W Z (Θ) 0102 *f*[1.13] Maj lat sy[c.p.h] co), while it is mainly "Western" witnesses (D it sy[s]) along with 33, Origen, and Syriac Eusebius that testify to its absence (or omission). Neither is it found in Irenaeus or Tatian's *Diatessaron*. While numbers favor the reading, the quality of those that express either no knowledge or deliberate excision of the reading deserves attention. It is fair to say that the external evidence is divided, with strong attestors on each side of the debate.

Examining the text from the perspective of intrinsic probabilities provides a slightly improved perspective on the matter. The text appears shortly following the account of Jesus cleansing the temple, and at the end of the second of a trio of parables: two sons asked to work in the vineyard, the tenant farmers who slay the heir, and the king who issued invitations for a wedding feast. The writer of Matthew connects the telling of the second parable with a powerful image from Psalm 118:22–23, the rejected rock that becomes the head of the corner, and concludes it with the fateful words, "When the chief priests and Pharisees heard his parables they realized he was speaking about them, but when they tried to arrest him, they feared the crowds, because they regarded him as a prophet." Albright and Mann regard this conjunction of parables as the watershed point in the Gospel. From this point on, discussion with Jesus is over, and the energy of his antagonists is directed toward entrapping, arresting, and destroying him. Pursuing this line of thought, it does not seem far afield to say that this rhetoric of violence complements the content of Matthew's narrative, and could well have rested in the "original" text. The likelihood that this is so is increased by the recognition that the violent imagery here appears to echo Daniel 2:34, 44 and Isaiah 8:14–15, 28:16. Since allusions to Daniel and Isaiah are frequent in Matthew, this fact increases the intrinsic probabilities in favor of the

---

[112]B. M. Metzger, *Textual Commentary*, 58.

"originality" of the verse.[113] Krister Stendahl adduces the possible influence of parallelism with Luke, but also advances the notion that Matthew was familiar with the tradition of testimonies that evolved into a more elaborate form in 1 Peter 2:7 and Romans 9:33.[114] Attribution of verse 44 to the writer of Matthew is also argued by S. G. F. Brandon.[115] Such testimony related to the intrinsic probabilities surrounding Matthew 21:44 may not prove conclusive, but they are enough to lead us to measure this dispute according to the third canon of criticism, that of transcriptional probabilities.

Here the question is whether a scribe is more likely to have added or deleted the verse. Considering the first option of scribal interpolation, the obvious suggestion is that a copyist assimilated the text of Matthew to that of Luke 20:18; but this has already been brought into question. Against this thesis is the fact that neither precise wording nor parallel location is in effect here. In Luke, the verse follows directly the quote of Psalm 118; the placement in Matthew removes it slightly. Certainly scribes could have assimilated from memory and not direct citation, which would therefore explain the slight difference in wording; but the matter of placement would remain. The theory that "original" Matthew did not include the verse but found its way into the tradition by way of scribal assimilation to Luke seems circuitous in comparison with the supposition that Matthew originally included 21:44 and that later scribes either

---

[113]For a compilation and treatment of some of the allusions to Daniel employed by the author of Matthew, see Robert Horton Gundry, *The Use of the Old Testament in St. Matthew's Gospel* (NovTSup XVIII; Leiden: E. J. Brill, 1967), *passim*, e.g., 207. Gundry believes the text issued from Matthew on the basis of the consistent messianic implications inherent in this verse and Daniel 7:13. He writes on p. 233, "Since Daniel 7 presents a Messianic figure as receiving the eschatological kingdom, it is only natural that we should see Messianic significance in the stone which smites the image in Dan 2 and becomes the kingdom of God (Mt 21:44)." For discussion of this verse in relation to the Isaiah texts, see Krister Stendahl, *The School of St. Matthew and Its Use of the Old Testament* (1st American ed.; Philadelphia: Fortress, 1968), 67–69.

[114]K. Stendahl, *The School of St. Matthew*, 68.

[115]S. G. F. Brandon, *The Fall of Jerusalem and the Christian Church* (London, 1951), 244 f.

accidentally or purposefully omitted it.[116] Applied here, Ockham's razor would support the "originality" of the verse.

If then, to begin at the opposite shore, the verse is considered "original," what are we to make of its omission? Metzger, it has already been noted, entertained the possibility of mechanical error. Perhaps here, though, a strong case can be made for the motivation of apologetic interests. In keeping with the descriptions and citations related above, copyists attuned to the theme of violence in apologetic-pagan discourse would have possessed ample reason to expunge this entire verse from their exemplars. It is noteworthy, in this regard, that included among those sources that would therefore bear witness to the deliberate excision of this violent verse would be the apologists Origen, Tatian (*Diatessaron*), and Eusebius (syr).[117]

In keeping with this theme but in a slightly different vein, variation in the manuscript tradition of Matthew 15:26 alters Jesus' reply to the Cananite woman of Tyre who pleads for help on behalf of her demon-possessed daughter. Some manuscripts report Jesus saying, "It *is* not *good/right* (ἔστιν καλὸν) to take bread from children and give it to the dogs," while others (D, it, sy^{s,c}) transmit the verse as, "It *is* not *lawful* (ἔξεστιν)...." This is also the reading known to the apologist Origen.

Determining the direction of this subtle shift is difficult. The judgment of the UBS[4] Committee in favor of the majority reading earned from themselves only a {C} rating. The antiquity of the "Western" witnesses that report the latter reading, along with the transcriptional argument that copyists may have recast the verse under the influence of Mark 7:27, constitute reasonable cause for favoring ἔξεστιν as "original." On the other hand, as the editors of UBS[4] contend, it appears more plausible that ἔξεστιν was introduced into the text to reinforce Jesus' reply, recasting it from rhetoric about what is morally fitting to what is lawful or permitted by social constraint.[118]

---

[116]For an extreme example of such a circuitous argument in favor of the interpolation of Matthew 21:44, see Willoughby C. Allen, *The Gospel According to St. Matthew* (ICC XXVI; New York: Charles Scribner's Sons, 1925), 232–33. Allen explains that Matthew 21:44 is best understood as an early editorial gloss. He argues that it is unlikely that the writer himself would have included verse 44, since it would carry the thought of the reader back to verse 42 and draw attention away from the writer's interpretation of the quotation from Psalms (21:42) in terms of verse 43. Allen then posits that a later copyist was reminded by the vocabulary of verse 43 of Daniel 2:44–45, which formed for him the nucleus of an explanatory gloss. Thus he argues that the textual history of 21:44 does not issue from efforts to assimilate the text to Luke 20:18, but to embellish Matthew 21:43. His conclusion, however, then makes it necessary for Allen to explain the development of Luke 20:18. He does so by arguing that the gloss found its way into Matthew early enough that it may have been read as part of Matthew by the author of the third Gospel. Finally, he ventures that there is no reason the same editor could not have added the gloss to both Matthew and Luke.

[117]Compare also the manuscripts here that favor the apologetic reading with those, e.g., in Mark 3:21 and Mark 6:3 below.

[118]B. Metzger, *Textual Commentary*, 40.

This admittedly conjectural supposition gains some reasoned momentum when it is coupled with the recognition that there appears to be no particular Roman law to which Jesus is referring. Since it does not appear to be Hebrew law (Torah) that is being referenced here, some other antecedent is called for. In this context, it does not seem unreasonable to suggest that this reference was directed to no specific law, but rather to the acceptable habits of well-mannered society. there were simply some things that, by well-bred citizens were not done. Read this way, the altered vocabulary would have functioned to introduce into the verse the theme of adherence to cultural norms and the notion of being law-abiding. The modified reading, then, would have imbued the text with the implication that Jesus was in some since deferential to the customs of the society around him and, in fact, did not view it as his mission to oppose the habits and attitudes associated with the customs of the land. This implication would, in turn, fit precisely within the contours of the apologetic motif that Christ and his followers were good, law-abiding citizens of the empire, and that they were totally without interest in overthrowing earthly power structures or directing irreverence at the prescribed dignities of Greco-Roman society.

Generally speaking, Greek intellectuals preferred gods that were rational, not emotional.[119] We can see this in the *Apology* of Aristides, where—in his effort to sharpen the distinction between the Christian god from the anthropomorphic deities of Greek myths—he reports, "And they say that some of them were lame and maimed; and some were wizards, and some utterly mad."[120] Aristides was therefore attempting to contrast his god with those mythologically deposed to be physically imperfect, magicians, or insane. Of course, each of these charges was leveled against Jesus by Celsus, who reported that he was ugly, performed miracles by means of necromancy, and was quite mad. Trypho directed this same charge against Justin when he says, "I wish you knew that you were *beside yourself*, talking like this...."[121]

The perception that Jesus was mad is reported in Mark 3:21. Variation in the text arises, interestingly enough, not on the matter of whether he was perceived so, but who it was that deemed him "mad." Scholars do not dispute the "original" text here. Clearly it reads, "And when his friends/ his relatives (literally, οἱ παρ αὐτοῦ) heard about him, they came out to seize him; for they said that he was mad (literally, 'beside himself,' ἐξέστη)." In an altered rendering of the verse, however, key representatives

---

[119]In contrast with the bulk of the populace who identified more easily with the anthropomorphic gods depicted in the epic poetry of Homer and Hesiod, Greek and Roman intellectuals gravitated toward the singular, transcendent, incorporeal deity that issued from Platonic philosophy. It was precisely this evolving philosophical monotheism that represented the central point of contact between Greco-Roman thinkers and the Christian apologists. Like their philosophical counterparts, defenders of the faith described their God in the language of negative theology. While it was difficult for mortal beings to express with precision what God was, it was easier to say what God was not. So, the deity was depicted as invisible, without rival, incapable of evil, unknowable.

[120]Aristides, *Ap.* VIII, cited from J. R. Harris, *Apology of Aristides*, 40. Greek text, 104.
[121]*Dial.* 39.

of the "Western" text (D W it) transmit a different subject. No longer is it οἱ παρ' αὐτοῦ who perceive him to be "beside himself," but "the scribes and the others around him" (περὶ αὐτοῦ οἱ γράμματεις καὶ οἱ λόποι) who regard him as such and therefore seek his capture.

The apologetic significance of this modification seems evident. In Metzger's words, the change is the result of the embarrassment to which this text lent itself. For Jesus' own friends or relatives to perceive him as "mad" would either lend suspicion to Jesus or make his associates look bad. On the other hand, attribution of this charge to his enemies would merely add more fuel to the fire that the opponents of Jesus contrived accusations against him.

CONCLUSION

The variant readings collected and explored in this chapter once again support the observation that some scribes were not merely unthinking transmitters of the texts placed in front of them. Beyond the changes that found their way into manuscripts by means of mechanical error, weariness, and accident were some modifications that appear best explained as deliberate alterations imposed by the purposeful actions of apologetically-minded scribes. Giving attention to the textual variants adduced in this chapter, the student of the scriptures will recognize modifications that can be classified accurately, in terms of activity, as deliberate, and, in terms of motivation, as apologetic. In the course of defending their text, their faith, and their Lord against pagan assault the scribes engaged in what I have termed "scribal apologetics." In so doing, they repaired and renovated the Gospel handed down to them, making it to pagan readers and critics more palatable, on the one hand, and more resistant to challenge, on the other.

It is with adequate reason, then, that scribes may be thought of as more than merely transmitters of an inherited textual tradition, but, at least on occasion, as themselves apologists and even evangelists. In the Gospel according to the Scribes, Jesus was portrayed emphatically as a person of reverence and not a revolutionary, a man of sacred disposition and not a sorcerer, and as a person whose temperament was most readily characterized not by extreme passions but sublime compassion.

4

FANATICS, FOOLS, AND FEMALES:
SCRIBES IN DEFENSE OF THE
FOLLOWERS OF JESUS

In addition to their efforts to impugn the character of Jesus, opponents of Christianity were unrestrained in their attempts to vilify his followers.[1] With conspicuous contempt, Greco-Roman intellectuals penned harsh historical assessments, teasing parodies, and scathing polemics that portrayed adherents of the Jesus movement as persons possessed of a blatant disregard for the law and for the public commonwealth, and characterized by their deficiencies of morality, class, intellect, and good humor. Practicing Christians were described variously as ethical libertines, sexual profligates, gullible fools, plyers of the magical arts, social miscreants, and political revolutionaries. Rumors ran rampant that in their secret gatherings they gave license to unspeakable acts of debauchery, infanticide, and cannibalism, and this calumny found its way into the published treatises of pagan antagonists. Female believers were expressly targeted as unreliable witnesses, possessed, fanatical, sexual libertines, domineering of or rebellious toward their husbands, and, in the familiar rhetoric of Celsus, "hysterical."[2]

The earliest extant pagan appraisals of adherents of the Christian movement took the form of blanket condemnations and sweeping dismissals. In his correspondence with Trajan, Pliny (62–113 C.E.) notified his emperor that his interrogations, which had featured the torture of two deaconesses, had uncovered nothing more than "a depraved and excessive superstition." In fact, his description of Christian assemblies sounds benign, if not laudatory.

---

[1] The literature on this subject constitutes an imposing corpus. The classic introduction remains P. Labriolle, *La Réaction païenne* (Paris: L'Artisans du Livre, 1948), while S. Benko, "Pagan Criticism of Christianity During the First Two Centuries A. D.," *ANRW* II.23.2 (Berlin: Walter de Gruyter, 1980), 1055–1118 has become a standard introduction in English. For other useful and informative overviews see idem, *Pagan Rome and Early Christians* (Bloomington, IN: Indiana University Press, 1984); Robert L. Wilken, *The Christians as the Romans Saw Them* (New Haven, CT: Yale University Press, 1984); and, most recently, Jeffrey W. Hargis, *Against the Christians: The Rise of Early Anti-Christian Polemic* (New York: Peter Lang, 1999) and many of the essays in Mark Edwards, Martin Goodman, and Simon Price, eds. *Apologetics in the Roman Empire: Pagans, Jews, and Christians* (Oxford: Oxford University Press, 1999).

[2] *Cels.* II.55.

They all asserted that all of their guilt and error was that they used to come together on a certain day before daylight to sing a song with responses to Christ as a god, to bind themselves mutually by a solemn oath, not to commit any crime, but to avoid theft, robbery, adultery, not to break a trust or deny a deposit when they are called for it. After these practices it was their custom to separate and then come together again to take food but an ordinary and harmless kind, and they even gave up this practice after my edict, when, in response to your order, I forbade associations.[3]

Still, Pliny was uncompromising in his condemnation of the sect. Even as he inquired as to whether punishment should be instituted simply on account of the name or was due because of crimes associated with the name, he did not hesitate to execute judgment.[4] Thus he informed Trajan:

In the meantime, I followed this method with those who were accused before me as Christians. I asked them whether they were Christians. Those who confessed I asked again and a third time, warning them of capital punishment; those who persevered I commanded to be led off to execution, for I had no doubt that whatever it were they believe in, stubbornness and inflexible obstinacy should be punished.[5]

This marked disdain for the *pertinacia et inflexibilis obstinatio* of the Christians would find voice again later in the writings of Marcus Aurelius (reigned 161–180 C.E.).[6] In discussing the honorable way to face death, the Stoic emperor contrasted "the reasoned and dignified decision" of a philosopher with the "obstinate opposition" associated with the martyrdom of Christians. The Roman historians Tacitus (55–117 C.E.) and Suetonius (70–160 C.E.) both labeled Christianity a *superstitio*, and both were aware that blame was placed upon the Christians for torching Rome during the reign of Nero.[7] Although Tacitus expressed awareness that it was in fact Nero who heaped the responsibility upon them in order to derail suspicion of his own culpability, he offered no sympathy for the scapegoat Christians. Instead he implied that, despite their

---

[3] Pliny, *Letters* 10.96. The translation is that of S. Benko, "Pagan Criticism of Christianity," 1069.

[4] Historians continue to puzzle over this question of why Christians were persecuted. Was it on account of the name alone, or the perceived obstinance associated with Christian exclusivity? Or were crimes (*flagitia*) so directly associated with the name that to confess the faith was to confess to a crime? The nuances of the discussion are represented well by the classic debate that ensued between A. N. Sherwin-White and G. E. M. de Ste. Croix. For references and a fuller discussion of this question see the next chapter.

[5] Pliny, *Letters* 10.96. The translation is that of S. Benko, "Pagan Criticism of Christianity," 1068.

[6] *Med.* 11.3.

[7] Tacitus, *Annals*, 15.44. Suetonius, *Nero* 16.2. See also the discussion of S. Benko, "Pagan Criticism of Christianity," 1056–1068.

innocence regarding the fire, they were deserving of arrest due to their hatred of the human race (*odium humani generis*).[8]

Among the surviving writings of Lucian of Samosata (115–200 C.E.), moving to a source of a different genre, is a satire whose subject—a cynic philosopher who ultimately ended his life in a flamboyant, fiery suicide during the Olympic Games of 165 C.E.—affiliated for a while with a Christian community. Though *Death of Peregrinus* is satirical in both form and content, between the jabs and jest Lucian provides us with some historically significant insights regarding pagan perceptions of Christians and their behaviors. Lucian's narrative, it should be noted, is less biography than drama, and seeks, not so much to criticize Christianity, as to ridicule those who are self-aggrandizing. Still, it effectively delivers insights into how second-century Romans regarded contemporary Christians.[9]

Early in Lucian's tale, Peregrinus, the pretentious son of a wealthy man, grew impatient for his inheritance and strangled his father. When the townspeople raised suspicions about the matter, Peregrinus banished himself, taking to the road and constantly moving from place to place. At this point in the narrative, Lucian recounts:

> During this period he apprenticed himself to the priests and scribes of the Christians in Palestine and became an expert in that astonishing religion they have. Naturally, in no time at all, he had them looking like babies and had become their prophet,

---

[8]Similar labels were pinned on Jews during the same time period, which serves as a reminder that during these early years of the Jesus movement, pagans recognized little distinction between Jews and Christians. See, e.g., the discussion of S. Benko, "Pagan Criticism of Christianity," 1056–1065. Benko points out that the *odium humani generis* Tacitus associates with Christians in his *Annals* (15.44) very closely approximates the phrase he uses to describe Jews in his *Histories* 5.5: *Apud ipsos, fides obstinata, misericordia in promptu, sed adversus omnes alios, hostile odium.* Elsewhere in the *Histories* he says of them, "Jews regard as profane all that we hold sacred; on the other hand, they permit all that we abhor" (*Hist.* 5.4; LCL, 178–9) In addition, Diodorus Siculus reports "hatred of mankind" as the most serious charge directed against the Jews, and Josephus in *Against Apion* 2.145–150 labors to defend Jews against the related accusations of atheism and misanthropy. John G. Gager in *The Origins of Anti-Semitism: Attitudes Toward Judaism in Pagan and Christian Antiquity* (New York and Oxford: Oxford University Press, 1983), 56–66, also provides a helpful discussion of why Jews were labeled as or for hatred of the human race. He avers that the spiteful attitude of Romans toward Jews that initially took the form of satire evolved into antagonism as a result of the Jewish War (66–73 C.E.) and the success of Jewish proselytism. Whether Rome issued a condescending glance, tempered tolerance, or volatile antagonism, they did so for selfish interests. Gager emphasizes, especially, the negative response of Roman intellectuals, the evidence for which may be found in Cicero (*Pro Flaccus*, 28.69), Petronicus (*Satyricon*, 68.8), and Seneca (preserved in Augustine, *City of God*, 6.11).

[9]For validation of this claim and additional insight into Lucian's perception and literary treatment of early Christians, see P. Labriolle, *La Réaction païenne*, 97–108; S. Benko, "Pagan Criticism of Christianity," 1093–97; idem, *Pagan Rome and Early Christians*, 30–53; and R. Wilken, *Christians as the Romans Saw Them.*

leader, Head of the Synagogue, and what not all by himself. He expounded and commented on their sacred writings and even authored a number himself. They looked up to him as a god, made him their lawgiver, and put his name down as the official patron of the sect, or at least vice-patron, second to that man they still worship today, the one who was crucified in Palestine because he brought this new cult into being.

Well, Proteus was arrested for being a Christian and thrown into jail, an event which set him up for his future career: now he had standing, a magic aura, and the public notice he was so passionately in love with. Once he was behind bars, the Christians, who considered this a catastrophe, moved heaven and earth to get him free. When this proved to be impossible they went all out to do everything else they could for him. From the crack of dawn on you could see gray-haired widows and orphan children hanging around the prison, and the bigwigs of the sect used to bribe the jailers so they could spend the night with him inside. Full course dinners were brought to him, their holy scriptures read to him and our excellent Peregrinus—he was still under that name at the time—was hailed as a latter-day Socrates. From as far away as Asia Minor, Christian communities sent committees, paying their expenses out of common funds, to help him with advice and consolation....

And so, because Peregrinus was in jail, money poured in from them; he picked up a very nice income this way. You see, for one thing, the poor devils have convinced themselves they are all going to be immortal and live forever, which makes most of them take death lightly and voluntarily give themselves up to it. For another, that first lawgiver of theirs persuaded them that they are all brothers the minute they deny the Greek gods (thereby breaking our law) and take to worshiping him, the crucified sophist himself, and to living their lives according to his rules. They scorn all possessions without distinction and treat them as community property; doctrines like this they accept strictly on faith. Consequently, if a professional sharper who knows how to capitalize on a situation gets among them, he makes himself a millionaire overnight, laughing up his sleeve at the simpletons.[10]

Reading Lucian as indicative of attitudes held by many of his intellectual contemporaries, this lengthy citation greatly informs our understanding of how at least some Roman intellectuals regarded Christians. Certainly, Lucian's individual bias comes through loud and clear. He perceived Christians to be unsophisticated and gullible, weak-minded simpletons who, more than figuratively, cast their pearls (their money, to be sure) before swine and who worshiped a "crucified sophist." Moreover, he painted them as a group whose most representative members were "gray-haired widows" and "orphan children," both of which were categories of persons who stood outside the *paterfamilias* so highly celebrated by Romans. Even those members of the cult who were viewed as persons of means are portrayed herein as fools who will soon be parted from their money. The "bigwigs of the sect," as he calls them, come across as impulsive, even whimsical, as they bribe guards for privilege of sleeping inside the

---

[10]Lucian, *Death of Peregrinus*, 11–13. The translation is that of Lionel Casson, *Selected Satires of Lucian* (New York: Norton, 1968), 368–9.

cell with Peregrinus. Lucian's satire, therefore, leaves the impression that Christians are not so much generous as they are gullible, and not so much faithful as they are foolish.

If Lucian, for the sake of comparison, may be described as painting his portrait with impressionistic strokes, those of Marcus Cornelius Fronto (100–166 C.E.) must be said to have issued from the school of stark realism. Incorporated into the *Octavius* of Minucius Felix is an extended critique presented by the author's literary antagonist, the pagan Caecilius. In it he refers to the report of "his friend from Cirta," a probable reference to Fronto, reportedly one of the foremost rhetoricians of his day. Its indicative and comprehensive summary of the standard slanders and graphic rumors directed against Christians once again merits quoting the passage at length.

> Already—for ill weeds grow apace—decay of morals grows from day to day, and throughout the wide world the abominations of this impious confederacy multiply. Root and branch it must be exterminated and accursed. They recognize one another by secret signs and marks; they fall in love almost before they are acquainted; everywhere they introduce a kind of religion of lust, a promiscuous 'brotherhood' and 'sisterhood' by which ordinary fornication, under cover of a hallowed name, is converted to incest. And thus their vain and foolish superstition makes an actual boast of crime. For themselves, were there not some foundation of truth, shrewd rumour would not impute gross and unmentionable forms of vice. I am told that under some idiotic impulse they consecrate and worship the head of an ass, the meanest of all beasts, a religion worthy of the morals which gave it birth. Others say they actually reverence the private parts of their director and high priest, and adore his organs as parent of their being. This may be false, but such suspicions naturally attach to their secret and nocturnal rites. To say that a malefactor put to death for his crimes, and wood of the death-dealing cross, are objects of their veneration is to assign fitting altars to abandoned wretches and the kind of worship they deserve.... Their form of feasting is notorious; it is in everyone's mouth, as testified by the speech of our friend of Cirta. On the day appointed they gather at a banquet with all their children, sisters, and mothers, people of either sex and every age. There, after full feasting, when the blood is heated and drink has inflamed the passions of incestuous lust, a dog which has been tied to a lamp is tempted by a morsel thrown beyond the range of his tether to bound forward with a rush. The tale-telling light is upset and extinguished, and in the shameless dark lustful embraces are indiscriminately exchanged; and all alike, if not in act, yet by complicity, are involved in incest, as anything that occurs by the act of individuals results from the common intention.[11]

The value of this lengthy citation is not that it correctly represents Christian practices during the apologetic era, but that it incorporates many of the typical accusations directed against the followers of Christ. The figure of Caecilius in his critique describes Christians as the dregs of society, a collection of ignorant fools and

---

[11]*Oct.* IX.1–7. The translation is from Minucius Felix, *Octavius* (LCL; Translated by Gerald H. Rendall; Cambridge, MA: Harvard University Press, 1960), 337–39.

gullible women, and a rabble of blasphemous conspirators. In practice, the author describes, they shun the light by assembling at night for periodic fasts and inhuman feasts. Speechless in public, in private they worship the head of an ass and the genitals of their father, venerate a condemned criminal and his cross, and initiate converts by means of sordid rituals. While prohibiting the consumption of ritually dedicated foods, they partake of cannibalistic victuals. Refraining from honest pleasure, they engage in promiscuous intercourse. Disregarding the obvious superiority of Roman might, they refuse to render reverence to the national deities or to participate in the festivals held in their honor. Charges of ignorance, gullibility (with an emphasis on women), low class, immorality (especially of a sexual kind), and treasonous attitude— these, à la carte or in tandem, were the stock accusations directed against the followers of Jesus.

Whether or not Aelius Aristides (129–181 C.E.) was referring to Christians in his "To Plato: In Defense of the Four," a paean to the golden age of Greece, is uncertain; but his words bear mention here because they express well the concern felt by many pagan intellectuals for their reverence of antiquity, their desire to preserve Hellenistic culture, and their struggle to maintain their preferred way of life. At one point he exclaims:

> They deceive like flatterers, but they are insolent, as if they are of higher rank, since they are involved in the two most extreme and opposite evils, baseness and willfulness, behaving like those impious men of Palestine. For the proof of the impiety of those people is that they do not believe in the higher powers. And these men in a certain fashion have defected from the Greek race, or rather from all that is higher....They are the most useless of all in helping to accomplish anything which is necessary. But they are cleverest of all at housebreaking, in upsetting those within and bringing them into conflict with one another, and in claiming that they can take care of everything....[12]

Even if, as Benko entertains and as Behr asserts, Aelius Aristides was directing these remarks to Cynic philosophers, the reference to "those impious men of Palestine" most certainly refers either to Christians or to Jews with whom they were associated and confused.[13] Behr is convinced that he is referring here to Christians, since they were more frequently persecuted during this time. Moreover, Behr points out, Polycarp was martyred in Smyrna, the home of Aelius Aristides, sometime after the middle of

---

[12] "To Plato: In Defense of the Four," Sections 671–73 (selections). For the translation see P. Aelius Aristides, *The Complete Works* (Translated by Charles A. Behr; Leiden: E. J. Brill, 1986), 275, and Behr's useful notes on 460, n. 1, 477, n. 745. Cf. the translation and comments of S. Benko, "Pagan Criticism of Christianity," 1097–98. For more extensive biography on Aelius Aristides, see C. A. Behr, *Aelius Aristides and the Sacred Tales* (Amsterdam: Adolf M. Hakkert, 1968).

[13] S. Benko, "Pagan Criticism of Christianity," 1097–98.

the second century,[14] lending credence to the contention that he would have more likely had Christians in mind in identifying them as "impious ones from Palestine."[15] In either case, his words offer one more illustration for how a conservative pagan intellectual of his era regarded the followers of Christ.

Celsus joined Aelius Aristides in his conservative devotion to the past and his appraisal of Christians as impious. His purpose in writing Ἀληθὴς Λόγος (ca. 177–180) was to commend the perennial wisdom of the ages to those who were, in his mind, misguided in pursuing this novel religious movement based on the life and teachings of Jesus. Much more will be said about Celsus below in the context of discussing textual variants. For now, let it suffice to say that Celsus debased Christianity for its lack of an adequate philosophical foundation, Christ for his propensity for magic and deceit, and Christians for their lack of intellect, courage, and moral scruples. One of the characteristics that most distinguishes Celsus from his contemporaries is his informed critique of Christianity. As has been established throughout this work and will be noted again below, Celsus based many of his attacks on an acquaintance with the sacred writings of the Christians.

Porphyry, too—with an even greater measure than Celsus—demonstrated in his polemic writings against Christianity a high degree of familiarity with both Testaments of the Christian scriptures. For studies such as this one, it is especially regrettable that so much of his *Against the Christians* has been lost, undoubtedly destroyed by Christians themselves. Were we to possess the complete work, we would know extensively more about how pagans read, understood, and took exception to the Christian scriptures, and we would have at hand much more data to analyze in reference to the thesis of this present work. What we do possess of his work, though, is enough to show clearly that he scrutinized the scriptures closely and identified inconsistencies of history, fact, or logic as reason to dismiss the new religion. Moreover, he announced that while Jesus himself proved to be a man of divine character, his disciples had miscarried his teachings and erroneously reformulated their religion. Porphyry's assaults, as we shall see, were aimed at the Bible and those who believed in it.[16]

---

[14]Although it seems clear that Polycarp was martyred at the age of 86, and Eusebius (*Hist. eccl.* 15.1) reports that his death occurred during the reign of Marcus Aurelius, the precise year of his execution remains disputed. T. D. Barnes ("A Note On Polycarp," *JTS* 18 (1967), 433–7) finds reason to place his martyrdom as early as 156, while H. Gregoire and P. Orgels ("La véritable date du martyre de Polycarpe (23 févr. 177) et le Corpus Polycarpianum," AnBoll 69 (1951), 1–38) locate it in the year 177. Herbert Musurillo, basing his contention on the premise that Ignatius' final trip through Smyrna coincided with the last years of the reign of Trajan when Polycarp was already bishop, favors a date sometime during the last quarter of the second century. For the discussion see idem, *The Acts of the Christian Martyrs* (Oxford: Clarendon Press, 1972), xiii.

[15]P. Aelius Aristides, *Complete Works*, 477, n. 745.

[16]For a useful overview see Milton V. Anastos, "Porphyry's Attack on the Bible," in *The Classical Tradition: Literary and Historical Studies in Honor of Harry Caplan* (Luitpold Wallach, editor; Ithaca, NY: Cornell University Press, 1966), 421–450. Although this article suffers from the

Such were the chief attitudes and issues raised by these second and third century pagans who wrote to discredit the Jesus movement and its adherents. In turn, Christian apologists in their writings framed carefully crafted responses to many of these same points. As we shall discuss below in greater detail, Athenagoras defended believers against attacks of atheism, cannibalism, and Oedipal intercourse. In the work of Minucius Felix, the character Octavius not only answered the slanderous charges Caecilius attached to Christians, but persuaded him to join the ranks of believers. Of course, Origen attempted to respond point by point to the libel of Celsus, and, along with Tatian, elevated Christian practices that were ascetic in nature. Other apologists, too, as we shall see, sought to offer direct rebuttal to pagan accusations that the followers of Jesus consisted of illiterate fools, drunken and perverse fanatics, and gullible females. Mindful of this, we now turn to the textual tradition, to see if and how this thesis—that the scribal tradition manifest in the Gospels at points reflects awareness of and concern for this critic-apologist discourse—locates evidence therein.

VARIANT READINGS

Of those variant readings in the textual tradition of the canonical gospels that in content deal with the followers of Jesus, it can be argued that a fair number show evidence of apologetically-driven influence, i.e. modifications that result in readings that reflect apologetic themes or strategies, or strengthen typical apologetic arguments. For purposes of convenience and organization, these readings will be considered under the following headings: Fanatics, Fools, and Females. This chapter will conclude with an examination of how these themes appear in the disputed endings of Mark's Gospel (Mark 16:9–20). I intend to proffer and support the contention that much of the content located in the various expanded conclusions to our earliest Gospel reflect apologetic strategy and content.

REGARDING THE FANATICS WHO FOLLOWED JESUS

Christians were damned if they did and damned if they did not. On the one hand, they were condemned for not attending and participating in public feasts and festivals, occasions that were in nature both civic and religious (pagan). As we shall discuss in greater detail below, Celsus and Aelius Aristides provide testimony that their absence was widely viewed as a form of anti-social truancy and even atheism.[17] In terms of their

---

writer's attribution of the pagan arguments located in Macarius Magnes directly to Porphyry, the study retains the merit of contributing insight to the authentic fragments derived from Jerome and Augustine and in his overall treatment of Porphyry's critique of the Bible.

[17]Celsus pleaded for Christian participation in pagan festivals. He argued that if, as Christians believed, pagan gods were only idols, what harm could there be in taking part in the festivals? If, on the other hand, they were in fact daemons or divine powers, then should proper homage not be paid them, since they must also extend from the common deity acknowledged

withdrawal from public celebrations, the charge was for the most part valid. Tertullian, in fact, forcefully advocated that Christians boycott pagan festivals.[18] On the other hand, Christians were accused of engaging in unbridled excess when it came to their own religious festivals. As we noted earlier, charges of cannibalism, incest, and drunkenness heaped upon believers have survived in the literary pogroms penned by pagan critics.[19]

Apologists, in turn, took their opportunity to defend themselves by explanation and even counter-claim. For their monotheistic devotion and purity of life Aristides lauded Christians as the most virtuous of persons, and even contended that the world continued to exist because of the prayers of Christians.[20] Athenagoras of Athens took it upon himself to refute false charges of atheism, cannibalism, and Oedipal incest. Christians, he reported, opposed exposure or child-murder, and engaged in sex solely for the purpose of procreation and not to satisfy any lustful appetite. Indeed, he praised virginity as among the most polished fruits of Christian ethics, and termed remarriage "a decent adultery."[21] In the narrative apology of Minucius Felix, Octavius insisted, "Our feasts are conducted not only with modesty but in sobriety. We do not indulge in delicacies or prolong conviviality with wine, but check our cheerful spirits by the sobriety of our manners."[22] Clement of Alexandria felt an obligation to address the apostle's advice to young Timothy to "use a little wine for your stomach's sake" (I Tim. 5:23) by cautioning against over-indulgence and strongly advocating temperance.[23] Water, he specified, remained the beverage of choice for the thirsty. Moreover, he emphasized that it was a mixed cup—wine diluted with water—that constituted the formula for the sacred chalice. Most especially, he warned against youth consuming wine, lest it fire their libidinous impulses. In short, although he did not insist on total abstinence, Clement urged that reason ought to chaperone the consumption of wine, "lest conviviality imperceptibly degenerate into drunkenness."[24] Tatian, taking the moral high ground, mocked pagan festivals as demonic and shameful.[25] Justin insisted that evil demons were responsible for plagiarizing the Christian Eucharist and ordering a similar rite to be performed by the Mithraic mysteries, and he drained a well of ink describing in detail the sacraments of Baptism and Eucharist.[26]

---

by all, even Christians? *Cels.* VIII.21, 24. See also Aelius Aristides, "To Plato: In Defense of the Four," 671–73. For an example of the charge of atheism directed at Christians, see Athenagoras, *Leg.* III.1.

[18]Tertullian, *Spect.*, 24.

[19]E.g., Athenagoras, *Leg.* III.1; Theophilus, *Ad Auto.* III.4; and Minucius Felix, *Oct.* IX.1–7.

[20]*Ap.* 15–16.

[21]*Ap.* 33, ANF 2, 146 f.

[22]*Oct.* XXXI.5.

[23]*Paed.*, II.2.

[24]*Paed.* II.2, ANF 244.

[25]*Or.* 22.1.

[26]*Ap.* I.65–66.

Thus the apologists reacted to pagan moral criticism against their behavior. Widespread as these topics appear in their writings, it is evident that concerns with questions of sobriety, promiscuity, and piety were foremost in their minds and vital to their arguments. If the thesis of this work is to any extent correct, then, we would expect to locate within the textual tradition scribal activity that reflected such concerns. Following is a discussion of the variant readings that, I believe, bear witness to how this apologetic motif influenced some of the scribes as they copied and transmitted the Gospel texts. Among these texts, it will be observed, are some particularly difficult and highly disputed textual problems. Let us begin, however, with less thorny matters.

Let us begin our textual considerations with the fairly straightforward modification located in Luke 5:33.[27] The pericope in which this verse occurs concerns the issue of fasting. It seems that certain interlocutors, presumably the Pharisees and scribes referred to in 5:30, wish to challenge the devotional and eating practices of Jesus' followers.[28] In contrast with the disciplined prayer lives and pious dietary habits of both the Pharisees and the disciples of John the Baptizer, who purportedly fast frequently and offer prayers (νηστεύουσιν πυκνὰ καὶ δεήσεις ποιοῦνται), they challenge, "but yours eat and drink" (οἱ δὲ σοὶ ἐσθίουσιν καὶ πίνουσιν). The Pharisees here appear to be castigating the disciples of Jesus for their disregard of devout dietary conventions. In tone and language they sound much like the pagan critics who accused believers who were their contemporaries with being gluttons and drunkards. It is interesting in light of this context, then, that Bezae, along with the Old Latin Codex Palatinus (e), supplants the phrase "yours eat and drink" with the innocuous words, "your disciples do not do these things" (μαθηταί σου οὐδεν τουτῶν ποιοῦσιν).[29] Such bland editorialization seems out of character for a witness so notorious for its garish embellishments. That is, it is not consistent with the stylistic tendency most commonly associated with the scribal activity preserved in Codex

----

[27]The verse also includes a minor modification not directly relevant to this discussion, in which διὰ τι ("Why?") appears to have been inserted into some manuscripts, thereby changing the statement of the Pharisees into a question. B. Metzger blithely suggests that this may have resulted from copyists who recalled the parallel text in Mark 2:18. *Textual Commentary*, 138.

[28]In Matthew, it is the disciples of John who pose this question. According to Mark, the disciples of John and the Pharisees together bring the challenge. Compare Matthew 9:14–17 and Mark 2:18–22. Moreover, John 3:26 portrays the disciples of John as envious of those who follow Jesus, and, in the view of Plummer, would have been ripe to criticize. He further suggests that the fast days that are being debated are Mondays and Thursdays, which were voluntary and not obligatory. He also indicates that ποιεῖσθαι δεήσεις in 1 Timothy 2:1 refers to prayers at fixed times according to rule, a practice Jesus' followers did not seem to respect. For additional useful exegetical insights see A. Plummer, *Luke*, ICC, 161.

[29]The fifth-century Codex Palatinus is an African Old Latin manuscript consisting of portions of the four Gospels in the sequence Matthew, John, Luke, and Mark. B. Metzger suggests that Augustine probably used a text of this sort prior to 400 C.E. See B. Metzger, *Early Versions*, 297, and idem, *Text of the New Testament*, 73.

Bezae, namely free expansion.[30] This clue suggests that the scribe responsible for this change had more on his mind than elements of style, quite probably apologetic interests. Notice that this change in wording suspends the very phraseology—eating and drinking—for which pagans criticized Christians. By recasting the contrast from "Ours fast and pray" while "Yours eat and drink" to "Ours fast and pray" while "Yours do not," the scribe has transformed an accusation of excess and gluttony into a more defensible question of piety and distinction.

Another variant reading related to fasting is located at Mark 9:29. At this point in Mark's narrative Jesus is explaining to his disciples why he was able to perform an exorcism that they were not able to bring off. "This kind," he specifies, "can be driven out only by means of prayer" ($\pi\rho\sigma\epsilon\upsilon\chi\tilde{\eta}$). So read the best witnesses. Scribal activity reflected in some manuscripts (P^{45vid} $\aleph^2$ A C D L W Θ Ψ $f^{1.13}$ 33 Maj lat sy[h] co), however, has embellished Jesus' explanation by adding the words, "and fasting" ($\kappa\alpha\iota$ $\nu\eta\sigma\tau\epsilon\acute{\iota}\alpha$). Both B. Metzger and B. Ehrman identify this gloss as one of the few recognizable traces of the influence of ascetic Christianity on the scribal transmission.[31] We should not overlook the fact, though, that some features of asceticism correspond closely to apologetic argumentation. Tertullian, for example, contrasts the pietistic behaviors of Christians and pagans during a time of summer drought. He writes:

> ...when summer days keep away the winter rain and men become anxious about the year's crops, this is your procedure: you eat your fill each day and are straightway ready to eat again; you keep the baths, taverns, and brothels constantly busy; you offer to Jupiter the so-called Aquilicia; you announce barefoot processions for the people; you investigate the sky near the Capitol; you watch for clouds from the paneled temple ceilings while you turn your back on heaven and God himself. Whereas we, grown lean with fastings and emaciated from all forms of self-restraint, abstaining from all the enjoyments of life, rolling in sackcloth and ashes, assail heaven with eager importunity and touch God's heart. And, when we have wrung from Him divine compassion, Jupiter gets all the honor![32]

Clement of Alexandria, too, signaled the vanity of allowing one's earthy passions to control one's directions and pursuits. He argued that God brought to nought the

---

[30]See for substantiation of this claim, D. C. Parker, *Codex Bezae: An Early Christian Manuscript and Its Text* (Cambridge/New York: Cambridge University Press, 1992), 284–86; J. N. Birdsall, "After Three Centuries of the Study of Codex Bezae: The *Status Quaestionis*," in D. C. Parker and C.-B. Amphoux, eds. *Codex Bezae: Studies from the Lunel Colloquium* (Leiden: E. J. Brill, 1996), xix–xxx, esp. xxv; and most especially Michael W. Holmes, "Codex Bezae as a Recension of the Gospels," also in Parker and Amphoux, *Codex Bezae*, 123–160. Here Holmes calls attention to the statistically-supported observation that the so-called "improvements" to the text contained in Codex Bezae "have been accomplished almost entirely by the addition and substitution of material, and only very seldom by omission" (154, cf. also n. 138) .

[31]B. Metzger, *Textual Commentary*, 101; B. Ehrman, "The Text of the Gospels at the End of the Second Century," *Codex Bezae*, Lunel Colloquium, 121.

[32]*Ap.* 40.14–15. ANF, 104–105.

labors of lust, such as obsession with money or winning or glory; the concupiscent craving after women or boys; gluttony; or profligacy.[33] Clement, though, it should be noted, advocated moderation, not abstinence. He believed, for example, that believers were to be responsible in marriage, propagate children, and live well.[34] Justin used "fasting" in a symbolic sense, identifying the nature of true fasting as clothing the naked, feeding the hungry, liberating the oppressed, and otherwise seeking after justice.[35]

At points, then, the line between ascetic and apologetic themes draws quite thin. A scribe more informed by apologetic discourse than ascetic practices could have also been inclined to offer just such an embellishment to his exemplar. In trying to offer some explanation for the impulse that prompted this scribal modification, then, perhaps we are wiser to assert a lesser claim that possesses the virtue of greater probability. Whether the scribe(s) responsible for the variant reading attached to Mark 9:29 was prompted by an austere piety or a defensive posture, it seems evident that we have here an instance of the deliberate corruption of his exemplar by a scribe who was both willing and able to make the text say what he read.

Let us now briefly shift our attention to the Fourth Gospel. The text of John 6:55–56 appears in N-A[27] as follows:

55 ἡ γὰρ σάρξ μου ἀληθής ἐστιν βρῶσις καὶ τὸ αἷμά μου ἀληθής ἐστιν πόσις. 56 ὁ τρώγων μου τὴν σάρκα καὶ πίνων μου τὸ αἷμα ἐν ἐμοὶ μένει κἀγὼ ἐν αὐτῷ.

[55]For my flesh is food indeed, and my blood is drink indeed. [56]He who eats my flesh and drinks my blood abides in me, and I in him.

Commentators offer no serious challenge to this constituting the "original" Johannine text.[36] That makes even more interesting, therefore, the modifications produced by the scribe responsible for the majuscule Bezae. Located in Codex D, along with a pair of Old Latin texts (a, ff²), appears the following insert:

καθὼς ἐν ἐμοὶ ὁ πατὴρ κἀγὼ ἐν τῷ πατρί. ἀμὴν ἀμὴν λέγω ὑμῖν ἐὰν μὴ λάβητε τὸ σῶμα τοῦ υἱοῦ τοῦ ἀνθρώπου ὡς τὸν ἄρτον τῆς ζωῆς οὐκ ἔχετε ζωὴν ἐν αὐτῷ.

---

[33]*Strom.* III.9.3. FC, 295.

[34]*Strom.* III.6.46.1. FC, 284.

[35]*Dial.* 15. ANF, I, 202. So also Origen in *Cels.* VIII.55. See H. Chadwick, *Origen: Contra Celsum*, 494.

[36]Verse 55 contains only a minor variation; some manuscripts substitute the adverbial ἀληθῶς for the adjective ἀληθής. The variant more germane to this work involves a gloss that almost certainly is the product of the scribe responsible for transcribing the Bezae majuscule. This will be discussed below.

Just as the Father is in me, so too am I in the Father. Truly, truly I say to you, unless you receive the body of the Son of Man as the bread of life, you do not have life in him.

Bruce Metzger is content to describe Bezae's gloss as a "homiletic expansion."[37] Raymond Brown echoes this view.[38] Still, more seems to be at stake here than benign embellishment. For one thing, both scholars fail to consider Bezae's modification of this verse in light of the variant reading in the previous verse. Codex D is alone in omitting the phrase, καὶ τὸ αἷμά μου ἀληθής ἐστιν πόσις, "and my blood is true drink." Of course, it is possible to attribute the deletion to homoeoteuleton.[39] One could reasonably argue that, in the process of moving from exemplar to manuscript and back, the eye of a weary scribe might have wandered from βρῶσις to πόσις, and therefore prompted this sin of omission. E. Haenchen also acknowledges this possibility.[40]

Yet, the coincidence of the substance that is omitted, particularly in light of the clearly intentional modification in the following verse, easily provokes suspicion. What the wielder of the stylus eliminated was a draft of blood! This editorial gesture seems blatantly apologetic, particularly in light of the stock accusations of many pagan critics that Christians participated in cannibalistic rituals.[41] Now, to be sure, the scribe did not extract all of the references to drinking blood; for instance, reference to blood remains in both 6:53 and 6:56. To John 6:56, notice however, the copyist did attach a relatively sophisticated conceptualization of sacramental union that, so to speak, fleshed out his pietistic understanding of the carnal imagery. Although Haenchen more mildly explains this interpolation as an attempt to mitigate the offensive mystical tone of this section,[42] it seems conspicuous that, in John 6:53, Bezae joins with Vercellensis (a) against the rest of the tradition in replacing φάγητε ("eat") with λάβητε ("receive"), once again mollifying language that could easily be interpreted as cannibalistic.

---

[37]B. Metzger, *Textual Commentary*, 214.

[38]R. Brown, *John*, AB, 29, 283. Brown's phrase is "a homiletic Western addition."

[39]M.-J. Lagrange, e.g., is of this opinion. See his *Évangile selon Saint Jean* (8th edition; Paris: Gabalda, 1948), 185.

[40]Both Ernst Haenchen, *John 1*, Hermeneia (Trans. Robert W. Funk: Philadelphia: Fortress, 1984), 295 and C. K. Barrett, *The Gospel According to St. John* (Second Edition; Philadelphia: Westminster, 1978), 299 subscribe to this explanation of omission by homoeoteleuton.

[41]For a highly useful study informed by both patristic studies and anthropological theories of "labeling," see Andrew McGowan, "Eating People: Accusations of Cannibalism Against Christians in the Second Century," *JECS* 2/3 (1994), 413–442. Here McGowan challenges the mainstream notion that the accusations of cannibalism directed against Christians resulted from a pagan misunderstanding of their eucharistic celebrations. Instead, he astutely argues, the charge of "cannibalism" stands in antiquity as one of the standard labels to attach to an individual or group in order to identify them as deviant. I find his discussion compelling and highly informative, though I am inclined to believe that, at least on the part of some, especially the pagan populace, there remained contention that Christians really were cannibals.

[42]E. Haenchen, *John 1*, 295–6.

In fact, this verse was so singled out and interpreted by the pagan critic whose polemic was preserved by Macarius. This anonymous critic labeled "beastly" as well as "absurd" Christian eucharistic practice as it was prescribed in John 6:53. He said:

> A famous saying of the Teacher is this one: "Unless you eat my flesh and drink my blood, you will have no life in yourselves." This saying is not only beastly and absurd; it is more absurd than absurdity itself and more beastly than any beast: that a man should savor human flesh or drink the blood of a member of his own family or people—and that by doing this he should obtain eternal life![43]

Thus, we see in this pagan critic identified by Macarius as Porphyry himself an accusation of cannibalism traceable directly to this verse. The Christian antagonist, in fact, heightens his polemic by contrasting the Eucharist with tales of Thyestes' banquet and others like it so familiar in antiquity. What is different in these accounts, he points out, is that diners consumed human flesh unknowingly and thus unwillingly; Christians, in contrast, voluntarily engage in cannibalistic practice. The writer even anticipates a defense on the basis of symbolic or allegorical meaning when he asserts:

> And so what does this saying mean? Even if it carries some hidden meaning, that does not excuse its appearance, which seems to suggest that men are less than animals. No tale designed to fool the simple-minded is crueler or more deceptive [than this myth of the Christians].[44]

The anticipation of the standard Christian reply suggests that both sides of this debate had become commonplace by the time of Macarius. Much earlier, we find evidence of these accusations in Tacitus,[45] Justin,[46] Tatian,[47] Athenagoras,[48] Theophilus,[49] Tertullian,[50] and Minucius Felix.[51] One of the fullest expressions of this theme is located in *Octavius*, in these words attributed to Fronto, as he relates this description of the Christian rite of initiation:

> And now, the stories told about the initiation of their novices: they are as detestable as they are notorious. An infant covered with a dough crust to deceive the unsuspecting is placed beside the person to be initiated into their sacred rites. This

---

[43] *Frag.* 69. Macarius, *Apocrit.* III.18. Translation is that of R. J. Hoffmann, *Porphyry's Against the Christians*, 49.

[44] *Apocrit.* III.18, cont. Again, the translation is that of R. J. Hoffmann, *Porphyry's Against the Christians*, 49–50.

[45] *Ann.* 15.44.

[46] *Ap.* I.26, II.12.

[47] *Or.* 25.

[48] *Leg.* 3.

[49] *Ad Auto.* 3.4–5, 15.

[50] *Ap.* 7; *Ad Nat.* I.15.

[51] *Oct.* 9, cf. 30.

infant is killed at the hands of the novice by wounds inflicted unintentionally and hidden from his eyes, since he has been urged on as if to harmless blows upon the surface of the dough. The infant's blood—oh, horrible—they sip up eagerly; its limbs they tear to pieces, trying to outdo each other; by this victim they are leagued together; by being privy to this crime they pledge themselves to mutual silence. These sacred rites are more shocking than any sacrilege.[52]

Whether pagans were genuinely confused about Christian sacramental practices and misunderstood the ritual language, or were consciously heaping upon believers stock accusations intended to bring out the differences between Christians and the mainstream pagan populace, second-century polemic literature indicates that cannibalism was a commonplace charge associated with the Jesus movement, and is one that Christian apologists expended great energy to refute.

Returning to the textual considerations, then, we should not miss the fact that the activity reflected in these variants produced the simultaneous effects of eliminating language offensive to pagans (and quite possibly some nascent converts), on the one hand, and, on the other, offering a carefully crafted codicil clearly intended to clarify, if not sanctify, this analogy of physical consumption with spiritual union.[53] In light of pagan depictions of the bloody victuals that purportedly graced the table of the early Christians, it seems a reasonable conjecture that an awareness on the part of some thinking scribe to pagan misconceptions and rumors regarding the Christian Eucharist and apologetic writers' attempts at explanation may well have influenced him to wilfully alter the sacred text that lay open before him.

Such regard for the Eucharist factors also into the analysis of one of the most notorious and complex text-critical problems distributed among the canonical Gospels. Textual scholars turn with endless fascination and continuing consternation to Luke's account of Jesus' last supper with the Twelve to explore the variant reading located in

[52]*Oct.* IX.5–6. The translation here is from *Tertullian: Apologetical Works and Minucius Felix: Octavius* (Translated by R. Arbesmann, et al., FC 10; Washington, DC: Catholic University of America Press, 1950), 337. The Latin text reads as follows: *Iam de initiandis tirunculis fabula tam detestanda quam nota est. Infans farre contectus, ut decipiat incautos, adponitur ei qui sacris inbuatur. Is infans a tirunculo farris superficie quasi ad innoxios ictus provocato caecis occultisque vulneribus occiditur. Huiu, pro nefas! sitienter sanguinem lambunt, huius certatim membra dispertiunt, hac foederantur hostia, hac conscientia sceleris ad silentium mutuum pignerantur. Haec sacra sacrilegiis omnibus taetriora. Et de convivio notum est, passim omnes locuntur; id etiam Cirtensis nostri testatur oratio....* This text is derived from G. Quispel, *M. Minucii Felicis Octavius* (Tweede Druk; Leiden: E. J. Brill, 1973), 19–20. Other critical editions include, in German, J. Lindauer, *M. Minucius Felix: Octavius* (München: Kösel-Verlag, 1964) and, in English, A. D. Simpson, *M. Minucii Felicis Octavius: Prolegomena, Text and Critical Notes* (New York: Columbia University Press, 1938).
[53]I invite further comparison of these reflections with the discussions of eating, drinking, and Eucharist located in Clement of Alexandria, *Paed.*, II.1–2.

Luke 22:19b–20.[54] The tradition has transmitted six distinct forms of this eucharistic narrative.

Most of the discussion focuses on the two major strands of transmission, the familiar longer reading and the shorter reading (sans 19b–20).[55] In the mind of J. Fitzmyer, the longer reading is not only the best attested (P[75] ℵ A B C K L T W X Δ Θ Π Ψ 063 $f^{1.13}$, many of the minuscules and versional witnesses), but also gains credibility on the basis of preference for the most difficult reading (*lectio difficilior*). This longer reading conveys a table paradigm of "cup-bread-cup." The bulk of the so-called "Western" witnesses (D, it$^{a, d, ff2, l, l}$) transmits a shorter reading that omits verses 19b–20 and thus describes the table distribution as "cup-bread." This abbreviated "Western" paradigm is located also in 1 Corinthians 10:16 and *Didache* 9.2–3. In their 1881 Greek text, Westcott and Hort favored this truncated reading and bracketed verses 19b–20 as a "Western Non-Interpolation." Their view carried the discipline for decades,[56] until eventually the pendulum of scholarly opinion swung back, and the verses were reinstated as "original" by Kurt Aland in N-A[26]. Snodgrass also spoke up for the "originality" of the longer text, submitting that scribal deletion was prompted by concern regarding the second cup.[57] Members of the UBSGNT committee were divided on their appraisal of this text. A minority sided with Westcott and Hort in favoring the shorter text and identifying it as a "Western non-interpolation"; whereas the majority affirmed the primacy of the longer reading on the basis of the external testimony and ease of attributing omission of verses to transcriptional accident or misunderstanding.[58] Current scholarship remains divided on the matter.

Among those who favor the shorter text as "original," Bart Ehrman constructs the most compelling case. He challenges those scholars who on the sole basis of its limited external support abruptly dismiss the shorter reading. To do so, he contends, misses the insight of Hort's genius on this point. Hort's "Western Non-Interpolations" consisted precisely of those variant readings characterized, in part, by their isolation in the "Western" tradition. What distinguished them within that tradition, however, was their dramatic brevity. For the textual tradition that was almost invariably expansionist to advance the shorter reading was striking to the point of earning it careful consideration on the basis of internal validation. Hort argued for nothing more,

---

[54]B. Metzger's *Textual Commentary* (173–77) provides a useful summary of the issues and reproduces a clear table, adapted from Kenyon and Legg, detailing in a parallel format the multitude of distinct readings. Traditionally, six separate readings are outlined. These need not be repeated here. For lucid historical background and commentary related to this pericope, see J. Fitzmyer, *Luke X–XXIV*, 1386–1403.

[55]As B. Ehrman explains in his article, "The Cup, The Bread, and the Salvific Effect of Jesus' Death in Luke–Acts," in Eugene H. Lovering, ed., *Society of Biblical Literature 1991 Seminar Papers* (Atlanta: Scholars Press, 1992), 577, n. 4.

[56]See, e.g., A. Plummer, *Luke*, ICC, 496–97.

[57]Snodgrass, *JBL*, 374.

[58]B. Metzger, *Textual Commentary*, 176.

and urged nothing less. Ehrman, on this basis, insists on weighing this problem in light of intrinsic and transcriptional probabilities.

In dealing with intrinsic probabilities, he devotes the bulk of his argument to the theological consideration of the longer text.[59] For Ehrman, the most telling point here is that the atonement motif associated with the longer reading occurs nowhere else in Luke, in either the Gospel or Acts.[60] Not only does Luke not portray Jesus' death as an atoning sacrifice, the evangelist, in the words of Ehrman, "has actually gone out of his way to eliminate just such a theology from the narrative he inherited from his predecessor, the Gospel of Mark."[61] In support of this claim, he points to Luke's modification of two references in Mark's narrative that indicate the saving effects of Jesus' death. Dealing with the first, where Mark quotes the declaration of Jesus, "The Son of Man came not to be served but to serve, and to give his life as a ransom for many" (Mark 10:45), Luke omits this verse altogether.[62]

The second reference consists of two distinct actions: the rending of the temple veil and the confession of the centurion. In Ehrman's view, these two events for Mark work in tandem to point to the atoning work of the cross. The ripping of the curtain marks the end of any requirement of an additional sacrifice to approach the deity; in the death of Jesus God has razed the barriers of access between heaven and earth. The confession of the centurion serves, then, to punctuate this saving event. "Truly this man was the Son of God" (Mark 15:39), he declares, and, in so doing, connects profession of faith, the key to salvation, with the death of Jesus. So is the death of Jesus according to Mark.

Luke, though, adapts both of these events to his own theology. First of all, Luke places the tearing of the curtain prior to the death of Jesus (Luke 23:45). For the evangelist, this dramatic event symbolizes something different than it does for his Synoptic counterparts. The veil is ripped not as a sign of perpetual access to divine mercy, but as an expression of divine judgment. Moreover, the evangelist alters the cry of the centurion from a confession of faith to a declaration of innocence (Luke 23:47). Luke's Jesus dies, then, not as an atoning sacrifice, but as a casualty of injustice. In death he is a victim, nothing more. It is in resurrection that he receives vindication and gains victory. Such is the Gospel according to Luke.

For Ehrman, what this means is that Luke never portrays the death of Jesus as an atonement for sin. And what this means for the textual conundrum presently before us is that only the shorter reading corresponds to Luke's theology of the cross. In

---

[59]B. Ehrman recognizes that difficulties in vocabulary and style belong to the longer reading, but deters in large measure on these points to Joel Green, "The Death of Jesus, God's Servant," in *Reimaging the Death of the Lukan Jesus*, ed. Dennis Sylva (Bonner biblische Beiträge 73; Frankfurt: Anton Hain, 1990) 4.

[60]Recognizing that Acts 20:28 is frequently cited in contradiction to this point, B. Ehrman treats this text with some care. See idem, "The Cup, The Bread and Salvific Effect," 582–84.

[61]B. Ehrman, "The Cup, The Bread and Salvific Effect," 579.

[62]But see the suggestion of Joel Marcus cited in B. Ehrman, "The Cup, The Bread, and Salvific Effect," 580, n. 13.

Ehrman's judgment, the longer reading emphasizes precisely the atoning relevance of Jesus' death. In his own words:

> How could Luke have blatantly eliminated from the accounts of Mark any notion of Jesus' death as an atoning sacrifice (Mark 10:45; 15:39) only to assert such a notion here in yet stronger terms? The conclusion appears unavoidable: Luke has either constructed his narrative with blinding inconsistency, or he has provided us with a shortened version of Jesus' last meal with his disciples.[63]

Turning, then, to transcriptional considerations, Ehrman declares, "In point of fact, no one has been able to provide a convincing explanation for how the shorter text came into existence if the longer text is original."[64] To the often adduced argument that a scribe either confused or concerned over the appearance of two cups simply eliminated one of them out of his own preference, he once again conjures the spirit of Hort to overturn the theory. Hort, he points out, wondered why a scribe concerned with harmony or precision would have expunged the second cup rather than the first, since it was the first cup that was problematic, particularly in light of the eucharistic formula of 1 Corinthians (11:23–26). Also unaccounted for, he adds, is the omission of verse 19b. Since here the cup is not yet mentioned, a scribe concerned with the second cup would have had no reason to subtract reference to the bread.[65] Thus, he declares, "...it is well-nigh impossible to explain the shorter text of Luke 22:19–20 if the longer text is original," but "it is not at all difficult to explain for an *interpolation* of the disputed words" into Luke's account of the last supper.[66]

Ehrman cinches his argument with an appeal to the "orthodox corruption of scripture." Here, his premise is that scribes who subscribed to proto-orthodox beliefs lengthened the text as they did, i.e. they inserted or manufactured 19b–20, out of anti-docetic concerns. Luke's account of the last supper was vulnerable to the docetic portrayal of a divine Christ tranquil in the face of his execution; but the interpolated passage reflecting the formula of 1 Corinthians 11:23–26 emphasized both the salvific effect of his death ("given for you") and that his death was physical in nature ("...in my

---

[63]B. Ehrman, "The Cup, The Bread and Salvific Effect," 584.

[64]B. Ehrman, "The Cup, The Bread and Salvific Effect," 587.

[65]Joachim Jeremias attempted to deal with this and other similar concerns by positing that scribes often omitted Christian liturgical passages from the text in order to preserve these formulae from the public forum and to safeguard them from abuse by non-believers who might wish to apply them toward magical ends. In this case, verse 19a was left intact to function as a kind of liturgical caret, a signal to Christian insiders regarding what ensued at the meal. See idem, *Eucharistic Words of Jesus*, 87–106 for further details regarding this theory identified as *disciplina arcani*. B. Ehrman, rightly in my mind, refutes Jeremias on this point. See B. Ehrman, "The Cup, The Bread and Salvific Effect," 588, especially n. 41.

[66]B. Ehrman, "The Cup, The Bread and Salvific Effect," 589.

blood poured out for you").[67] As further evidence he points to how both Tertullian and Irenaeus drew upon the concepts reflected, among the locations in the Gospels, within this textual variant to refute Marcion's heretical docetic christology.[68] Thus it is clear in his own mind that the shorter text is "original," and that the longer text represents a proto-orthodox interpolation designed to thwart docetic heretics engaged in doctrinal polemic.

Ehrman's arguments I find compelling, insofar as they treat the two forms of the variants he isolates. Yet, I wonder if there is not more to be discovered here by more closely examining the additional forms of variation related to this text.[69] In chart form B. Metzger outlines a total of six forms of variation. The first column he labels the Majority Text, by which he means the consensus of P^{75} ℵ A B C K L T W X Δ Θ Π Ψ 063 $f^{1.13}$ vg syr^{pal} cop^{sa,bo} arm geo, all the minuscules, and the remainder of the Latin versions that do not appear elsewhere. The second column consists of the reading attested by D it$^{a, d, ff2, l, 1}$ and reports the shorter reading that Ehrman believes to be "original." The third column includes the other Old Latin witnesses (it^{b,e}) and, except for verse order (19 is placed before 17 so that the bread prefaces the cup), follows the reading in Bezae almost verbatim.[70] The fourth, fifth, and sixth columns report Syriac readings rendered in Greek, specifically and in order those of the Curetonian, Sinaitic, and Peshitta. Since the Greek form of the Syriac is conjectural, little can be made of certain minor grammatical differences.[71] What we can make something of, however, are features that bear the mark of one textual tradition over against the other, such as parallel word order, deletions, or expansions.

---

[67]Ehrman does not mention here that, in addition, the reference to "the new covenant" could be taken as representative of the kind of anti-Judaic bias frequently associated with the "Western" text, especially Codex Bezae. It would be a surprise to some extent that, if a phrase so well-suited to his purposes had been located in his exemplar, the scribe of Bezae would have dropped it. In reference to this bias see E. J. Epp, *Theological Tendency*, esp. 41–164.

[68]B. Ehrman, "The Cup, The Bread and Salvific Effect," 590. Here he cites Tertullian, *Adv. Marc.* 40 and Irenaeus, *Adv. Haer.* IV 33.2.

[69]The chart appearing in B. Metzger, *Textual Commentary*, 175, adapted from Frederic G. Kenyon and S. C. E. Legg, *The Ministry and the Sacraments*, ed. by Roderic Dunkerly (London, 1937), 284 f., greatly aids the analysis of this complex constellation of readings. For the most thorough delineation of the textual witnesses see IGNTP, *Luke*, II, 176–178.

[70]Especially noteworthy is the fact that, in those places shared by the Bezae reading and that of the Majority text (17–19a), where Bezae differs from the Majority text, the reading reported in column three most frequently follows Bezae. The only exceptions are the insertions of an article and a conjunction, both of which could be explained as either the result of Latin translation or the perceived grammatical improvements of an idiosyncratic scribe.

[71]For example, in their comparison of verse 19, where the first three columns report the participle, λέγων, all three Syriac columns are rendered by the imperfect, ἔλεγεν. But is this really accurate or useful? Syriac and Greek tense systems differ considerably. For the problems see Sebastian P. Brock, "Limitations of Syriac in Representing Greek," in B. Metzger, *Early Versions*, 83–98.

In such a comparison of the Curetonian, Sinaitic, and Peshitta versions to the Majority text and Bezae group, the following traits may be observed. First of all, all three Syriac texts invert the verse order from both Bezae and the Majority text in such a way that each introduces bread before cup.[72] Secondly, both the Curetonian and Sinaitic witnesses in their treatment of verse 18 mirror the word order of the Bezae group reading rather than that of the Majority text. Specifically, the telling elements are that the Syriac witnesses here follow Bezae's phrasing ἀπὸ τοῦ νῦν οὐ μὴ πίω in lieu of the word order located in the Majority reading (4 5 6 1 2 3). Next, the Bezae group and the consensus reading are identical in their witness to the first part of verse 19; in the second half of the verse, however, their paths diverge. Each of these Syriac witnesses testifies to a knowledge of the Majority text, yet each includes its own rendering of at least some part of Luke 22:19b–20. The Peshitta, the Syriac Vulgate, despite its complete omission of verses 17–18, follows the Majority text almost verbatim in transmitting verse 19b–20.[73] The Curetonian Syriac manifests no parallel with verse 20, but except for the omission of the participle διδόμενον parrots verse 19b word for word. The Sinaitic text renders 19b exactly, but splits and alters verse 20. The precise differences are detailed in the following chart:

Majority Text	Sinaitic Syriac
20 καὶ τὸ ποτήριον ὡσαύτως	20 καὶ [omit cup]
μετὰ τὸ δειπνῆσαι,	μετὰ τὸ δειπνῆσαι
λέγων,	[insert v. 17][74]
Τοῦτο	τοῦτο
τὸ ποτήριον	[no mention of cup]
[see line 8 below]	ἐστιν τὸ αἷμά μου
ἡ καινὴ διαθήκη	ἡ διαθήκη ἡ καινὴ
ἐν τῷ αἵματί μου,	[see line 6 above]
τὸ ὑπὲρ ὑμῶν ἐκχυννόμενον.	[no parallel]

Notice the differences in how the two strands of tradition treat the cup and blood. Twice the scribe responsible for the Sinaitic Syriac has omitted reference to the cup. Where in the Majority text we locate the peculiar cup-bread-cup pattern, and three

[72] Using the Majority text and Bezae group as a base, the Curetonian verse order is 19–17–18; the Sinaitic is 19–20a–17–20b–18; and the Peshitta simply 19–20, with no parallel at all to verse 18.

[73] The only slight difference being one of word order: καὶ τὸ ποτήριον ὡσαύτως in the Majority reading, with 1 4 [1] 2 3 in the Peshitta.

[74] The Sinaitic witness *appears* to follow the Majority text here, if the translation of the dative and accusative are properly mirrored in moving from the Syriac to Greek as conjectured here. Where Bezae transmits the dative "distribute this among yourselves" (διαμερίσατε ἑαυτοῖς), the Majority reading employs the accusative "share this with each other" (διαμερίσατε εἰς ἑαυτούς).

times attend the term ποτήριον ("cup") in its account—indeed, twice in this verse—the Sinaitic text offers us only a single passing glimpse of the cup. In point of fact, the cup of which he affords a glance is not the so-called second cup, but the earlier, so-called first cup. The Sinaitic text offers no parallel to the references to ποτήριον in verse 22:20. So, either the scribe responsible for the Sinaitic text was not familiar with the Majority text, or he modified the text, either by accident or design. Which was it? Let us hold that question in abeyance for a moment as we return to the rest of the Syriac tradition for additional insight.

Thus far our investigation has disclosed the following facts. (1) With regard to verse order, the entire Syriac tradition inverts the traditional flow in order to substitute a bread-cup pattern for either a cup-bread (Bezae) or a cup-bread-cup (Majority) table paradigm. None of the Syriac witnesses mentions a second cup. The scribes who produced these versional witnesses, then, imposed on their exemplar an act of quill. If their original contained the Bezae reading, they inserted a different table paradigm, and, if the Majority reading lay open before them, they did away entirely with a second cup. (2) With regard to verse 19a, the Syriac tradition agrees with both the Majority text and the Bezae group reading. Little is to be learned here. (3) With regard to verse 19b, which serves as the line of demarcation between the Majority and Bezae texts, both the Old Syriac (sy^{c.s}) and the Peshitta (sy^p) virtually duplicate the consensus reading. This seems telling. At the very point at which the road of transmission forks, the entire Syriac tradition follows the tracks laid down by the Majority text in publishing verse 19b. (4) With regard to verse 20, each witness to the Syriac tradition offers a distinct reading. The Peshitta virtually replicates the Majority text, while the Curetonian bears no trace of the verse. It is left to the Sinaitic text to locate a middle ground. The scribe of this text relayed verse 20, but not before he recast it according to his own idiosyncratic agenda. But what was that agenda?

Consider the likelihood of apologetic motivation. Something similar occurs in Justin, where we locate a bread-cup paradigm, a table model that reverses the elements of the "original" text. We noted above in Celsus and Fronto the caustic tirades directed at followers of Jesus by some pagan intellectuals regarding the drunkenness and debauchery presumed to occur at Christian assemblies. We also marked reference to accusations that Christians were cannibals who ingested human flesh and blood. Moreover, in Justin, we locate a table model that reverses the presentation of elements in the shorter text and portrays a bread-cup paradigm.[75]

There appears to exist in this variant reading a point of contact with these apologetic dynamics. The precise features of deviation between the Sinaitic Syriac and the consensus text concern cup and blood. By omission and inverted word order sy^s excises reference to a second cup and separates the blood from the chalice. It seems evident that the effect of these changes would potentially reduce the perception of either drunkenness or blood ingestion. The evidence presented here strongly indicates that this reading resulted from the efforts of a scribe who was aware of or attuned to

---

[75] *Ap.* I.62.

such pagan accusations directed against Christians. No mechanical cause seems to lie behind the Sinaitic Syriac text, nor does harmonization to Paul or Synoptic parallels explain these particular changes. The motivation of apologetic interests, however, affords a reasonable explanation for the scribal amendment recorded in the Sinaitic Syriac reading of Luke 22:17–20.

Next, we shift focus to a group of readings, related to one another by a common theme of prostration. Among those practices of Christians with which Celsus found fault was this physical gesture of submission. As recorded in *Contra Celsum*, he declared, "the humble man humiliates himself in a disgraceful and undignified manner, *throwing himself headlong to the ground upon his knees* (χαμαιπετὴς ἐπὶ τῶν γονάτων καὶ πρηνὴς ἐρριμμένος), clothing himself in a beggar's rags, and heaping dust upon himself."[76] Origen, of course, responded with the claim that Celsus had misunderstood the doctrine of humility. Falling to one's knees was merely an outward expression of human subjugation to the will of God as it had been modeled by Christ. Tertullian, also, in *de Paenitentia*, went to great lengths to lay out in detail the proper obligation of self-abasement and penitence.[77] Even some Christians, though, found such kneeling disgraceful, and Greeks generally associated it with barbarian superstition.[78]

So, although some Christians understood the gesture as an humble act of piety, the practice of falling to one's knees was regarded with suspicion by a portion of the pagan populace and unfavorably even by some within the movement itself. Although apologists such as Origen and Tertullian attempted to explain the Christian belief that lay behind the custom, theirs was an uphill struggle.

This dynamic offers us reason to pause, then, before a trio of variant readings that surface in Mark's Gospel that deal with this matter of prostration. At first glance, they appear benign, so far as historical significance is concerned. With regard to reflecting apologetic interests, however, such a cursory reading may prove deceptive. Each centers around the act of falling to one's knees or prostrating oneself in pious (or, in one case, feigned) reverence. Before proceeding to the texts, though, it seems prudent to recall the Greek locutions involved. Various Greek terms are used in the Septuagint (LXX), New Testament, and Greco-Roman literature for genuflection, including γονυπετέω, προσπίπτω, τιθέναι ἐπὶ τὰ γόνατα, κάμπτειν τὰ γονάτα and ὀκλάζειν ἐπὶ τὰ γόνατα.[79] Such variety of terminology is represented in the modified readings we are about to peruse. Yet, all of these terms in one way or another communicate the act of kneeling or falling to one's face in homage or supplication,

---

[76]*Cels.* VI.15. H. Chadwick, *Origen: Contra Celsum*, p. 328. M. Borret, Vol. III, 214.

[77]*Paen.* 9. As H. Chadwick notes, however, it is evident from section 11 of this same work that some Christians found this custom unseemly and shameful.

[78]Both Plutarch and Theophrastus, e.g., denoted prostration as characteristic of a person of superstition. See Plutarch, *Mor.* 166A. Theophrastus, *Char.* 16.

[79]The following discussion of these Greek terms is based on entries located in G. W. H. Lampe, *A Patristic Greek Lexicon*, 322, 1174–6, 1181; Heinrich Schlier, "γόνη, γονυπετέω," I.738–40, and Wilhelm Michaelis, "πίπτω, κτλ.,"VI.161–73, and H. Greever, "προσκυνέω," VI.758–66, in G. Kittel, *TWNT*.

either as a slave to one's master or as a suppliant to one's deity. A synonymous term relevant to this discussion, one which occurs in both pagan and Christian canonical sources, is προσκυνέω, a term which although associated with a demonstration of pious adoration traces its etymology to the act of "kissing" rather than "kneeling." The Septuagint at various points employs the term to translate the Hebrew words for "bow," "kiss," "serve" or, most often, "worship." Almost always in the New Testament, the word features an object of veneration. Christian writers frequently employed the term in reference to pagan devotional practices.[80]

A series of textual variants arises around this theme of worship and prostration. The first of these occurs in the Markan narrative of the woman with the hemorrhage. In touching Jesus' garment she is healed, but she becomes shaken when Jesus, sensing that power has gone out of him, seeks her out. What is clearly the "original" text of Mark 5:33 reads, "But the woman, with fear and trembling, knowing what had happened to her, came and *fell before him* (προσέπεσεν αὐτῷ) and told him the whole truth." Two extant manuscripts—the fifth century Codex Ephraemi Rescriptus (C) and the fourth century Old Latin Codex Vercellensis (a)— however, bear witness to transcriptional activity.[81] In each of these manuscripts the phrase "fell before him" (προσέπεσεν αὐτῷ) has been changed to a synonym best translated "worshiped him" (προσεκύνησεν αὐτῷ).

The second instance arises in Mark's account of the soldiers mocking Jesus (Mark 15:19). Having costumed him with a purple cloak and a crown of plaited thorns, the governor's guards, the evangelist reports, "struck his head with a reed, and spat upon him, *and knelt down in homage to him*" (καὶ τιθέντες τὰ γόνατα προσεκύνουν αὐτῷ). There should be no dispute that the author's text read so. The Matthean parallel suggests strongly that there was in Mark reference to the soldier's scornful parody of prostration. In addition, the external evidence consistently supports this contention. Except, that is, for certain "Western" witnesses. Codex Bezae, k, and vg^ms fail to record this clause. The most immediate explanation for this is scribal error. Since the second part of the verse begins and ends with the same words (καί...αὐτῷ), omission is readily accounted for by either homoeoarcton and/or homoeoteuleton.

A similar set of variant readings is located at Mark 1:40. The verse begins the Markan version of the healing of the leper, and reads, "And there came to him a leper who called out to him [*v. l.* and fell to his knees] and said to him, 'If you wish to you have the power to make me clean.'" Here, the textual question consists of whether the phrase καὶ γονυπετῶν represents the Markan "original" or a scribal gloss. The fact that the parallel accounts rendered by Matthew and Luke contain a reference to "kneeling" makes it highly likely that the phrase was Markan in origin.[82] Yet, the UBS[4]

---

[80]H. Greever, "προσκυνέω,"*TWNT*, VI.758–66.

[81]Report of this variant is absent in the apparatus of both UBS[4] and N-A[27]. For citation see the apparatus of von Soden, *Die Schriften des Neuen Testaments*, p. 146, and K. Aland, *Synopsis Quattuor Evangeliorum*, p. 191.

[82]As noted by J. Marcus, *Mark 1–8*, 205.

Committee, although it opted to retain the phrase as "original," indicated some misgivings by enclosing the phrase in square brackets and rating it only a {C}, a slight improvement over the {D} it had been given in the previous edition. Their hesitation surfaced from the strong counter-testimony brought by the absence of the reading in the highly-regarded Alexandrian and "Western" witnesses, B and D. Other strong witnesses, though—including ℵ, L, Θ, f, and 565—support inclusion. Moreover, as noted previously, those who adhere to the theory of Markan priority should find the support of the Synoptic parallel accounts compelling. Matthew 8:1 reads προσεκύνει ("worshiped"); Luke 5:12, πεσὼν ἐπὶ πρόσωπον ("falling prostrate"). Elsewhere we have observed the pattern that Matthew and Luke tend to follow Mark by copying verbatim or importing synonyms, except when stylistic or tendentious reasons lead them to do otherwise. Therefore, it is fair to state—with a greater degree of confidence than is reflected by the committee of UBS[4]—it seems highly likely that Mark's "original" text included καὶ γονυπετῶν.

What remains is to wonder what forces may have prompted the change. Certainly, as in the previous citation, omission as a result of homoeoarcton is a strong possibility; a scribe could have skipped from one καί to another. Metzger explains the omission as the result of homoeoteuleton, but Joel Marcus questions this, since the preceding word αὐτὸν shares only its final letter with γονυπετῶν.[83] Mechanical error there-fore serves as *one* plausible explanation for the omission, though it is by no means certain.

Nor does it constitute the *only* reasonable one. Marcus suggests the possibility of assimilation to Mark 10:17 or as a tendentious embellishment to highlight the divinity of Jesus.[84] Also, I would add, the evidence adduced in the references to Origen and Tertullian produce sound reasons for postulating that apologetic interests shaped this reading. In the writings of these two apologists we locate concern on the part of some defenders of the faith regarding the Christian practice of "kneeling." Informed of this dynamic, therefore, we should not rush to assign mechanical origin to these specific variants currently under review.

Now, to be sure, not every canonical report of pious kneeling or prostration bears the mark of scribal alteration. Matthew 17:14 and Mark 10:17 serve as examples where no apparent scribal activity has occurred in descriptions of "falling to ones knees" (in both instances the verb is a form of γονυπετέω). Here, though, it is important to remember the caveat of Eldon Epp, that because the scribal transmission of sacred texts is a relatively conservative enterprise, premeditated alterations are more likely to be introduced "with cautious subtlety than with rigid consistency."[85] Moreover, examination of the textual tradition, as we have seen, clearly demonstrates that scribes were neither systematic nor exhaustive in their purposeful modifications of exemplars.

---

[83]B. Metzger, *Textual Commentary*, 76; J. Marcus, *Mark 1–8*, 206.

[84]J. Marcus, *Mark 1–8*, 206.

[85]E. J. Epp, *Theological Tendency*, 38. See also K. Lake, "The Influence of Textual Criticism on the Exegesis of the New Testament," 10 f.

Bearing this in mind, this fact remains: in three separate instances located in the earliest of the canonical Gospels reference to kneeling has been displaced in transcription, either by omission or word substitution. Although the latter two of these *can* (but by no means *must*) be explained mechanically, the first of the trio is not so easily accounted for. This instance bears the unmistakable marks of deliberate modification. With premeditation, in probably more than one of these instances, scribes have *chosen* to substitute one word for another. That is, copyists have intentionally altered the text. Of this there is no dispute.

The lingering historical question is "Why?" What I have attempted to demonstrate here is how the motivation of apologetic concerns offers one plausible and reasonable explanation for this transcriptional activity. Both vocal pagan critics and some adherents (perhaps even some transcribers!) of the movement found the particular practice of prostration distasteful. The efforts apologetic writers expended to explain the custom and make it palatable to Hellenized observers was met evidently with only limited success.[86] Therefore, it is not far-fetched to conceive of apolo-getically sensitive scribes altering the gospel descriptions of this practice in just the way the tradition indicates, either by verbal amendment or deletion. Indeed, several changes to the language and practice of prostration that occur in the textual tradition coincide precisely with apologetic concerns related to pagan distaste for the behavior of genuflection. Although it must be admitted that the evidence does not permit certification of *intentional* scribal activity in two of these three readings, neither does it dismiss outright the possibility. Commitment to thoroughness dictates that the impulse to attribute these transmissional changes to technical error should be balanced with the realistic possibility that apologetic interests could well have driven the intentional modification of one or more of these readings.

Pagans also found disgusting the practice on the part of Christians to recognize one another as sisters and brothers.[87] Fronto's scandalous depiction of the behavior of believers cited in *Octavius* includes the charge that followers "indiscriminately call each other brother and sister, thus turning even ordinary fornication into incest...."[88] Margaret MacDonald finds this a telling example of how pagans believed that Christians blurred the lines of distinction between, in the contemporary terminology of social anthropologists, public and private spheres of society. By doing so, early Christians in the minds of some of their contemporaries threatened some of the social norms that lay at the foundation of Greco-Roman society.[89]

---

[86]See, e.g., the references to Tertullian and Irenaeus above, n. 68.

[87]Yet, at least some apologists boasted of the behavior as indicative of their high moral character and godly affection. Aristides, e.g., reports how masters of a Christian household win their servants to Christ not by fiat but by their loving example, and that, when slaves do submit to baptism, they are "called without distinction brothers." *Ap. Aristides* 15, J. R. Harris, TS I, 49.

[88]*Oct.* 8. LCL, 413.

[89]M. MacDonald, *Early Christian Women*, 61.

It is interesting, in this light, that several textual variants involve the editorial revision of language related to "brothers." Certain scribes (B* 0128* 1424 ff¹ ff²), for example, excised the familial language in Matthew 25:40, so that the phrase "the least of these my brothers" was left simply "the least of these."[90] Also reflected in some later manuscripts (157, l2211 pc) is evidence of scribal activity that changed the reference to "brothers" in Matthew 28:10 to read "disciples."[91] This pattern repeats itself in Acts 1:15, where Peter is said to rise to address "the brothers" regarding the replacement of Judas. Numerous are the witnesses here that report a change either to "apostles" (P⁷⁴) or "disciples" (C³ᵛⁱᵈ D E Ψ 1739ˢ Maj it sy mae; Cyp). Admittedly, the evidence for these cases is less convincing than others I have adduced above, but I proffer them here for the sake of thoroughness and for their potential origin in apologetic motivation.

The textual variants brought together under this rubric have all in some way dealt with pagan perceptions of the behavior of the followers of Jesus. Where they were accused of drunken excess and promiscuity, defenders of the faith replied with characterizations of themselves as a community of moral discipline, sobriety and piety. Where pagans heaped suspicion on Christians by describing their regular gatherings in the standard rhetoric of Thyestian banquets, cannibalistic feasts, and incestuous orgies, apologetic authors sought to defend themselves by explaining the benign character of their gatherings, the allegorical meaning of their Eucharist, and the great reverence they attached to this meal. We have seen these themes played out in the works of Justin, Athenagoras, Origen, Minucius Felix and Tertullian, just to name a few. We have also detailed how, occasionally at points, copyists of the canonical Gospels intentionally modified their exemplars in ways that mirror these same strategies and motifs. Let us turn now to another group of variant readings, the content of which we shall see reflects how debate concerning the emotional and intellectual composition of the followers of Jesus played itself out in the apologetic wars.

---

[90]Those who would argue that this change is due to assimilation to verse 45 can make a case, but it would be hindered by the fact that the harmonization would be directed forward rather than backward, which is the more likely (though admittedly not only) direction of modification. It is also interesting here that, among patristic sources, Clement (pt) and Eusebius are two apologetically-minded writers who bear witness to this amended reading.

[91]It is difficult to know whether the modification of Luke 22:32 may be adduced here or not. Codex Δ bears witness to a scribe who altered Jesus' words to Peter, "...when you have turned again, strengthen your *brothers* (ἀδελφούς)" to "...strengthen your *eyes* (ὀφθαλμούς)." The produced reading is so strange that I hesitate to adduce it as evidence, but I report it here for the sake of thoroughness.

REGARDING THE FOOLS WHO FOLLOWED JESUS

A brief survey of the following collection of variant readings suggests a pattern in which scribes altered their exemplars with an agenda to mollify negative character traits on the part of the disciples—traits such as an insecure bashfulness around adults, fear, indignance, or intellectual bewilderment. To some pagan intellectuals, such characteristics made Christians appear foolish.

Pagan critics frequently described Christianity as a religious movement embraced mostly by women, children, and gullible males. Moreover, Christians were disparaged as persons who preyed on little children and others of malleable wills but shied away from rational adults. Certainly Lucian displayed this opinion.[92] Celsus, in particular, mocked Christians for proselytizing "only the foolish, dishonourable and stupid, and only slaves, women, and little children."[93] Continuing his assault, he asserted:

> Moreover, we see that those who display their secret lore in the market-places and go about begging would never enter a gathering of intelligent men, nor would they dare to reveal their noble beliefs in their presence; but whenever they see adolescent boys and a crowd of slaves and a company of fools, they push themselves in and show off.[94]

Finally, exhibiting severe disdain, Celsus defamed:

> In private houses also we see wool-workers, cobblers, laundry-workers, and the most illiterate and bucolic yokels, who would not dare say anything at all in front of their elders and more intelligent masters. But whenever they get hold of children in private and some stupid women with them, they let out some astounding statements as, for example, that they must not pay attention to their father and school-teachers, but must obey them; they say that these talk nonsense and have no understanding, and that in reality they neither know nor are able to do anything good, but are taken up with empty chatter. But they alone, they say, know the right way to live, and if the children would believe them, they would become happy and make their home happy as well. And if just as they are speaking they see one of the school-teachers coming, or some intelligent person, or even the father himself, the more cautious of them flee in all directions; but the more reckless urge the children on to rebel....[95]

Origen extended his response to these charges over several pages, suggesting the high level of concern he felt about this issue.[96] While he acknowledged that Christians sought to encourage all to wisdom (i.e. faith in Jesus), and therefore taught slaves,

---

[92]Lucian, "Death of Peregrinus," 13; see L. Casson, ed., *Selected Satires*, 369.
[93]*Cels.* III.44.
[94]*Cels.* III.50. The translation here belongs to H. Chadwick, 162.
[95]*Cels.* III.55; H. Chadwick, 165–66.
[96]*Cels.* III.44–58; H. Chadwick 158–68.

women, and children, he insisted that Christians would not hesitate to teach their lessons in front of fathers and teachers who themselves exhibited virtue.[97]

Key elements of this discourse between Celsus and Origen, related in particular to the accusation that Christians were prone to retreat from adults, can arguably be observed in the variant reading of Mark 10:13. This verse introduces the Markan account of Jesus blessing the children. Scholars voice no dispute here as to the direction of scribal shift. The "original" text tells of a time that, when some people (the use of a pronoun here leaves them unidentified) brought their children in hopes that Jesus would touch them, the disciples rebuked them (ἐπετίμησαν αὐτοῖς). It is difficult to understand why the disciples would have been so guarded of Jesus in this instance, unless it was for protection (unlikely in the face of children) or simply to shield him from a ceaseless barrage of people wanting something from Jesus.[98] R. H. Gundry states straightforwardly that Mark offers no explanation for why the disciples rebuked those attending to the children.[99] Ben Witherington ventures that what prompted their rebuke was "a typical ancient attitude" that children were less important than adults, and that renowned teachers like Jesus should not have to bother with them.[100]

The greater issue for scribes, however, appears to have been the ambiguity of the pronoun, αὐτοῖς. Grammatically, it is possible to understand the pronoun here as referring to "the children" rather than their anonymous adult ushers. As evidenced in a wide variety of witnesses, however, certain scribes exhibited a sensitivity to this potential misunderstanding, and therefore clarified the object of the disciples' chastisement by amending the reading, ἐπετίμων τοῖς αὐτοῖς προσφέρουσιν, "they were rebuking those who brought them."[101] This expansion serves clearly to isolate the adult attendants as the recipients of the apostles' reprimand.[102] Despite the fact that in the story, ultimately, Jesus rebuffs the disciples, there is a sense in which this scribal modification potentially improves the lot of Jesus' followers. Even if misdirected, their concern is clearly for Jesus; it is just that, and this is the point of the pericope, Jesus is concerned for the children. More to the point for this study, though, is that the text as these scribes refined it now conveys the sense that the disciples did not dismiss the children but rebuked the adults who had brought them. Moreover, as is indicated by the masculine dative plural pronoun in "original" Mark (αὐτοῖς), at least some of those adults they confronted were males.[103] Thus, in the hands of these

---

[97]*Cels.* III.57–58.

[98]See, e.g., C. S. Mann, *Mark*, 396.

[99]R. H. Gundry, *Mark*, 544.

[100]B. Witherington, *Mark*, 279.

[101]See B. Metzger, *Textual Commentary*, 105 for his brief but vital discussion, and his delineation of manuscript witnesses. Notable among the list of those that testify to the amended reading are several important "Western" and Caesarean sources, including D W Θ *f*[13] 565 700.

[102]This is a commonly held view. For example, see B. Metzger, *Textual Commentary*, 105; V. Taylor, *Mark*, 422; C. E. B. Cranfield, *Mark*, 323; and W. Lane, *Mark*, 358–59.

[103]See, e.g., C. E. B. Cranfield, *Mark*, 323; W. Lane, Mark, 358–59.

copyists, the edited story presented his disciples as persons who were willing to stand up for Jesus even in the face of adults who had their own agenda. This mirrors precisely the features of Origen's reply to Celsus—that Christians did in fact teach and confront adversarial adults—and suggests once again that apologetic interests may have triggered a particular scribal revision.

The determination by the UBSGNT Committee to assign its rendering of Mark 14:4 only a {C} rating seems reserved, given that Metzger's explanation rests firmly on both external and intrinsic evidence.[104] The variant occurs in the pericope narrating the anointing at Bethany. In Mark's account, Simon the leper is entertaining Jesus when unannounced a woman bearing a costly alabaster flask of ointment broke the flask and poured its contents upon the head of Jesus. Then follows Mark 14:4, which reports the reaction of some who were present, saying, "But there were some who began speaking indignantly with each other, 'Why was this ointment thus wasted?'" (ἦσαν δέ τινες ἀγανακτοῦντες πρὸς ἑαυτούς....) In what appears to be the secondary reading, however, the speakers are identified as not merely some guests but Jesus' disciples. The variant reads, "But his disciples had become annoyed, and said, "Why was this ointment wasted?'" (οἱ δὲ μαθηταὶ αὐτοῦ διεπονοῦντο καὶ ἔλεγον....).

First of all, D, Θ, and 565 are the best of the few witnesses that testify to the alternate reading; this is a feeble defense against the rest of the textual tradition. Moreover, Metzger asserts that the secondary nature of the reading is exposed by the substitution of the Matthean οἱ μαθηταί (Mt 26:8) in place of the more typical Markan indefinite subject τινες. This point is confirmed by the conflate reading located in W, f^{13}, and a few others, τινες τῶν μαθητῶν. Another mark of its scribal origins is found in the substitution of the non-Markan διαπονεῖσθαι for ἀγανακτεῖν, a verb which does appear elsewhere in Mark (10:14, 41). Though an indication of its secondary character, this exchange of verbs can be traced to neither mechanical error nor assimilation. The words are too dissimilar for their exchange to have resulted from confusion, and, as noted earlier, διαπονεῖσθαι occurs nowhere else in Mark so that a scribe might have erred by glancing even several verses away. Also, the verb διαπονεῖσθαι occurs in no parallel text; indeed, it occurs nowhere else in any of the Gospels, though it is used by the writer of Acts (4:2, 16:18).

What then could explain this intentional modification? Apologetic motives suggest a reason. First of all, let us explore the definitions. The term ἀγανακτεῖν means to be "indignant," "vexed," "angry," "violently irritated," or "showing outward signs of grief."[105] Cast in this language, the reaction of the onlookers is cast as negative, tendentious, dark, and oppositional. Though Mark does not indicate who these onlookers are—he employs here the indefinite pronoun, τινες—it seems likely, especially when one compares this text with the pericope just discussed, that the writer

---

[104]B. Metzger, *Textual Commentary*, 112.
[105]Liddell-Scott, *Greek-English Lexicon*, 5–6.

has in mind the disciples.[106] Recall that in the story of Jesus blessing the children, "the disciples" rebuked (ἐπετίμησαν) some adults (some of whom were male) bringing children to Jesus. In that pericope his followers were recognized as persons who, even if as the result of good intentions, were capable of misunderstanding and getting in the way of his ministry. Moreover, it bears repeating, this confusion on the part of his followers evoked from Jesus a response of indignation (ἠγανάκτησεν), a form of the same verb presently under discussion. As noted above, it is striking that Matthew and Luke altered their Markan source by omitting any mention of Jesus growing angry in this context. So, we have a verb indicating violent or negative emotion and evidence that some users of Mark found reason to avoid applying the term, ἀγανακτεῖν, to Jesus. We also have reason to suspect that readers, at least some, would have had reason to understand the antecedent of the indefinite pronoun τινες in Mark 14:4 to have been "the disciples."[107] This being said, it does not require much of a leap in logic to advance the notion that other users of Mark, namely copyists of the Gospel, might also have felt compelled to avoid applying ἀγανακτεῖν to Jesus' followers. This proposition accrues interest when one considers an apparent evolution in the meaning of the word substituted by those scribes, διαπονέω. Verbal and nominative forms of this term encompass a wide range of meanings, most of which are related to labor and achievement, including "achieve," "cultivate," "work out with labor," and "the reward of toil." Its passive form, διαπονεῖσθαι, implies being "worn out from labor."[108] In Acts, though, the author twice uses the word in a sense that closely approximates ἀγανακτεῖν. The first of these (Ac 4:2) occurs in the wake of Peter's miraculous healing of a crippled man and his stirring sermon at Solomon's portico. The concerned and troubled reaction on the part of the priests, Samaritans and captain of the temple is characterized as διαπονούμενοι. The second time the word is used (Ac 16:18) occurs in reference to Paul's surly response to a spirit-possessed female diviner. She has been, we are told, following after him and his company for several days, promoting their identity as preachers of salvation by shrieking, "These men are servants of the most high God...." Finally, we are told, Paul, described as διαπονηθείς, exorcises from the female the spirit of divination, to the economic consternation of her male handlers. Translators frequently render both of these forms of διαπονέω "annoyed," accurately enough conveying the sense of the antecedent party feeling irritated beyond limits, badgered, and harassed.

---

[106]This probability increases when one compares this pericope with its parallel versions in the other canonical Gospels. While Luke reports that it was Jesus' Pharisee host who harbored resentment toward the anointing, the writer of Matthew ascribes the negative reaction to Jesus' disciples, while the author of the Fourth Gospel declares that it was Judas alone from whom this response issued. This is noteworthy, considering that in Mark and Matthew, this event is followed immediately by the account of Judas presenting before the Jewish authorities his offer to hand Jesus over to them.

[107]For further evidence of this point see, C. E. B. Cranfield, St. Mark, 415–16.

[108]Liddell-Scott, Greek-English Lexicon, 408.

Yet, notice the very different meaning in the term when applied by the Christian apologist, Clement of Alexandria (ca. 150–215 C.E.). In *Paedagogus* he employs forms of the term (διαπόνησις, διαπονητέον) in reference to the kinds of "toil" and "exercise" appropriate to the godly life.[109] Here the term lacks any sense of vexation or irritation, but conveys instead a sense of dutiful and fruitful labor and exercise on the part of the believer.

Limited as this evidence is, it seems at least within reason to surmise that the more familiar nuances of this term had evolved between the time Luke used it in Acts and Clement used it in *Paedagogus*. Moreover, there can be no doubt that scribes did intentionally alter the term; no mechanical explanation is evident. If we are correct in tracing this development in the meaning of διαπονέω between the time of Acts and Clement, then the exchange of terms goes a long way toward toning down the hostile character of those onlookers who witness this woman so lavishly anointing Jesus. Thus, it seems reasonable to conjecture that defensively-minded scribes felt compelled to mollify the character of the disciples here in Mark 14:4. So the scribes recast the dynamics of this interchange. In seeing the woman anoint Jesus, his disciples did not become vexed, annoyed, and angry; rather, they began discussing with each other in an attempt to figure out what was going on.

A number of other variant readings appear to display this concern with reactions on the part of the disciples. At Matthew 17:23, an omission of the phrase καὶ ἐλυπήθησαν σφόδρα ("they were greatly distressed") has been preserved in Codex Cyprius (K), a ninth or tenth century uncial manuscript generally associated with the Byzantine or Majority textual tradition. Davies and Allison point out that this verse in Matthew already represents a mollified reading of Mark 8:32, "and they were ignorant about the saying and feared to ask him."[110] This prior attention to the verse with regard to mollifying perceptions indicates that something more deliberate than mechanical error is involved here. Moreover, the omission fits this paradigm witnessed earliest in Matthew and Luke but maintained and expanded by the apologists.

A few, mostly "Western" witnesses (D W $f^{1.13}$ lat) disclose a revision of Mark 9:10 that consists of the subtle substitution of ὅταν...ἀναστῇ for τὸ...ἀναστῆναι. Thus, the phrase "questioning among themselves what rising from the dead was" was altered to read "questioning among themselves about when he might rise from the dead." E. Schweizer's insight that no Jew would have needed to ask what the resurrection meant indicates that the evangelist himself had composed this dialogue in order to make a point.[111] Ostensibly, some scribes sensed a need to transpose this dialogue, but to what end? The substance of the change hints at apologetic motives. The effect of this

---

[109]*Paed.* 3.10.

[110]W. D. Davies and D. Allison, *Matthew* 2, 734. Already for the evangelists some concern is in evidence for perceptions related to the disciples.

[111]For Schweizer that point is that the disciples were blind to the revelation of God. Eduard Schweizer, *The Good News According to Mark* (Translated by Donald H. Madvig; Atlanta: John Knox Press, 1977), 184–85.

alteration was that it transformed the disciples from persons who were dumbfounded by Jesus' proclamation into men who were curious about the time when it would take place. Thus, with a dash of reflection and a pass of his pen, this unnamed scribe managed to make the disciples appear smarter.

Later in that same chapter is related a story of Jesus interrupting a dispute between his followers and some of the teachers of Torah. It should be noted that this story follows close upon the heels of the transfiguration account (Mark 9:2–8). In their transcriptions of Mark 9:15, several Old Latin witnesses join Codex Bezae in replacing προστρέχοντες with προσχαίροντες, thereby transforming an amazed mass of people running up to Jesus into a crowd of rejoicing devotees. M. Hooker calls attention to the unusual placement of the reaction of the crowd at the beginning of the story, rather than the more characteristic Markan style of so closing his narratives.[112] B. Witherington follows R. H. Gundry in attributing the astonishment of the crowds to his transfigured countenance, an intentional reminiscence on the part of the author of reactions to Moses' descent from Sinai (Ex 34:29–30).[113] Yet, where Mark may have wished his readers to share a sense of awe in the face of Christ, the scribes responsible for this revision shifted the reaction from one of awe-struck astonishment to that of gleeful celebration. Once again, this reflects the apologetic concern to improve perceptions related to the followers of Jesus. They want to communicate that Christians do not consist solely of gullible masses easily amazed and swayed, but who understand what Jesus is about and who rejoice in his presence.

The fifteenth chapter of the third Gospel consists of a triad of Luke's best known parables—the Lost Sheep, Lost Coin, and the Lost Son. While the Lost Sheep has a Matthean parallel (Mt 18:12–14) and therefore issues from the Q-source, the Lost Coin and Lost Son are unique to Luke (L). All three of these parables are addressed to a group of Pharisees and scribes who are murmuring about the fact that Jesus keeps company and dines with sinners and tax collectors (Lk 15:1–2). In most manuscripts, the chapter begins, "Now the tax collectors and sinners were *all* (πάντες) drawing near to hear him." The crisp omission of πάντες in a few transcriptions of Luke 15:1 (W lat sy[s.c.p] sa[ms]), however, merits attention. A. Plummer comments that how the term is understood greatly determines the reading of the sentence. If it is regarded hyperbolically to mean, "very many," or is taken to refer to "all the publicans and undesirables in that specific locale," the verb indicates that some number of tax collectors and sinners "were drawing near" to him on a particular occasion. On the other hand, if the term is taken literally to refer to "the whole class of tax collectors and sinners," then the verb can be translated, "used to draw near," indicating the

---

[112]Morna Hooker, *The Gospel According to Mark* (Peabody, MA: Hendrickson, 1991), 222.

[113]Ben Witherington, III, *The Gospel of Mark: A Socio-Rhetorical Commentary* (Grand Rapids, MI: Eerdmans, 2001), 266. Robert H. Gundry, *Mark: A Commentary on His Apology for the Cross* (Grand Rapids, MI: Eerdmans, 2000), 487–88.

repeated action of a pattern.[114] Either way, Plummer's observations demonstrate that πάντες in its clause is not a wasted word easily dismissed. So, although its omission could easily be the result of scribal accident, it is also reasonable to recognize the omission to be deliberate, and possibly apologetically-driven. The omission, if intentional, would have served effectively to sidestep the standard pagan critique that Christians consisted only or entirely of sinners, tax collectors, and members of the lowest classes.

Finally, in Luke 9:26, may be observed a scribal rendering that elevates the status of the twelve and of all subsequent followers. Here, in the narrative context of Jesus discussing the need to follow him with no regard for the cost, the "original" text reads, "Whoever is ashamed of me and my *words* (λόγους), of him shall the Son of Man be ashamed when he comes in his glory...." Certain witnesses, however, omit λόγους, and thus redirect the requirement to honor "my words" to simply "mine." The loss of the noun could conceivably be attributed to mechanical error, but we should not disregard the fact that the omission of the noun produces the effect of transferring the honor applied to Jesus' words to his disciples and followers.

Enemies of Christianity could not do enough to disparage the social class to which the disciples belonged.[115] In turn, apologetically-minded writers urged that the apostles, in the words of Walter Bauer, "were by no means sprung from wholly impecunious circles." Clement of Alexandria, he further points out, described Matthew as "rich," and in the apocryphal First Book of Jeu 2, the apostles say:

We...have forsaken father and mother...have forsaken goods, have forsaken the splendor of a king and have followed you.[116]

It was noted earlier that Athenagoras insisted that Christianity embraced all classes, not only the lowly.[117] Tertullian, also, sought to defend the social status of Christians, insisting that Christians labored in society, paid taxes without deceit, and otherwise participated in the economy. "We are sailors," he wrote, "we serve in the army; we

---

[114]A. Plummer, *Luke*, ICC 29, 367–68. Plummer also reports that πᾶς is a favorite Lukan term (38).

[115]See, e.g., *Cels.* I.62, 63; II.46; Julian, *C. Christianos*, 199, 200, 226. See also the lucid and compelling discussion in Wayne Meeks, *The First Urban Christians* (New Haven: Yale University Press, 1983), 51–73, where he argues that early Christian congregations consisted of a cross section of Greco-Roman society, exclusive of the extreme top and bottom of society.

[116]W. Bauer, "The Picture of the Apostle in Early Christian Tradition," Hennecke-Schneemelcher, eds. *New Testament Apocrypha*, Vol II. (Philadelphia: Westminster, 1964) p. 35–74 [esp 39–40]. The citation of Clement is from *Quis div.* 13, and the reference to First Book of Jeu 2 is GCS 45, 258. On the other hand, however, the Pseudo-Clementine literature (*Hom.* XII.6) reports that Peter and Andrew grew up as orphans in poverty.

[117]*Leg* 11:3–4.

engage in farming and trading; we share with you our arts; we place the products of our labor at your service."[118]

In this regard, additional evidence for our thesis may be derived from the next grouping of variant readings in which social and economic considerations constitute the common theme. These texts appear to have been altered in precise agreement with the contours of apologetic interests related to how early Christians were perceived to fall into these categories. One, in fact, is the product of an apologist. Origen, in treating the Lord's Prayer in Matthew 6:12, in place of the term, τὰ ὀφειλήματα, "debts," substituted παραπτώματα, "misdeeds" or "trespasses."[119] Origen's exchange of terms appears quite intentional, but is not readily explained as an act of harmonization with the Lukan text. The parallel text (Luke 11:4) offers a plea for forgiveness of τὰς ἁμαρτίας, "sins," not παραπτώματα. Moreover, the variant readings that might signal a harmonization of the Lukan text to that of Matthew feature the term τὰ ὀφειλήματα. Similarly, the version of the prayer located in *Didache* also employs a form of τὰ ὀφειλήματα.[120] The term παραπτώματα does occur later in the Matthean pericope (6:14), which could have brought the term to mind for Origen, but would not necessarily account fully for his intentional choice to use the term in this place. Of course, as is frequent in analyzing patristic sources, it is difficult to know whether Origen is quoting or paraphrasing a text, or citing it or recalling it from memory; yet, considering how significant the Lord's Prayer would have been for third-century Christians at worship, it is difficult to imagine that Origen would not have known the reading by heart.[121] Yet, it seems possible, given Origen's apologetic concern for precision of language, that he may have altered this text in light of his own sensitivity to the pagan attacks on the poverty and low social standing of Christians. Origen may have been moved to avoid the ambiguity of a term wrought with economic meaning (debts) by substituting a term that was clearly ethical in content (misdeeds). In praying the Lord's Prayer, then, no one could think that Christians were pleading for God to rid them of their economic burdens; it would be evident that they were asking for forgiveness from their trespasses.

The texts of Mark 1:18/Matthew 4:20 also appear to have been altered with possible attention to economic sensitivity. These texts feature Jesus' call of the fishers Simon and Andrew. The narrator describes their decisive response to follow Jesus with the phrase, οἱ δὲ εὐθέως ἀφέντες τὰ δίκτυα ἠκολούθησαν αὐτῷ, "And immediately, leaving the nets, they followed him." Certain scribes, however, apparently

---

[118]*Ap.* 42.

[119]See, in fact, how Origen engages in word plays on this economic imagery throughout his exposition of the Lord's Prayer. See his treatise "On Prayer," *Or.* 28.1.

[120]*Did.* 8.2. For additional commentary see W. D. Davies and D. Allison, *Matthew* I, 597.

[121]On the basis of the use of the Lord's Prayer in early Christian worship, some scholars have questioned whether the prayer can be attributed with accuracy to the Q-source. It is possible that the evangelists (and later scribes?) inserted the version of the prayer known to them from their own worship services. See W. D. Davies and D. Allison, *Matthew* I, 591.

felt compelled to insert the possessive pronoun αὐτῶν after τὰ δίκτυα, thereby creating the reading, "And immediately, leaving *their* nets, they followed him."[122] Granted, this change is subtle, but the effect is worth noting. Inclusion of the possessive pronoun implied that what Simon and Andrew were leaving behind was not merely a job but their own nets, i.e., their own business. Some manuscripts (D, it) imply this even more strongly, where at Mark 1:18 they replace τὰ δίκτυα with πάντα, thus producing the reading, "And immediately, leaving *everything*, they followed him." Given Celsus' proclivity for assailing the low class of Christians, and his tendency to point out the fishermen (sometimes he referred to them as "sailors") as particularly telling examples of this, it appears plausible to think that these scribal changes may well have been intended to elevate social perceptions of these disciples, Peter in particular. To hear these scribes relate the story, these disciples were not merely common laborers; they owned their own business. Yet, they were willing to drop everything and leave it all behind in order to trace the footprints of this Rabbi from Nazareth.

A small number of witnesses (D d k) omit the remainder of Mark 9:35 following δώδεκα. This creates a reading lacking the words, "and he said to them, 'He who would be first is to be last of all and servant of all.'" Though it has been argued that these words did not belong to the "original" text, the sparse manuscript evidence in support of that contention would invite us at least to consider other reasons for exclusion. Homoeoarcton is one possibility; since the omission begins with καì as does the next word after the lost phrase, a scribe could have easily had his eye skip from one to the other. Another possibility worthy of consideration is that the words have been excised deliberately. M.-J. Lagrange explains the lacuna as result of assimilation to Matthew and Luke.[123] The phrase is indeed absent from parallels in both Matthew and Luke. This suggests that, if the words were located in their Markan exemplars, both Matthew and Luke chose to pass over them. Why might they have done so? Taylor matter-of-factly suggests they did so to improve the order of the narrative.[124] Yet, in light of the acerbic barbs directed at Christians as last among the economic ranks, is it not plausible to think that it was for defensive reasons that they eliminated the phrase (...καì λέγει αὐτοῖς, Εἴ τις θέλει πρῶτος εἶναι ἔσται πάντων ἔσχατος καὶ πάντων διάκονος) from Mark, and for those same reasons that later scribes either followed Matthew and Luke or arrived independently at the decision to similarly modify their exemplars? After all, did not Celsus imply that slaves constituted a high

---

[122]This scribal activity in Matthew is represented by K W 565 *al* it sy[s.c.p] co; in Mark, it is to be found in A *f*¹ Maj f l sy sa bo[mss].

[123]L'omission de D et k καì λεγει...διακονος, si ce n'est un pur accident, a été entraînée par l'imitation de Mt. et de Lc. M.-J. Lagrange, *Évangile selon Saint Marc*, 245.

[124]V. Taylor, *Mark*, 405.

percentage of the male Christian population?[125] Yet, did not Athenagoras testify that some members of the believing community themselves owned slaves?[126]

Similar dynamics may have been involved in modifications to John 9:8 in the pericope of the man born blind. A number of witnesses report readings that may have issued from a concern to emphasize the blindness rather than the beggarly status of this hapless individual. The "original" text read, "Therefore, his neighbors and those who had seen him before when he was a *beggar* (προσαίτης) said, 'Is this not the one who was sitting and begging?'" In its modified forms, though, the text reads, "Therefore, his neighbors and those who had seen him before when he was *blind* (τυφλός)/*blind and a beggar* (τυφλὸς ἦν καὶ προσαίτης) said, 'Is this not the one who used to sit and beg?'" Both the substitution and conflated reading have the effect of emphasizing his physical condition of blindness and muting his economic condition as a mendicant. This corresponds to apologetic propensities for both countering pagan contentions that Christians consisted almost exclusively of the impoverished lower classes and extolling the miracle-working power of Jesus.

THE FEMALES WHO FOLLOWED JESUS

Tatian devoted a chapter of his *Address to the Greeks* to the vindication of Christian women. "All our women are chaste," he wrote.[127] Clearly this apologist was concerned to defend the virtue of Christian women. There was, as we shall see, good cause.

Female followers, as indicated by both pagan and Christian sources, supplied opponents of the Jesus movement with a particularly vulnerable point of attack. Women for Christianity stood, as Margaret Y. MacDonald points out, both at the center of the movement's public controversy as well as at the heart of its egalitarian appeal.[128] The observation of Dieter Georgi, who points out that Juvenal (ca. 60–140 C.E.) in some of his satires scolded the missionary practices of Greco-Roman cults for preying almost exclusively on the curiosity of women, could well be applied to pagan attitudes toward Christian evangelistic efforts.[129] We noted above, in our discussion of

---

[125]See, e.g., *Cels.* III.50.

[126]*Leg.* XXXV. Against the charge that Christians are murderers, Athenagoras asserts, "And yet we have slaves, some more and some fewer, by whom we could not help being seen; but even of these, not one has been found to invent such things against us." The translation is from ANF II.147. The Greek, according to J. Geffcken, *Zwei griechische Apologeten*, 153, reads καίτοι καὶ δοῦλοί εἰσιν ἡμῖν τοῖς μὲν καὶ πλείους τοῖς δὲ ἐλάττους, οὓς οὐκ ἔστι λαθεῖν· ἀλλὰ καὶ τούτων οὐδεὶς καθ' ἡμῶν τὰ τηλικαῦτα οὐδὲ κατεψεύσατο.

[127]*Or.* 35.2.

[128]M. MacDonald, *Early Christian Women*, 13.

[129]In point of fact, Georgi notes, Juvenal was incorrect. The conversion of Apuleius to Isis, for example, demonstrates how an educated male could locate appeal in alien cults. Still, in this case, perceptions may be more important than truth. See Dieter Georgi, "Socioeconomic Reasons for the 'Divine Man' as a Propagandistic Pattern," in *Aspects of Religious Propaganda*, ed. E. S. Fiorenza (Notre Dame, IN: University of Notre Dame Press, 1976), 27–42, esp. 37–38.

Mark 10:13, Celsus' derision of the feminine constituency of the Christian cult. To be sure, Celsus directed one of his most barbed criticisms at what he believed was the frail foundation of Christianity, i.e., belief in Jesus' resurrection, by assailing its claim to veracity on the grounds that it was based on the testimony of a "hysterical" woman. With reference to the resurrection of Jesus, he wondered:

> But who saw this? A hysterical female, as you say, and perhaps some other one of those who were deluded by the same sorcery, who either dreamt in a certain state of mind and through wishful thinking had a hallucination due to some mistaken notion (an experience which has happened to thousands), or, which is more likely, wanted to impress the others by telling this fantastic tale, and so by this cock-and-bull story to provide a chance for other beggars.[130]

Origen recognized that Celsus had directed this malediction at Mary Magdalene[131], but he disagreed with his adversary's appraisal of Mary as "hysterical," saying, "But there is no evidence of this in the scriptural account which was the source upon which he drew for his criticism."[132]

This is but one example of how pagan opponents sought to discredit Christianity by disgracing its female face. In the male-dominated Greco-Roman world, antagonists could easily call into question the credibility of one of the key witnesses to the resurrection merely by pointing out her gender. Apologists, therefore, faced an uphill battle as they were forced to contend with numerous accusations related to female followers and adherents. In light of this dynamic, disputed readings that both dealt with women and reflected themes and concerns indicative of the apologetic corpus would lend additional support to the thesis of this work. In fact, several instances do surface in which scribes appear to have manipulated terms and verses related to the presence of γυναîκες (women or wives) and sexual content in ways consistent with apologetic themes.

Prior to examining those variant readings, however, a bit more needs to be said with regard to women in early Christianity. Among the many recent and fine works dedicated to the subject of women in early Christianity, MacDonald's possesses particular virtue for this present study because it focuses attention on female visibility in pagan critiques of early Christianity with an eye toward informing our knowledge of early Christian texts.[133] In her treatment of works by Pliny the Younger, Galen,

---

[130]*Cels.* II.55, translated by H. Chadwick, *Origen: Contra Celsum*, 109.

[131]*Cels.* II.59; H. Chadwick, *Origen: Contra Celsum*, 112.

[132]*Cels.* II.60; H. Chadwick, *Origen: Contra Celsum*, 113.

[133]M. MacDonald, *Early Christian Women*, 51. Though well beyond the limits of this study, it is incumbent upon us here to recognize at some point the complex difficulties inherent in the study of women in antiquity. Another strong feature of MacDonald's study is her due concern for methodological issues related to these complexities and her prescription that a system of checks and balances be maintained among anthropological, social-scientific, feminist, and historical modes of interpretation. Each discipline, she recognizes, offers insights and points of

Lucian, Apuleius, and Celsus, she asserts that pagan males in general negatively appraised the presence and visibility of women in the Jesus movement. For example, Pliny saw women as inclined toward religious excesses and prone to superstition, while Galen described them as biologically inferior to males. Apuleius depicted them as sexually promiscuous sorceresses. Lucian mocked them as naive and susceptible to the spells of charlatans such as Peregrinus. Celsus, as noted above, criticized Christianity itself as a religion born of the dubious initiative of a hysterical female, and, in MacDonald's understanding, connected the secrecy of Christian gatherings with the illegitimate exercise of power by women in the public sphere. MacDonald, then, argues that pagan perceptions of female believers significantly shaped their perceptions of Christianity as a whole and led to their conclusions that Christianity was a movement that was dangerous, promiscuous and seditious.[134]

Numerous other fine studies in the last quarter century have reached similar conclusions with regard to how women were treated in nascent Christianity, particularly in terms of their roles as leaders in the early church. In particular, Karen Jo Torjesen with compelling force showed how the migration of Christianity from the private, domestic, female-oriented sphere to the public, male-dominated sphere coincided directly with the ecclesiastical subjugation of women, particularly in terms of their relegation from leadership roles.[135] Also, Elizabeth Schüssler Fiorenza, in regard to the paucity of references to women in Christian sources, described what she accurately terms an "androcentric selection and transmission of early Christian traditions."[136] Here she challenged the verdict that infrequent references to women in canonical sources accurately represent the secondary and relatively inconsequential place females held in the early Jesus movement. The legitimacy of such a judgment would, she noted, necessarily rest on the presupposition that Christian writings consisted of objective factual accounts. This presupposition, however, would deny completely the insights gleaned from biblical criticism that have exposed the pastoral and propagandistic functions of the canonical scriptures as well as the influence of social forces upon the historical church. Continuing her forthright appraisal, she wrote:

> The early Christian authors have selected, redacted, and reformulated their traditional sources and materials with reference to their theological intentions and practical objectives. None of the early Christian writings and traditions is free from any of these tendencies. All early Christian writings, even the Gospels and Acts, intend to speak to actual problems and situations of the early church and illuminate them

---

correction and control for the other. On methodological considerations see idem, *Early Christian Women*, 13–27.

[134]M. MacDonald, *Early Christian Women*, 29.

[135]Karen Jo Torjesen, *When Women Were Priests* (San Francisco: HarperSanFrancisco, 1993). But see Elaine Pagels, *The Gnostic Gospels* (New York: Random House, 1979), who argues that much of the bias against women that evolved in early Christianity was rooted in the church's struggle with Gnosticism.

[136]Elizabeth Schüssler Fiorenza, *In Memory of Her* (New York: Crossroad, 1983), 48–53.

theologically. We can assume, therefore, that this methodological insight applies equally to the traditions and sources about women in early Christianity. Since the early Christian communities and authors lived in a predominantly patriarchal world and participated in its mentality, it is likely that the scarcity of information about women is conditioned by the androcentric traditioning and redaction of the early Christian authors. This applies particularly to the Gospels and Acts, since they were written toward the end of the first century. Many of the traditions and information about the activities of women in early Christianity are probably irretrievable because the androcentric selection or redaction process saw these as either unimportant or as threatening.[137]

The evidence Fiorenza marshaled in support of her lucid discussion included, in part, reference to variant readings in the New Testament tradition that exhibit "an active elimination of women from the biblical text."[138] For example, she conducted the reader to Colossians 4:15 and pointed out how feminine elements in the text had been either omitted or replaced in "Western" and Byzantine manuscripts with masculine elements. Codex Bezae is particularly notorious in this regard. To Acts 1:14, the phrase "and children" is affixed to "the women" said to be gathered with the apostles. The effect of this change is that it makes it appear that these women constitute part of the "wives and families" of the apostles rather than that they are followers in their own right. In similar fashion, Codex D also edits Acts 17:4 and 17:12 so "not a few of the noble women" are subserviently reclassified as "wives of the noble men."[139]

Other scholars have affirmed Schüssler Fiorenza's observations about how androcentric selection influenced scribes in their transmission of the text of the New Testament, some with reference to the Gospels. Let us turn to some of the variant readings that apprise us regarding how scribes treated some of the women they encountered in their exemplars.

Most commentators make little over the variant readings located in Matthew 19:29 and Mark 10:29, where ἢ γυναῖκα ("or woman/wife") is inserted into the list of sacrifices persons may be forced to make in order to follow Jesus. The amendment is easily and most often attributed to assimilation to Luke 18:29.[140] Yet, it should be noted, first, that the more common pattern of assimilation is Luke and Mark to Matthew, not Matthew and Mark to Luke.[141] Also, we should not overlook how this

---

[137]Elizabeth Schüssler Fiorenza, *In Memory of Her* (New York: Crossroad, 1983), 49.

[138]Elizabeth Schüssler Fiorenza, *In Memory of Her* (New York: Crossroad, 1983), 51.

[139]Elizabeth Schüssler Fiorenza, *In Memory of Her*, 52. Schüssler Fiorenza also reports how Bezae eliminates reference to a female convert named Damaris in Acts 17:34, and inverts the order of Prisca and Aquila in Acts 18:26 out of an apparent concern to insure that Aquila be viewed as the primary teacher of Apollos.

[140]See, e.g., B. Metzger, *Textual Commentary*, 50 in reference to the Matthean text; V. Taylor, *Mark*, 433–34, and C. S. Mann, *Mark*, 403 in reference to Mark.

[141]This was also true for Mark. Since among the Gospels Matthew was the best-known and most frequently cited, the general tendency (though certainly not without exception) is that Mark and Luke were assimilated to Matthew. See J. K. Elliott and Ian Moir, *Manuscripts and the*

insertion changes the previously expressed attitude of these Gospels with respect to wives or women. Even if they are following Luke, a point of which I remain unconvinced, the fact remains that some scribes have intentionally chosen to include "wives/women" among the things one will be rewarded for giving up in pursuit of the Jesus and the gospel.[142] "Husbands," it should be noted, are not mentioned in any of the Synoptic Gospels.[143] The adjusted readings, therefore, generate in both Matthew and Mark a portrayal of a comprehensive willingness on the part of believers to submit to ascetic discipline, even to the repudiation of nuptial union. This stands in sharp contrast to the pagan perception that Christians were profligate in satisfying their lustful appetites. It also echoes the sentiments of Christian apologists who offered direct commentary on the willing celibacy of Christians.

This willingness to surrender pleasures of the flesh in deference to pursuing intimacy with God is seen with the greatest clarity in Athenagoras. Christians, he describes, are persons far removed from promiscuous activity; even a lustful glance is forbidden.[144] Married Christians engage in coitus for the sole purpose of procreation (παιδοποιήσασθαι).[145] Yet, "If to remain a virgin (παρθενία) and abstain from sexual intercourse brings us closer to God, and if to allow ourselves nothing more than a lustful thought leads us away from God, then, since we flee the thought, much more will we refuse to commit the deed."[146] Similar sentiments may be located in Tatian, as noted above, and Theophilus of Antioch.[147]

Ben Witherington not only echoes Schüssler Fiorenza's treatment of the variant readings in Acts (and comments on some additional ones), but he invites consideration of additional disputed readings beyond the confines of Acts. One to which he directs attention is Jesus' teaching on divorce expressed in Matthew 5:32, a text that in its "original" form castigates as an "adulterer" either a woman or a man who divorces a mate. The text translates, "But I say to you, 'Any man who divorces his wife (except for fornication) causes her to commit adultery, *and any man who might marry a woman so*

Text of the New Testament (Edinburgh: T&T Clark, 1995), 67.

[142]For Matthew, ℵ C*.3 L W Θ *f*[13] (33) Maj 579 892 lat sy[c.p.h] sa mae bo testify to the inclusion of "or wife/woman." For Mark the witnesses for like amendment are A C Ψ *f*[13] Maj f q sy[p.h] bo[ms]. The witnesses that support exclusion as the "original" reading include the best of the Alexandrian, Caesarean, and "Western" witnesses and appear compelling.

[143]Perhaps the failure of any evangelist or scribe to add "husbands" to this list merely reflects the male-dominant culture of the era. Yet, it is also possible that this omission is itself apologetic in character, reflecting the concern expressed by pagan critics that Christianity is destructive of the *paterfamilias* so revered in Greco-Roman culture.

[144]*Leg.* 32.2. W. R. Schoedel, 78–79.

[145]*Leg.* 33.2. W. R. Schoedel, 80–81.

[146]*Leg.* 33.3. W. R. Schoedel, 80–81.

[147]*Ad Auto.* III.15.

divorced himself commits adultery.'"[148] Codex Bezae and several Old Latin witnesses, however, omit the second half of the verse (in italics). B. Metzger explains the omission as the product of overly-scrupulous scribes who believed the second half of the verse proved the natural consequence of the first half of the verse; thus, they erased it as redundant.[149] Witherington, though, in keeping with Schüssler Fiorenza's obser-vations, offers an alternative explanation. He suggests that it may result from "the tendency of the Western text to highlight and protect male privilege, while also relegating women to a place in the background."[150] Along with his further observation that what is omitted here is material that reflects negatively on men, we are left with a reading that renders adultery a crime that is in praxis exclusively female.[151] To be sure, the male might cause his wife to sin by putting her aside with a bill of divorce, but the "scarlet letter" may never be assigned to his forehead.

For another example of the scribal treatment of women, B. Ehrman directs our attention to a subtle modification that occurs in Luke 8:3.[152] As information for historians, the pericope in which this verse is located has been of no small importance. Luke, with his penchant for elevating—at least in comparison to his peer evangelists—the role of women in the ministry of Jesus, reports that Jesus, for the financial support of his ministry, depended upon a group of female benefactors.[153] H.

---

[148]Minor variations appear in various manuscript traditions, but the vast majority of readings apart from several "Western" witnesses incorporates some version of this phrase (5:32b). See UBS[4] for a fuller citation of witnesses and minor variations.

[149]B. Metzger, *Textual Commentary*, 13–14.

[150]Ben Witherington, "The Anti-Feminist Tendencies of the 'Western' Text in Acts," *JBL* 103 (1984), 82–84.

[151]For another treatment of this reading that arrives at a similar conclusion see B. Ehrman, "The Text of the Gospels," *Codex Bezae*, Lunel, 116. W. F. Albright and C. S. Mann, on the other hand, treat it casually with the report that the sentence is omitted in some manuscripts. Idem, *Matthew*, 65.

[152]B. Ehrman, "Text of the Gospels," *Codex Bezae*, Lunel, 116. See also Ben Witherington III, "On the Road with Mary Magdalene, Joanna, Susanna, and Other Disciples—Luke 8:1–3," *ZNW* 70 (1979), 243–248. Moreover, I am indebted for part of the following discussion to my colleague, L. Stephanie Cobb, whose insights were summarized and shared with me in her unpublished paper, "...Also Some Women: An Investigation of Luke 8:3," University of North Carolina at Chapel Hill, April 1997.

[153]Although, it should be noted, in recent years scholars have begun to question the positive appraisal of Luke's view of women. See, e.g., Elizabeth Tetlow, *Women and Ministry in the New Testament* (New York: Paulist Press, 1980); Mary Rose D'Angelo, "Women in Luke–Acts: A Redactional View," *JBL* 109 (1990) 441–61; Ross Shepard Kraemer, *Her Share of the Blessings* (New York: Oxford University Press, 1992); and Elizabeth Schüssler Fiorenza, *In Memory of Her*. Reflecting on his survey of the pertinent literature, Robert Karris characterizes the debate as "a new storm center." For his balanced, insightful remarks and extensive bibliography see idem, "Women and Discipleship in Luke," *CBQ* 56 (1994) 1–20.

Conzelmann even locates in this pericope the foundations of the later ecclesiastical office of "deaconess."[154]

The disputed reading of interest to us here consists of a presumably inconsequential exchange of dative pronouns, the singular αὐτῷ to or from the plural αὐτοῖς. It is conceivable, in noting that the variation consists of a mere one to three letters, to dismiss this variation as mechanical in nature. Yet, the substance of the change proves weighty. The plural pronoun locates its antecedent in Jesus and the Twelve, while the singular pronoun refers solely to Jesus. Both A. Plummer and J. Fitzmyer consider the plural the better attested reading, and views the singular with suspicion on the basis of its presumed harmonization to Matthew 27:55 and/or Mark 15:41.[155] B. Metzger includes the suggestion that introduction of the singular pronoun may have been due to "Christocentric correction, due perhaps to Marcion."[156]

B. Ehrman, however, sees in the reference to Marcion evidence of the prior text, one clearly attested as early as the mid-second century.[157] R. Karris, drawing extensively on the work of Carla Ricci, also questions the consensus reading.[158] The structure of the lengthy sentence in Luke 8:1–3 is fashioned around two subjects, Jesus and the women, each governing a verb; the phrase, "and the Twelve with him," appears structurally as a tacked on afterthought. Yet, most English translations, Karris points out, make this phrase the main clause, and reduce the clause featuring the women to a dependent clause. C. Ricci, according to Karris, also points out that the contention that αὐτῷ stems from harmonization with Mark 15:41 and Matthew 27:65 is flawed. If the tradition behind Mark and Matthew had specifically mentioned that the women served not only Jesus but also his disciples, then the evangelists could have reported this—i.e., used the plural pronoun—in the context of the passion, even after the departure of the Twelve. Thus, even if the singular pronoun owes its immediate location in Luke 8:3 to scribal harmonization, it conveys authentic tradition, and the plural pronoun αὐτοῖς is secondary.[159]

Such reasoning calls us to reconsider the consensus and entertain the strong possibility that the scribal modification of pronouns in Luke 8:3 moved in the direction from the singular to the plural. If this view is correct, despite the subtlety of the change, it portends weighty ramifications. Where the singular pronoun has the effect of identifying the women as the personal patrons of Jesus himself, and ostensibly places them on an equal footing with his male followers, the plural pronoun serves to redistribute their vassalage among Jesus and the Twelve. This, in practical terms,

---

[154]Hans Conzelmann, *The Theology of St. Luke* (Translated by Geoffrey Buswell; New York: Harper & Row, 1961), 47.

[155]A. Plummer, *Luke*, 216–17; J. Fitzmyer, *Luke I–IX*, 698.

[156]B. Metzger, *Textual Commentary*, 144.

[157]B. Ehrman, "Text of the Gospels," *Codex Bezae*, Lunel, 116.

[158]R. Karris, "Women and Discipleship in Luke," 6–7, who follows Carla Ricci, *Maria di Magdala e le molte altre: Donne sul cammino di Gesù* (La dracma 2; Naples: D'Auria, 1991), 167–69.

[159]See R. Karris, "Women and Discipleship in Luke," 7.

assigns their ministry to the traditional domestic sphere, which to the vast majority of the Greco-Roman populace would have been perceived as secondary in nature. The women serve and support the men, who in turn engage in direct, peer partnership with Jesus. The shift of pronouns in Luke 8:3 represents, therefore, an example of the scribal relegation of women.

This contention is made even more likely when one compares this reading with two other texts, beginning with Mark 15:41. In speaking of the women viewing the crucifixion from afar, the evangelist lists among them three particular women, Mary Magdalene, Mary the mother of James the younger and Joses, and Salome. The writer continues his identification of these women by pointing out that these were the ones "who, when he was in Galilee, followed him *and ministered to/ with him*" (καὶ διηκόνουν αὐτῷ).

Yet, once again Codex Bezae, in the company of a few other witnesses (C Δ 579 n), can be seen modifying a reference to three named women serving Jesus (=him, αὐτῷ). Also, in the modification of Luke 23:55, we view evidence of scribes tampering with a pronoun. Against the rest of the tradition that translates, "The women, who had come *with him* (αὐτῷ) from Galilee followed, and saw the tomb, and how his body was laid...," Bezae and a few other witnesses omit αὐτῷ, "with him." Although most commentators make nothing of this change, George Rice observes that the effect of this omission is to distance the association between Jesus and these women. The absence of the dative pronoun removes any trace of a connection to Jesus; they are connected only to one another as traveling companions from Galilee, nothing more.[160]

Still another variant reading worth considering in this regard is located in the Dura fragment (Parchment 24) believed by some to be from Tatian's *Diatessaron*.[161] The first

---

[160]G. Rice, "Western Non-Interpolations," 8.

[161]For a facsimile, text, and critical introduction to the fragment see Carl H. Kraeling, *A Greek Fragment of Tatian's Diatessaron from Dura* (SD III; London: Christophers, 1935). For a lucid and insightful discussion of the questions and arguments regarding the relationship of the Fragment to Tatian's Diatessaron and its implications see William L. Petersen, *Tatian's Diatessaron: Its Creation, Dissemination, Significance, and History in Scholarship* (Leiden: E. J. Brill, 1994), esp. 196–203. I borrow heavily from his discussion in order to offer this brief summary. Unearthed in excavations conducted in 1933, this revealing fragment is arguably only eighty years removed from Tatian's harmony and offers sufficient evidence for some scholars to surmise that his *Diatessaron* was composed originally in Greek and not Syriac, as had been previously supposed. Kraeling supports this his thesis, in part, with what William Petersen terms "a rhetorical argument" favoring a Greek original; Kraeling conjectures that "from the beginning there existed a need for a Greek Diatessaron if Christianity was to spread in the cities of the Mesopotamian lowlands" (Kraeling, *A Greek Fragment*, 17). D. Plooij ("A Fragment of Tatian's Diatessaron in Greek," ET 46 (1934/5), 471–6) challenged this position, however, with his observation that one reading in the Fragment could not be located in any reading of the *Diatessaron*, but did agree with a reading in the *Gospel of Peter*. Plooij argued further that, in sharp contrast to the numerous Diatessaronic readings located in the writings of Aphrahat and

line of the reconstructed fragment reads as follows:

...Ζεβεδαῖου καὶ Σαλώμη καὶ αἱ γυναῖκες τῶν συνακολουθησάντων αὐτῷ ἀπὸ τῆς Γαλιλαίας...[162]

In comparing this with the relevant canonical parallels (Mark 15:40–41, Matthew 27:55–56, and Luke 23:49), Carl Kraeling identified this as a modification that, in his words, "so drastically changes the statements of the Gospels concerning the women

---

Ephrem, no Greek Father quotes a single line from Tatian's *Diatessaron*. In his judgment, this cast serious doubt on the likelihood that the Diatessaron was penned originally in Greek. Moreover, he declared against Kraeling that a Gospel produced for the benefit of evangelizing the native population would have more likely been written in Syriac.

F. C. Burkitt ("The Dura Fragment of Tatian," *JTS* 36 (1935), 255–9) disagreed, arguing that disagreements between the Old Syriac and the Fragment indicated that their textual *Vorlage* was not the same. M.-J. Lagrange ("Deux nouveaux textes relatifs à l'Évangile. I. Un fragment grec du Diatessaron de Tatien," *RB* 44 (1935), 321–7), following the evidence adduced by Burkitt, nevertheless settled on Greek as the original language in which Tatian produced his *Diatessaron*. W. L. Petersen (*Tatian's Diatessaron*, 200) qualifies the data adduced by Plooij that no Greek Father reproduces Diatessaronic readings, noting that more recent scholarship has located such citations in the *Homilies* of Macarius and in the hymns of Romanos Melodos. Still, he notes further, both have links with Syria.

Petersen reports finding compelling the additional linguistic arguments favoring a Syriac original produced by A. Baumstark ("Ein weiteres Bruchstück griechischen 'Diatessaron' textes," *Oriens Christianus* 36 (1939), 115, n. 1). Petersen then states, "Together with Plooij's arguments, Baumstark's evidence has convinced a majority of experts that the Dura Fragment is not proof of a Greek original Diatessaron—if, indeed, it is part of a Greek Diatessaron at all, and not, as Plooij suggested, part of an independent Passion Harmony" (Petersen, *Tatian's Diatessaron*, 225). D. C. Parker, D. G. K. Taylor, and M. S. Goodacre ("The Dura-Europos Gospel Harmony," in D. G. K. Taylor, ed. *Studies in the Early Text of the Gospels and Acts: The Papers of the First Birmingham Colloquium on the Textual Criticism of the New Testament* (Atlanta: SBL, 1999), 192–228), in fact, conclude that the Dura Fragment does represent a Greek original of a Gospel harmony, but specifically one distinct from Tatian's *Diatessaron* (228).

The implications of these arguments for the variant reading currently under consideration consist mainly of how they frustrate any attempt to locate the variant reading chronologically and/or contextually with any confidence. If dependence on the *Diatessaron* could be determined with a greater degree of certainty, we could with some assurance posit very narrow temporal parameters and a fairly certain context that gave rise to this particular variant reading. As it stands, however, the Fragment still serves linguistically and literarily as a witness to the practice on the part of some scribe of intentionally modifying his exemplar of the New Testament in concert with his own agenda related to the perception of women in the movement, whether he was reproducing Tatian or some other Gospel harmony.

[162]C. Kraeling's reconstruction of this line of Dura Fragment 24 appears as follows: [ζεβεδ] ΑΙΟΥ ΚΑΙ ΣΑΛΩΜΗ Κ[α]Ι ΑΙ ΓΥΝΑΙΚΕΣ [των συ]ΝΑΚΟΛΟΥΘΗΣΑΝΤΩΝ Α[υτ]Ω. C. H. Kraeling, *Greek Fragment*, back coverlet.

who followed Jesus to Jerusalem."[163] What he was referring to is how Tatian's text, in place of "the *women* who were traveling with him," reads "the *wives of those* who were traveling with him." A. F. J. Klijn minimized the variation, identifying it merely as the result of a mechanical error, the product of the omission of a single letter in the Syriac original.[164] Kraeling, though, had argued that Greek was the original language of the work. E. C. Colwell joined ranks with Kraeling, against Klijn and theorized that the reading more likely stemmed from what he called "vital interests in the church."[165] Specifically, he expressed the probability that Tatian considered the report of the presence of women as "a liability to the Christian movement." "I am convinced," he explained further, "that the variant in the Dura fragment is an evidence of apologetic interest either on the part of Tatian or on the part of the scribe who wrote this copy."[166]

Of similar mind but pressing this matter even further, M.-J. Lagrange traced the source of the textual modification to the apologist himself, arguing that Tatian sought to remove all elements of suspicion of immorality from the account.[167] Colwell and Lagrange, then, would convince us that this reading resulted from a concern with how the presence of women in the Christian movement could be potentially misunderstood by outsiders. These three variant readings, two of which appear in Codex Bezae, all appear to be the result of a desire on the part of scribes—or in the case of the Dura fragment, an apologetically-driven harmonizer—to place distance between Jesus and his female followers. These readings also provide additional transcriptional support for Ehrman's external argument for the "originality" of the singular pronoun in Luke 8:3.

Changing course slightly, let us examine how Codex Bezae treats the text of Luke 4:39. Most manuscripts describe Jesus healing Peter's mother-in-law as follows:

καὶ ἐπιστὰς ἐπάνω αὐτῆς ἐπετίμησεν τῷ πυρετῷ καὶ ἀφῆκεν αὐτήν·
παραχῆμα δὲ ἀναστᾶσα διηκόνει αὐτοῖς

"And he stood over her and rebuked the fever and it left her; and immediately she rose and served them."

Codex D, however, transmits the verse as follows:

...καὶ ἀφῆκεν αὐτήν [semi-colon omitted] παραχρῆμα ὥστε ἀναστᾶσαν αὐτήν διακονεῖν αὐτοῖς.

---

[163]C. H. Kraeling, *Greek Fragment*, 8.

[164]A. F. J. Klijn, *A Survey of the Researches into the Western Text of the Gospels and Acts* (Utrecht, 1949), 101.

[165]E. C. Colwell, "Method in Locating a Newly Discovered Manuscript," 38.

[166]E. C. Colwell, "Method in Locating," 39.

[167]M.-J. Lagrange, "Deux nouveaux textes relativs à l'Évangile," *Revue Biblique*, XLIV (1935), 325. Cited by E. C. Colwell, "Method in Locating," 39.

"...and immediately it (the fever) left her so that (with the result that) she rose and served them."

Notice here that the scribe has transformed the second half of the compound sentence into a result clause.[168] Although some might dismiss this as a stylistic idiosyncracy on the part of the scribe, I am struck by how this editorial change in at least two ways alters the narrative. First, in Bezae's version, Jesus does not merely bring the woman from illness to health; her healing results also in her becoming one who serves Jesus and his followers. Thus, what is transmitted by all the other manuscripts as simply the first of Mark's healing miracles may be said in Codex D to perform double duty as both a healing miracle and a type of call narrative. Second, however, this slight but significant shift of emphasis also results in reducing the narrative identity of Peter's mother-in-law. Where her act of service in the "original" text is an independent act of will on her part—an act of reverence of gratitude, perhaps, but nonetheless an act of *her* will—in its modified form the action of Peter's mother-in-law becomes a result of a mere reaction to Jesus' act of healing. She is rendered all but invisible, while Jesus is elevated as the singular focal point of the story. This is no longer *quid pro quo*, no longer an interaction between peers. Her serving is, in Bezae's rendering, no longer an active and deliberate response to the merciful healing power of Jesus; it is merely the reactive, almost passive, result of being healed by him. Thus, in the miracle story as it is rendered by the scribe responsible for this portion of Codex Bezae, the dynamic influence of Jesus is elevated while the narrative identity of Peter's mother-in-law is substantially reduced. This narrative shift reflects the evolutionary shifts we outlined earlier in which the visible status and presence of women in the church were reduced and depreciated.

Another informing reading appears in some transcriptions of John 4:25. This modified reading occurs in the Johannine account of Jesus' conversation with the Samaritan woman. At one point in this discussion, the Samaritan woman responds "*I know* that Messiah, the one called Christ, is coming; whenever he might come, he will disclose to us all things." So reads a highly impressive cadre of witnesses, including P^{66*} P^{75} $\aleph^*$ A B C D W^s Θ Ψ 086 f^1 Maj lat sy$^{c.p.h}$ pbo Or^{pt}.[169] Apparently this set of witnesses is impressive enough that most commentators simply accept it as the "original" text and fail to treat the variant. Yet, the alternate reading, which I agree appears on the basis of inferior witnesses to be clearly secondary here, once again seems to adapt the testimony of a female character in a way that mirrors the social conventions of the apologetic era. A number of witnesses (among them P^{66c} $\aleph^c$ L N

---

[168]Grammatically, ὥστε with the infinitive indicates result. See F. Blass and A. Debrunner, *A Greek Grammar of the New Testament and Other Early Christian Literature* (Robert W. Funk, trans.; Chicago: The University of Chicago Press, 1961), Section 391, 197–99.

[169]It is interesting to note that the witness of Origen is split with regard to this reading. In fact, his acquaintance of both readings is reflected in his Commentary on John. For the citations see Bart Ehrman, Eldon Epp, and Gordon Fee, *The Text of the Fourth Gospel in the Writings of Origen, Volume I*, SBLNTGF 3 (Atlanta: Scholars Press, 1992), 129.

f^{13} 33 1241 it^f sy^{hmg} cop^{sa} ac^2 Or^{pt} Cyr^{lem}) indicate that certain scribes modified the singular first person οἶδα, "I know," to the plural form, οἴδαμεν, "we know." The potential significance of this subtle change rests in the fact that this transcription produces a reading in which the individual expression of personal belief issuing from a lone and morally suspect woman is recast as a corporate creed, i.e., the expression of faith that represented the established beliefs of a religious community. In this way, from a narrative perspective, the presence of this woman at the well is reduced, in a way that mirrors the efforts of the early church to placate pagan sensitivities to the visibility and leadership status of women in nascent Christianity.

Another instance of this pattern may have been imposed on the text at the beginning of the annunciation narrative in the modification of Luke 1:28. Let me acknowledge at the outset that the following discussion involves some speculation, but it is speculation mindful of the *Sitz im Leben* with which we are dealing and of the variant readings we have just discussed. Luke narrates that the angel Gabriel approaches Mary in Nazareth and addresses her, "Hail, O favored one!" A. Plummer rightly calls attention to the alliteration and verbal connection between Χαῖρε and κεχαριτωμένη.[170] Indications are that Luke has carefully crafted his story, paying close attention to language. Then follows the benediction, "The Lord is with you" (ὁ κύριος μετὰ σοῦ). At this point it can be observed by the testimony of certain witnesses (A C D X Γ Δ Π latt syr eth goth Tert Eus) that some scribes have duplicated Elizabeth's outburst, "Blessed are you among women" (1:42), and placed it upon the lips of the angel Gabriel. The UBSGNT committee expresses confidence that this is the case, giving their appraisal of the transcriptional genesis of the phrase a {B} rating. B. Metzger adds that members could offer no plausible reason for why such a wide range of witnesses (א B L W Ψ *f*1 565 700 1241 syr^{pal} cop^{sa}, bo arm geo) would have omitted it if it were original.[171] Manuscript 565 even included in its margin the note, "not found in the ancient copies."[172] Plummer rests after labeling this an interpolation borrowed from verse 42.[173] J. Fitzmyer is similarly content.[174]

Although these scholars offer solid reasons for resolving the *textual* question, their observations beg the *historical* question of why these scribes went to the trouble of borrowing the content of verse 42 and inserting it earlier in the text. What motive could have inspired this exercise? On this matter they are mute. If, however, we recognize once again that our context is a Greco-Roman world in which the male is considered superior to the female, we may unearth a clue. The words the scribes intentionally imposed on their exemplar were, εὐλογημένη σὺ ἐν γυναιξίν, "Blessed are you *among women*" (my italics). What scribes have added, therefore, is a phrase that qualifies the status of Mary. She remains blessed, to be sure, and is raised above all her

---

[170]A. Plummer, *Luke*, 22.
[171]B. Metzger, *Textual Commentary*, 129.
[172]B. H. Streeter, *The Four Gospels*, 123–24.
[173]A. Plummer, *Luke*, 22.
[174]J. Fitzmyer, *Luke I–IX*, 346.

peers; but her peers are singularly identified to be women only. She is elevated above all women, perhaps; but she remains privileged only in relation to other females. As the scribes have rewritten the story, they have insured that no one can think she has been raised to a higher status than that possessed by males.

Admittedly, not all scribal variants relegated women to an inferior status. For instance, scribes who omitted "and he did not know her until..." in Matthew 1:25 and "firstborn" in Luke 2:7 appear to have subscribed to a belief in the perpetual virginity of Mary, a belief that developed alongside the evolving high christology of proto-orthodoxy.[175] Davies and Allison address both of these texts on precisely this point.[176] They point out that, although ἕως following a negative does not necessarily indicate that there did come a point at which marital relations ensued, had the evangelist maintained a belief in perpetual virginity (as did the second-century writer of the *Protoevangelium of James*), Matthew would "have almost certainly chosen a less ambiguous phrase."[177] Likewise Luke, they continue, would scarcely have written "firstborn" to identify Jesus if the matter of Mary's continuing chastity was an issue. Yet, it became an issue early on, certainly by the second century. Already in *Protoevangelium of James*, as noted, we can observe this interest in Mary's maintained virginity, and in Aristides we observe reference to Mary as the *theotokos*.[178]

In reviewing the relationship of these amended readings to apologetic interests, recall that the Roman Empire was a man's world, a male world. Consider how these scribal modifications altered the perception of women portrayed in the Gospels. Most often, the scribally-engineered text renders women subservient to males or moves them to the background of the Gospel tradition. Females are elevated, in general, only when it serves a larger (read male) purpose, such as the heightened deification of Jesus through emphasis on his virgin birth. Otherwise, their leadership roles are down-played; their maternal instincts and spousal relationships are lifted up as definitive; and, when in doubt, they are ushered into the shadows. Some scribes, it appears, even reconfigured the healing of Peter's mother-in-law from an invitation to health into a call to service. As benefactors, women were shifted away from an intimate association with Jesus himself and recast as peripheral supporters of the general cause mainly led and carried out by men. As witnesses to the resurrection, their voices were rendered adjunct to those of the men who saw the risen Christ, even if scribes had to introduce such male witnesses into their exemplars.

In short, it can be observed that, on occasion, scribes modified their exemplars in order to put women in a place condoned by Greco-Roman culture. In many respects, this pattern closely mirrors treatment of women by various Christian

---

[175]It deserves mention here that some manuscripts assimilate Matthew 1:25 to Luke 2:7, adding "her firstborn son" at this point. See B. Metzger, *Textual Commentary*, 8.

[176]W. D. Davies and D. Allison, *Matthew*, 219.

[177]W. D. Davies and D. Allison, *Matthew*, 219. For the reference to the *Protevangelium* see *Prot. Jas.* 19.3–20.2.

[178]J. R. Harris, *Ap. Aris.* TS I, 29. Cf. 2, 3, 79, 25.

apologists. In applying scriptural exegesis to their discussions of women, patristic writers generally turned to texts that offered the basis for limiting rather than liberating women.[179]

ALL'S WELL THAT ENDS WELL: MARK 16:9–20

In concluding this chapter, I would like to bring together several motifs that have surfaced previously in this discussion and apply them to a series of variant readings widely recognized by members of the guild as one of the most compelling conundrums faced by textual critics—the several and distinct endings of the Gospel according to Mark. Scholars locate within the textual tradition four distinct endings to Mark's Gospel. For purposes of this discussion I will, for the most part, follow Vincent Taylor's nomenclature. To the verses traditionally identified as Mark 16:9–20 Taylor attaches the name, "The Longer Ending." This reading is derived from a number of witnesses (most notably A C D Δ Θ f^{13} 28 33 565 700 Maj aur c ff^2 vg syr$^{c.p.h.pal}$ cop^{bo,fay}) and is referenced by Irenaeus, Didymus, Epiphanius, Ambrose and Augustine. In addition, both Jerome and Eusebius report knowing about manuscripts containing the ending. By his tag, "The Shorter Ending," Taylor refers to the relatively terse conclusion that reads as follows:

> But they reported briefly to Peter and those with him all that they had been told. And after these things Jesus himself sent out through them, from east to west, the sacred and imperishable proclamation of eternal salvation.[180]

This Shorter Ending is found in conjunction with verses 9–20 in most of the sources that include it (L Ψ 083 099 0112 274^{mg} 579 k sy$^{hl\,mg}$ cop^{samss} bo^{mss} eth^{mss,TH}), although it serves as the final words of the Old Latin manuscript k. Taylor employs the familiar phrase "The Freer Logion" to identify the scribal embellishment of verse 16:14 that is located only in Codex W, although evidence in Jerome demonstrates that the reading was in circulation during the fourth century. The text reads as follows:

---

[179]As noted by Elizabeth A. Clark, *Women in the Early Church* (Wilmington, Delaware: Michael Glazier, 1983), 16. Prior to advancing this notion, however, she enlisted the term "ambivalence" as the most fitting characterization of the attitude of the Church Fathers toward women. These writers, she noted, portray females as both gift and curse, brimming with lust and fleeing sexual encounter, weak-willed on the one hand, unwavering in the face of martyrdom on the other (p. 15). Certainly, she is accurate here. In my discussion of women in the context of apologetic interests, therefore, I do not mean to imply either a consistency or a unilateral approach on the part of Christian apologists. Rather, I am highlighting what I do believe is the more dominant theme located among apologetic writers and how those themes correspond to scribal emendations of the text.

[180]The translation is from B. Metzger, *Textual Commentary*, 123–24.

And they excused themselves saying, "This age of lawlessness and unbelief is under Satan, who does not allow the truth and power of God to prevail over the unclean things of the spirits. Therefore reveal thy righteousness now"—thus they spoke to Christ. And Christ replied to them, "The term of years of Satan's power has been fulfilled, but other terrible things draw near. And for those who have sinned I was delivered over to death, that they may return to the truth and sin no more, in order that they may inherit the spiritual and incorruptible glory of righteousness which is in heaven."[181]

Although Codex Washingtonianus (W) constitutes the sole witness to this reading, evidence in Jerome demonstrates that this reading was in circulation during the fourth century. Finally, and this is the single amendment I will offer to Taylor's nomenclature, there is the text that ends quite suddenly with 16:8 that I prefer to label the "Abrupt Ending."[182] Strikingly, it will be seen, some of the most dramatic examples of apologetic textual reinforcement occur in the notorious amendments to the ending of Mark's Gospel.

Scholars have long recognized the strong resemblance that certain features of these Markan appendages bear to other parts of the canon. Westcott and Hort, for example, extricated the quandary of the shorter ending by asserting that it resulted from a scribe who, dissatisfied with the abrupt conclusion of 16:8, constructed his own denouement out of the contents of Matthew 28:19; Luke 24:9–12, 47; and John 20:21. The longer ending, they found much more trying, but finally settled on the notion that a scribe located this "condensed fifth narrative of the Forty Days" in another source and conscripted it as a more fitting conclusion to Mark. Much more has been written on this conundrum since the days of Westcott and Hort, and to delve too deeply into this maze of readings would be to open Pandora's box.[183]

---

[181]Again, I have employed the translation of B. Metzger, *Textual Commentary*, 124.

[182]Although in large measure I subscribe to the opinion embraced by the vast majority of scholars that this is, in fact, Mark's "original" ending, I do not wish to poison the well or fail to acknowledge that the question remains a sensitive and controversial one to some members of the guild. I therefore choose here to affix to this ending a more neutral label.

[183]The literature on this topic is vast and complex. Westcott and Hort dedicated their longest (by far) note to this issue, describing it as "almost unrivalled in interest and importance," stating further that "no other that approaches it in interest and importance stands any longer seriously in need of full discussion." [*Introduction*, "Notes," 28–51]. Caspar René Gregory asserted that the closing verses of Mark neither belonged to the Gospel nor deserved to be included in the New Testament, and Vincent Taylor was led to speak of the "decisive" nature of the evidence in supporting "the almost universally held conclusion" that these verses were not part of 'original' Mark [C. Gregory, *The Canon and Text of the New Testament* (New York: Scribner, 1924), 513; V. Taylor, *Mark*, 610]. William R. Farmer, however, in his classic study on the subject, took exception with these statements, believing that the evidence for drawing this conclusion was at the very least indecisive. Moreover, he determined that, to the extent the evidence could be considered to favor one side or the other, it favored inclusion [*The Last Twelve Verses of Mark*, SNTSMS 25 (London and New York: Cambridge University Press, 1974), 109].

Still, despite the complexities related to this constellation of variant endings, contemporary scholarship widely agrees that "original" Mark ended with 16:8 and that Mark 16:9–20 in its several forms is the product of scribal interpolation.[184] Even swimming against this current, W. R. Farmer invoked the methodology we are currently employing as offering some hope for shedding light on this textual problem when he declared:

> The best hope seems to lie in new papyrological discoveries, and in further progress in our understanding of the history of the development of text types emerging in the second and third centuries. The place of patristic studies in this development, and especially that of Origen, would seem to be especially important.[185]

It is beyond the scope of this work to untangle this Gordian knot of textual problems.[186] It seems adequate here, however, to recognize with the vast majority of scholars that the disputed endings of Mark all represent the products of scribal labors. Yet, the determination that Mark 16:9–20 is either a montage constructed out of material from the other Gospels or an independent compressed narrative is, in my judgment, at best an intermediate conclusion. We are still faced with a text in need of a context. That is, we still need to understand what forces have motivated and influenced the construction and interpolation of these verses. My contention, of course, is that apologetic interests constituted, at least in part, a force that encouraged these scribes. Therefore, the task left to us here is to compare the content of these readings to apologetic themes and strategies in order to discover whether and to what

---

W. Lane contends that the "originality" of the abrupt ending is supported by the fact that Matthew and Luke follow Mark until verse 8, and then fork in completely independent directions [W. Lane, *Mark*, NICNT, 601]. C. E. B. Cranfield conjectures that 16:9–20 constitute an early but non- Markan catechetical summary that was probably attached to the Gospel before the middle of the second century [*Mark*, Cambridge Greek Testament Commentary, 472]. Bruce Metzger's *Textual Commentary on the Greek New Testament* offers a brief but informing consideration of the four endings of the Markan Gospel (122–128). For more on the manuscript evidence see also J. K. Elliot, "The Text and Language of the Endings to Mark's Gospel," *TZ* 27 (1971), 255–62.

[184]C. S. Mann (*Mark*, AB, 673) expresses the consensus well: "Not even among writers who reject the notion that Mark deliberately ended his gospel at 16:8 is there to be found any suggestion that vv. 9–20 are from the hand of the evangelist. The vocabulary is not Markan, the whole tenor of the pericope is far different in tone from all we have seen of Mark, and even at first glance it appears to be a collage of a series of resurrection traditions." Again, though, see W. R. Farmer, *Last Twelve Verses*, 109.

[185]W. R. Farmer, *Last Twelve Verses*, 109.

[186]For other useful, more thoroughgoing discussions of the issues related to these verses see, e.g., B. H. Streeter, *The Four Gospels*, 333–360, and Frederick Wisse, "The Nature and Purpose of Redactional Changes in Early Christian Texts: The Canonical Gospels," in *The Gospel Traditions in the Second Century: Origins, Recensions, Text, and Transmission*, ed. William L. Petersen (South Bend, Ind.: Notre Dame University Press, 1989), 39–53.

extent apologetic motives may have influenced the fashioning of the finale to Mark's Gospel.

THE SHORTER ENDING

Let us consider, first, "The Shorter Ending."[187] Attested mainly by four Uncials dating from the seventh to ninth century (L Ψ 099 0112), Old Latin k, the margin of the Harclean Syriac, several Sahidic and Boharic manuscripts, the reading once again translates as follows:

> But they reported briefly to Peter and those with him (literally "those around Peter") all that they had been told. And after these things Jesus himself sent out through them, from east to west, the sacred and imperishable proclamation of eternal salvation.

At least three features of this construction reflect apologetic themes. Foremost is the indication that testimony to the resurrection and responsibility for its proclamation is transferred from the female followers to the male disciples. Second, the Gospel is a universal message that is to be directed westward, i.e. in the direction of Rome. Third, Peter is singularly identified as leader of the apostolic pack.

We may locate all of these themes in Christian apologetic writings. First, we have already witnessed how Celsus spurned Christianity as a religion built on the tenuous foundation of a deranged woman's testimony, and how Origen replied by insisting that Jesus had appeared to others, including Thomas and the men on the road to Emmaus whom he identified as Simon and Cleopas.[188] Second, the universal scope of the great commission is repeated frequently among apologists. Origen, for example, employed the concept of universality to explain why Christianity consisted of all nations and races of persons.[189] Third, the disciples are identified as "those around Peter." Recognizing here the primacy of Peter not only recalls his revered status in the early church, a status shared among most apologists,[190] but also stands against pagan rhetoric

---

[187]Kurt Aland affords a positive appraisal for the "originality" of the shorter ending in his article, "Bemerkungen zum Schluss des Markusevangeliums," in *Neotestamentica et Semitica, Studies in Honor of Matthew Black*, ed. by E. Earle Ellis and Max Wilcox (Edinburgh, 1969), 157–180.

[188]*Cels.* II.61–63. In this section Origen also alludes to the Pauline tradition from 1 Corinthians 15:3–8 in which Jesus is reported to have appeared to Cephas, the twelve, to about 500 brothers at once, then to James, and then to the apostles, and then to Paul himself.

[189]*Cels.* II.13.

[190]Origen defended the reputation of Peter against Celsus by recalling the prophetic words of John 21:18–19 that Peter would die a martyr's death (*Cels.* II.45) and allegorized Peter as the rock upon which Christ would build his church as a promise issued to all believers (*Comm. Matt.* XII.10–11). Though Tertullian remains more literal and personal in his understanding of the power of the keys being conferred on Peter uniquely, he nevertheless reveres Peter as the one by whom the church was reared (*Pud.* XXI). Clement of Alexandria refers to him as "the blessed

directed specifically at Peter. Both Celsus and Porphyry are known to have ridiculed him. If, as most scholars conclude, the so-called Shorter Ending is an editorial or scribal embellishment of Mark's Gospel, it should be noted that the literary masons responsible for constructing this addition crafted their edifice out of apologetic brick.

THE LONGER ENDING

Vincent Taylor's "Longer Ending," sometimes identified as the "Traditional ending," established itself in many versions of the New Testament as a result of its inclusion in the Textus Receptus. It, too, includes features that may rightly be identified as apologetic in character. Scholars note that these twelve verses fall naturally into four brief accounts: (1) the appearance to Mary Magdalene; (2) The appearance to two disciples; (3) the appearance to and commissioning of the eleven; and (4) an ascension narrative. Let us reflect upon each of these from the standpoint of Christian apologetics.

We discussed earlier how pagan critics, especially Celsus, scorned Christians for relying for evidence of the resurrection upon the testimony of a "hysterical" (πάροιστρος) woman. Notice, though, that this embellishment accomplishes two things in that regard. First, the narrative testifies to the sanity of Mary by reporting that prior to her ever seeing the risen Christ he had driven seven demons out of her. As in the Lukan text (8:2) which appears to bear a direct influence upon this verse, Mary is being identified here as a person purged of those forces that would make her hysterical. She is a sane, reliable witness.

Yet, and this is the second point, despite this affirmation, the male disciples refuse to believe her. They do not believe her in the same way they would subsequently dismiss the testimony of two other disciples walking in the country who relate to them the same story. It seems evident that these verses constitute a compressed account of the Lukan story of the Emmaus Road encounter.

Indeed, the eleven come to faith only when Jesus himself appears to them, a story which extends the features of the Johannine "Doubting Thomas" story to all eleven disciples.[191] From an apologetic point of view, though, this serves as a sort of back-handed compliment. Faith in the resurrection is not the product of irrational men falling for the fanciful tale of a mad woman. These men consistently yield to their own reason until a resurrected Jesus rebukes them for their incredulity and stiff-necked stubbornness. Compare this to the contention of Theophilus of Antioch that "historical writers," a category into which he placed himself, ought to have either been eye-witnesses to the events they transmitted, or at least to have received accounts of

---

Peter" and testifies to his hope in the resurrection by recalling his exhortation to his wife at her death to remember the Lord (*Strom*. XI).

[191]Notice, once again, that these stories of doubting Thomas and the two men on the road to Emmaus are precisely those Origen uses in refuting Celsus' assertion that Christianity is founded on the testimony of a hysterical woman. See *Cels*. II.61–63.

those events from credible eye-witnesses.[192] Moreover, Theophilus declared that he himself did not trust in the resurrection of the body until he understood it as the fulfillment of the prophets.[193]

Immediately following this tongue-lashing, however, Jesus authorizes the eleven to travel to the corners of the earth (κόσμος, a word used only twice in Mark) on a mission to proclaim the gospel. Although Mark 16:15–16 bears some resemblance to Matthew 28:18–20, certain Johannine features have located here, as well (cf. Jn 3:17 f.). The themes of universality and baptism included in these verses, as noted above, resonate with apologetic writers.

Also finding its way into this story is the characteristic Johannine reference to "signs" (σημεῖα). The embellisher of the Markan text declares:

> And these *signs* will accompany those who believe: in my name they will cast out demons; they will speak in new tongues; they will pick up serpents, and if they will drink any deadly thing, it will not hurt them; they will lay their hands on the sick, and they will recover.

Speaking in tongues, of course, also recalls the Pentecost narrative of Acts 2:1 ff., and reference to surviving the bite of a serpent and laying hands on the sick mirrors activities of Paul on the island of Malta (Ac 28:3–10), as well as the "power to tread upon snakes and scorpions" (Lk 10:19). Celsus ridiculed Christians for not making a positive difference in the world. Tatian, in his own inimitable style of turning the other cheek, took the offensive and inquired of the Greeks, "What are your philosophers doing of any significance or note?"[194] Origen drew a direct connection between Jesus intending his followers to serve as ministers of his teaching and conveying upon them miracle-working powers.[195] The promise that bold signs and life-changing deeds will accompany the missionary activity of the apostles serves as an important theme in apologetic writings.

Finally, an abbreviated ascension narrative concludes the Longer Ending. Examination of references to the ascension within the textual tradition proves illuminating. Three times in writings attributed to the canonical evangelists is the ascension reported: here in Mark 16:19–20, as well as Luke 24:50–52 and Acts 1:6–11. Keeping in mind the high probability that Mark 16:19–20 is derived from scribal amendment, it is striking to recall that the key verse in Luke's account, Luke 24:51, constitutes another of Hort's "Western Non-Interpolations." The shorter "Western" reading in this instance consists of the omission of the phrase, καὶ ἀνεφέρετο εἰς τὸν οὐρανόν, "and he was carried up into heaven." If, as Hort believed, ℵ* D it sys report the authentic Lukan text, then the "original" Gospels would have contained no

---

[192] *Ad Auto.* III.2.
[193] *Ad Auto.* I.14.
[194] *Or.* 25.1.
[195] *Cels.* I.38.

account of the Ascension.[196] Apart from two variant readings widely recognized as inauthentic, therefore, the account of the ascension occurs only in Acts and nowhere in the Gospels.[197]

Yet, despite the fact that the tradition treats the ascension almost as an afterthought, Jesus' transmission into heaven was adduced frequently to serve the cause of the apologists. For example, where pagans, as exhibited in Porphyry, contended that his disciples distorted and corrupted the message of Jesus, the early apologist Aristides drew a direct connection between the ascension and the commission to teach, as well as the content of the message. He stated specifically that it was after his followers witnessed Jesus go up into heaven that they went forth into the world teaching the majesty of Christ (τὴν ἐκείνου μεγαλωσύνην) and proclaiming the doctrine of truth (τὸ δόγμα κηρύττων τῆς ἀληθείης).[198]

Again, then, the four major elements that constitute the Longer Ending (16:9–20) of Mark's Gospel all appear as important features in apologetic discourse. The earliest certain evidence we have for this ending is an apologist, Tatian.[199] Both internal and external evidence, then, suggest the plausible conclusion that apologetic interests played a role in the formulation and transmission of the Traditional Ending.

THE FREER LOGION

The so-called "Freer logion" also bears marks of apologetic considerations. Taylor reads the Freer logion as an effort on the part of some scribe to, in his words, "soften the severe condemnation of the Eleven" in 16:14.[200] Albeit so, details related to the content of their defense should not be overlooked. The disciples based their appeal in the face of Jesus' rebuke on the notion that they had been dwelling under the

---

[196]See Westcott and Hort, *Introduction*, 73.

[197]See, however, John 6:62 and 20:17. These can be said to represent Johannine references to Jesus ascending, although there is no direct narrative in the Fourth Gospel of the ascension itself. Elsewhere in the New Testament, implicit references may be detected in Ephesians 4:8–10; Hebrews 4:14, 7:26, 8:1; 1 Peter 3:22; and 1 Timothy 3:16.

[198]In addition to those apologists discussed here, the fragmentary *On the Resurrection* also speaks of Jesus being taken up into heaven while the disciples beheld (see ANF, I.298). Three large fragments of this treatise survive solely in the writings of St. John of Damascus, who attributes them to Justin. Although the authenticity of this work is highly questionable (see Quasten, *Patrology*, I.205), the content of the fragment demonstrates the polemic value that was made of the ascension narrative and its witness by the disciples, and could point to a time much earlier than John of Damascus (*ca.* mid-seventh to mid-eighth century C.E.). Even as early as the second century, Irenaeus reported that the risen Jesus appeared to his disciples and in their sight ascended (*Ad Haer.* XXXII.3).

[199]Although C. S. C. Williams believed that Justin alluded to verse 20 and may have even been responsible for authoring the longer ending. C. S. C. Williams, *Alterations to the Text of the Synoptic Gospels and Acts*, 42.

[200]V. Taylor, *Mark*, 615.

oppression of a Satanic dispensation, and were therefore unable to believe and act as they would have otherwise willed. The Freer logion portrayed this Satanic era as an age in which demonic powers actively refused to permit the truth and power of God to prevail.

Compare this discussion of a sinful evil age with these apologetic writings. Tatian spoke of an end time when the present age of demons would cease and God's judgment would prevail.[201] So, too, did Origen, who declared that Jesus died in order to "destroy a great daemon, in the fact the ruler of daemons, who held in subjection all the souls of men that have come to earth."[202] Athenagoras also talked of demons whose business it was to delude humanity and to overwhelm the soul with illusion and deceit.[203] Thus, the central theme of the Freer logion resonates with a frequency shared by early Christian apologists.

CONCLUSION

Greco-Roman intellectuals derisively characterized the followers of Jesus, in sum, as gullible poverty-stricken fools, immoral fanatics, and hysterical females. The statements by Lucian of Samosata, Marcus Fronto, Apuleius, Celsus, and Porphyry adduced above confirm this digest of pagan opinion. They also, particularly in the cases of Celsus and the learned Porphyry, betray on the part of pagan opponents a familiarity with certain parts of the Christian scripture. Apologists who struggled to answer these charges frequently offered a contrary explanation of behaviors or interpretation of certain biblical narratives. Aristides, Athenagoras, Minucius Felix and Clement of Alexandria, among others, took great pains to claim the moral high ground and portray Christians as sober, pious, and chaste. Apologists defended the temperament of the disciples, asserted their boldness before non-believing adults, and explained in terms of reverent humility the practices of prostration and referring to one another as "sisters and brothers," both of which were perceived by many ancients as disgusting. Also, defenders of the faith addressed the perceived isolation of Christians among the lower classes with the claim that adherents of the movement could be found among all social and economic classes. Naturally, the burden of proof lay in showing that some Christians were indeed people of means. With regard to the female followers of Jesus, apologists were careful both to acknowledge the excellent moral character of those women who confessed the faith, and to buttress Christian claims rooted in female testimony by corroborating their stories with the support of male witnesses.

The variant readings adduced and analyzed in this chapter have in terms of content concerned persons who followed Jesus. In each instance I have sought to demonstrate the plausibility if not strong likelihood that the scribes responsible for

---

[201]Cf. *Or.* 6.1, 12.4, 14.2, 16.1, 26.2, and, especially, 29.2.
[202]*Cels.* I.31; trans. H. Chadwick, *Origen: Contra Celsum*, 31.
[203]*Leg.* 27.2.

these amended readings transposed their texts to the pitch of apologetic interests. The voices of Origen, Tatian, and Athenagoras may be discerned echoing through these scribal compositions. As if members of an orchestra before the concert, certain scribes tuned their manuscripts to match the apologetic chords resonating in their minds. With deliberation and yet subtlety, the scribes whose actions have been reported here effectively fortified strengths and minimized weaknesses inherent in the texts where they recognized the need and opportunity. Sometimes they replaced troublesome words; other times they improved the depicted character of a disciple or introduced an explanation for a socially offensive behavior. Most notably, perhaps, is how the various embellishments to the finale of Mark's Gospel—each of which (except for the "abrupt ending") is viewed by the consensus of textual scholars as a scribal product—all consist in large measure of content that follows the contours of apologetic interests.

5

WHEN QUIRE MEETS EMPIRE:
SCRIBAL TRADITION AND THE ROMAN STATE

In the earliest years of the Christian movement, the Roman attitude toward followers of Jesus appears to have been marked by casual indifference. Most of the residents of the Empire were, in the words of T. D. Barnes, "either unaware of or uninterested in the Christians in their midst."[1] Those hostilities that were directed at believers in those initial years consisted mostly of fallout issuing from internecine controversies that broke out among Christians and Jews. Only when such disturbances disturbed the Roman peace did authorities intervene.[2] Canonical Acts reports how such tensions provoked the violent deaths of Stephen and James, but these were

---

[1]T. D. Barnes, "Pagan Perceptions of Christianity," in Ian Hazlett, ed., *Early Christianity: Origins and Evolution to AD 600* (London: SPCK, 1991), 232. Despite the fact that Christians were present in Rome at least by the time of Claudius, Barnes points out, no clear reference to them can be located in the extant pagan writers of the first century, including Martial, Juvenal, Dio Chrysostom, and Plutarch.

[2]W. H. C. Frend, *Martyrdom and Persecution in the Early Church: A Study of a Conflict from the Maccabees to Donatus* (New York: New York University Press, 1967). Frend's thick volume reads like a seismographic chart displaying, in terms of the hostile attitudes and actions of the Roman state toward nascent Christianity, numerous shifts in intensity and scope. At times Frend's narrative resembles a steady, smooth line, reflecting the simple fact that earliest Christianity merited little consideration from Roman authorities or their enforcing legions. That is to say, in the beginning, the number of Christian adherents was small and their impact on the empire was inconsequential. Where they did come to the attention of the political or peacekeeping establishment during the first two-thirds of the first century, such incidents usually resulted from some sort of local commotion related to their often zealous evangelical efforts. What might be classified as an empire-wide ennui, therefore, constitutes the most consistent attitude of the Roman state toward Christianity prior to the Decian persecution, apart from occasional sporadic and scattered pogroms and persecutions.

In Frend's description, these periodic afflictions—such as those appearing, for example, at points during the reigns of Nero, Trajan, Domitian, Marcus Aurelius, and Maximin, to name some major ones—can be characterized as sharp spikes on the historical graph. Even most of these, though, it should be emphasized, were local and therefore limited in scope. Similarly, the famous martyrdom of the saints in Lyons and Vienne, for all its notoriety, remained geographically confined. To continue to borrow the language of seismology, the Richter scale would have failed to register peak numbers until the first empire-wide persecution under Decius (249–251 C.E.), and the later, so-called "Great Persecution" under Diocletian (303–312).

deaths carried out by Jewish crowds and not Roman legions. Although the *Annals* of Tacitus inform us that, as early as 64 C.E., Nero lay blame for the fire of Rome at the Christians' doorstep, the historian himself notes that the accusation was politically motivated and unfounded, and all indications are that the prescribed retribution against them was confined to Rome.[3] Before the fire, the antagonism that was directed toward Christians happened on a small scale, and appears to have been generated as the result of local disturbances, led usually by Jews.

Roman writers seem to have considered Christianity a topic of interest only when it became a perceived threat to Rome. For example, Roman historians gave serious treatment to none of the failed messianic movements in Palestine during the first century.[4] Only later, the extant evidence shows, did the practice grow widespread among Romans to target Christians as deserving capital sentence. How, when, and why this escalation occurred has been the subject of a great deal of scholarly reflection and dispute, especially since the middle of the twentieth century. This bewildering issue remains in dispute, but is important enough to merit a brief excursus, following which we shall pursue a search for the stances taken most frequently by Christian apologists in relation to the Roman state.

EXCURSUS: WHY WERE EARLY CHRISTIANS PERSECUTED?

As indicated by his reply to Pliny, *c.* 111 C.E., Trajan affirmed the execution of accused persons who remained adamant in their claim of faith, but he also insisted that any accused person who denied the faith and who publicly demonstrated his denial by honoring Roman deities should be released. Moreover, he forbad either unfounded accusation or government-sponsored investigations.[5] In addition to those under Nero and Trajan, data support the dual contention that, on the one hand, Christians endured periodic hardships under Domitian,[6] Marcus Aurelius,[7] and Septimus Severus,[8] to name

---

[3]Tacitus, *Annals* XV.44. See the critical edition of the Latin text in Karl Niperdey and Georg Andresen, eds. *P. Cornelius Tacitus: Annalen*, Zweiter Band (Freiburg, Germany: Weidmann, 1978), 263–265; and the text and English translation in Tacitus, *The Annals*, Volume V, (Translated by John Jackson; LCL; Cambridge, MA: Harvard University Press, 1937), 282–285.

[4]As so clearly summarized in the recent introduction by Robert E. Van Voorst, *Jesus Outside the New Testament: An Introduction to the Ancient Evidence* (Grand Rapids, MI: Eerdmans, 2000): 70–1.

[5]Pliny, *Letters* 97.

[6]Although some recent scholarship has rejected the occurrence of persecution under Emperor Domitian (81–96 C.E.), Robin Lane Fox points out that phrases in 1 Clement 1.1 indicate that persecution within the city of Rome did indeed transpire during his reign. Idem, *Pagans and Christians* (San Francisco: Harper & Row, 1986), 433. See also L. W. Barnard, *Studies in Church History and Patristics*, 139–42, in support of this contention by Lane Fox. Kirsopp Lake, in discussing the date of 1 Clement, entertains the possibility of associating the persecutions referred to in 1 Clement 1.1 with the reign of Domitian, probably around 96 C.E.; but he

a few; but, on the other, it was for the first time in the middle of the third century, during the short-lived reign of Decius (249–251), that an emperor ordered an empire-wide pogrom against Christians.[9]

Thus, prior to the tolerance for them prescribed by the edict of Galerius in 311 and their subsequent elevation to favored status under Constantine, Christians were generally treated by the Roman state with either widespread indifference or violent contempt. On and off again during the first four centuries of the common era, Christians suffered at the hands of Roman authorities. That this occurred is clear enough; but the template for how, why, and to what extent it occurred remains unsettled. The lacunae in our knowledge regarding this issue have prompted fierce and long-standing discussions among members of the academy about the scope and motives for Roman intervention in the Christian enterprise. The question is often framed, "Why were early Christians persecuted?" A brief review of the classic debate between A. N. Sherwin-White and G. E. M. de Ste. Croix serves as a point of smooth entry into the white water currents of this discussion.[10]

---

cautions that "we know very little about the alleged persecution in the time of Domitian, and it would not be prudent to decide that the epistle cannot be another ten or fifteen years later." Idem, ed. and trans., *The Apostolic Fathers* (LCL 2 vols.; Cambridge, MA: Harvard University Press, 1985), 5. For additional ancient source material on Domitian see Suetonius, *De Vita Caesarum*, VIII and Eusebius, *Hist eccl.* III.13–20.

[7]Eusebius (*Hist. eccl.* IV.15.1) refers to disturbing persecutions associated with the joint reign of Lucius Verus (161–169) and Marcus Aurelius (161–180). W. H. C. Frend (*Persecution and Martyrdom*, 198–9) indicates that over time the prescriptive practices directed by Trajan and Hadrian that Christians were to be punished but not sought out for punishment began to be discarded in favor of more active investigation. He cites the persecutions in Smyrna (166–7) and Lyons (177) as evidence in support of his contention. Frend goes on to point out, however, that under Marcus Aurelius, recantation still earned the accused a pardon, unless allegations of criminal behavior (*flagitia*) had also been charged.

[8]Only briefly, however. Except for the years 202–3, the reigns of Septimus Severus and his son demonstrated tolerance toward Christians. W. H. C. Frend, *Martyrdom and Persecution*, 242.

[9]R. Lane Fox describes the publication of Decius' edict as part of his effort to construct for himself a deliberate public image harking back to the piety and prosperity of the Antonine dynasty. He notes that only a fragment of actual text of the edict has survived, and thus the precise nature of its purpose remains disputed. Idem, *Pagans and Christians*, 452. W. H. C. Frend (*Persecution and Martyrdom*, 300–301) in general concurs with Lane Fox, although he emphasizes even more the political motives behind the edict and its call for sacrifice, namely to unite support behind him as a usurper to the imperial throne, and downplays the edict as being "aimed negatively against the Christians." Nevertheless, its application led to persecution.

[10]Prior to 1952, motivation for Roman carnage against Christians was generally attributed to one of three factors: (1) "general law," the belief that there was enacted a widespread legislation forbidding the practice of Christian religion; (2) "*coercitio*," Mommsen's theory that Christians were punished at the discretion of local governors on the basis of their ordinary power to enforce public order (*imperium*); and, (3) "specific offenses," the belief that Christians were prosecuted for specific offenses such as child-murder, incest, magic, illegal assembly, and treason—a charge generally based on a Christian's refusal to worship the emperor.

In his 1952 article that rekindled interest in this question, Sherwin-White argued that, prior to the empire-wide edicts issued by Decius, Romans persecuted early Christians on account of their *contumacia*, i.e. their excessive obstinacy at refusing an official request to perform a reasonable order. In support of his thesis, he cited as primary evidence that Christians were executed only when they proved obstinate, particularly in failing to pay homage to the Roman cult. Pliny's correspondence from Bithynia-Pontus, e.g., disclosed that neither for their name (*nomen*) nor past actions (*flagitia*) were Christians executed if they merely carried out the command of the governor to offer up incense. Also, with regard to the Scillitan martyrs, he noted, reference was made to the proconsul affording Christians time to return to the Roman tradition. Thus, for Sherwin-White, Christians were persecuted on the basis of gubernatorial discretion not imperial edict, and they were persecuted, not so much for their crimes or for merely bearing the name "Christian" *per se*, but for their obstinacy.[11]

Sherwin-White's arguments failed to convince G. E. M. de Ste. Croix. In a 1961 paper read to the Joint Meeting of Hellenic and Roman Societies and the Classical Association at Oxford and published as an article in 1963, Ste. Croix challenged several features of Sherwin-White's case. In particular, he clarified the point that Pliny did not offer a test to those who professed to be Christians but only to those who claimed *not* to be. The test, then, was not a means of pardon for professing Christians, but a test of sincerity on the part of those who denied association with the movement. Equally challenging was Ste. Croix's stern reminder that the question under investigation involved the impulse behind the *initial* arrest of Christians, i.e., why they were brought to trial in the first place. While it was possible, Ste. Croix conceded, that obstinacy in the face of judicial review might provoke the temperamental wrath of a governor in the heat of dispute, the concept of *contumacia* failed to explain why believers were initially summoned before the provincial administrator.

What did account for their initial summons, at least in part, according to Ste. Croix, was the monotheistic exclusivism of the Christians.[12] Their singular devotion to one god to the exclusion of all others was incomprehensible to the polytheistic majority. Moreover, by a population rooted in the belief that harmony between humans and their deities was brought about by the regular exercise of traditional cultic practice, it was believed that Christian truancy from public religious rites alienated the affections of the traditional gods and thus jeopardized the *pax deorum*. As Christians

---

For the classic exchange between Sherwin-White and Ste. Croix, see A. N. Sherwin-White, "The Early Persecutions and Roman Law Again," *JTS*, n. s. III,2 (October, 1952), 199–213; G. E. M. de Ste. Croix, "Why Were the Early Christians Persecuted?" *Past and Present*, 26 (1963), 6–38; A. N. Sherwin-White, "Why Were Early Christians Persecuted?—An Amendment," *Past and Present*, 27 (1964), 23–27; and G. E. M. de Ste. Croix, "Why Were Early Christians Persecuted—A Rejoinder," *Past and Present*, 27 (1964), 28–33. All four of these articles appear together in Everett Ferguson, ed., *Church and State in the Early Church* (Studies in Early Christianity, Volume VII; New York and London: Garland, 1993), 1–59.

[11]A. N. Sherwin-White, "Early Persecutions and the Roman Law Again," 210–11.

[12]G. E. M. de Ste. Croix, "Why Were the Early Christians Persecuted?" 24.

openly vented their denigration of pagan gods as loathsome demons or publicly declared their assertion that these deities did not exist at all, such brazen disregard of their traditions provoked among many pagans simmering disdain if not boiling hostility. Also, unlike their religious progenitors with whom they shared an emblematic exclusivism, Christians did not enjoy the degree of tolerance pagans afforded Jews on the basis of the antiquity of their religion and its practices. Christians, then, garnered neither the respect attached to antiquity nor the public attitude of *laissez faire* generally associated with mutual indifference. Instead, tensions mounted. In refusing altogether to participate in the religious rites of their local communities, followers of Jesus threatened to add injury to insult. As numerous sources from the mid-second century to the fifth century demonstrate, the pagan populace feared that when the gods inevitably chose to rain punishment down upon these irreverent Christians they might get hurt from the fallout.[13] Other factors, such as economic issues, may have played a minor part in the growing tensions, but chiefly it was this fear of innocently suffering from a divine retribution deserved by and directed at irreverent Christians that inflamed the sensitivities of the pagan populace.

This served Ste. Croix as a satisfactory explanation for why the *masses* developed hostility toward Christians, but there remained for him the question of the *official* reaction of the Roman state. With the single and very different exception of the Jews, he noted, Rome possessed no precedent for dealing with this maverick brand of religious exclusivism. He also acknowledged that different members of the governing establishment may have been driven or moved by different motivations. Finally, though, for Ste. Croix, the attitude of the state in persecuting Christians stemmed from the latter's denigration of traditional religion. Two points prompted his conclusion. One was his observation that official representatives of the state, unlike pagan adversaries like Celsus and Porphyry, did not attack the positive aspects of the religion; only its refusal to honor the pagan gods was confronted. Second was his recognition that most sects of Gnostic Christians escaped persecution, apparently on the grounds that their expression of the faith did not insist on being exclusive.[14]

Sherwin-White's reply to Ste. Croix was immediate. While he affirmed Ste. Croix's overall treatment of the question, and acknowledged that his thesis prevailed following the reign of Marcus Aurelius, he charged that the author's criticism of his basic thesis missed the mark due to a methodological flaw, namely that of working backward historically. "The belief that 'godlessness' was at the core of the matter," he writes, "depends entirely upon the evidence of the later period....But for the earliest period of Christian persecution we have the testimony of three highly placed Roman

---

[13]Probably the most familiar of these sources is located in Tertullian, *Ap.* 40.1–2, where he puts these words into the mouths of pagans who blame every misfortune upon Christians: "If the Tiber overflows or the Nile does not, if there occurs a drought or an earthquake, famine or pestilence, at once the cry goes up, 'The Christians to the lion.'" See also Augustine, *Civ.* II.3 and Origen, *Cels.* III.15.

[14]G. E. M. de Ste. Croix, "Why Were the Early Christians Persecuted?", 28–9.

administrators," whom he names as Pliny, Tacitus, and Suetonius. "In all three," he continued, "the only ground indicated for the proscription of the cult is its association with crimes and immoralities—*flagitia, scelera, maleficia.*"[15] Before addressing Ste. Croix's question about why the masses disdained and the authorities arrested Christians in the first place, Sherwin-White insisted, one needed to face a prior question, which he phrased, "When did the central government perceive that the extensiveness of the Christian following required that their exclusive godlessness was in itself not to be tolerated, apart from other associated offences?"[16] Pliny's letter, Sherwin-White declared, made clear that this did not occur before his time, i.e. 112 C.E. His *contumacia* theory, he argued, was proposed to explain the transition among Romans from the earliest indictments that centered on *flagitia* to charges related to *godlessness* that emerged later.

Once again, though, Sherwin-White's "amendment" failed to persuade Ste. Croix. In a "Rejoinder" that appeared in the same issue as Sherwin-White's "Amendment," Ste. Croix once again dismissed the *contumacia* theory on the basis of vocabulary (*obstinatio* not *contumacia* occurred in the relevant source material) and for lack of any firm evidence that Christians were ever executed because they were guilty of disobedience.[17] Moreover, Ste. Croix noted that in both Pliny and Tacitus there was clear indication that Christians could be duly punished even in the absence of being found guilty of any immediate crimes or abominations (*flagitia*) merely on the basis that the name Christian itself implied inherent abominations. Ste. Croix distinguished this behavior of the Roman state from its approach to other "superstitions," such as the Bacchanalia or the Isis cult. Roman action against these groups was always directed toward specific offenses (*flagitia*), and neither cult was ever made altogether illegal. This, he emphasized, was different from the Roman ban against professing to be a Christian.[18] For Ste. Croix, then, both prior to and after the response of Trajan, Christian confession was enough to merit arrest and punishment; any reaction to *contumacia* constituted an afterthought. Ste. Croix remained convinced that at the heart of what he called the "unique offense" of Christianity was its atheism (ἀθεότης).[19] Its failure to peacefully co-exist within a religiously pluralistic society constituted not only, in the words of Tacitus, a "detestable superstition" (*exitiabilis superstitio*), but also a treasonous threat.

For some time, then, Ste. Croix's thesis constituted the mainstream of discourse on the subject until, more recently, T. D. Barnes attempted to cut a fresh channel into

---

[15] A. N. Sherwin-White, "Amendment," 23.

[16] A. N. Sherwin-White, "Amendment," 24.

[17] G. E. M. de Ste. Croix, "Rejoinder," 28–29.

[18] G. E. M. de Ste. Croix, "Rejoinder," 32–33.

[19] G. E. M. de Ste. Croix, "Rejoinder," 33.

this braided river of thought.[20] Barnes approached the question by searching for any evidence of Roman legislation against Christianity prior to Decius in 250 C.E. Both Tertullian (*Ap.* 4.4) and Athenagoras (*Leg.* 7), Barnes pointed out, indicated that Christianity was illegal, but failed to explain how it came to be so. Unfortunately, his analytical trek through source references to emperors—among them Tiberius, Nero, Domitian, Trajan, Hadrian, Antoninus Pius, Marcus Aurelius, Commodus, Septimus Severus, and Maximin—and what he considered the most reliable of martyr accounts produced little fruit. His sober but rather anticlimactic conclusion was that, until the persecution of Decius, the legal position of Christians within the empire remained that of Trajan's prescription to Pliny.[21]

Finding no definitive answer in his research into imperial legislation led Barnes to seek more decisive conclusions elsewhere, however, most immediately in clues located in the canonical Acts of the Apostles (16:16 ff., 17:5 ff.). Thessalonian Jews, he noted, charged Paul and Silas with illegal activity for proclaiming Jesus as their king, and at Philippi, after Paul's effective exorcism rendered their slave-girl useless to them, her owners brought Paul and Silas before the magistrate for "disturbing our city and for advocating customs which it is not lawful (οὐκ ἔξεστιν) for us Romans to accept or practice" (Ac 16:21). The resulting punishments before local officials—a moderate flogging and a night's imprisonment—showed him that local responses to Christian missionary activity could result in the sort of disturbances that had to be enforced by local peacekeepers. Moreover, Acts offers evidence of abuse on strictly religious grounds. Because the communities were divided over their teachings and acts of power, Paul and Barnabas were cast out of Pisidian Antioch, Iconium, and Lystra, where in this last instance Paul was stoned and left for dead. At Athens and Ephesus, also, religious tensions incited crowd reactions to Paul.

Barnes located in these stories the foreshadowing of a future and more severe prejudice against Christianity as he recalled the proconsul of Africa, Vigellius Saturnus, who in the year 180 truncated a Christian's attempt to espouse his faith with the assertion, "I shall not listen if you speak evil of what is sacred to us." There was, in addition, the juxtaposition discernible in Pliny of his celebration of the revival of interest in pagan temples and cults with his concern for the residence of Christians in his province. Even in the absence of evidence for clear definitive legislation that supported his thesis, Barnes substantiated his opinion on what he saw as a common thread that united virtually every layer of official Roman response to Christians—whether it was that of a local magistrate, provincial governor, or the Emperor himself. He concluded:

---

[20]T. D. Barnes, "Legislation Against the Christians," 32–50. Reprinted in Everett Ferguson, ed., *Church and State in the Early Church* (Studies in Early Christianity Series, Volume VII; New York and London: Garland Publishing, 1993): 60–78.

[21]T. D. Barnes, "Legislation," 48.

The relevance of these facts to the problem of the legal basis of the condemnation of Christians ought to be clear. A provincial governor was predisposed to punish those who attacked the established religions, and would do so without waiting for a legal enactment by the Senate or the emperor. *Mos maiorum* was the most important source of Roman law, and it was precisely *mos maiorum* in all its aspects that Christians urged men to repudiate. The theory of 'national apostasy' fails as an explanation of the legal basis of the condemnation of Christians; but it comes close to the truth if it is applied, not to the law, but to the attitudes of men. It is in the minds of men, not in the demands of Roman law, that the roots of the persecution of the Christians in the Roman Empire are to be sought.[22]

From this brief survey of the issues arising from the effort to characterize the relationship of the Roman state and early Christianity it may be seen easily enough why this riddle remains unsolved. Despite the sweeping research and probing analyses of Sherwin-White, Ste. Croix, and Barnes, no categorical case has been constructed and loose ends remain. Yet, it may be stated fairly that tying together this web of investigation is the thematic thread rooted in the writings of Pliny. All three scholars return to this provincial governor's correspondence with Trajan as the underpinning of their arguments, and each, in his own way, understands that there lies beneath Pliny's swift execution of Roman justice some unwritten but preconceived notion that persons unwilling to deny their Christianity deserve to die. Capital punishment is earned not for any crime they have committed but for the specific creed they continue to confess; and not for what they have done but for what they have left undone.

Roman justice was at its foundation practical. Christians as they were perceived may or may not have deserved to die, but they needed to be eliminated, because they would not "live and let live." Every convert to this novel superstition added to a growing number of persons intolerant of the beliefs of the majority and of those unwilling to adhere to the traditions that helped make the empire great and insure its ongoing stability.

CHRISTIANS THROUGH THE EYES OF PAGAN DESPISERS

Whatever uncertainties remain about why they were persecuted, it is clear that by the early second century, along with being despised, Christians were suspected and feared. For example, the aforementioned correspondence between Pliny and Trajan provides an early Roman record of government-inflicted punishment on adherents of the faith.[23] Here we are informed that Roman leadership early in the second century

---

[22]T. D. Barnes, "Legislation," 50.

[23]For the relevant English text of Pliny's letters see *The Epistles of Pliny*, Volume III (Translated by William Melmouth and edited by Clifford H. Moore; Boston: Bibliophile Society, 1925), 166–170, and S. Benko, "Pagan Criticism of Christianity,"1068–69. For commentary on the Latin text of Epistles 96 and 97 see A. N. Sherwin-White, *The Letters of Pliny: A Historical and Social Commentary* (Oxford: Clarendon Press, 1985): 691–712.

understood Christians to be a menace to society, to the extent that the very confession of the name Christian merited capital punishment.[24] Also, the literary invention of Minucius Felix , the pagan Caecilius, gave voice to a form of pagan criticism that viewed Christians as a rabble of blasphemous conspirators, whose secret nocturnal orgies provided settings for their immoral, anti-social behaviors.[25] The Cynic philosopher Crescens, known to posterity only through Justin's reference to him as an opponent of the Jesus movement, publicly declared Christians to be "impious" and "atheistic."[26] These were labels that had political as well as religious implications. Separation of church and state was a concept foreign to the ancient mind.

Thus, literary defenders and despisers of Christianity both recognized that there were political implications associated with their religious convictions. Failure on the part of Christians to revere Roman deities was believed to jeopardize the ongoing stability and prosperity of the empire. Their truancy from pagan festivals, processions, and games; their obsession with a future afterlife to the point of eschewing pleasure in the present; their irreverent disregard for pagan gods and temples; and their refusal to offer incense to the emperor connoted treason against Rome. Tacitus represented this view in his *Annals* when he described how blithely Nero was able to transfer blame for the torching of Rome to the Christians because they were widely viewed by the masses as *odio humani generis*," the hatred of the human race."[27] Even more to the point, Caecilius (in *Octavius*) defined Christianity as a rabble of blasphemous conspirators who practiced the adoration of an executed criminal.[28]

In order to propagate this specter that the Jesus movement constituted a menace to society, pagan intellectuals liberally applied to Christ or his followers pejorative labels such as criminal, charlatan, friend of sinners, magician, or revolutionary. Celsus was particularly fond of invoking this theme of insurrection. He described certain teachings of Jesus as "*rebellious utterances*,"[29] and frequently labeled him a "sorcerer," an appellation that we noted previously was in terms of its content not merely pejorative but criminal. At one point Celsus draws what was in his mind a dramatic contrast between adherents of the [other] mystery religions and Christians. Celsus declares:

> Those who summon people to the other mysteries make this preliminary proclamation: Whosoever has pure hands and a wise tongue. And again, others say: Whosoever is pure from all defilement, and whose soul knows nothing of evil, and who has lived well and righteously. Such are the preliminary exhortations of those who promise purification from sins. But let us hear what folk these Christians call. Whosoever is a sinner, they say, whosoever is unwise, whosoever is a child, and, in

---

[24]For an English translation of the relevant text of Pliny's letters see S. Benko, "Pagan Criticism of Christianity,"1068–69. See also the footnote immediately above.

[25]*Oct.* VIII.

[26]Justin Martyr, *2 Ap.* See Benko, "Pagan Criticism of Christianity," 1078.

[27]Tacitus, *Ann.* 15.44, cited from S. Benko, "Pagan Criticism of Christianity," 1063.

[28]*Oct.* VIII.

[29]*Cels.* VIII.2.

a word, whosoever is a wretch, the kingdom of God will receive him. Do you not say that a sinner is he who is dishonest, a thief, a burglar, a poisoner, a sacrilegious fellow, and a grave-robber? What others would a robber invite and call?[30]

In another particularly inflammatory passage in which he calls Christians to perform their civic duty and serve the emperor, Celsus dared:

If everyone were to do the same as you, there would be nothing to prevent him [meaning the emperor] from being abandoned, alone and deserted, while earthly things would come into the power of the most lawless and savage barbarians....[31]

For Celsus, then, Christian behavior represented activity that if emulated would threaten the stability of Rome and pose a danger to the emperor himself. Roman civilization would fall into the hands of lawless barbarians, and the only *kingdom* that would be left—the one of Christians' making—would consist of unwise wretches, misled children, and a host of social miscreants. Yet another pagan critic, recorded in the *Octavius* of Minucius Felix, voiced that "Christians do not understand their civic duty."[32] Porphyry, too, particularly in his *Philosophy from Oracles*, called attention to the implicit dangers in a movement that turned citizens away from traditional piety and urged exclusive commitment to Jesus. Curiously, in this work, it was not with Christ that Porphyry found fault; indeed, Porphyry's perception was that the gods themselves honored Jesus. It was with his followers, whom the Neo-Platonist believed had corrupted the Nazarene's teachings, blasphemously declaring him to be a god.[33] It was they who were leading people astray, religiously and politically.

CHRISTIAN APOLOGISTS AND THE ROMAN STATE

Recognizing the stakes inherent in the treasonous and criminal accusations of their opponents, defenders of the faith in an effort to stave off police actions against believers frequently appealed directly to imperial justice. Thus, many of the preserved apologies were addressed to emperors, and, though bold in their arguments, were crafted with a deferential respect for Roman authority.

Though a venerated figure of the second century and a prolific writer, only fragments of the works of Melito, bishop of Sardis, have survived. From Eusebius, we know that around the year 170 C.E. Melito addressed to Marcus Aurelius his defense of the Christian faith. Of our extant sources, Melito was the first to champion belief

---

[30]*Cels.* III.59.

[31]*Cels.* VIII.68.

[32]Minucius Felix, *Oct.*, 12.

[33]See G. Wolff, ed. *Porphyrii de Philosophia Ex Oraculis Haurienda* (Hildeshiem: Georg Olms, 1962; Original edition 1856): 180–81; and the discussions in J. Bidez, *Vie de Porphyre.* (Hildesheim: Georg Olms, 1964; Original edition 1913): 19–22; and Robert L. Wilken, *The Christians as the Romans Saw Them* (New Haven: Yale University Press, 1984): esp. 148–56.

in the symbiotic relationship of the Christian religion and the Roman state. In his defense addressed to Marcus Aurelius, he portrayed the chronological coincidence of Augustus and Jesus as a good omen for the empire, noting that since that time Rome had suffered no mishap but only flourished.[34] Also, for all of Melito's well-known polemical passion, he dutifully prostrated himself before Caesar. To the emperor about the brutal treatment of Christians, he submissively fawned, "If it is your command that this is done, let it count as rightly happening."[35]

The unknown writer of the *Epistle to Diognetus* embarked on a slightly different course, drawing an analogy between the relationship of the soul to the body and that of Christians to the world. Although they resided in this world, he explained, it was merely as sojourners; Christians innately belonged to another sphere of existence. Indeed, it was because of their alien nature that they were so blatantly misunderstood and so condemned. Still, even when reviled, they blessed. Despite being condemned as evildoers, theirs was a record of doing good. And as dutiful servants in this alien existence, the writer asserted, Christians were committed to take full part as citizens.[36]

Respect for the imperial office may also be witnessed in the writings of Theophilus of Antioch. Although he asserted unequivocally that God alone was to be worshiped, he added in no uncertain terms that the emperor deserved honor and should be wished well, obeyed, and prayed for; indeed, to do so was to perform the will of God.[37] Of course, this attitude toward Rome had been expressed early on by Paul in his letter to the believers in the capital city (Rom 13:1–7), and echoed with enthusiasm in the general epistle designated as 1 Peter (2:11–17). Theophilus, though, made sure this attitude was known to Roman principalities.

Athenagoras, devoting most of his apology to refuting charges of immorality directed against Christians, closed his defense with a plea for imperial approval, which, he insisted, was well deserved. He argued:

> Who ought more justly to receive what they request than men like ourselves, who pray for your reign that the succession to the kingdom may proceed from father to son, as is most just, and that your reign may grow and increase as all men become subject to you? This is also to our advantage, that we may lead a quiet and peaceable life and at the same time may willingly do all that is commanded.[38]

Christian apologists recognized their vulnerability to the charge of treason, particularly in light of the potential misunderstanding of how Christians intended the term, "kingdom" (βασιλεία). In his *First Apology*, Justin labored to be lucid in regard

---

[34]See the fragment of Melito preserved in Eusebius, *Hist. eccl.* 4.26.7–8.

[35]Melito, Fragment 1.6, recorded in Eusebius, *Hist. eccl.* 4.26.5–11.

[36]*Diog.* 5.

[37]*Autol.* I.10. The verbs used by the apologist for how to honor (τίμα) the emperor here are εὐνοῶν, ὑποτασσόμενος (cf. Rom 13:1,5), and εὐχόμενος. Cf. Grant, *Theophilus*, OECT, 14–17.

[38]Athenagoras *Leg.* 37.2–3. For the translation see W. R. Schoedel, *Athenagoras: Legatio*, 87.

to this matter. "When you hear we look for a kingdom, you suppose (without inquiry) it is a human one. No, it is a *kingdom* with God."[39]

Origen was similarly concerned. In reply to Celsus' charge that Christians were "mad" and "rushed forward to arouse the wrath of an emperor or governor that brings upon us blows and tortures and even death,"[40] he pleaded sanity and devotion, citing in reply Romans 13:1–2, "Let every soul be subject to the higher powers; for there is no power except by God's permission; the powers that be are ordained of God; so that those who resist the power resist the ordinance of God."[41] At Origen's editorial discretion, the closing paragraphs of *Contra Celsum* feature Celsus exhorting Christians to "accept public office...if it is necessary to do this for the sake of the preservation of the laws and piety."[42] The crux of this appeal clearly indicates Celsus' impassioned desire for the preservation of his nation and his religion.

Thus, where many pagans viewed Christianity as a threat to the social order, traditional religion, and the security of the Empire, apologetic voices attempted to mollify their concerns. They explained that Christians met to worship not plot. Yes, they admitted, Christians speak of and seek a "kingdom," but only one beyond the sphere of this world. Meanwhile, Christians live as loyal citizens by praying on behalf of the emperor. Those who decried Christianity as a movement initiated by an executed rebel would be reminded that Pilate was coerced into acting as he did; in his own mind, Jesus was innocent. Indeed, it was the enemies of Christianity that were in fact hypocritical and evil.

VARIANT READINGS

In what follows I collect a number of variant readings that in my judgment reflect these apologetic themes. I have grouped them around four major themes: "Kingdom" (βασιλεία) Language in Luke, The Exoneration of Pilate, Secrecy, and Scribal Characterization of Opponents as Evil, Hypocritical and Violent. I intend to solicit from these readings support for my claim that scribes sometimes changed their texts due to apologetic motivation.

"KINGDOM" (βασιλεία) LANGUAGE IN THE GOSPEL OF LUKE

The Christian gospel declared with bold anticipation that the advent of a divine kingdom would soon take place. Christians disobeyed Roman law when they met in

---

[39] *Ap.* I.11.

[40] H. Chadwick hints that this line may have been directed toward Christians who deliberately courted martyrdom and reports that the name martyr was withheld from those who initiated their own demise. He references *Mart. Pol.* I.4 and Clement of Alexandria, *Strom.* IV.17.1.

[41] *Cels.* VIII.65.

[42] *Cels.* VIII.75.

secret and when they refused to offer sacrifice to the emperor, and they posed a threat to the welfare of the realm when they neglected their civic responsibility of participating as full citizens in service to the state and participation in pagan religious festivals.

A careful inspection of the scribal activity associated with the verses in the third Gospel in which the term βασιλεία occurs has uncovered an interesting pattern: every otherwise unqualified occurrence of the word "Kingdom" (βασιλεία) in Luke's "original" text has been modified by some scribe in the process of transcription. The specific variants to which I refer appear in the following texts: Luke 9:27; 11:2; 12:31; 19:38; 22:29, 30; and 23:42.

Luke 9:27 is situated in the pericope featuring Jesus' call to his followers to take up their crosses and follow him. He warns them against being ashamed of the Son of Man and urges them to commitment. In fall, the verse reads:

λέγω δὲ ὑμῖν ἀληθῶς, εἰσίν τινες τῶν αὐτοῦ ἑστηκότων οἳ οὐ μὴ γεύσωνται θανάτου ἕως ἂν ἴδωσιν τὴν βασιλείαν τοῦ θεοῦ [ν. ι. τὸν υἱὸν τοῦ ἀνθρώπου ἐρχόμενον ἐν τῇ δόξῃ αὐτοῦ].

But I tell you truly, there are some standing here who will not taste death before they see *the kingdom of God* [*v. l.* replace with *the Son of man coming in his glory*].

This is the reading of virtually all witnesses to this verse except for the frequently exceptional Codex Bezae (D). The copyist of this "Western" manuscript replaced the phrase, τὴν βασιλείαν τοῦ θεοῦ, with a reference to "the Son of Man coming in his glory," τὸν υἱὸν τοῦ ἀνθρώπου ἐρχόμενον ἐν τῇ δόξῃ αὐτοῦ.

Since mechanical error does not readily explain the genesis of this variant reading, it appears to be the product of intentional scribal modification. Its similarity to its counterpart in Matthew might at first glance prompt one to account for the reading as a product of harmonization, but careful appraisal shows that this explanation proves insufficient. The Matthean parallel to this verse, Matthew 16:28, reads:

ἀμὴν λέγω ὑμῖν ὅτι εἰσίν τινες τῶν ὧδε ἑστώτων οἵτινες οὐ μὴ γεύσωνται θανάτου ἕως ἂν ἴδωσιν τὸν υἱὸν τοῦ ἀνθρώπου ἐρχόμενον ἐν τῇ βασιλείᾳ αὐτοῦ.

Truly, I say to you, there are some standing here who will not taste death before they see the Son of man coming in his kingdom.

Comparison of the Matthean reading with that of Codex Bezae reveals that the harmonization is not exact. Indeed, the divergence between the two consists precisely of kingdom language. The differences between the readings are slight until, where Matthew reads "coming *in his kingdom*" (ἐν τῇ βασιλείᾳ αὐτοῦ), the parallel as attested in Codex D reads "coming *in his glory*" (ἐν δόξῃ αὐτοῦ). Therefore, although the Lucan reading in Bezae shows signs of assimilation to its Q-counterpart, there remains another facet of this modification for which we must account. The effect of the variant reading is to replace the term βασιλείαν—a word that is at its core political and would have undoubtedly been understood by outsiders as such—with language that is inherently theological and rooted in Jewish and Christian eschatological tradition, namely "the coming of the Son of man." Admittedly, pagan readers may have judged the altered phrase as alien or even superstitious, perhaps accounting for why Luke may have omitted it "originally" in his treatment of the Q passage; but in Bezae's version of Luke, another—and perhaps more consequential—effect, was produced: any inference that Jesus and his movement sought to supplant Roman rule would have been avoided. This "clarification" corresponds to the apologetic theme repeated with frequency in Tertullian, Origen, Melito of Sardis, and to a lesser extent in Athenagoras and Theophilus.[43]

Appearing in the context of the Lucan version of the Lord's Prayer, Luke 11:2 cradles the second petition, ἐλθέτω ἡ βασιλεία σου, "May your kingdom come." While it is well known that a large number of manuscripts show the affects of assimilating the Lucan Lord's Prayer to the Matthean version, no imposed agreement was in this case required. Luke's words here are exactly those of Matthew 6:10. Certain scribes, though, were not content to leave well enough alone. Something about this verse provoked them to alter it. The copyist of Codex Bezae affixed to the beginning of this plea, ἐφ᾽ ἡμᾶς, so that the invocation reads, "*Upon us* may your kingdom come" (my emphasis). The addition by D of the prepositional phrase is not dramatic, but it may have been introduced to clarify the apolitical intention of the petitioner that he himself (and not the Roman empire) was to serve as ground zero for the advent of God's kingdom. Verbally, it also drew attention to the parallelism of this plea to the following one, one that Bezae assimilated into his text from the Matthean parallel, "as your will is done in heaven, let it be so on earth" (i.e., ἐπὶ τῆς γῆς = ἐφ᾽ ἡμᾶς).

A more striking variation of this verse, however, displaces "Kingdom" language altogether and replaces it with the vocabulary of "Spirit." The variant text reads, ἐλθέτω τὸ πνεῦμά σου τὸ ἅγιον ἐφ᾽ ἡμᾶς καὶ καθαρισάτω ἡμᾶς, "May your Holy Spirit come upon us and cleanse us." Though this reading is preserved by only two minuscules (the eleventh century Caesarean ms 700 and ms 162, dated 1153 C.E.), a few patristic citations suggest that the reading was familiar to readers of Luke in the fourth and fifth centuries.[44] The earliest account of this reading resides in Tertullian, and it may or may not point to Marcion's text of Luke.

The sparse nature of the external evidence is of little concern here. Quite clearly this remnant in Tertullian does not convey the "original" reading; no such case is being broached. What is of concern here is an attempt to recognize and, where possible, analyze the nature of various influences on the transmission of the New Testament text. We are trying to learn more about the history of the text.

---

[43]For sample references see Tertullian, *Ap.* 29.1–7; Origen, *Cels.* VIII.65; Melito of Sardis in Eusebius, *Hist. eccl.* IV.26.7–8; Athenagoras, *Leg.* 37; and Theophilus, *Autol.* I.11.

[44]For a lucid and fuller treatment of this variant see B. Metzger's discussion in *Textual Commentary*, 154–55. See also J. Fitzmyer, *The Gospel According to Luke*, 903–4.

Bruce Metzger and Joseph Fitzmyer conclude that this variant reading issues from a liturgical adaptation of the Lord's Prayer used at baptisms or during the rite of laying on of hands. Moreover, Metzger points out that reference to this text in Tertullian emanated from his Montanist period when matters of the Spirit would have been of prime importance for him.

Although these ideas are reasonable, juxtaposed alongside them with tantamount plausibility is the premise that apologetic interests influenced the formation of this variant. While the insertion of "Spirit" language into this verse may well indeed accommodate liturgical usage, the modification also fits the contours of apologetic concerns. The change removes from the central prayer of the early church the phrase that would have sounded most politically threatening to outsiders. Also, the location of this reading in the corpus of the first great Latin *apologist* should not be overlooked, especially since a leitmotif in the apologetic works of Tertullian is that Christians represent no threat to the state. The fact that in his work resides the earliest trace of this reading locates the likely *Sitz im Leben* for the derivation of this reading in or around Carthage. By the time of Tertullian, Carthage was next to Rome the greatest city in the western empire. It is precisely in this sort of high profile Roman urban center in which distress over the mis-perception of Christians as a political threat would have been a major concern for early believers. While none of these data contradict the liturgical relevance of the textual variant, they do offer a complementary and equally feasible explanation for the origin of the reading. Scribes concerned with the political implications of the *kingdom* language in this verse may have for apologetic reasons supplanted it with the vocabulary of the *Spirit*.

An analogous transmutation occurs in Luke 12:31. By a substitution of genitives deft as the sleight of hand in an urban shell game, the vague reference into *"his* kingdom" was changed to "kingdom *of God."* This subtle shift expunged any hint that Jesus might have been seeking to supplant the Roman throne and ratified the Johannine theme that the kingdom Jesus preached was *not* of this world (Jn 18:36).

Yet another instance occurs within Luke's account of the Palm Sunday entrance into Jerusalem. Luke 19:38 recounts the welcoming shouts of the crowd as, εὐλογημένος ὁ ἐρχόμενος ὁ βασιλεὺς ἐν ὀνόματι κυρίου, "*Blessed is the King who comes in the name of the Lord,*" or as the majority of manuscripts read by merely omitting an article, "*Blessed be he who comes as <u>king</u> in the name of the Lord.*" Bruce Metzger acknowledges that a constellation of variants surrounds this verse, but that the former reading best explains the others. One of the other variants, however, relates to our discussion. A few witnesses (W 1216 it vg[mss] bo[mss]) omit ὁ βασιλεὺς altogether, so that the text reads, "*Blessed is the one who comes in the name of the Lord.*" Although it could be argued that homoeoarcton explains the omission, the significant change in meaning wrought by the omission should be considered. This modification not only brings the verse into harmony with its Synoptic counterparts (Mt 21:9; Mk 11:10) but also removes from the verse the term which would undoubtedly have proven the most problematic for defenders of the faith. Much more than accident seems involved here.

Still another reading to be considered under this rubric is that of Luke 22:29. In this pericope Jesus responds to the dispute among the disciples over which of them is the greatest. Jesus quells the argument by distinguishing his followers from pagan benefactors who do good in order to gain personal prestige and by injecting the paradoxical query, "Who is greater? The one who serves or the one who sits at table? Yet I am here among you as one who serves" (Lk 22:27). Thus, Jesus drives home the point that greatness in the kingdom is related to service. In this context he then says, "And I confer on you a *kingship* (βασιλείαν) such as my Father has conferred on me, that you may eat and drink at my table in my *kingdom* (βασιλεία) and sit upon thrones as the judges of the twelve tribes of Israel" (Lk 22:29–30). Some copyists, though, as attested by A Θ 579 and sy[h], inserted into this verse the word, "covenant" (διαθήκην), so that the altered text read, "I make a *covenant* with you just as my father conferred on me a kingship" or "I leave you a last will and testament...." Ms 579 even replaces the second occurrence of kingdom language (βασιλείαν) with διαθήκην. Yet again, then, these changes involve the insertion or substitution of religious language for language that could be misconstrued as (or antagonistically manipulated into) the idiom of political threat, thus reflecting the concerns of early Christian apologists.

The final instance of this pattern of substitution in Luke occurs in the plea of the so-called penitent thief on the cross that he be remembered by Jesus (Lk 23:42). Gaining certainty as to which reading constitutes the "original" is difficult. The stalwarts Vaticanus and P[75] along with L and Latin witnesses bear witness to the reading, "...remember me when you come *into your kingdom*," εἰς τὴν βασιλείαν σου. This is the reading selected by the UBS[4] Committee, but they grade their choice only a {C}.[45] This low rating is due in part to the notion that the change in preposition from εἰς into ἐν has the appearance of a scribal grammatical improvement, but the committee opted for it on the grounds of intrinsic probability, preferring it as more congruent with Luke's theology (cf. 24:26). The great majority of witnesses (ℵ A C² R W Ψ 0124 0135 *f*[1.13] and the Majority tradition) however, render the preposition ἐν, which alters the meaning slightly to, "...when you come *in/with your kingdom*." Some commentators have argued for this as the reading that issued from the pen of Luke.[46] Which of these came first, however, is of no great consequence for this study, though the latter sounds slightly more like an apocalyptic return to the Roman earth while the former intimates an ascension into heavenly bliss. Therefore, if the judgment of the committee was reversed, the scribal shift from ἐν to εἰς would more consistently mirror the more common apologetic depiction of eschatology, i.e. God receiving his own into divine paradise rather than imposing on the Greco-Roman world an earthly hegemony.

More telling for our purposes, though, is the variant reading located in Codex Bezae. Here once again we observe the transcriptional pattern of replacing "Kingdom" language with theological idiom. The text of Codex D reads, ἐν τῇ ἡμέρᾳ τῆς ἐλεύσεώς σου, "*in the day of your coming*." Clearly the secondary reading, Bezae's rendering of this pericope completely omits the term βασιλεία. The witness of this

---

[45]B. Metzger, *Textual Commentary*, 181.

[46]See J. Fitzmyer, *The Gospel of Luke*, 1510 for references to those who make such a case.

codex exposes once again a deliberate effort on the part of a scribe to discard the political vernacular in favor of theological phraseology.

In each of these variants a similar dynamic appears to have been at work in shaping the textual transmission. Examination of the textual tradition indicates a proclivity on the part of some specific scribes for modifying ambiguous "Kingdom" language. Analysis of this constellation of variants suggests that these scribes were concerned that βασιλεία might have been interpreted politically rather than theologically, and altered their exemplars to circumvent this potentially threatening misunderstanding.

Recognition of this pattern, though, in some ways raises more questions than it answers. While it illuminates the influence of apologetic interests on the transmission of the New Testament text, it also begs the question of why this particular phenomenon seems to occur most frequently in Luke.[47] The pattern, if it can rightly be called that, is not associated with any single text-type or maverick manuscript. Nor was it applied systematically or exhaustively. Copyists made no sweeping effort to expunge the term βασιλεία from the pages of their transcribed canon. In all four gospels the term continued to appear imbued with theological substance. What does seem to have occurred, though, is that, occasionally, use of the word βασιλεία (or its corollaries) struck a particular scribe as precariously political in meaning in such a way that it prompted him to shave the stubbly substance of political treason from the face of the text by omitting the word altogether or introducing into the reading a theological surrogate.

---

[47]Granted, sensitivity to the political echoes of Gospel readings can be discerned in the transmissional manipulations of scribes other than those of Luke. For example, scribes appear to desire that Jesus be viewed as a sober peacemaker, not a threatening figure of violence. Consider, for example, the lineage of Matthew 10:34, in which the author reports the apocalyptic announcement of Jesus, "*I have come to bring strife and a sword,*" but where the scribe responsible for the Curetonian Syriac substituted, "*I have come to bring division of mind.*" This account transforms Jesus from a figure whose arrival breeds contention to one whose presence induces a deeper, more precise way of thinking. See also Origen's commentary on Matthew 27:16–17, in which he argues that no one who is a sinner is called Jesus; and Matthew 27:24, where the movement in the tradition appears to be from the blood of Jesus being "innocent" (ἀθῷον) to "righteous" (δίκαιον) and "blameless" (ἀναίτιον). See also Luke 23:2, 5, where the charges added to Jesus reflect those directed against early Christians by pagan despisers; when Jesus rises, therefore, it serves to vindicate him and exonerate him of those charges, and by way of association, exonerate the early Christians, as well. See also Mark 4:9/Matt 9:12–3, where the insertion of "into repentance" expresses sacred purpose of Jesus' gathering of persons. This same concern surfaces in Origen's treatment of this activity (*Cels.* III.60–61). It is not for sharing secret wisdom that we call thief, burglar, etc but for healing!

THE EXONERATION OF PILATE

Although in all four canonical Gospels he sits squarely at the center of the passion narrative in his judgment seat at the Praetorium, it is ironic that Pilate was even in Judea at all. He owed his assignment there, in large measure, to the bungled regency of the ethnarch Archelaus. He, alone among the three sons of Herod I who inherited the rights to administer a portion of their father's kingdom, proved unequal to the task. Though the details of his deficiency remain incomplete, they somehow proved damning,[48] so that by the year 6 C.E., Caesar Augustus summoned Archelaus to Rome, subsequently banished him to Gaul, and reestablished his territory, which included Judea, as a Roman gubernatorial province.

As the fifth of those prefects assigned to oversee this province, Pilate had hardly been issued a plum. Bond labels it, in the parlance of Strabo, "a third-class imperial province."[49] His was not a large province, but the mercurial zeal of its citizenry belied its small size. Thus, yet another irony is to be observed: despite its inconsequential character as a desolate outpost on the far-flung fringes of the empire, the man who administered Judea for a decade in the early part of the first century (ca. 26–37 C.E.) is remembered in many lands some two thousand years later as a household word. Still another is that, though his official records have long been lost, and the only real archaeological record of his earthly sojourn consists of a few coins and an inscription unearthed in Caesarea, his prescribed involvement in the execution of a Nazarene prophet has indelibly etched his name in the chronicles of history. So too, however, is the reverse true. This odd coupling of Jewish peasant and Roman equestrian, Galilean and Governor, Jesus and Pilate is almost universally recognized among scholars as the single, most recoverable and incontrovertible historical fact of the life of Christ: "he was crucified under Pilate." This *factum*, though, found its way into the formulas of the Christian *credo*, ergo constituting perhaps the oddest irony of all: the man who bore the historical responsibility for sending Jesus to his death was later portrayed variously in Christian evangelical, apologetic and apocryphal literature as

---

[48]The sources convey mixed messages. Josephus portrays Archelaus as a brutal, self-indulgent ruler (*J.W.* 2.11–13; *Ant.* 17.213–18, 17.339–41), while Dio Cassius intimates that the seed of his fall lay in plots against him (55.27.6). For a brief discussion of the sources followed by her own view that political intrigue did play a hand in Archelaus' fate, see Helen K. Bond, *Pontius Pilate in History and Interpretation* (SNTS Monograph Series 100; Richard Bauckham, gen. ed.; Cambridge: Cambridge University Press, 1998): 1–4. Raymond Brown, on the other hand, describes Archelaus as proving such a "bad ruler" that a delegation of Jews and Samaritans requested he be deposed. Raymond Brown, *The Death of the Messiah*, 2 Vols. (ABRL; New York: Doubleday, 1994): 334, 336, 340, 342, 677, 678, 763.

[49]H. Bond, *Pontius Pilate*, 4. Her reference is to the classification in Strabo, *Geog.* 17.3.25. She notes that the imperial provinces were generally characterized by more turbulence than the more subdued senatorial provinces. A heavier deployment of troops was generally required to keep the peace.

increasingly exonerated of responsibility for the death of Jesus, as a person who ultimately became a believer, and even as one who became a martyr for the faith.

Early in the evolution of the gospel tradition, for example, there gained in momentum an effort to shift responsibility for the death of Jesus away from Pilate and the Romans and onto the Jewish leadership and/or people. This has long been recognized and frequently discussed. Whatever impulse originally lay behind this migration of responsibility, the shift had the practical effect of serving apologetic interests. Plainly, the exoneration of Pilate implied the innocence of Jesus. That is to say, looking at matters from a Roman perspective, the perception that a Roman governor wielding his best judgment determined that the crucifixion of Jesus was necessary for the stability of his territory would have confirmed the impression that he was a political threat. On the other hand, reports indicating that the governor acted reluctantly and under duress in ordering his troops—or permitting others—to execute the Nazarene would have similarly suggested that Jesus was the innocent victim of a lynch mob. Certainly, when one traces Pilate's role in the developing canonical Passion Narrative from Mark through Matthew, Luke, and John, even the casual observer cannot fail to notice a pattern of shifting blame away from Pilate and onto others. Matthew and Luke transfer accountability to the select party of Jewish leaders, while the tradition of the Fourth Gospel assigns blame more broadly to the "the Jews" (οἱ Ἰουδαῖοι).

Some scholars, it should be noted, interpret this shift of responsibility as indicative of an early "anti-Judaic" bias among Christians.[50] Others, like Raymond Brown, argue that Pilate is not exculpated in any of the canonical accounts.[51] Mark, he writes, portrays Pilate as one who, although he recognizes the clear innocence of Jesus, yields quickly to the cries to surrender him. Brown interprets the Matthean interpolations of Pilate washing his hands and his wife's dream as further evidence of the governor's spineless character. Despite believing in the Nazarene's innocence, he still hands him over to be crucified. Nor is the author of Luke striving to exonerate Pilate. Brown declares, "The primary motive in this portrayal is not the exculpation of the Romans; rather we learn from the examples of Pilate, Herod, the wrongdoer on the cross, and the centurion that anyone (Jew or Gentile) who judges in an unprejudiced manner could immediately see that Jesus was a just man."[52] Likewise in the Fourth Gospel, Pilate's declaration that he finds no fault in Jesus fails to exonerate him; rather, the author uses Pilate to typify the person who in failing to decide for truth decides against it. Brown's read of the evangelists, therefore, is that they not only resist any impulse

---

[50]See, e.g., Eldon J. Epp, *Theological Tendency*, for a description of this bias. But cf. D. Moody Smith, *John* (Abingdon New Testament Commentaries; Nashville: Abingdon, 1999): 34–38, for his discussion of the treatment of Jews in the Fourth Gospel, where he concludes, "The obvious hostility toward Judaism in John is then not a function of their remoteness from one another but of a one-time close relationship gone sour."

[51]R. Brown, *Death of the Messiah*, 387–391.

[52]R. Brown, *Death of the Messiah*, 390.

to exculpate him, but also consistently portray Pontius Pilate as craven and unwilling to stand up for truth and justice.

For Helen K. Bond, the canvas of the canonical Gospels does not contain a monolithic portrayal of Pilate. Located within each text is a visage of the governor drawn within the frame of each evangelist's design and purpose. For her, Mark's Pilate appears, not as weak and vacillating, but as a shrewd politician. With imperial interests securely in mind, he manipulates the Jewish crowd in order to defuse a potentially explosive situation. Although the evangelist places primary responsibility for the death of Jesus on the Jewish leadership, Pilate is not released from his role in this fatal, fateful chain of events.[53] Nor is he exonerated in Matthew. Though seen here as less calculating than in Mark, Bond assesses the Matthean governor as sometimes gaunt and colorless, sometimes indifferent. Once again, he gains no pardon from the evangelist because of his willingness to allow Jewish authorities to have their way with an innocent man.[54] In Bond's appraisal of the Lucan Pilate, she highlights the evangelist's "major apologetic purpose" to employ Pilate as the official witness to the innocence of Jesus. With C. H. Talbert, she views the prefect of Luke "more as an advocate...than as a judge."[55] Still, she determines that Luke's portrait of Roman administration remains unflattering. She points, first, to Pilate's attempt to pass off the burden of judgment onto Herod, and, when that fails, to succumb to the will of the Jewish tribunal. "In the end," she writes, "Jewish mob pressure triumphed over Roman justice." Finally, she likens the Johannine Pilate to the one found in Mark, a nimble bureaucrat willing to forfeit the life of an innocent man in order to patronize local leaders and to placate a restive crowd.[56] Thus, she concludes, "...there is no evidence of a linear progression throughout the gospels in which Pilate becomes progressively friendlier towards Christianity."[57]

To the extent that Brown and Bond may be right in their unequivocal judgments that Pilate is never exonerated in any of the Gospel accounts, they appear to be denouncing "a Pilate of straw." Much of their appraisal relies on the fact that, no matter how or to what extent an evangelist may have air brushed his image of Pilate, his action of handing over Jesus to be executed remained the scar that could not be removed. His choice to give in to manipulated lies and mob violence rather than to stand firm in the face of truth and innocence conveyed to him an intractable guilt from which he could not be exculpated.

This, in my judgment, begs the question. Jesus was crucified, after all, under Pontius Pilate. Whether Pilate acted directly or indirectly, or played an active or passive role in the event, is open for discussion; but whether he ultimately acted in a way that

---

[53]H. Bond, *Pontius Pilate*, 117.

[54]H. Bond, *Pontius Pilate*, 159–62.

[55]H. Bond, *Pontius Pilate*, 159. See also C. H. Talbert, *Reading Luke: A New Commentary for Preachers*. (London: SPCK, 1982): 217.

[56]H. Bond, *Pontius Pilate*, 192–3.

[57]H. Bond, *Pontius Pilate*, 206.

resulted in the execution of Jesus is not subject to dispute. No evangelist could have told the story any other way. According to the prophets, their scriptural traditions affirmed, Jesus had to be crucified, and that required the authorization of a Roman authority.[58] Therefore, the issue at the core of what is generally referred to as "the exoneration of Pilate (and the Romans)," in my judgment, does not consist of what political and judgmental action Pilate ultimately did or did not take with respect to Jesus, but the characterization of him in terms of his personal feelings and convictions as he made that decision. That a politician would subjugate his personal convictions for reasons of expediency, albeit sadly, should not surprise anyone today; nor, would it necessarily have proved striking to members of a Greco-Roman audience.

What remains to be seen, then, is whether there can be traced in the Gospels a pattern from the earliest Gospel, Mark, to and through the later Gospels that exhibits an evolution or modification in how Pilate was portrayed to have felt about turning Jesus over to be crucified. If "exoneration" is understood in these terms, the evidence seems conclusive. According to Matthew, the Roman governor—having been cautioned by his wife as a result of her own disturbing dream to have nothing to do with Jesus, whom she refers to as "that righteous man" (ὁ δίκαιος ἐκεῖνος) —symbolically washes his hands of the whole matter. To this gesture the people respond with the shout, "His blood be on us and our children" (Mt 27:19, 24–25). In the Lukan account, three times Pilate declares Jesus innocent (Lk 23:4, 13, 22), and the centurion overseeing the execution is in the end moved to exclaim, "Certainly this man was *innocent* (δίκαιος)" (Lk 23:47). This pattern continues in the Fourth Gospel, where, after a philosophical discussion with Jesus about truth, Pilate straightforwardly declares, "I find no crime in him" (Jn 18:38). Later, he even exhibits awe in the face of the announcement that Jesus declared himself the Son of God (Jn 19:7–8). Thus, there does exist within the editorial features and narrative interpolations of the Gospel tradition a linear pattern that serves, not only to shift accountability for the death of Jesus from Pilate to the Jews, but also to underscore Pilate's own view that Jesus was innocent.

Thus, however disputable the motif of the exoneration of Pilate is among the scholars of the Gospels, there can be little doubt that effort was made among the apologists and non-canonical writers to grant Pilate some measure of amnesty for allowing the execution of Jesus. Paul Winter informs this claim. He insists that making sense of the sharp distinctions between the ruthless Pilate of Philo, Josephus, and the sources for Luke 13:1–2 and the perceptive politician of the canonical Gospels requires

---

[58]For discussion of whether or not the Sanhedrin had the power to execute capital sentences see, R. Brown, *Death of the Messiah*, 363–372, 747–748. Brown's evaluation of the evidence is that, in fact, the Sanhedrin did possess some restricted rights to put to death offenders of certain religious laws and perhaps adulterers. He continues, though, that with regards to Jesus, because of the political nature of the crimes for which he was being accused, it is likely that the Sanhedrin would have been exceeding its authority to slay him.

examination of the transformation in the character of Pilate through early Christian traditions.

> We should not confine ourselves to the portrayal of the procurator's character and actions in the canonical Gospels if we wish to elucidate the motives behind that pattern; we have also to consider the role assigned to Pilate in post-evangelical Christian traditions, for the motives which were operative in the minds of the evangelists continued to influence the communal activities of Christian believers for a long time after the Gospels had been written. It is only by considering later records in conjunction with the Gospels that we can arrive at a clear appreciation of the factors that governed the continually changing representation of Pilate's personality.[59]

On the basis of his study of the Gospels, patristic sources, Christian apologists and non-canonical literature, Winter claims, "the more Christians are persecuted by the Roman state, the more generous becomes the depiction of Pontius Pilate as a witness to Jesus' innocence." Clues from early Christian sources—e.g., the *Gospel of Peter*, Melito, Tertullian, and the *Acts of Pilate/ Gospel of Nicodemus*—indicate the marked rise in Pilate's stock, a trend that continued noticeably until the time of Eusebius, when the consequences of Constantine's victory at the Milvian Bridge and the ensuing Edict of Milan rendered inconsequential the testimony of the Roman governor on behalf of Jesus. Until then, however, the strategy of manipulating Pilate's character and actions for purposes of serving the Christian cause was frequently employed. Christian writers often adapted his role in the story of Jesus' trial and death, no longer presenting him as the unjust judge of Christ, but as an advocate and a witness for the defense. The Roman governor's testimony was reworked in such a way as to imply that "the profession of Christian beliefs and attendance at Christian cultic practices was non-subversive...."[60] Thus it was that efforts on the part of Christian writers to exonerate Pilate served apologetic interests on behalf of Christians.

Let us review some of those writers. Although he objectively reported that Jesus was judged by Pilate (ὁ ὑπὸ Πιλάτου ἀνακριθείς), Melito of Sardis was vituperative in his insistence that Jews rather than Romans were responsible—and thus accountable—for his death. He wrote, "The king of Israel has been put to death by the right hand of an Israelite" (ἀνήρηται ὑπὸ δεξιᾶς Ἰσραηλίτιδος).[61] Similarly, he dislodged even from the shoulders of Nero and Domitian culpability for their capital assault against Christians, arguing that it was not by force of imperial will but "in

[59]Paul Winter, *On the Trial of Jesus* (Berlin: Walter de Gruyter, 1961): 55.
[60]P. Winter, *On the Trial of Jesus*, 61.
[61]Melito of Sardis, Fragment 15 and *Peri Pascha* 96. See Stuart George Hall, ed. and trans. *On Pascha and Fragments* (OECT, ed. Henry Chadwick; Oxford: Clarendon Press, 1979): 82–84 and 50–51.

yielding to the persuasion of malicious persons" that they participated in pogroms against believers.[62]

Justin Martyr twice summoned the purported writings of Pilate to corroborate the facts of his case, i.e., to demonstrate that the death and deeds of Jesus occurred as they did in fulfillment of ancient Hebrew prophecy. The specific content of these passages merits attention. In *Ap*. I.35, Justin compares certain details of the crucifixion, such as piercing the hands and feet of Jesus and casting lots for his clothing, to those oracles located in Isaiah 9:6, 65:2, 58:2 and Psalms 22:16; analogy of Jesus' acts of healing to those predicted in Isaiah 35:6 is the subject of *Ap*. I.48, which reads:

> And it was predicted that our Christ should heal all diseases and raise the dead. Hear what was said; these are the words: "At his coming the lame shall leap as a hart, and the tongue of the one who stammers shall speak clearly. The blind shall see, and lepers shall be cleansed; and the dead shall rise and walk about." And that he did those things you can learn from the Acts of Pilate.[63]

Writing in the middle of the first century, Justin either felt compelled to, or felt that he could as ready currency, adduce Pilate as an authoritative source to support his defense of Christianity. Moreover, he summoned him for support precisely at points in Justin's argument where tensions with the Roman state would have been most evident: (1) in relation to miraculous events, which could easily be recast in the harsh vernacular of "magic";[64] and (2) in relation to the crucifixion, a Roman form of punishment reserved for only the most heinous of criminals. Justin slyly invoked the witness of a Roman authority to secure the most vulnerable planks of his platform.

---

[62]Melito of Sardis, Fragment 1.9, in S. G. Hall, ed. *On Pascha and Fragments*, 64–5. See also the discussion of R. M. Grant in which he situates the apology of Melito in the context of the attempted coup of Avidius Cassius against Marcus Aurelius and Commodus that occurred shortly after 176 C.E. His suggestion is that Melito as well as several other apologists are aware that fallout from this revolt had led to the persecution of Christians, particularly in Gaul, and craft their works accordingly. Robert M. Grant, "Five Apologists and Marcus Aurelius," *VC* 42 (1988): 1–17.

[63]Justin, *Ap*. I.48. Cf. ANF, Vol. 1, 179.

[64]As further evidence for this point, it is interesting to observe that located in the apocryphal *Acts of Pilate* is a very similar collection of healing miracles that are adduced by the Jews to accuse Jesus before Pilate. Moreover, they specifically attach to them the label of sorcery. The text reads:

> "But this man with evil deeds has healed on the Sabbath the lame, the bent, the withered, the blind, the paralytic, and the possessed." Pilate asked them, "With what evil deeds?" They answered him, "He is a sorcerer, and by Beelzebub the prince of devils he casts out evil spirits, and all are subject to him." Pilate said to them, "This is not to cast out demons by an unclean spirit, but by the god Asclepius."

See *Acts Pil./Gos. Nic.* 1, in Hennecke-Schneemelcher, eds., *New Testament Apocrypha*. Vol. I. (Trans. by R. McLean Wilson; Philadelphia: Westminster, 1963): 451.

Tertullian pressed this strategy even further. "Yes," he wrote in his *Apology*, "and we shall prove that even your own gods are effective witnesses for Christ. It is a great matter if, to give you faith in Christians, I can bring forward the authority of the very beings on account of whom you refuse them credit."[65] Thus, this Latin apologist sought to turn the tables on the enemies of the faith by intentionally adducing Roman deities and authorities as bearing positive testimony on behalf of Christians and their beliefs. Trajan, as Tertullian told it, in essence repealed any sort of imperial acrimony directed against Christians when he forbid Pliny to hunt them down, and Marcus Aurelius he portrayed as the protector of Christians.[66] It was in this light, then, that the author acknowledged that it was indeed Pontius Pilate who tried, crucified, and secured with an armed guard the burial chamber of Jesus, but, he insisted that Pilate's complicity resulted from the violent outcries of the leading Jewish citizens. Moreover, he implied, there was more to the story.

> All these things Pilate did to Christ; and now in fact a Christian in his own convictions, he sent word of him to the reigning Caesar, who was at the time Tiberius. Yes, and the Caesars too would have believed on Christ, if either the Caesars had not been necessary for the world, or if Christians could have been Caesars.[67]

Thus Tertullian unabashedly declared that Pilate held not only sympathy for Christ, but faith in him.

Numerous legends surfaced among Christian storytellers that similarly conveyed this central theme. One example, the Christian *Acts of Pilate*, is paired in some manuscripts with an independent treatise about the Descent of Christ into Hell, and the two together are known as *The Gospel of Nicodemus*.[68] Regarding the date of the work, some scholars locate in a reference from Justin (*Ap.* I. 35, 48; see above) reason for establishing an early date for the work, perhaps early in the second century; but others suggest that Justin had in mind official records from Pilate's tenure. Still other

---

[65]Tertullian, *Ap.* 21.

[66]Tertullian, *Ap.* 5.

[67]Tertullian, *Ap.* 21.

[68]For the translated text of *The Gospel of Nicodemus* and other apocryphal literature related to Pilate, see F. Scheidweiler, "The Gospel of Nicodemus: Acts of Pilate And Christ's Descent Into Hell," in Hennecke-Schneemelcher, *New Testament Apocrypha*, I.444–484 (all citations refer to this volume); and J. K. Elliott, *The Apocryphal New Testament*. (Oxford: Clarendon Press, 1993): 164–225. Elliott dates the current recension of the document no earlier than the fifth century, and he benignly expresses for the motivation of the work a creative engagement of the natural curiosity that, he believes, must have emerged among Christians about Pilate. But if P. Winter is correct in his assertion that Christian interest in Pilate waned in the post-Constantinian era, Elliott seems mistaken on both fronts. For one, the clearly positive spin the author puts on Pilate reflects the concerns of the pre-Constantinian period, and therefore suggests an earlier date (at least for the *Grundschrift*), and, secondly, much of the content of the work mirrors the apologetic themes discussed herein.

scholars argue that the Christian *Acts of Pilate* may have been inscribed to counter a pagan version that circulated during the reign of Emperor Maximin.[69] It is equally likely, however, that the pagan version was composed to rebut the Christian narrative. Scheidweiler argues persuasively on the basis of some exact wording shared between Epiphanius, writing around 375 C.E. (*Haer.* 50.1) and this work that at least the *Grundschrift* of the *Acts of Pilate* was certainly in existence by the late fourth century.[70] Thus, a fourth century date is likely, though some of the traditions included in this work may, as suggested by Justin, be much older.

At points a piece of highly lavish fiction, this apocryphal Gospel relates an inventive and purposeful account of the trial, death, and resurrection of Christ. Of particular relevance for this study is the author's treatment of Pilate, or more accurately, how Pilate in this narrative treats Jesus. For example, when the Jewish leaders implore Pilate to interrogate Jesus, he replies, "How can I, a governor, examine a king?" (I.2) He orders that Jesus be brought before him "with gentleness," and when Jesus finally enters the room the imperial images on the standards bow in homage to him (I.5). Against those who testify that Jesus was born of fornication Pilate believes those who insist that he was not. When his accusers charge him as a sorcerer and a would-be king, the governor dismisses all the Jews except the twelve who defended the legitimacy of his birth. They respond to the governor's inquiries that the Jews wish to kill Jesus because he healed on the Sabbath. Pilate wonders, "For a good work do they wish to kill him?" They answered, "Yes." (II.5). The Nicodemus narrative expands the dialogue between Jesus and Pilate at several points, most notably adding an exchange surrounding the question, "What is truth?" Strikingly, this Gospel embellishes the pronouncement of Matthew's Pilate, "I am innocent of the blood of this man" (Mt 27:24) in exactly the same way, as we shall see below, the variant tradition does; thus, it reads, "I am innocent of the blood of this *righteous* man" (IV.1). These examples suffice to indicate that, in the *Acts of Pilate*, the prefect is presented as a reasonable judge vainly disputing with an unyielding mob determined to do away with Jesus. Moreover, his disposition toward Jesus is reported as one of gentleness and mutual respect, and his own personal appraisal of the accused is evident and unequivocal: Jesus is a "righteous" man. Evidence of this apologetic dynamic is also discernible in the textual tradition. At several points in the various canonical Passion Narratives, most notably that of Matthew, variant readings serve to dilute tensions between Pilate and other Roman authorities, on the one hand, and Jesus and his followers, on the other. Throughout the Matthean Passion Narrative, for example, there can be observed a subtle but consistent pattern of exaggerating the reported difference of opinion existing between Pilate and the crowd about what fate is owed Jesus of Nazareth. This subtle scribal activity serves to erode what remnants remain in Matthew of the culpability for the death of Jesus that was attached to Pilate by the evangelist Mark.

[69]As described in Eusebius, *Hist. eccl.* IX.5. Cf. LCL, II.338–9.
[70]Hennecke-Schneemelcher, *New Testament Apocrypha*, 447.

In the context of Pilate responding to the crowd after they have selected Barabbas for release, the "original" text of Matthew 27:22 reads, "Pilate said to them, 'What then *shall I do* (ποιήσω) to Jesus the one called Christ?'" Pilate here speaks in the singular first person, thus denoting his individual authority—and thus culpability—for that which is about to transpire. Witnesses of the "Western text" (D, it), however, substitute for the verb the plural first person, so that the text reads, "Pilate said to them, 'What then *shall we do* (ποιήσωμεν) to Jesus the one called Christ?'" Use of the plural form in this verse effectively draws the will of the crowd into the process of decision making. Thus, by scribal decree, no longer is Pilate as sole authority about to do something to Jesus; the throng has been drawn into the act of determining his fate. When, therefore, Pilate orders a basin to wash his hands of the entire affair, culpability is lifted from his shoulders and left solely on those of the gathered mass. With this, Pilate is subtracted from the equation, and the calculus of crucifixion becomes the exclusive function of willful Jewish leaders and a willing Jewish crowd. Thus, the scribal editorialization of the Passion Narrative portrays the death of Jesus not as a Roman execution but as a public lynching, and is carried out not as much by soldiers under orders as by a crowd characterized by disorder.

Another instance of transcriptional activity amplifying the contrary attitudes of Pilate and the homicidal horde results from the insertion of dative pronouns and a subject in Matthew 27:22–23. Thus, the reading of verse 22 is embellished from "everyone said, 'Let him be crucified'" to "everyone said *to him* (αὐτῷ), 'Let him be crucified.'" Verse 23 is similarly altered from "But he (i.e., Pilate) said, 'What evil has he done?'" to "But he said *to them* (αὐτοῖς), 'What evil has he done?'" Some manuscripts further accentuate the distinction in parties by replacing the subject pronoun with "the governor" (ὁ ἡγεμών). This conspicuous introduction of a subject and indirect objects effects—or at the very least draws attention to—a polarization of Pilate and the crowd. In turn, heightening the opposition between Pilate and the multitude suggestively reduces the enmity between Jesus and Pilate, and therefore, by implication, Christians and Rome.

This pattern continues to be reflected in the manuscript tradition of Matthew 27:24. The text of this verse as recorded in N-A[27] can be translated as follows:

> But Pilate, seeing that he could accomplish nothing and that moreover a riot was brewing, had water brought and washed his hands before the *crowd* (ὄχλου [*v. l.* substitute λάου]) as he said, "I am innocent of the blood of *this man* (τούτου [*v. l.* substitute τοῦ δικαίου τούτου]). You see to it yourselves."

Alterations by copyists of the words in italics serve to distance Pilate even further from the determined rabble. First, the most compelling of the emendations to 27:24 is to be observed in the dramatic stroke of the transcriber—attested by ℵ L W *f*[1.13] 33 Maj lat sy[p.h] sa[mss] mae bo—who seized the opportunity to place into the mouth of Matthew's Pilate a declaration of the innocence of Jesus. Merely by embellishing the "original" demonstrative pronoun τούτου with the substantive τοῦ δικαίου τούτου, the adjusted reading placed on the lips of the Matthean Pilate an unambiguous pronouncement of the uprightness of Jesus. Whether one sees this scribal gesture as one of harmonization to the Lukan proclamations of innocence on the part of Pilate (three times) and the centurion (once) or as the copyist's own creative impulse, that the resulting reading serves apologetic interests is undeniable.

Secondly, the hand of the copyist preserved in Codex Koridethi (Θ) changed the word designating the "crowd" from ὄχλου to λαοῦ ("people"). The possible significance of this modification rests in the observation, most thoroughly outlined in the work of Eldon Epp, that λαός was sometimes used by Christian writers as the Greek rendering of the Hebrew עם, used almost as a technical term for "the Jews."[71] If this usage may be applied here, the modification emphasizes the ethnic makeup of the crowd, thereby distinguishing in yet another way the Roman Pilate from the Jewish "people" who insist on Jesus' crucifixion.

Finally, the exoneration of Pilate is punctuated in the boldest way possible in the language of the "Western" tradition of Matthew 27:26. Recognizing the force of this transcriptional episode requires a brief comparison with Mark. Where Mark in 15:13, 15 reports that the crowd in response to Pilate's inquiry concerning the fate of Jesus shouted "Crucify him!" (σταύρωσον αὐτόν), Matthew in 27:23 revises it to read, "Let him be crucified!" (σταυρωθήτω). Although some commentators have viewed this revision as an effort on the part of Matthew to exculpate Pilate of and burden the multitude with responsibility for Jesus' death, Albright and Mann report difficulty seeing how the passive verb brings about such a reading.[72] Such cause for hesitation was eliminated altogether, however, in the stroke of the scribe recorded in certain "Western" witnesses (D, Θ, *pc*, it) who modified Matt 27:26 from ἵνα σταυρωθῇ, "in order that *he might be crucified*," to ἵνα σταυρώσωσιν αὐτόν, "in order that *they might crucify him*." The willful quill of this copyist not only transposed the mood of a verb but transferred accountability for the death of Jesus. For the scribe, Jesus' tortured demise issued not from the orders of a Roman governor but at the insistence of a disorderly crowd; his was not an execution at the hands of Roman soldiers but a lynching by a riotous mob.

The evidence amassed here seems to indicate that some transmitters of the Matthean Passion Narrative, with meticulous attention to detail, modified their exemplars to the support of the apologetic themes of the recognized innocence of Jesus by Pilate and the governor's unwillingness to be a party to his execution. Already adduced as evidence for rooting this theme in the apologetic corpus have been the works of Melito, Justin, and Tertullian. Moreover, we saw clear evidence of Pilate's exoneration in the apocryphal tradition and the Ethiopic and Coptic lists of saints.

Transferring culpability for the death of Jesus to Jewish rather than Roman authorities may be appear to some the strict result of an "anti-Judaic" bias, but this appears to me a narrow view. Apologists fashioned accounts that recast and accented in new ways the Gospel narratives toward the end of making them palatable to, and,

---

[71]Eldon J. Epp, *Theological Tendency in Codex Bezae*, 76–9.
[72]W. F. Albright and C. S. Mann, *Matthew*. 345.

whenever theologically possible, compatible with Roman ways. The ambition of their literary labors was to blaze trails in religious discourse toward the end of safeguarding Christians from persecution and delivering the Gospel from extinction. Making Jewish leaders or even "the people" scapegoats for the execution of Jesus did not, *per se*, aid the Christian cause. Apologists sought urgently to remove the onus of blame from Rome; sadly and unfairly, Jerusalem was conscripted as the new custodian. History after Constantine would, in time, associate heinous consequences with that action. Meanwhile, transferring blame for Jesus' execution was not as much about inculpating Jews as much as it was distancing Pilate and Rome from willing participation in the verdict and execution of Jesus. In subtle but potent ways, scribes worked at removing hints that Pilate was an accomplice in the crucifixion of the Christ. Moreover, they inserted elements that transformed Pilate from the judge of Jesus to his advocate, from one who executed an innocent to one who exclaimed his innocence. Finally, by underscoring the opposition of the Jewish and Roman forensic decisions directed toward Jesus, as well as the ethnic breach that lay between Pilate and "the people," these transcribers dramatized that the operative philosophical breach that drove this verdict existed, not between Romans and Christians, but between Romans and the Jewish opponents of Christ.

SECRECY

The custom of Christians to gather regularly in private assemblies exposed them to the risk of inculcating suspicion among outsiders. Pagan writers recognized this vulnerability and heightened public apprehensions with their uninhibited speculations. Phrased in a way to raise eyebrows, it was repeated widely that Christians met "in secret." Celsus provocatively designated Christians as "a secret doctrine" (κρύφιον τὸ δόγμα).[73] As was acknowledged by Fronto above, innocent or not, nocturnal assemblies presented the appearance of impropriety. Referring to rumors about them worshiping the head of an ass or venerating the private parts (Latin, *genitalia*) of their high priest he admits, "This [story] may be false, but such suspicions naturally attach to their secret and nocturnal rites."[74] In other words, whether or not Christians actually do the things gossip relates, they deserve the slander because they make themselves vulnerable to it by meeting in secret at night. This practice also reflected behavior commonly associated with magic. Ancient magical rites were usually performed at night in quiet seclusion.[75]

That Christians met and met privately could not, and usually was not, denied by apologists. Nor did it necessarily need to be. Those affiliated with certain mystery cults met privately and engaged in undisclosed rituals. Baptism and the Eucharist were reserved for the initiated, again, in much the same way that certain practices among

---

[73]*Cels.* I.7. Cf. the translations by H. Chadwick, 10–11, and M. Borret, 92–95.
[74]*Oct.* IX.4, LCL 336–7.
[75] S. Benko, *Pagan Rome*, 125–6.

mysteries were restricted. Admission into the community served as only the beginning stages of the catechumenate; adherents came to more complete knowledge of the doctrines over time. Bearing witness to this is Hippolytus (ca. 170–236), who in the third century document *The Apostolic Traditions* wrote:

> And we have delivered to you briefly these things concerning Baptism and Oblation because you have already been instructed concerning the resurrection of the flesh and the rest according to the Scriptures. But if there is any other matter which ought to be told, let the bishop impart it *secretly* to those who are communicated. (My emphasis)[76]

Therefore, it was not unique or peculiar that Christians met privately so much as this fact was manipulated by antagonists to cultivate mistrust and apprehension among the masses. For this reason, then, the commonplace charge that Christians were a secret society required a swift reply. In rebutting Celsus, for example, Origen acknowledged that certain doctrines lay beyond the grasp of outsiders, but in this fact compared Christianity favorably with respected philosophies.[77] Moreover, Origen insisted that the basic message of the faith—including virgin birth, crucifixion, resurrection, and final judgment—had become familiar to almost the whole world. In view of this, Origen summarized, "it is quite absurd to say that *the doctrine is secret.*"[78]

Attention to the matter of secrecy, then, is rightly listed among themes of apologetic interest. Thus, it is incumbent upon this study here to examine the textual tradition of the New Testament Gospels with an eye toward locating any scribal alterations that might have been prompted by this concern. A small number surface as possibilities. Evidence of scribal alteration intersects texts in which the language or theme of secrecy occurs in the following texts: Mark 1:44, Mark 5:33, and John 11:28. Admittedly, in none of these variant readings can it be said that apologetic motives appear as the conspicuous cause, but attention to the subtleties in some of these altered verses leaves open the possibility that apologetic interests may well underlie these transcriptional changes.

Let us turn first to a minor variant that occurs in Mark's account of the healing of the leper. In the Majority text, the strongest of the Caesarean witnesses and Vaticanus, among others, Mark 1:44 reads, ὅρα μηδενὶ μηδὲν εἴπῃς ἀλλὰ ὕπαγε... ("See that you say nothing to anyone, but go..."). V. Taylor argues convincingly on the basis of intrinsic probabilities that this is the "original" text. The asyndetic construction is characteristic of Mark's style, as is the motif of secrecy (Messianic Secret).[79] In

[76]Hippolytus, *The Apostolic Tradition* 23:13–14. Gregory Dix, ed. *The Treastise on the Apostolic Tradition of St. Hippolytus of Rome* (Second Edition revised by Henry Chadwick; London: SPCK, 1968), 42–43.
[77]In this sense borrowing, perhaps, from the tradition associated with Galen.
[78]*Cels.* I.7. See the translations by H. Chadwick, 10–11, and M. Borret, 92–95.
[79]V. Taylor, *The Gospel According to Mark* (Second Edition; New York: St. Martin's Press, 1966): 189.

contrast to this rendering, and joined by both Matthew and Luke, another assortment of manuscripts discards the characteristic double negative, omitting the word μηδέν. Thus, the revised text says, "See that you speak to no one, but go...." The change is subtle, to be sure, and can reasonably be explained on the basis of homoeoarcton, μηδενί/μηδέν; but that there is a change in meaning wrought by the change should not be overlooked. Expunged with the pronoun is the strong appearance that Jesus was concerned with concealing his work of healing, a behavior with which pagan critics would have recognized as argue bore strong resemblance to that of a magician. The scribal modification potentially avoids this pitfall. The omission of the second pronoun shifts the emphasis of the command from secrecy to immediacy. "See that you speak to noone, but go..." presses the straightforward nature of Jesus' words. It suggests, "Do not let anyone detain you or impede your way. Go directly there," or, in a slightly more vernacular expression, "Don't tarry talking to anybody. Get out of here and go where I told you. Now!"

Another textual variant relevant to this discussion of secrecy occurs in Mark 5:33. The context for the reading is the story of the woman with the issue of blood who secures healing for herself by worming her way through a pressing crowd and touching the hem of Jesus' garment. Her plan to slink away, however, backfires when Jesus halts abruptly and inquires, "Who touched me?" Reluctantly, the woman approaches him, "trembling with fear" (φοβηθεῖσα καὶ τρέμουσα). At this point in the story, several sources include an explanation for her frightened state.[80] They propose that she was afraid διὸ πεποιήκει λάθρα, "because she had acted in secret." Most commentators completely gloss over this variant reading.[81] V. Taylor acknowledges it, but finds this to be a speculative and unnecessary emendation insofar as it attempts to explain the underlying reasons for the woman's frightened reaction. Such an explanation is unnecessary, because—in Taylor's judgment—the author of Mark has provided sufficient explanation for the woman's trembling, namely, that it is the result of her amazing healing and Jesus' penetrating glance.[82]

If the scribe's interests lay only in explaining the woman's reaction, Taylor's verdict that the reading is speculative and unnecessary could probably stand. Is such an explanation, however, the scribe's only concern? Could it be, that where this scribe appears out of step, he might be marching to a different cadence?

Let us consider this line of reasoning by revisiting some of the matters discussed in the previous chapter about how the socially-structured paradigm of male:public/female:private affected the perceptions of Christian women. Among others, the compelling discussions of Margaret MacDonald and Karen Jo Torjesen demonstrate how, for first-century Romans, the private sphere of the home was the

---

[80]Among them D (Θ) 28 50 124 348 565 (700) 1071 a ff i r¹ geo arm. Compare N-A²⁷, 104 and V. Taylor, *Mark*, 292.

[81]Among them Mann, Marcus, Gould, C. H. Turner, and Wellhausen.

[82]Taylor, *Mark*, 292.

only socially-acceptable arena in which women, generally, were to exercise influence and be noticed. Almost exclusively, the public sphere belonged to men.

Based upon this view, it seems reasonable to entertain the notion that outsiders may have perceived the behavior on the part of the woman who was healed as an act of social indiscretion. Up to this point in the narrative, nothing in the story has suggested that she has acted with restraint. The story makes clear that she acts out of desperation: she has suffered from a flow of blood twelve years, a malady not only physically draining but rendering her ceremonially unclean. Mark's story also indicates that she acts with premeditation: having heard reports about him, she determines that if she touches his garment she can be made well. She even says so out loud.[83] A pagan could have easily detected in that assertion features of contagious magic, on the one hand, and, on the other, verification that she was, like most women were commonly believed to be, openly vulnerable to superstition. Moreover, she acts aggressively, if surreptitiously; she sneaks up from behind and touches (ἥψατο) his garment. Now, although in the synoptic Gospels, ἅπτομαι is most often used in association with the healing touch of Jesus (Mt 8:3, 15; 9:20, 21, 29; 14:36; 17:7; 20:34; Mk 1:41; 3:10; 5:27, 28, 30, 31; 6:56; 7:33; 8:22; 10:13; Lk 5:13; 6:19; 7:14, 39; 8:44, 45, 46, 47; 18:15; 22:51), it is not used so exclusively in the New Testament or in patristic sources. The word conveys the act of touching in a variety of ways, including embracing, being affected, and even partaking of the sacraments.[84] When in John 20:17, for example, Jesus, because he has not yet ascended, directs Mary to refrain from touching him, the implication is that she yearns to embrace him with joy, not merely to gently brush the hem of his garment. Finally, the woman—suddenly healed from her hemorrhage— ends up singled out by Jesus and falling at his feet. We have already seen in the previous chapter how unseemly Celsus found this gesture of prostration. Add to that her complete lack of decorum at gaining the attention of a previously occupied crowd. As the "original" text tells the story, then, or, better said, as a Roman might have perceived the Markan account, this woman, in the act of securing healing from Jesus, acted in breech of Roman etiquette. In her leap of faith she committed a *faux pas*.

Before continuing, I want to anticipate the concern of readers who may deem this reasoning adrift. Compare the Markan account with that of the evangelist most often associated with apologetic concerns and a noble treatment of women, Luke (8:42b–48). Notice that the "original" text of the third Gospel spares any mention of her spending her livelihood on the futile efforts of physicians,[85] eliminates any report of her talking until after Jesus singles her out (and even then Luke grants her no direct

---

[83]Mark reads, "For she said (ἔλεγεν), 'If I touch even his garments, I shall be made well.'" There is nothing here about thinking to herself or speaking to herself. Though the impression of self-reflection can be inferred, it is not enforced by the words alone.

[84]See G. W. H. Lampe, *A Patristic Greek Lexicon*, 222. See also Jn 20:17, I Cor 7:1, II Cor 6:17, Col 2:21; and I Jn 5:18.

[85]If we read as the "original" text that witnessed by P[75] B (D) 0279 sy[s] sa and Origen, against the Majority text, א* (C) A L W Θ Ξ (Ψ) f[1.13] 33 (1424) (lat sy[c.p.h] bo).

voice), and omits any reference to her perceiving that her blood stopped (Luke simply informs the reader that it did). Jesus, in Luke, does not ask, "Who touched me?", but declares to the crowd that someone did, explaining openly, "For I perceived that power has gone forth from me." Luke explains that the woman comes forth only when she realizes that she was no longer hidden. Yes, she does tremble and fall down before Jesus (so Celsus would still be upset about her prostration), but she immediately declares in the presence of the people why she touched him and how she had been immediately healed. In Luke, then, she secretly approaches, is inauspiciously discovered, and only then humbly confesses why she did what she did. She ends her nervous outpouring with the report that she is healed, thereby vindicating her action and putting the attention back on Jesus, who offers her a benediction. Luke's reading, then, effectively—and, I presume, quite deliberately—excises and mollifies many of the elements of the Markan account that pagans could have found coarse, insolent, and disturbing. The actions of the woman with the hemorrhage are softened, her voice is muted, and she is made humble. All of these would have made the story more palatable to listeners from a male-dominated Roman audience.

Quite similarly, I wish to argue, so would the textual variants located in this verse. Reviewing the variant in Mark 5:33 in light of the foregoing discussion, it may be seen that the scribe(s) who inserted διὸ πεποιήκει λάθρα similarly softened the actions of the woman as she was portrayed in the Markan account. The mere report that she intended to do what she did discreetly (λάθρα) alters the details of the story. Her gestures may now be more rightly perceived as purloined movements. Her strain to touch his garment can more likely be interpreted as an act of pious humility than of occult contagion. All because she intended to act privately, she comes across as submissive and, in the anthropological rhetoric employed by M. MacDonald, respectfully bearing her burden of shame. Thus, the softer, more submissive traits that Luke imputed upon this woman through his editorial modification of Mark were similarly introduced by the scribe responsible for this variant reading; with the inclusion of this potent phrase, διὸ πεποιήκει λάθρα, he tempered her assertiveness and rendered her humble. Such editorializing adapted the behavior of this woman to the protocols and social mores of the dominant pagan culture, a characteristic mark of mindful apologetic strategy.

Yet another scribal adjustment to the vocabulary of secrecy occurs in John 11:28. Occurring in the context of the story of Jesus raising Lazarus, this verse marks the point in the story at which Martha notifies her sister Mary that Jesus has arrived and wishes to see her. The relevant words read:

...καὶ ἐφώνησεν Μαριὰμ τὴν ἀδελφὴν αὐτῆς λάθρα [ν. l., οιωπῇ] εἰποῦσα· ὁ διδάσκαλος πάρεστιν καὶ φωνεῖ σε.

...and she called her sister Mary secretly [v. l., quietly] saying, "The Teacher is here and would speak with you."

The variant reading involves a change of adverb in several "Western" witnesses (D lat syˢ) from λάθρα, meaning "secretly," to σιωπῇ, a term rooted in "silence" and perhaps best translated here as "quietly." Even though what sits before us, in terms of external probabilities, appears to be the classic case of a few "Western" witnesses standing against all the rest of the textual tradition, this does not constitute a "Western Non-interpolation." The transcriptional alteration in this instance neither abbreviates or omits textual material resident elsewhere; rather, the variant reading consists of one adverb substituted for another. In considering which reading was "original," C. K. Barrett entertains the possibility that σιωπῇ "may well be right," but he offers no argument to support his hypothesis.[86] Stylistic preference could be adduced to explain the change in either direction. Certainty on this matter is difficult, although external evidence weighs most heavily in support of λάθρα as the product of the author. If this is so, apologetic concern with the appearance of secrecy language being ascribed to Christians might explain the substitution of σιωπῇ. The effect of the change is precisely to eliminate the vocabulary of "secrecy" by replacing it the rhetoric of serene gentility. In the amended text, therefore, Martha approaches her grieving sister gently and quietly, not covertly or surreptitiously.

These verses demonstrate that scribes, on occasion, modified from their exemplars certain texts that featured the theme or rhetoric of secrecy. These editorial alterations served, on the one hand, to discard nuances that intimated secrecy as a subversive pattern on the part of Christians; and, on the other hand, to define features of secrecy commonly associated with Christians as expressions of humility and piety, not insubordination or insurrection.

SCRIBAL CHARACTERIZATION OF OPPONENTS AS EVIL

"Sometimes," today it is commonplace to say, "the best defense is a great offense." In ancient campaigns of verbal mudslinging, Christian apologists frequently applied the principles that lie at the foundation of this familiar adage. Again and again, defenders of the faith depicted themselves and their fellow believers as innocent victims of grave misunderstandings among the uninformed masses and as the righteous prey of deliberate malfeasance on the part of corrupt authorities. Examples abound, but certainly the most dramatic is Melito, who in his *Peri Pascha* portrayed Jews as cruel adversaries who in no uncertain terms were "Christ-killers." Athenagoras accused the opponents of Christ of acting out of their own evil impulses (κατὰ τὰς ἐπιθυμίας αὐτῶν τὰς πονηράς) to commit the most dreadful acts of evil, including adultery, pillaging, and murder.[87] Theophilus declared that "godless mouths falsely accuse" believers, and redirects accusations of cannibalism, atheism, and unlawful intercourse toward pagans devoted to their corrupt polytheistic myths.[88] Aristides

---

[86]C. K. Barrett, *The Gospel According to John*, 331.
[87]*Leg.* 11.3; cf. W. R. Schoedel, 25.
[88]*Autol.*, III.4, 9.

projected many of the pejoratives pointed at Jesus—e.g., that he was a sorcerer and mad—onto Greek deities; moreover, he labeled the Greeks themselves laughable, foolish and impious (γέλοια καὶ μωρὰ καὶ ἀσεβῆ), and described them as quick to take occasion to commit fornication and abominable acts.[89]

Since it is evident that Christian apologists made full use of this rhetorical strategy, the following catalogue of variant readings that betray this same offensive scheme serves as additional support for my thesis. In these verses we will see how scribes have modified their texts by either introducing into or emphasizing within their texts the characterization of adversaries as in some way evil. At these several points copyists have used their transcriptional changes to sharpen the distinction between Jesus and his opponents, toward the end of presenting Jesus as a good person who fell victim to wicked people. This depiction once again serves the apologetic purpose of presenting the death of Jesus not as an execution under Roman authority, but as a premeditated lynching at the hands of a manipulated, violent mob. In other words, in subtle ways scribes are trying to enforce the apologetic message, "*We* are not the bad guys; *they* are."

Luke 5:22 serves as one example. Here in this Gospel's depiction of Jesus first forgiving and then healing a lame man, scribes and Pharisees murmur under their breath that Jesus speaks blasphemy. Aware of their musings, Jesus addresses them, "Why do you question in your hearts?" (τί διαλογίζεσθε ἐν ταῖς καρδίαις ὑμῶν;). Certain witnesses of the "Western" tradition, though, heighten the tension in this question by inserting the object πονηρά, so that the text translates, "Why do you ponder *wicked things* in your hearts?" Here, the transcriptional characterization of the scribes and Pharisees leaves nothing to the imagination. Their musings consist of malevolence.

In similar fashion, Codex Bezae (D) and the Old Latin manuscript b embellish the text of Luke 11:39 by inserting after "Pharisees" the added modifier "hypocrites" (ὑποκριταί). Although this interpolation may be explained in terms of assimilation to Matthew (23:25), the effect of the insertion is not benign and should not be so easily dismissed. Something similar can be said with regard to the almost identical assimilation to Matthew that appears in Luke 11:44, where A (D) W Θ Ψ f[13] Maj sy[p.h] bo[pt] infix γραμματεῖς καὶ Φαρισαῖοι ὑποκριταί at a point "original" Luke did not have it. Again in Luke 20:23, predominantly "Western" witnesses (C* D *pc* a e l r[1] sy[s.c.hmg]) alter the report that, in the face of those seeking to entrap him, Jesus perceived not their *craftiness* (πανουργίαν), as other manuscripts read, but their *evil* (πονηρίαν). A related change is located in Luke 6:11. When Jesus heals a man with a withered hand on the Sabbath, the on looking scribes and Pharisees begin to talk amongst themselves what they are going to do with Jesus. What is evidently the "original" Greek reads matter-of-factly enough, διελάλουν πρὸς ἀλλήλους τί ἂν ποιήσαιεν τῷ Ἰησοῦ,

---

[89] *Ap. Aristides* VIII. For both the English translation and Greek text see J. R. Harris, *Apology of Aristides*, (TS 1; J. A. Robinson, ed.; Cambridge: Cambridge University Press, 1891), 41 and 104.

"They began talking with one another about what to do with Jesus." Codez Bezae, though, transforms this otherwise benign verse into a precursor of violence. Manuscript D reads, διελογίζοντο πρὸς ἀλλήλους πῶς ἀπολέσωσιν αὐτόν, "They began to discuss with each other *how they might destroy* him."

Scribes have similarly modified the Johannine account of Jesus healing on the sabbath. Where what is accepted as the "original" text of John 5:16 reads, "And this was why the Jews persecuted Jesus, because he performed these acts on the sabbath," scribes represented by the Majority text along with A Θ Ψ (ƒ¹³) e q (f r¹) syᵖʰ boᵖᵗ have changed the text to read, "And on account of this, because he performed these acts on the Sabbath, the Jews persecuted Jesus *and sought to kill him*" (καὶ ἐζήτουν αὐτὸν ἀποκτεῖναι).

Other examples of ascribing wickedness to the scribes and Pharisees, in particular, may be located in Matthew 23:25 and Matthew 26:3. The first of these occurs in the Matthean collection of woes, and finds Jesus directly accusing the scribes and Pharisees of hypocrisy. "Woe to you, scribes and Pharisees. Hypocrites! For you purify the outside of the cup and plate, while outside they remain full of extortion and void of discipline" (ἀρπαγῆς καὶ ἀκρασίας). Scribal tampering, however, has resulted here in several variant readings, in which the term ἀκρασίας (lack of self-control) has been either altered or embellished. The sources C K Γ 579 700 f syᵖ substitute ἀδικίας (unrighteous) for ἀκρασίας, while W (syʰ) transmit both terms. Clement of Alexandria as well as Σ / 844* lat syˢ co report the reading that replaces ἀκρασίας with ἀκαθαρσίας (unclean). Finally, M *pc* bear witness to πλεονεξίας (greed, covetousness, the proclivity to seek advantage or grab more than ones share) in lieu of ἀκρασίας. Each of these readings somehow intensifies a negative trait on the part of Jesus' enemies. What begins as a lack of discipline attributed to the scribes and Pharisees escalates into spiritual and moral decay. By the stroke of a pen, they are declared unrighteous, unclean, or greedy to the point of covetousness (thereby breaking one of the ten commandments). With the result of similar character assassination, some scribes amplified the guest list of those chief priests and elders who assembled at the home of Caiaphas to plot against Jesus. The Majority text, Old Latin, Peshitta and Harklean Syriac report the insertion of καὶ οἱ γραμματεῖς (the scribes), while the Freer Codex announces the presence at this gathering of the Pharisees (καὶ οἱ Φαρισαῖοι). It is possible in this last instance that Christian scribes here were influenced by the other evangelists. Mark and Luke report that it was the chief priest and scribes who took counsel how to eliminate Jesus, while John reports that the chief priests and Pharisees called the Sanhedrin into session.[90] Still, based on previously cited examples, it lies well within the scope of reason and the confines of scribal practice to speculate that Christian copyists may have borrowed from Synoptic sources for the specific purpose of expanding the noose of culpability, in order to loop it as well around the necks of the scribes and Pharisees.

---

[90]Mk 14:1, Lk 22:2, and Jn 11:47.

In each of this series of variant readings, there may be observed an effort on the part of scribes to intensify the breach that exists between his adversaries and Jesus. To be sure, they did not create the breach. Resistant opposition resided at the most foundational level of the gospel narrative. Prior to any evidence of scribal tampering, these texts reported friction between Jesus and the scribes and Pharisees, or, in the case of the Fourth Gospel, "the Jews" and Jesus. Christ, readers are informed, sensed in their questions and murmurs wily antagonism. For his compulsion to heal on the Sabbath he was persecuted. When thwarted, his adversaries held counsel as to what their next move should be. Christian copyists did not import conflict into the story. What they *did* do, though, as evidenced in these variant readings, was to heighten the tensions and raise the stakes of this conflict. Thus, they characterized the breach that existed between Jesus and his enemies in the dialect of good and evil. Jesus sensed on the part of his opponents not merely cunning but concupiscence. They were not merely wily but wicked. Where Jesus acted out of a ready compassion willing to disregard ritual regulations if they stood in the way of alleviating human suffering, his opponents staunchly clung to the law with an "at all costs" attitude that spawned violence. Repeatedly, scribes altered the text to sharpen the contrast between Jesus and his Jewish adversaries. Jesus, they cast, as good, compassionate, openly ready to help; the Jews were wicked, hard-hearted, and desperately afraid of this good man with his eager dedication to heal. They were so wicked, the scribes inserted as fact, that they began to plot his murder.

The origin of these variants clearly lies beyond the scope of mechanical explanation. They have found their way into the textual tradition at the hand of scribes who were, arguably, motivated by apologetic interests.

CONCLUSION

In this chapter I have sought to demonstrate a direct correlation between the content and/or effects associated with a select quantity of textual variants and certain major themes and strategies Christian apologists employed in constructing their pleas and defenses to Roman authorities. The data marshaled here seems more than sufficient, both by degree of correlation and sheer mass, to indicate that these canonical products of scribal labor undeniably manifest the influence of apologetic interests.

Scribes interjected into the scriptures rhetoric that accentuated the corrupt character of Christian adversaries and emphasized that the death of Jesus was not a case of Roman justice but mob violence. Also, they input subtleties that interpreted perceptions of *secrecy*, not as the clandestine atmosphere of moral turpitude, magic, or political intrigue, but as the natural, ordained nesting place for Christian piety and humility. Even more conspicuously, copyists of the New Testament Gospels borrowed key terms from apologetic discourse to imbue scriptural personalities or events with features more desirable or palatable to Romans. Scribes arranged for the declaration from Pilate's own lips that Jesus was δίκαιος, and, in the precise contours of Justin's diatribe, modified instances where βασιλεία insinuated political implications. Finally, reflected in the scribal tradition are small signs of the impulse that prevailed until the events surrounding Constantine rendered it superfluous: the so-called exoneration of Pilate. Sometimes bold, often oblique, but generally consistent signs entered the corpus of Christian literature that portrayed Pilate not as the judge whose verdict proved fatal for Christ, but as a Roman witness whose testimony left incontestable the matter of Jesus' innocence. Following the lead of many literary defenders of the faith, certain concerned copyists of the New Testament Gospels revised their exemplars in accord with the apologetic hermeneutic that was quickly, and quite necessarily, gaining currency in their day. After all, to carry out their labors in ways that rendered both reverence to God and honor to the emperor, as Theophilus had insisted, was directed by scripture. In a sense, then, altering the text was for them keeping the faith.

6

THE INFLUENCE OF APOLOGETIC INTERESTS ON THE TEXT OF THE CANONICAL GOSPELS

The scribes of our era have names, such as Hewlett–Packard, Canon, and Xerox. Such was not the case long ago. Little is known of the ancient copyists who manually reproduced documents—New Testament manuscripts in particular—and who, for the most part, remain anonymous.[1] So, although the character of the New Testament as a work of literature and historical significance might rightfully be said to reflect a long and distinguished heritage, the fact remains that we are incapable of tracing with precision its genealogical origins. Those persons most responsible for propagating this corpus of literary work are least known. Despite the traditional sobriquets we assign the Gospels, both their birth mothers (evangelists) and foster parents (scribes) remain faceless and nameless.

Among the sketchy knowledge we do possess is the recognition that these scribes were counted among the very slight but significant minority of ancients whom we would deem literate.[2] Yet, while their abilities to read and write distinguished them as members of a slender segment of the population, this distinction did not necessarily correspond to an elevated social status. We must not confuse literacy with superiority of rank or intellectual ability. Still, no complete or accurate history of the New Testament text can be written without devoting adequate attention to these unknown scribes. In the end, though, we know them only by their works, and their works we know only by means of the historical process of textual transmission. Thus, the study of the New Testament textual criticism—whether it is acknowledged or not—is necessarily a study of evolution, of scribes, and of words that have been altered in their transmission. Despite theological declarations to the contrary, no one speaking from a historical perspective may deny the editorial character and changing face of the New Testament text. We simply do not possess the autographs. Period.

---

[1] For the most recent (and quite thorough) investigation into the ancient scribes who copied sacred texts see Kim Haines–Eitzen, *Guardians of Letters: Literacy, Power, and the Transmitters of Early Christian Literature* (Oxford: Oxford University Press, 2000). Haines–Eitzen laments the dearth of direct evidence about scribes, yet observes that many clues about them may be located in the mountain of manuscripts produced by their hands. From these clues she gleans a number of historical insights about scribes and certain dynamics lying back of the transmission of the New Testament text.

[2] For a thorough discussion of literacy in antiquity see William Harris, *Ancient Literacy* (Cambridge: Harvard University Press, 1989).

Therefore, textual criticism is at its essence not only a literary enterprise, but a historical discipline as well. Yet, for most of the history of the critical discipline, the majority of textual scholars focused exclusively on the singular task of recovering the "original" text of the New Testament.[3] Only in the past century have scholars of the New Testament text begun to harvest the potential of examining formerly discarded variant readings for what they tell us about how historical and social forces shaped the text. Various studies have shown how the evolving Christian reactions to Judaism,[4] efforts to suppress the public role of women in the early church,[5] asceticism,[6] and the christological controversies of the second and third centuries[7] impacted and transformed the text of the canonical New Testament.

---

[3]I have used the publication of Kirsopp Lake's *The Influence of Textual Criticism on the Exegesis of the New Testament* (Oxford: Parker and Son, 1904) as the watershed for this line of inquiry. Although one may discern even earlier in the work of Westcott and Hort sensitivity to historical forces, Hort's declaration that "there are no signs of deliberate falsification of the text for dogmatic purposes" (WH, Introduction, 282–83) served as an obstacle to this line of inquiry that was challenged eloquently and admirably by Lake when he termed the text of Westcott and Hort a "failure, though a splendid one"(3).

[4]The primary work is that of Eldon J. Epp, *The Theological Tendency of Codex Cantabrigiensis in Acts*. (SNTSMS 3; Cambridge: Cambridge University Press, 1966). See, however, C. K. Barrett, "Is There a Theological Tendency in Codex Bezae?" in *Text and Interpretation: Studies in the New Testament Presented to Matthew Black*, E. Best and R. McL. Wilson, eds. (Cambridge: Cambridge University Press, 1979), 15–27, who challenges Epp's thesis on the grounds that the redactor responsible for Codex Bezae may have been exaggerating tendencies already located in Acts rather than imposing his own anti-Judaic bias. Still, in my judgment and that of many others, Epp's basic thesis stands. Historical and social forces may be reflected in what tendencies a scribe or editor mollifies or emphasizes in the process of transmission. Epp is not suggesting that Codex Bezae has been rewritten anew; he is noting that many of the changes in Acts underscore and enhance an anti-Judaic bias.

[5]For the influence of this dynamic on the text see, e.g., Elizabeth Schüssler Fiorenza, *In Memory of Her: A Feminist Theological Reconstruction of Christian Origins* (New York: Crossroad, 1983), 51–52; Ben Witherington, "The Anti-Feminist Tendencies of the 'Western' Text in Acts," *JBL* 103 (1984), 82–84, and idem, "On the Road with Mary Magdalene, Joanna, Susanna, and Other Disciples—Luke 8:1–3," *ZNW* 70 (1979), 243–48. For full–scale studies of how the subordination of women evolved in early Christianity see E. S. Fiorenza, *In Memory of Her*, Karen Jo Torjesen, *When Women Were Priests: Women's Leadership in the Early Church and the Scandal of Their Subordination in the Rise of Christianity* (San Francisco: Harper, 1993); and Ross Shepherd Kraemer, *Her Share of the Blessings: Women's Religions Among Pagans, Jews, and Christians in the Greco-Roman World* (New York and Oxford: Oxford University Press, 1992).

[6]Although this dynamic has been studied less than some of the others, Bart Ehrman signals the potential of this avenue of study in his article, "The Text of the Gospels at the End of the Second Century," in D. C. Parker and C.-B. Amphoux, eds. *Codex Bezae: Studies from the Lunel Colloquium 1994* (Leiden: E. J. Brill, 1996) 95–122, esp. 121–22.

[7]Bart D. Ehrman, *The Orthodox Corruption of Scripture: The Effect of Early Christological Controversies on the Text of the New Testament* (New York and Oxford: Oxford University Press, 1993).

Also among those historical and editorial influences upon the New Testament texts were dynamics that proceeded from a defensive posture against pagan opponents of the Jesus movement. In the process of locating, juxtaposing, comparing, and analyzing intentional variant readings produced by copyists of the canonical Gospels with the dominant themes and strategies of second and third century Christian apologists, this study has sought to inform our understanding of the extent to which, the frequency with which, the methods by which, and the reasoning behind which scribes sometimes modified their exemplars under the influence of apologetic interests.

The New Testament was not completely unfamiliar to or ignored by pagan critics of the movement. Among such critics, Celsus and Porphyry demonstrated a particularly keen acquaintance with Christian sacred writings, and it appears that in some clear cases scribes may well have modified their exemplars in direct reaction to their informed assaults.[8] Celsus, in fact, was aware that such amendments were being effected. Origen in his *Contra Celsum* preserved this declaration from the learned critic's *True Logos*:[9]

> Although you lied you were not able to conceal plausibly your fictitious tales. Some believers, as though from a drinking bout, go so far as to oppose themselves and alter the original text of the gospel three or four or several times over, and they change its character to enable them to deny difficulty in the face of criticism.[10]

To the extent that the thesis of this volume has been demonstrated, Celsus was in this assertion correct. Some copyists of New Testament Gospels did in fact, on occasion,

---

[8]Several instances have been suggested in this volume. Perhaps the most obvious are the altered readings of John 7:8 and Mark 6:3. See the discussions above, pp.132–42 and 185–88, respectively.

[9]Among those provocative ironies of history resides this fact: the sole reason there remains extant any single phrase from Celsus' *True Logos*, a work that proved significant in generating pagan hostilities against nascent Christianity, is that much of its content was preserved verbatim in the Christian apology *Contra Celsum*, a work penned as a favor to his friend and benefactor Ambrose by the learned Origen, who was himself later declared a heretic. Much has been said about *True Logos* and *Contra Celsum* throughout this volume. For the critical Greek text see M. Borret, *Contra Celse*, and for the English translation H. Chadwick, *Contra Celsum*. See also the background discussion in the initial chapter of this volume, pp. 38–40, and the notes there for other relevant bibliography.

It bears repeating here that scholars continue to dispute the lasting effects of *True Logos* and puzzle over why Ambrose commissioned Origen to craft an address to a polemical work nearly eighty years old. Joseph W. Trigg, *Origen*, 52–61, points out, however, that despite Origen's hesitation "to rescue from oblivion a work he had never heard of before" (53) revival of the critique of Celsus does appear to have played a part in engendering among the Roman ruling class a new wave of antipathy against Christians (61). Trigg notes further that *Contra Celsum* (ca. 248 or 249 C.E.) appeared in close chronological proximity to the advent of the Decian persecution (249–51 C.E.).

[10]*Cels.* II.27. The translation is that of H. Chadwick, *Contra Celsum*, 90.

alter their exemplars to avoid or reduce "difficulties in the face of criticism;" that is, *some scribes occasionally modified the text of the Gospels under the influence of apologetic interests.*

Such scribes, therefore, proved neither benign nor mechanical in their transmissional labors; they often showed themselves to be sentient, mortal beings subject to both banal error and creative outbursts. The same scribes that, more than any other group, are the reason the text of the New Testament survived to the present are also almost exclusively responsible for the various and numerous flaws and corruptions that found their way into the textual tradition—errors, omissions, harmonizations, corrections, editorial and stylistic changes, and intentional modifications. Thus, it is their story in relationship to the texts they copied that must be understood if the history of the transmission of the New Testament is ever to be written, and if "the historical significance of the altered text" is ever to be measured.[11] This study has been an effort to contribute to this symbiotic tale of the scribes and their texts.

Methodologically, the foundation of this study has been rooted in the recognition that textual transmission did not occur in a historical vacuum. Our efforts have built on this astute observation of J. Rendel Harris:

> The Bible of any given church becomes affected by the church in which it circulates. The people who handle the text leave their finger–prints on the pages, and the trained detective can identify the criminal who made the marks.[12]

This study has consisted in large measure of a scrupulous search for those fingerprints, and in the course of this investigation certain scribes have been implicated. Despite their anonymity, their marks have been found all over the textual tradition of the canonical Gospels. The nearly one hundred variant readings adduced in this volume consist of modifications to the text that arguably appear both intentional in nature and apologetic in character. In other words, these readings attest to alterations of the canonical Gospels effected by copyists who, in their work of transmitting them, edited their exemplars with apologetic interests clearly and consciously in mind.

The precise strategies by which they effected these changes, we have noted, were widely diverse and, usually, quite subtle; yet, in the course of reproducing the text certain scribes honed or refined the narrative to the apologetic advantage of the Christian cause. We located evidence in some readings that scribes occasionally corrected, refined, or harmonized their exemplars in ways that addressed criticism directed at the intellectual integrity of the early Christian movement and its sacred writings. We uncovered other variant readings that appear to have been shaped in

---

[11]The quoted phrase is borrowed from the 1997 Kenneth W. Clark Lectures given at Duke University given by Bart D. Ehrman, the title of which was "Text and Transmission: The Historical Significance of the 'Altered' Text." These lectures were delivered February 13–14, 1997.

[12]J. Rendel Harris, "Was the Diatessaron Anti-Judaic?," 103.

accordance with the Christian claim to antiquity and prophetic fulfillment, both of which were central themes in early apologetic literature.

In others we observed Christian scribes airbrushing the portrait of Jesus, smoothing from certain angles of his profile features that gave the appearance of him resembling a man of profane temperament, acting indecisively, practicing the arts of thaumaturgy or deception, or leading a band of miscreants into treasonous rebellion. By omission, correction, embellishment, and other forms of editorial repair, these copyists refined the Jesus fashioned by the "original" evangelists into a "kinder, gentler Jesus." To be sure, they did not completely reinvent Jesus; his essence remained intact. Akin to cooks adapting a recipe, though, some scribes on occasion chose to eliminate harsh spices and bitter flavors in order to serve up a Jesus that was less unsavory and more tolerable to the distinctive palates of the Greco-Roman establishment.

Located also were textual modifications designed to defend Christian disciples against the perceptions that followers of Jesus consisted of rabid fanatics, pedestrian fools, and hysterical females. Christian transcribers once again tweaked elements of their narratives in order to reduce the validity of the affronts directed at disciples of Christ. Women were acknowledged as followers, but their high visibility and intimacy with Jesus—rendered problematic in pagan rhetoric—was reconfigured into more acceptable social categories. For example, the report of women who took the initiative in following Jesus from Galilee, an image repugnant to many in the pagan public, was edited to read "wives of those who followed Jesus from Galilee," thus rendering a more conventional description of the females of antiquity.[13] Similarly, scribes improved the ethical and moral perceptions of Jesus' disciples by depicting them as persons representing more than the lowest social classes, and as people of sobriety and piety. In the context of this conversation it was also recognized how many of the features that constitute the various scribal compositions that extended the Gospel of Mark beyond 16:8 mirror the content and rhetoric of Christian apologetic discourse.[14] Scribes also modified their exemplars mindful of the political environment in which they dwelled and to which they were vulnerable. Sources reflect how the evolution in pagan reactions to Christianity from indifference to infuriation shaped the official state reaction of Rome to the new faith, and in turn led scribes to modify their exemplars to soften and mollify some of the implications of subversion and societal threat resident in the text. Here we located scribal changes in the New Testament text that rooted secrecy in piety and not sedition; that exonerated Pilate from direct responsibility for the sentence and execution of Jesus, thus making him and his

---

[13]See above, pp. 282–3, the discussion of Mark 15:40–41 and parallels in light of the Fragment believed by many to be part of Tatian's *Diatessaron* found at Dura-Europus. See especially Carl H. Kraeling, *A Greek Fragment of Tatian's Diatessaron from Dura*, and E. C. Colwell, "Method in Locating a Newly Discovered Manuscript," 38–9.

[14]See the discussion above, pp. 287–97, in which attention is paid to the so-called Shorter Ending, Longer Ending, and Freer Logion, pointing out features of each that reflect apologetic concerns and discourse.

movement seem less subversive to Roman authorities; and that revised occurrences of "Kingdom" (βασιλεία) language in such a way as to emphasize the divine nature of Jesus' message and reduce any political misunderstandings that might be derived from it. Some variant readings even showed that scribes occasionally followed apologists in "fighting fire with fire," occasionally embellishing descriptions of Jesus' opponents within the Gospels by attaching *ad hominem* labels to them.

In no small measure, then, the history of the transmission of the text is as much a story of scribes as it is manuscripts. The innumerable variant readings are each and every one the product of some scribe somewhere in some time engaged for some reason in the sober enterprise of transcribing scripture. Those committed to the goal of reconstructing the "original" text, then, must perform exegesis on the variant readings themselves. They must seek to place the variant readings as accurately as possible within a bona fide *Sitz im Leben* so that they may be fully regarded and evaluated as components of the "original" or an amended text.

Once recognized as part of the "altered" text, however, those variant readings should not be randomly discarded, but carefully sifted through a sieve of historical examination toward the end of unearthing clues and insights into the unfolding history of nascent Christianity. The constraints of cultural norms and the pressures of historical forces informed and motivated scribes engaged in reproducing sacred texts sometimes to modify their exemplars to correct, harmonize, mollify, satisfy, or otherwise ameliorate polemic tensions. Textual transmission did not occur in a historical vacuum.

Therefore, textual criticism is necessarily a historical discipline. It is not enough for textual scholars to gain acquaintance with manuscripts; it is incumbent upon those who attempt to recover the "original" text to comprehend, to the extent the evidence affords, the historical events, circumstances, and forces that constituted the dynamic contexts out of which these texts and copies were first written and then transcribed.

Traditional exegetes have long recognized this. They have advocated that the text cannot be understood apart from its *Sitz im Leben*, i.e., from history, from its context, from the setting of its author and audience. What has been often overlooked by these same exegetes, however, is that before the text can be read in its historical setting it must be reconstructed, and to do so is no small feat. Such textual reconstruction requires assembling—or, for the optimist, reassembling—so many jigsaw pieces strewn broadly in a seemingly cavalier fashion across the manuscript tradition, fitting together this reading from that codex, borrowing that phrase from this papyrus, and so forth, guided not by a preconceived pattern but by methodological principles.[15] To continue

---

[15]This statement betrays my bias against this feature of the local-genealogical method subscribed to by the Alands, whereby they do, in measuring variant readings, assume a prior pattern. For them the so-called "Strict text," which corresponds generally to the text-type known as Alexandrian (or in Westcott and Hort's nomenclature, "Neutral"), serves as the point of departure for all textual analysis. For the description of this method see Kurt and Barbara Aland, *The Text of the New Testament*. (Leiden, 1989, 280–81; and Barbara Aland, "Die

the analogy, this is akin to piecing together a puzzle on the basis of shape alone, with no colors or pattern to provide direction.

What should be clear by now is that the text has not survived as a relic of a distant past, but as something that lived and was adapted in response to change, much like an evolutionary species adapting to its environment.[16] This analogy, of course, threatens to break down in the assertion that manuscripts do not possess life, but that assertion holds true only if one fails to see that manuscripts do not exist at all except as the products of trained, sentient, vulnerable, reactionary human beings. There is a sense, then, in which it is fair to say that manuscripts are "begotten, not made," brought into being by human beings and brought forward through history by them, as well. Surviving ancient texts, then, result from labor—tedious, intense, focused, and wearisome labor. Pressing this analogy only slightly further, although the evangelist may be thought of as the birth mother of the Gospel, the scribe functions in a number of other roles in maintaining this newborn entity, including at times midwife, wet nurse, and even adoptive parent. The human infant will not survive unless it is held, kept warm, duly nurtured, and, occasionally and quite necessarily, changed. Ancient texts, too, in order to survive to the next generation had to be handled frequently and carefully; they had to be transmitted, transcribed, copied by hand. And sometimes—again much like an infant—they had to be changed.

Sacred texts, although born of natural parents (their authors), all too quickly leave the secure possession of their first home and become the possession of an extended family (the community for whom they are authoritative). Leaving its home and evolving under the influence of an extended and diverse religious community, the text gains a new life of prominence in that community when it is determined to be authoritative. This new life, though, is symbiotic in character. Sacred texts both shape and are shaped by the communities and believers who locate authority in them. They levy a certain influence over and benefit to those communities, but those communities also define and propagate their sacred texts. The texts are preserved as they are passed on, transmitted, and copied by Christian scribes. The text may itself pass on life or be given new life when a scribe copies it, transferring its life to what was a *tabula rasa*, the scribe serving sometimes as midwife, and sometimes as stepparent.

Münsteraner Arbeit am Text des Neuen Testaments und ihr Beitrag für die frühe Überlieferung des 2. Jahrhunderts: Eine methodologische Betrachtung," *Gospel Traditions in the Second Century* (W. L. Petersen, ed.; South Bend, IN: University of Notre Dame Press, 1989), 55–70. For an insightful treatment of this method see Jacobus H. Petzer, "The History of the New Testament Text—Its Reconstruction, Significance, and Use in New Testament Textual Criticism," *New Testament Textual Criticism, Exegesis, and Church History: A Discussion of Methods* (B. Aland and J. Delobel, eds.; Kampen, The Netherlands: Pharos, 1994), 1–32. For an animadversion see Bart D. Ehrman, "A Problem of Textual Circularity: The Alands on the Classification of New Testament Manuscripts," *Biblica* 70 (1989) 377–88.

[16]This is the theme of the recent book by D. C. Parker, *The Living Text of the Gospels* (Cambridge: Cambridge University Press, 1997).

The purpose of this study has been to extend our current understanding of the history of the New Testament text. More and more the fog has dissipated and it has grown clear that a calculus of personal interests, historical forces, and social dynamics functioned to produce and shape the canonical text. That is to say, the text currently before us represents a product of evolution, not a *de novo* creation. Present-day readers of the New Testament Gospels encounter a cloned subject, something that in the process of being duplicated has been both diluted and enhanced. As such, it can be said to bear a marked resemblance to the "original," but it should never be equated with the "original." To the extent that it has become clear that apologetically-driven concerns number among those forces that shaped the evolution of the text, my thesis has been demonstrated: *Christian copyists engaged in the reproduction of the New Testament Gospels sometimes altered their texts in the interest of apologetic concerns.*

IMPLICATIONS OF THIS STUDY

In the final analysis, the value of this study will be measured by the academy. Meanwhile, I offer the following reflections on what I believe are the lasting effects and contributions of this study. In addition, I suggest ideas for further work to build on this project.

TEXTUAL IMPLICATIONS

First, and perhaps most obviously, this study has implications for reconstructing the text of the New Testament. With regard to several variant readings in the textual tradition of the Gospels, I have made a case for adopting a reading different from that opted for currently by the editors of UBS[4] and N-A[27]. In such instances, I have either consolidated the arguments of others or mounted my own arguments for revisiting and revising the text of the Greek New Testament as it currently appears in these editions. Of particular interest in this regard are the following: Matthew 9:34, 13:35, 15:26, 21:44; Mark 1:41, 14:4; and John 4:25. It is my expectation that, to the extent this volume is considered by colleagues in the guild, there will be other textual critics who will find merit in at least some of these arguments and who will join me in taking up the gauntlet to revise the text accordingly. Until a manuscript autograph is unearthed from its resting place in the sand, or transcriptional and intrinsic probabilities can somehow be transformed into certainties, our labors as producers of a canonical text will continue to be a work in progress, *semper reformanda.* Subsequent published editions of the New Testament text should incorporate the modifications suggested here that as they are ratified by a consensus of New Testament textual critics.

In the case of some variant readings, I have attempted to construct a thoroughgoing argument for establishing the "original" reading or for interpreting the modified reading in a fresh way. In other instances, however, much remains to be done. For example, although I believe that what I have suggested with regard to the influence of apologetic interests on the composition of the various extensions of Mark's Gospel is viable and promising, the complexities associated with the closure of

Mark's Gospel transcend the scope of this work. In fact, I hope to focus more attention and study on this constellation of readings in a future project. Meanwhile, I remain convinced that each of the so-called endings (with the exception of that ending marked by the punctuation of Mark 16:8) represents a composition designed, at least in part, with apologetic interests in mind.

METHODOLOGICAL IMPLICATIONS

This study also has produced at least two methodological implications for conducting the labor of textual reconstruction. First, the evidence and arguments presented in this study serve to validate further the claims of those textual scholars who rightly insist that the text of the New Testament must be discerned, evaluated, and reconstructed on the basis of principles that go beyond (yet work in tandem with) the criterion of external probabilities. The research that provides affirmation of the thesis of this work in turn supports reasoned eclecticism as the most rational and effective method for determining the text of the New Testament. By extension, the conclusion that apologetic interests influenced scribes in transmitting the text implies that scholars who are engaged in textual reconstruction and committed to accuracy must dedicate renewed energy to the task of weighing transcriptional probabilities on the sensitive scale of historical awareness.

During the course of this study, I should interject, I have taken great pains to avoid the denunciation of constructing "circular" arguments. Therefore, when faced with a disputed reading, I have looked to discern the "original" and scribally-altered readings without reference to transcriptional arguments based on evidence of apologetic interests. Only after evaluating readings on the bases of external evidence and intrinsic probabilities did I make an effort to explain the resulting variant reading in the vernacular of apologetic interests.

Now, however, that a reasonably compelling case has been made for the influence of apologetic interests on the text of the New Testament, it appears very much in order to suggest that textual critics should be attuned to the possible influence of apologetic concerns when adjudicating variant readings elsewhere in the New Testament. Although similar full-scale studies will need to be conducted with regard to the Pauline corpus, Acts, the Deutero-Pauline writings, Hebrews, the Catholic Epistles, the Johannine Letters, and the Apocalypse, the continuing evaluation of New Testament variant readings in light of transcriptional probabilities should take into consideration the possible influence of apologetic interests as they have been surveyed here. Second, the beginnings of being able to locate the origins of some few variant readings in relatively small chronological windows may be emerging. It is well known within the guild of textual critics that among our sources for textual reconstruction—manuscripts, versions, and patristic sources—only patristic writings can be fixed in chronology and location with any degree of precision.[17] Except for rare instances, therefore, scholars have seldom been able to date with any desirable degree of precision at what point particular scribal modifications entered the textual tradition. Yet, by carefully constructing the sorts of intersections represented by this study—intersections between the undatable textual tradition and the datable patristic (in this case apologetic) corpus—some hope of locating some variants in time (and even space) might be possible. I do not mean to promise too much. In addition to the unyielding chronological mysteries connected to the manuscript tradition, difficulties arise also from the fact that very little pagan polemical prose survived the exigencies of history or the book burnings mandated by bishops or emperors. Since we do not have a complete corpus of pagan anti-Christian writings, we cannot with absolute certainty directly associate changes in the text that appear to have been motivated in response to a specific challenge from a particular pagan writer simply on the basis that his work survived to the present. Is Celsus, in fact, the first pagan writer to assail the character of Jesus? Is Porphyry original in his specific attacks on scriptural integrity? Can the arguments recorded in the *Apocriticus* of Macarius Magnes be connected with any accuracy to Porphyry? Fortunately, our judgments on these questions can achieve a high level of *probability* based on our efforts to apply strictly the calculus of plausibility. Still, we must be careful not to assert more than we can positively maintain; we must balance our zeal to know with an admission of what we do not know.

With that caveat issued, there do appear to be some conclusions we can draw with a large measure of confidence. Particularly in the ways Christian writers address, respond to, and reflect on pagan critics, it seems clear that certain censures and denouncements were, in fact, associated with individual pagan critics. In particular, I am thinking of Eusebius and his treatment of Porphyry, and even more especially the retort of Origen to Celsus. In these cases we can with some confidence identify a historical window in which certain specific disputes are given temporal location. In these cases, it becomes theoretically feasible to locate the scribal origins of certain intentional variant readings that feature the contours of this specific pagan-apologetic discourse within this same window of time. With additional investigation and increasing knowledge it might prove possible in some cases to "connect the dots" between certain transcriptional readings and related pagan and patristic sources in such a way that additional light might be shed on particular readings, manuscripts, manuscript traditions, or versional witnesses. For example, the modification of Mark 6:3 may with high probability have been introduced into the textual tradition sometime

---

[17]See, e.g., discussions in Gordon D. Fee, "The Use of the Greek Fathers for New Testament Textual Criticism," in Bart Ehrman and Michael Holmes, eds. *The Text of the New Testament in Contemporary Research: Essays on the* Status Quaestionis (Grand Rapids, MI: Eerdmans, 1995) 191–207; and Bart D. Ehrman, "The Use and Significance of Patristic Evi-dence for NT Textual Criticism," in B. Aland and J. Delobel, eds. *New Testament Textual Criticism, Exegesis, and Early Church History* (Kampen, The Netherlands: Pharos, 1994).

between the publication of Celsus' *True Doctrine* (*ca.* 170 C.E.) and Origen's *Contra Celsum* (*ca.* 248–249 C.E.), most likely motivated by apologetic interests.[18]

HISTORICAL IMPLICATIONS

This study serves to ratify what the last century of scholarship discovered and maintained: that New Testament textual criticism is no longer an independent literary discipline with its singular task being that of reconstructing the canonical text.[19] It is no longer possible to ignore the historical forces that directed the evolution of the text. Reconstructing the text consists no more of merely constructing stemmata, categorizing family trees of manuscripts, and evaluating readings on the basis of external and literary evidence alone. Transcriptional probabilities especially must be determined, understood, and evaluated against the backdrop of a scribal *Sitz im Leben*, with particular attention to the dynamic social and historical energies that motivated and directed scribes in their work.

In pursuit of this line of investigation, I appreciate in particular the efforts of Kim Haines-Eitzen in her attempt to shed light on the anonymous scribes who are ultimately the subject of every textual scholar's labor.[20] Efforts to recover the "original" text must begin to resemble more and more the labors of archaeologists, who recognize better than most who seek knowledge of the past that the only way to go backward in time is to dig downward through history. Such investigation is not confined, however, to the perusal of ruins and solid artifacts; variant readings themselves are artifacts, products of people writing at a time and place in history.

Despite their anonymity, therefore, the historical dynamics and social forces that influenced these scribes must be understood, or at the very least recognized. Copyists labored for a variety of reasons—from profit to piety; and, in some cases, their own personal agendas or concerns gave rise to an intentional choice to change the exemplar they were engaged in copying. In most cases, the sorts of deliberate changes which have been the focus of this study—particularly those resulting from christological concerns and apologetic interests—would have more likely been produced by copyists who had the most invested in the texts themselves, i.e., who had something to gain or lose from what was penned on the page. Therefore, these acts of intentional modification of canonical writings—readily observable not only to the trained eye but to the attentive reader—stand as historical artifacts, and teach us something important about how these early believers viewed the sacred texts they were copying.

---

[18]See the discussion of this variant reading above, pp. 185–88.

[19]Very recently this has been affirmed by Larry W. Hurtado, "Beyond the Interlude? Developments and Directions in New Testament Textual Criticism," in *Studies in the Early Text of the Gospels and Acts*, D. G. K. Taylor, ed. (Atlanta: Society of Biblical Literature, 1999) 26–48, esp. 43–6.

[20]K. Haines–Eitzen, *Guardians of Letters*.

One of the most dramatic historical (and theological) lessons is this: whatever it was that was sacred to them about those writings did not reside in the actual words of the exemplars themselves. For some scribes at least, the exacting word of God was not equivalent to the exact words of scripture. The sacred message was transmitted in and through words of scripture, but the medium was not the message. The degree of homage with which many in today's world view the canonical text should not obfuscate this fact.

The data adduced and analyzed in these chapters has brought some clarity to how and why Christian scribes commissioned with transcribing the Gospels were influenced by apologetic interests. Moreover, we have learned something of the nature and extent to which they did so. Such changes were neither systematic nor comprehensive, and in most cases they were subtle rather than blatant. With respect to apologetic influences, textual transmission remained a conservative enterprise.

Another lesson gleaned from this study is the validity as well as the importance of claiming the historical component of the discipline of New Testament Textual Criticism. As history informs the discipline, so the discipline can release clues and insights that shed light on history. This is a reciprocal relationship: textual critics must claim the historical component of their labors and engage more actively in dialogue with their historian colleagues; similarly, church historians are invited to glean fresh new insights into their subject matter from deliberate exchanges with New Testament textual critics.

Toward this end, though, this volume serves as but a small step. Great potential, I believe, resides in the venture of pursuing this intersection of disciplines.[21] For example, the frequency with which "Western" witnesses in general, and Codex Bezae and the Syriac traditions in particular, have testified to the "apologetic" variant reading invites further study, particularly by those with the interests and linguistic capabilities to explore in depth the Syriac versional witnesses alongside the historical, cultural, and sociological factors that shaped the community of faith out of which those scribes that produced these manuscripts emerged.[22]

---

[21]Along these lines, more in-depth studies focused on specific manuscripts are needed, such as that of D. C. Parker, *Codex Bezae: An Early Christian Manuscript and Its Text* (Cambridge: Cambridge University Press, 1992). So also the continuing investigation into the texts associated with various Greek fathers, studies currently being affirmed by their publication in the SBL "New Testament in the Greek Fathers" series, the most recent of which is Roderic L. Mullen, *The New Testament Text of Cyril of Jerusalem* (SBLNTGF 7; Atlanta: Scholars Press, 1997).

[22]Much fruitful work has already been conducted on Syriac versional tradition. See, e.g., Tjitze Baarda, "The Syriac Versions of the New Testament," and Sebastian P. Brock, "The Use of the Syriac Fathers for New Testament Textual Criticism," both in B. Ehrman and M. Holmes, *The Text of the New Testament in Contemporary Research*, 224–36; J. W. Childers, "The Syriac Evidence for the 'Pre-Johannine Text' of the Gospel: A Study in Method," in *Studies of the Early Text of the Gospels and Acts*, D. G. K. Taylor, ed., 49–85; Matthew Black, "The Syriac New Testament in Early Patristic Tradition," in *La Bible et les Pères*, A. Benoit and P. Prigent, eds. (Paris: Presses Universitaires de France, 1971) 263–78; and Arthur Vööbus, *Studies in the History*

There is potential also for clarifying the relationship between nascent Christianity and evolving Judaism. Recognizing the extent to which apologetic dynamics shaped the textual tradition might lead to a nuanced reappraisal of the nature and scope of the influence of anti-Judaic tendencies on the New Testament text. We might inquire, for example, how some of those readings traditionally determined to be "anti-Judaic" in character might plausibly be viewed as efforts on the part of apologetically-minded scribes to elevate the status of Christianity by claiming the legacy of antiquity and prophetic authority rooted in Judaism.[23]

SUMMARY

In summary, the textual evidence garnered for this study bears testimony to the fact that historical influences affected those anonymous scribes who were busy about transcribing the Gospels. These were not merely disinterested copyists. To them it was a *sacred* text they reproduced, but a text, too, that was open and vulnerable to outside criticism. Certainly they understood their function to be that of copyists, not authors, and certainly not evangelists. Yet, the survival of the movement and the perpetuity of the Gospel appears to have been for them a more profound responsibility than the stoic reproduction of a manuscript. For them, it seems, a text that bore testimony to a living spirit could easily afford a measure of liquidity in transmission. In a sense each word mattered, yet in another sense no word mattered; only The Word mattered, only the *Logos*.

So I offer this conjectural image:

In a room lit by the sunshine through a translucent window and the dim light of a candle, a scribe sits at an angled table bent over parchment dipping his quill in ink. As he has been assigned, he copies a copy of the Gospel of Mark. Dutifully, painstakingly, faithfully, artistically yet swiftly, sometimes wearily, sometimes mindlessly but sometimes clearly mindful of something being at stake, he copies. Hour after hour he copies. Oh, he has made his share of errors: an omission here, a mechanical modification there. Rarely but occasionally, though, something—a word, an error, a fact, a phrase, a phrasing, a description, or an opportunity—brings him to a pause. Perhaps it has something to do with his own cultural sensitivities. Perhaps his long-standing acquaintance with the writings of Justin or Tatian, or something he just read or heard recently that issued from Origen made him take notice and think twice. Perhaps he himself has felt tensions recently related to pagan criticism, from the old arguments of Celsus that never seem to go away, or from the fresh and informed assaults of Porphyry that bear witness to a dangerous pagan familiarity with this book he is copying. Perhaps at this juncture he glances back over his exemplar and, in his own mind, thinks,

---

of the Gospel Text in Syriac. 2 vols. (CSCO 128, 496, Subsidia 3, 79; Louvain: Imprimerie Orientaliste L. Durbecq and Peeters, 1951, 1987).

[23]The foundations for such labor have been well established, as can be seen in the content and bibliographies located in Eldon J. Epp, *Theological Tendency in Codex Cantabrigiensis in Acts*, and John Gager, *The Origins of Anti-Semitism: Attitudes Toward Judaism in Pagan and Christian Antiquity* (Oxford: Oxford University Press, 1985).

"There is a better way to say this." And so he does. His stroke varies from that of the author of his exemplar. He writes it anew, differently, his way.

Thus the text of the Gospel was reproduced and transmitted, but not without first being interpreted and modified—revised, buttressed, corrected, harmonized, refined, polished, stylized, abbreviated, enhanced, or otherwise altered.

To conclude with an analogy, if these copyists of Gospel texts may be compared to chefs, it is fair to say that they are not in the business of creating new recipes, but merely recreating old ones. Still, like relocated chefs who are forced to adapt their old recipes to a new locale by incorporating spices popular to that region, these scribes occasionally introduced new spices and accents to their exemplars, making them more acceptable to the pagan palate. They tempered their recipes and changed the flavor, ever so slightly; but, those who bore an appetite for things apologetic must surely have welcomed these enhancements with the greeting, *"Vive la différence!"*

BIBLIOGRAPHY

Aland, Barbara, and Joël Delobel, eds. *New Testament Textual Criticism, Exegesis and Church History: A Discussion of Methods*. Kampen, The Netherlands: Pharos, 1994.

Aland, Barbara. "Die Münsteraner Arbeit am Text des Neuen Testaments und ihr Beitrag für die frühe Überlieferung des 2. Jahrhunderts: Eine methodologische Betrachtung." *Gospel Traditions of the Second Century*, William L. Petersen, ed. South Bend, IN: University of Notre Dame Press, 1989: 55–70.

Aland, Kurt. "Bemerkungen zum Schluss des Markusevangeliums." *Neotestamentica et Semitica, Studies in Honor of Matthew Black*. E. Earle Ellis and Max Wilcox, eds. Edinburgh: T&T Clark, 1969, 157–80.

———. "The Twentieth Century Interlude in New Testament Textual Criticism." In *Text and Interpretation: Studies in the New Testament Presented to Matthew Black*, ed. Ernest Best and R. McL. Wilson. Cambridge: Cambridge University Press, 1974, 1–14.

———. "Die Bedeutung des P^{75} für den Text des Neuen Testaments: Ein Beitrag zur Frage des 'Western non-interpolations,'" in idem ed., *Studien zur Überlieferung des Neuen Testaments und seines Textes* (Berlin: Walter de Gruyter, 1967), 155–72.

Aland, Kurt and Barbara Aland. *The Text of the New Testament: An Introduction to the Critical Editions and to the Theory and Practice of Modern Textual Criticism*. Grand Rapids, Michigan: Williams B. Eerdmans, 1987.

Albright, W. F. and Mann, C. S. *Matthew*. AB 26. Garden City, NY: Doubleday, 1971.

Allen, Willoughby C. *The Gospel According to St. Matthew*. ICC 26. New York: Charles Scribner's Sons, 1925.

Allison, Dale and Davies, W. D. *A Critical and Exegetical Commentary on the Gospel According to Matthew*, 3 Volumes. ICC; Edinburgh: T&T Clark, 1988.

Altaner, Berthold. *Patrology*. Eng. trans. Hilda C. Graef; Freiburg: Herder & Herder, 1960.

Anastos, Milton V. "Porphyry's Attack on the Bible." *The Classical Tradition: Literary and Historical Studies in Honor of Harry Caplan*. Luitpold Wallach, ed. Ithaca, NY: Cornell University Press, 1966: 421–50.

Anderson, Hugh. *The Gospel of Mark*. New Century Bible. Greenwood, SC: Attic Press, 1976.

Andresen, Carl. *Logos und Nomos: Die Polemik des Kelsos wider das Christentum*. Munich: Walter de Gruyter, 1955.

Arbesmann, R., *et al.*, trans. *Tertullian: Apologetical Works and Minucius Felix: Octavius*. FC 10. Washington, DC: Catholic University of America Press, 1950.

Aune, David E. "Magic in Early Christianity," *ANRW* II.23.2 (1980) 1507–57.

Baarda, Tjitze. "ΔΙΑΦΟΝΙΑ ΣΥΜΦΟΝΙΑ: Factors in the Harmonization of the Gospels, Especially in the Diatessaron of Tatian," *Gospel Traditions in the Second Century*. William L. Petersen, ed. Notre Dame: University of Notre Dame Press, 1989: 133–154.

————. "The Syriac Versions of the New Testament." *The Text of the New Testament in Contemporary Research: Essays on the* Status Quaestionis. Bart D. Ehrman and Michael W. Holmes, eds. Grand Rapids, MI: Eerdmans, 1995:97–112.

Bammel, Ernst and Moule, C. F. D., eds. *Jesus and the Politics of His Day.* Cambridge: Cambridge University Press, 1984.

Barnard, Leslie W. *Athenagoras: A Study in Second Century Christian Apologetic.* ThH 18. Paris: Beauchesne, 1972.

————. *Justin Martyr: His Life and Thought.* Cambridge: Cambridge University Press, 1967.

Barnes, Timothy D. "Porphyry Against the Christians: Date and Attribution of Fragments," *JTS* n.s. 24 (1973), 424–42.

————. "Pagan Perceptions of Christianity." *Early Christianity: Origins and Evolution to AD 600.* London: SPCK, 1991.

————. "Legislation Against the Christians." *Journal of Roman Studies* 58 (1968): 32–50.

————. *Tertullian: A Historical and Literary Study.* Oxford: Clarendon Press, 1971.

Barrett, C. K. "Is There a Theological Tendency in Codex Bezae?" *Text and Interpretation: Studies in the New Testament Presented to Matthew Black.* Ernest Best and R. McL. Wilson, eds. Cambridge: Cambridge University Press, 1979: 15–27.

————. *The Gospel According to St. John.* Second Edition. Philadelphia: Westminster, 1978.

Bauer, Walter. *Das Leben Jesu im Zeitalter der neutestamentlichen Apocryphen.* Tübingen: J. C. B. Mohr (Paul Siebeck), 1907; reprinted Darmstadt, 1967.

————. *Rechtgläubigkeit und Ketzerei im ältesten Christentum.* BHT, 10. Tübingen: J. C. B. Mohr (Paul Siebeck), 1934; English translation, *Orthodoxy and Heresy in Earliest Christianity.* Trans. Robert Kraft, *et al.* Philadelphia: Fortress, 1971.

————. "The Picture of the Apostle in Early Christian Tradition," in E. Hennecke and W. Schneemelcher, eds. *New Testament Apocrypha,* 2 Volumes. Philadelphia: Westminster, 1964, 35–74.

Behr, Charles A., ed. and trans. *P. Aelius Aristides: The Complete Works.* Leiden: E. J. Brill, 1986.

————. *Aelius Aristides and the Sacred Tales.* Amsterdam: Adolf M. Hakkert, 1968.

Bellinzoni, Arthur J. *The Sayings of Jesus in the Writings of Justin Martyr.* Leiden: E. J. Brill, 1967.

Benko, Stephen. "Pagan Criticism of Christianity during the First Two Centuries A. D." *ANRW* II.23.2 (1980): 1055–1118.

————. *Pagan Rome and Early Christians.* Bloomington: Indiana University Press, 1984.

Betz, Hans Dieter, ed., *The Greek Magical Papyri in Translation.* Chicago: University of Chicago Press, 1996.

————. "Secrecy in the Greek Magical Papyri," *Secrecy and Concealment: Studies in the History of Mediterranean and Ancient Near Eastern Religions.* Studies in the History of Religions, *Numen* Book Series 64. Leiden: E. J. Brill, 1995: 153–75.

Bidez, J. *Vie de Porphyre.* Hildesheim: Georg Olms, 1964.

Birdsall, J. Neville, "The Recent History of New Testament Textual Criticism (from Westcott and Hort, 1881, to the Present)," *ANRW* II.26.1: 99–197.

————. "After Three Centuries of the Study of Codex Bezae: The *Status Quaestionis.*" *Codex Bezae: Studies from the Lunel Colloquium.* D. C. Parker and C.-B. Amphoux, eds. Leiden: E. J. Brill, 1996: xix–xxx.

Bond, Helen K. *Pontius Pilate in History and Interpretation.* SNTSMS 100. Richard Bauckham, gen. ed. Cambridge: Cambridge University Press, 1998.

Borret, Marcel. *Origène. Contre Celse,* 5 Volumes. Sources Chrétiennes; Paris: Les Éditions du Cerf, 1968.

Brandon, S. G. F. *The Fall of Jerusalem and the Christian Church.* London, 1951.

Brock, Sebastian P. "Limitations of Syriac in Representing Greek," in Bruce M. Metzger, *The Early Versions of the New Testament: Their Origin, Transmission, and Limitations.* Oxford: Clarendon Press, 1977, 83–98.

———. "The Use of the Syriac Fathers for New Testament Textual Criticism." *The Text of the New Testament in Contemporary Research: Essays on the* Status Quaestionis. Bart D. Ehrman and Michael W. Holmes, eds. Grand Rapids, MI: Eerdmans, 1995: 224–36.

Brown, Milton. "Matthew as ΕΙΡΗΝΟΠΟΙΟΣ." *Studies in the History and Text of the New Testament in honor of Kenneth Willis Clark, Ph. D.* Boyd Daniels and Jack Suggs, eds. SD XXIX. Salt Lake City: University of Utah Press, 1967: 39–50.

Brown, Raymond E. *The Death of the Messiah.* 2 Volumes. Anchor Bible Reference Library. Garden City, NY: Doubleday, 1994.

———. *The Gospel According to John.* Anchor Bible 29–29A; Garden City, NY: Doubleday, 1966.

———. "The *Gospel of Peter* and Canonical Gospel Priority," *NTS* 33 (1987): 321–43.

Burke, Gary T. "Walter Bauer and Celsus: The Shape of Late Second-Century Christianity," *Second Century* 4 (1984): 1–7.

Burkill, T. A. *New Light on the Earliest Gospel.* Ithaca: Cornell University Press, 1972.

Cadbury, H. J. *The Making of Luke–Acts.* London: SPCK, 1961.

Carroll, Kenneth L. "Tatian's Influence on the Developing New Testament." *Studies in the History and Text of the New Testament in Honor of Kenneth Willis Clark, Ph.D.* SD XXIX. Salt Lake City: University of Utah Press, 1967: 59–70.

Carter, Warren. *Matthew: Storyteller, Interpreter, Evangelist.* Peabody, MA: Hendrickson, 1996.

Casey, P. M. "Porphyry and the Origin of the Book of Daniel," *JTS* n.s. 27 (1976): 15–33.

Casson, Lionel. *Selected Satires of Lucian.* New York: W. W. Norton, 1962.

Chadwick, Henry. "Justin Martyr's Defence of Christianity." *BJRL* 47 (1965): 275–97.

———. "The Evidences of Christianity in the Apologetic of Origen," in Studia Patristica II, K. Aland and F. L. Cross, eds. *Texte und Untersuchen zur Geschichte der altchristliche Literatur,* 64; Berlin: Akademie-Verlag, 1957: 331–39; Reprinted in H. Chadwick, *Heresy and Orthodoxy in the Early Church.* Hampshire, Great Britain: Variorum Reprints, 1991.

———. *Christianity and the Classical Tradition,* Oxford: Clarendon Press, 1966.

———. *Origen: Contra Celsum.* Oxford: Clarendon Press, 1953.

Clark, Elizabeth A. *The Origenist Controversy: The Cultural Construction of an Early Christian Debate.* Princeton, NJ: Princeton University Press, 1992.

———. "Eusebius on Women in Early Church History," in Harold W. Attridge and Gohei Hata, eds. *Eusebius, Christianity and Judaism.* Detroit: Wayne State University Press, 1992: 256–269.

———. *Women in the Early Church.* Wilmington, DE: Michael Glazier, 1983.

Clark, Kenneth W. "The Theological Relevance of Textual Variation in Current Criticism of the Greek New Testament," *JBL* 85 (1966): 1–16.

———. "The Text of the Gospel of John in Third-Century Egypt," *NovT* 5 (1962): 17–24.

Clarke, G. W. "The Literary Setting of the *Octavius* of Minucius Felix." *Studies in Early Christianity, Vol II: Literature of the Early Church.* Everette Fergusen, ed. New York: Garland, 1993: 127–43.

———. "The Historical Setting of the *Octavius* of Minucius Felix." *Studies in Early Christianity, Vol II: Literature of the Early Church.* Everette Fergusen, ed. New York: Garland, 1993: 145–64.

Cobb, L. Stephanie. "...Also Some Women: An Investigation of Luke 8:3." Unpublished Paper presented at the University of North Carolina at Chapel Hill, April, 1997.

Colwell, E. C. *Studies in Methodology in Textual Criticism of the New Testament.* NTTS 9; Grand Rapids, MI: Eerdmans, 1969.

———. "External Evidence and New Testament Textual Criticism." Boyd L. Daniels and M. Jack Suggs, eds. *Studies in the History and Text of the New Testament in honor of Kenneth Willis Clark,* Ph.D. SD XXIX. Salt Lake City: University of Utah Press, 1967: 1–12.

Conybeare, F. C. "Three Doctrinal Modifications of the Text of the Gospels," *Hibbert Journal* 1 (1902–03): 96–113.

Conzelmann, Hans. *The Theology of St. Luke.* Geoffrey Buswell, trans. New York: Harper & Row, 1961.

———. *Gentiles, Jews, Christians: Polemics and Apologetics in the Greco-Roman Era.* M. E. Boring, trans. Minneapolis: Fortress, 1992.

Craddock, Fred. *Luke.* Interpretation Series. Louisville, KY: John Knox, 1990.

Cranfield, C. E. B. *The Gospel According to St. Mark.* Cambridge Greek New Testament Commentary. Cambridge: Cambridge University Press, 1959.

Croke, Brian. "The Era of Porphyry's Anti-Christian Polemic," *JRH* 31/1 (1984): 1–15.

Crouzel, Henri. *Origen.* Trans. A. S. Worrall. San Francisco: Harper & Row, 1989.

———. *Bibliographie critique d'Origène.* Hagae Comitis: Martinus Nijhoff, 1971.

Culpepper, R. Alan. *Anatomy of the Fourth Gospel: A Study in Literary Design.* Philadelphia: Fortress, 1983.

D'Angelo, Mary Rose. "Women in Luke–Acts: A Redactional View." *JBL* 109 (1990): 441–61.

Dix, Gregory, ed. *The Treatise on the Apostolic Tradition of St. Hippolytus of Rome.* Second Edition revised by Henry Chadwick. London: SPCK, 1968.

Dodds, E. R. *Pagan and Christian in an Age of Anxiety.* New York: Norton, 1970.

Drijvers, Hans. *East of Antioch: Studies in Early Syriac Christianity.* London: Variorum Reprint, 1984.

Droge, A. J. *Homer or Moses? Early Christian Interpretations of the History of Culture.* Hermeneutische Untersuchungen zur Theologie 26. Tübingen: J. C. B. Mohr (Paul Siebeck), 1989.

———. "Apologetics, NT." *Anchor Bible Dictionary,* Volume I, David Noel Freedman, ed. New York: Doubleday, 1992: 302–07.

Easton, Burton Scott. *The Gospel According to St. Luke.* New York: Charles Scribner's Sons, 1926.

Edwards, Mark, Goodman, Martin, and Price Simon, eds. *Apologetics in the Roman Empire: Pagans, Jews, and Christians.* Oxford: Oxford University Press, 1999.

Edwards, M. J. "Justin's Logos and the Word of God," *JECS* (1995): 261–80.

Ehrman, Bart D. *The Orthodox Corruption of Scripture: The Effect of Early Christological Controversies on the Text of the New Testament.* New York: Oxford University Press, 1993.

————. "The Text of the Gospels at the End of the Second Century." *Codex Bezae: Studies from the Lunel Colloquium, June 1994.* D. C. Parker and C.-B. Amphoux, eds. Leiden: E. J. Brill, 1996: 95–122.

————. "Textual Criticism of the New Testament," in Joel Green, ed. *Hearing the New Testament: Strategies for Interpretation.* Grand Rapids, MI: Eerdmans, 1995: 127–45.

————. "The Use and Significance of Patristic Evidence for NT Textual Criticism," in B. Aland & J. Delobel, eds., *New Testament Textual Criticism, Exegesis, and Early Church History: A Discussion of Methods.* Kampen, The Netherlands: Pharos, 1994: 118–35.

————. "The Cup, The Bread, and the Salvific Effect of Jesus' Death in Luke–Acts," *Society of Biblical Literature Seminar Papers.* Atlanta: Scholars Press, 1991: 576–91.

————. "The Text of Mark in the Hands of the Orthodox," in *Biblical Hermeneutics in Historical Perspective*, ed. Mark Burrows and Paul Rorem. Philadelphia: Fortress, 1991:19–31.

————. "Jesus' Trial Before Pilate: John 18:28–19:16," *BTB* 13 (1983): 124–31.

Ehrman, Bart D., and Holmes, Michael W, eds. *The Text of the New Testament in Contemporary Research: Essays on the Status Quaestionis.* Grand Rapids, MI: Eerdmans, 1995.

Ehrman, Bart D., Holmes, Michael W., and Fee, Gordon D. *The Text of the Fourth Gospel in the Writings of Origen.* Atlanta: Scholars Press, 1993.

Ehrman, Bart, Epp, Eldon, and Fee, Gordon. *The Text of the Fourth Gospel in the Writings of Origen, Volume I.* SBLNTGF 3. Atlanta: Scholars Press, 1992.

Elliott, J. K. *The Apocryphal Jesus: Legends of the Early Church.* Oxford: Oxford University Press, 1996.

————. *The Apocryphal New Testament.* Oxford: Clarendon Press, 1993.

————. *A Bibliography of Greek New Testament Manuscripts.* Cambridge: Cambridge University Press, 1989.

————. "An Eclectic Textual Commentary on the Greek Text of Mark's Gospel," *New Testament Textual Criticism: Its Significance for Exegesis.* Eldon J. Epp and Gordon D. Fee, eds. Oxford: Clarendon Press, 1981: 47–60.

————. "The Text and Language of the Endings to Mark's Gospel," *TZ* 27 (1971): 255–62.

Elliott, J. K. and Moir, Ian. *Manuscripts and the Text of the New Testament.* Edinburgh: T&T Clark, 1995.

Epp, Eldon J. *The Theological Tendency of Codex Bezae Cantabrigiensis in Acts.* SNTSMS 3; Cambridge: Cambridge University Press, 1966.

————. "The 'Ignorance Motif' in Acts and the Anti-Judaic Tendencies in Codex Bezae." *HTR* 55 (1962): 51–62.

————. "The Twentieth Century Interlude in New Testament Textual Criticism." *JBL* 93 (1974): 386–414.

————. "The Papyrus Manuscripts of the New Testament," *The Text of the New Testament in Contemporary Research: Essays on the Status Quaestionis.* Bart D. Ehrman and Michael W. Holmes, eds. Grand Rapids, MI: Eerdmans, 1995: 3–21.

Epp, Eldon J. and Fee, Gordon D., eds. *New Testament Text Criticism: Its Significance for Exegesis. Essays in Honor of Bruce M. Metzger.* Oxford: Clarendon, 1981.

Ernst, J. *Das Evangelium nach Markus.* Regensberg: Pustet, 1981.

Evans, Craig A. "Patristic Interpretation of Mark 2:26 'When Abiathar Was High Priest,'" *VC* 40 (1986): 183–86.

Fall, Thomas, ed. and trans. *Writings of Saint Justin Martyr*. FC 6. Washington, DC: Catholic University of America Press, 1948.

Farmer, W. R. *The Last Twelve Verses of Mark*. Cambridge: Cambridge University Press, 1974.

Fee, Gordon D. "The Text of John in Origen and Cyril of Alexandria: A Contribution to Methodology in the Recovery and Analysis of Patristic Citations," *Biblia* 52 (1971): 353–73.

———. "Modern Textual Criticism and the Synoptic Problem." *J. J. Griesbach: Synoptic and Text-Critical Studies 1776–1976*. B. Orchard and T. Longstaff, eds. Cambridge: Cambridge University Press, 1978: 154–69.

———. "Origen's Text of the New Testament and the Text of Egypt," *NTS* 28 (1981): 348–64.

Fergusen, Everett, ed. *Church and State in the Early Church*. Studies in Early Christianity Series VII. New York: Garland, 1993.

———. *In Memory of Her*. New York: Crossroad, 1994.

Fitzmyer, Joseph A. *The Gospel According to Luke*. 2 Volumes. Anchor Bible 28/28a. Garden City, NY: Doubleday, 1981.

Frede, M. "Origen's Treatise Against Celsus." M. Edwards, M. Goodman, and S. Price, eds. *Apologetics in the Roman Empire: Pagans, Jews, and Christians*. Oxford: Oxford University Press, 1999: 131–55.

———. "Celsus' Attack on the Christians." Jonathan Barnes and Miriam Griffin, eds. *Philosophia Togata II: Plato and Aristotle at Rome*. Oxford: Clarendon Press, 1997: 218–40.

Frend, W. H. C. *Martyrdom and Persecution in the Early Church: A Study of a Conflict from the Maccabees to Donatus*. New York: New York University Press, 1967.

———. *The Rise of Christianity*. Philadelphia: Fortress, 1984.

———. "Prelude to the Great Persecution: The Propaganda War." *JEH* 38/1 (1987): 1–18.

Gager, John G. *Kingdom and Community: The Social World of Early Christianity*. Englewood Cliffs, NJ: Prentice–Hall, 1975.

———. *The Origins of Anti-Semitism*. New York: Oxford University Press, 1983.

Gallagher, Eugene. *Divine Man or Magician? Celsus and Origen on Jesus*. SBLDS 64. Chico, CA: Scholars Press, 1982.

Gamble, Harry. *Books and Readers in the Early Church*. New Haven: Yale University Press, 1995.

Garrett, Susan. *The Demise of the Devil*. Minneapolis: Fortress, 1989.

Geffcken, Johannes. *Zwei griechische Apologeten*. Leipzig: Teubner, 1907. Reprinted Hildesheim: Georg Olms Verlag, 1970.

Georgi, Dieter. "Socioeconomic Reasons for the 'Divine Man' as a Propagandistic Pattern," in *Aspects of Christian Propaganda in Judaism and Early Christianity*, E. Schüssler Fiorenza, ed. Notre Dame, IN: University of Notre Dame Press, 1976: 27–42.

Gnilka, Joachim. *Das Evangelium nach Markus*. 2 Volumes. Zürich: Benziger Verlag, 1979.

Goodenough, E. R. *The Theology of Justin Martyr*. Jena: Frommann, 1923.

Grant, Robert M. *Greek Apologists of the Second Century*. Philadelphia: Westminster, 1988.

———. "Five Apologists and Marcus Aurelius," *VC* 42 (1988): 1–17.

———. "Theological Education at Alexandria," *The Roots of Egyptian Christianity*, Birger A. Pearson and James E. Goehring, eds. Philadelphia: Fortress, 1986: 178–89.

———. "Paul, Galen, and Origen." *JTS* 34 (1983): 533–36.

———. *Theophilus of Antioch: Ad Autolycum*. Oxford: Clarendon Press, 1970.

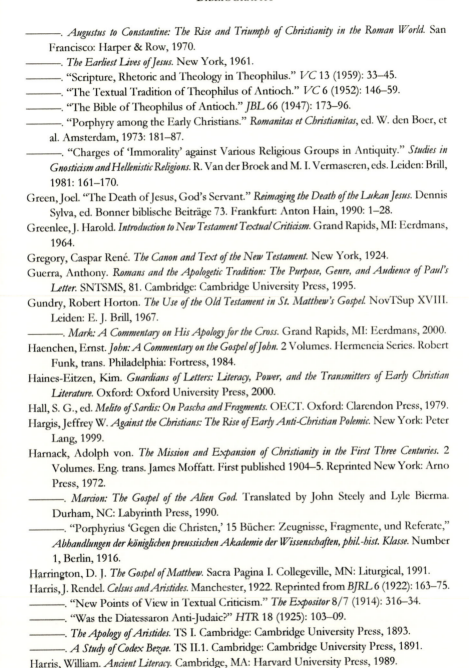

——. *Augustus to Constantine: The Rise and Triumph of Christianity in the Roman World.* San Francisco: Harper & Row, 1970.

——. *The Earliest Lives of Jesus.* New York, 1961.

——. "Scripture, Rhetoric and Theology in Theophilus." *VC* 13 (1959): 33–45.

——. "The Textual Tradition of Theophilus of Antioch." *VC* 6 (1952): 146–59.

——. "The Bible of Theophilus of Antioch." *JBL* 66 (1947): 173–96.

——. "Porphyry among the Early Christians." *Romanitas et Christianitas*, ed. W. den Boer, et al. Amsterdam, 1973: 181–87.

——. "Charges of 'Immorality' against Various Religious Groups in Antiquity." *Studies in Gnosticism and Hellenistic Religions.* R. Van der Broek and M. I. Vermaseren, eds. Leiden: Brill, 1981: 161–170.

Green, Joel. "The Death of Jesus, God's Servant." *Reimaging the Death of the Lukan Jesus.* Dennis Sylva, ed. Bonner biblische Beiträge 73. Frankfurt: Anton Hain, 1990: 1–28.

Greenlee, J. Harold. *Introduction to New Testament Textual Criticism.* Grand Rapids, MI: Eerdmans, 1964.

Gregory, Caspar René. *The Canon and Text of the New Testament.* New York, 1924.

Guerra, Anthony. *Romans and the Apologetic Tradition: The Purpose, Genre, and Audience of Paul's Letter.* SNTSMS, 81. Cambridge: Cambridge University Press, 1995.

Gundry, Robert Horton. *The Use of the Old Testament in St. Matthew's Gospel.* NovTSup XVIII. Leiden: E. J. Brill, 1967.

——. *Mark: A Commentary on His Apology for the Cross.* Grand Rapids, MI: Eerdmans, 2000.

Haenchen, Ernst. *John: A Commentary on the Gospel of John.* 2 Volumes. Hermeneia Series. Robert Funk, trans. Philadelphia: Fortress, 1984.

Haines-Eitzen, Kim. *Guardians of Letters: Literacy, Power, and the Transmitters of Early Christian Literature.* Oxford: Oxford University Press, 2000.

Hall, S. G., ed. *Melito of Sardis: On Pascha and Fragments.* OECT. Oxford: Clarendon Press, 1979.

Hargis, Jeffrey W. *Against the Christians: The Rise of Early Anti-Christian Polemic.* New York: Peter Lang, 1999.

Harnack, Adolph von. *The Mission and Expansion of Christianity in the First Three Centuries.* 2 Volumes. Eng. trans. James Moffatt. First published 1904–5. Reprinted New York: Arno Press, 1972.

——. *Marcion: The Gospel of the Alien God.* Translated by John Steely and Lyle Bierma. Durham, NC: Labyrinth Press, 1990.

——. "Porphyrius 'Gegen die Christen,' 15 Bücher: Zeugnisse, Fragmente, und Referate," *Abhandlungen der königlichen preussischen Akademie der Wissenschaften, phil.-hist. Klasse.* Number 1, Berlin, 1916.

Harrington, D. J. *The Gospel of Matthew.* Sacra Pagina I. Collegeville, MN: Liturgical, 1991.

Harris, J. Rendel. *Celsus and Aristides.* Manchester, 1922. Reprinted from *BJRL* 6 (1922): 163–75.

——. "New Points of View in Textual Criticism." *The Expositor* 8/7 (1914): 316–34.

——. "Was the Diatessaron Anti-Judaic?" *HTR* 18 (1925): 103–09.

——. *The Apology of Aristides.* TS I. Cambridge: Cambridge University Press, 1893.

——. *A Study of Codex Bezae.* TS II.1. Cambridge: Cambridge University Press, 1891.

Harris, William. *Ancient Literacy.* Cambridge, MA: Harvard University Press, 1989.

Hauck, Robert J. "'They Saw What They Say They Saw': Sense Knowledge in Early Christian Polemic," *HTR* 81:3 (1988): 239–49.

Head, Peter M. "Christology and Textual Transmission: Reverential Alterations in the Synoptic Gospels," *NovT* XXXV, 2 (1993): 105–29.

Hill, David. *The Gospel of Matthew.* New Century Bible. London: Oliphants, 1972.

Hoek, Annewies van den, "The 'Catechetical' School of Early Christian Alexandria and Its Philonic Heritage," *HTR* 90 (1997): 59–87.

Hoffmann, R. J. ed. and Eng. trans. *Porphyry Against the Christians: The Literary Remains.* Amherst, NY: Prometheus Books, 1994.

———. ed. and Eng. trans. *Celsus: On the True Doctrine.* New York: Oxford University Press, 1987.

Holmes, Michael W. "Codex Bezae as a Recension of the Gospels." *Codex Bezae: Studies from the Lunel Colloquium.* D. C. Parker and C.-B. Amphoux, eds. Leiden: E. J. Brill, 1996: 123–60.

Hooker, Morna. *The Gospel According to Saint Mark.* Black's New Testament Commentary. Peabody, MA: Hendrickson, 1991.

Horbury, William. "Christ as Brigand in Ancient Anti-Christian Polemic," in Ernst Bammel and C. F. D. Moule, eds. *Jesus and the Politics of His Day.* Cambridge: Cambridge University Press, 1984: 183–95.

Hornschuh, M. "Das Leben des Origenes und die Entstehung der alexandrinischen Schule," *Zeitschrift für Kirchengeschichte* 71 (1960): 193–214.

Howard, Wilbert F. "The Influence of Doctrine upon the Text of the New Testament." *The London Quarterly and Halborn Review* 166 (1941): 1–16.

Hull, John M. *Hellenistic Magic and the Synoptic Tradition.* Studies in Biblical Theology. Second Series 28. London: SCM, 1974.

Hunger, Herbert. "Zur Datierung des Papyrus Bodmer II (P 66)," *Anzeiger der Österreichischen Akademie der Wissenschaften,* phil.-hist. Kl. 4 (1960): 12–33.

Hurtado, Larry. "Beyond the Interlude? Developments and Directions in New Testament Textual Criticism." *Studies in the Early Text of the Gospels and Acts,* D. G. K. Taylor, ed. SBLTS 1. Atlanta: Society of Biblical Literature, 1999: 26–48.

———. *Mark.* Good News Commentary. San Francisco: Harper & Row, 1983.

Jackson, John, trans. *Tacitus: The Annals.* LCL. Cambridge, MA: Harvard University Press, 1937.

Janssen, L. F. "'Superstitio' and the Persecution of the Christians." *VC* 33 (1979): 131–59.

Jensen, E. E. "The First Century Controversy over Jesus as a Revolutionary Figure," *JBL* 60 (1941): 261–72.

Jeremias, Joachim. *The Eucharistic Words of Jesus.* Translated from the German by Norman Perrin. New York: Charles Scribner's Sons, 1966. German edition *Die Abendmahlsworte Jesu,* Rev. 3rd ed. Göttingen: Vandenhoeck & Ruprecht, 1964.

Jervell, Jacob. *Luke and the People of God: A New Look at Luke–Acts.* Minneapolis: Augsburg, 1972.

Joly, R. *Christianisme et Philosophe: études sur Justin et les apologistes grecs du deuxième siècle.* Brussels: Editions de l'Université Bruxelles, 1973.

Karris, Robert. "Women and Discipleship in Luke." *CBQ* 56 (1994): 1–20.

Kenyon, Frederic G. And S. C. E. Legg. *The Ministry and the Sacraments.* Roderic Dunkerly, ed. London, 1937.

Keresztes, P. "The Imperial Roman Government and the Christian Church. I. From Nero to the Severi. II. From Gallienus to the Great Persecution." *ANRW* 23.2 (1980): 247–315, 375–86.

———. "The Literary Genre of Justin's First Apology." *VC* 19 (1965): 99–110.

———. "The 'So-Called' Second Apology of Justin." *Latomus* 24 (1965): 858–69.

Kilpatrick, G. D. "Western Text and Original Text in the Gospel and Acts," in J. K. Elliott, ed. *The Principles and Practice of New Testament Textual Criticism: Collected Essays of G. D. Kilpatrick.* Leuven: Leuven University Press, 1990: 113–27.

Klijn, A. F. J. *A Survey of the Researches into the Western Text of the Gospels and Acts.* Utrecht, 1949.

Koester, Helmut, "The Text of the Synoptic Gospels in the Second Century," *Gospel Traditions in the Second Century.* William L. Petersen, ed. Notre Dame: University of Notre Dame Press, 1989: 19–37.

———. "ΓΝΩΜΑΙ ΔΙΑΦΟΡΟΙ: The Origin and Nature of Diversification in the History of Early Christianity," in H. Koester and James M. Robinson, eds. *Trajectories Through Early Christianity.* Philadelphia: Fortress, 1971:114–57.

Kraeling, Carl H. *A Greek Fragment of Tatian's Diatessaron from Dura.* Studies and Documents III. London: Christophers, 1935.

Kraemer, Ross Shepard. *Her Share of the Blessings.* New York: Oxford University Press, 1992.

——— and D'Angelo, Mary Rose. *Women and Christian Origins.* New York: Oxford University Press, 1999.

Labriolle, Pierre de. *Le Réaction païenne. Etude sur la polemique antichrétienne du I au VI siècle.* Second edition. Paris, 1948.

Lagrange, M.-J. *Évangile selon Saint Marc.* Ninth edition. Paris: Libraire Lecoffre, 1966.

———. *Évangile selon Saint Matthieu.* Third Edition. Études Bibliques. Paris: Librarie Lecoffre, 1927.

———. *Évangile selon Saint Jean.* Eighth Edition. Paris: Gabalda, 1948.

———. "Deux nouveaux textes relativs à l'Évangile." *Revue Biblique* XLIV (1935).

Lake, Kirsopp, "ΕΜΒΡΙΜΗΣΑΜΕΝΟΣ and ΟΡΓΙΣΘΕΙΣ, Mark 1, 40–43," *HTR* (1923): 197–8.

———. *The Influence of Textual Criticism on the Exegesis of the New Testament.* Oxford: Parker & Sons, 1904.

———, ed. and trans. *Eusebius: Ecclesiastical History.* 2 Volumes. LCL; Cambridge, MA: Harvard University Press, 1949.

Lane, William. *Mark.* NICNT. Grand Rapids, MI: Eerdmans, 1974.

Lane Fox, Robin. *Pagans and Christians.* San Francisco: Harper & Row, 1986.

LaPorte, Jean. *The Role of Women in Early Christianity.* Studies in Women and Religion 7. New York: Edwin Mellen Press, 1982.

Liddell, Henry George and Scott, Robert. *A Greek-English Lexicon.* Revised by Sir Henry Stuart Jones, *et al.* Oxford: Clarendon press, 1968.

Lightfoot, R. H. *St. John's Gospel: A Commentary.* C. F. Evans, ed. Oxford: Clarendon Press, 1956.

Lindauer, J. M. *Minucius Felix: Octavius.* München: Kösel-Verlag, 1964.

Lindsay, Jack, trans. *Apuleius: The Golden Ass.* Bloomington: Indiana University Press, 1962.

Long, A. A. *Hellenistic Philosophy,* 2nd ed. Berkeley: University of California, 1986.

Long, George, trans. *Marcus Aurelius: Meditations.* Amherst, NY: Prometheus, 1991.

Luck, Georg. *Arcana Mundi: Magic and the Occult in the Greek and Roman Worlds.* Baltimore, MD: Johns Hopkins University Press, 1985.

Luz, Ulrich. *Matthew.* A Continental Commentary. Wilhelm C. Linss, trans. Minneapolis: Fortress, 1992.

MacDonald, Margaret Y. *Early Christian Women and Pagan Opinion: The Power of the Hysterical Woman.* Cambridge: Cambridge University Press, 1996.

MacMullen, Ramsey. *Paganism in the Roman Empire.* New Haven: Yale University Press, 1981.

————. *Christianizing the Roman Empire.* New Haven: Yale University Press, 1984.

————. *Enemies of the Roman Order.* Cambridge, MA: Harvard University Press, 1966.

Mann, C. S. *Mark.* AB 27. Garden City, NY: Doubleday, 1986.

Marcovich, Miroslav. *Tatiani: Oratio ad Graecos.* PTS 43; Berlin: Walter de Gruyter, 1995.

————, ed. *Theophili Antiocheni: Ad Autolycum.* PTS 44; Berlin: Walter de Gruyter, 1995.

————, ed. *Iustini Martyris Apologiae pro Christianis.* Berlin: Walter de Gruyter, 1994.

Marcus, Joel. *Mark 1–8.* Anchor Bible 27. New York: Doubleday, 1999.

Martini, Carlo M. "Is There a Late Alexandrian Text of the Gospels?" *NTS* 24 (1978): 285–96.

McGowan, Andrew. "Eating People: Accusations of Cannibalism Against Christians in the Second Century." *JECS* 2:3 (1994): 413–42.

Meeks, Wayne. *The First Urban Christians: The Social World of the Apostle Paul.* New Haven: Yale University Press, 1983.

Melmouth, William, trans. and Moore, Clifford H., ed. *The Epistles of Pliny.* Boston: Bibliophile Society, 1925.

Meredith, Anthony. "Porphyry and Julian Against the Christians." *ANRW* II.23.2 (1981): 1119–49.

Metzger, Bruce M. *The Text of the New Testament: Its Transmission, Corruption, and Restoration.* New York: Oxford University Press, 1993.

————. *A Textual Commentary on the Greek New Testament.* London: United Bible Societies, 1975.

————. "Explicit References in the Works of Origen to Variant Readings in the New Testament Manuscripts." *Biblical and Patristic Studies in Memory of Robert Pierce Casey.* J. Neville Birdsall and Robert W. Thompson, eds. Freiberg: Herder, 1963: 78–95.

————. "St. Jerome's Explicit References to Variant Readings in Manuscripts of the New Testament." *Text and Interpretation.* Ernest Best and R. McLean Wilson, eds. Cambridge: Cambridge University Press, 1979: 179–90.

————. "Names for the Nameless in the New Testament: A Study in the Growth of Christian Tradition," in *Kyriakon: Festschrift Johannes Quasten.* Patrick Granfield and Josef A. Jungman, eds. Münster, 1970: 79–99.

————. "Literary Forgeries and Canonical Pseudepigrapha," *JBL* 91 (1972): 3–24.

————. *The Early Versions of the New Testament: Their Origin, Transmission, and Limitations.* Oxford: Clarendon Press, 1977.

————. "The Caesarean Text of the Gospels," *JBL* 64 (1945): 457–89.

Miura-Stange, Anna. *Celsus und Origenes.* Giessen, 1929.

Musurillo, H. A., ed. and Eng. trans. *The Acts of the Christian Martyrs.* Oxford: Clarendon Press, 1972.

Mullen, Roderic. *The New Testament Text of Cyril of Jerusalem.* SBLNTGF 7. Atlanta: Scholars Press, 1997.

Nautin, P. "Trois autre fragments de livre du Porphyre 'Contre les Chrétiens.'" *Revue Biblique* 57 (1950): 409–16.

Nestle, Wilhelm. "Die Haupteinwände des antiken Denkens gegen das Christentum." *Archiv für Religionswissenschaft* (Leipzig) 73 (1941–42): 51–100.

Niperdey, Karl and Georg Andresen, eds. *P. Cornelius Tacitus: Annalen*. Two Volumes. Freiburg, Germany: Weidmann, 1978.

Nock, Arthur Darby, *Conversion: The Old and the New in Religion from Alexander the Great to Augustine of Hippo*. Oxford: Clarendon, 1933.

Norris, Frederick W. "Black Marks on the Communities' Manuscripts," *Journal of Early Christian Studies* 2:3 (1994): 443–66.

O'Flaherty, Wendy D. *The Critical Study of Sacred Texts*. Berkeley, California: Graduate Theological Union, 1979.

Osborn, G. T. "Why Did Decius and Valerian Proscribe Christianity?" *CH* 2 (1933): 67–77.

Pagels, Elaine. *The Gnostic Gospels*. New York: Random House, 1979.

Painter, John. *Mark's Gospel: Worlds in Conflict*. London: Routledge, 1997.

Palmer, Darryl W. "Atheism, Apologetic, and Negative Theology in the Greek Apologists of the Second Century," *VC* 37, 3 (1983): 234–59.

Parker, D. C. *Codex Bezae: An Early Christian Manuscript and Its Text*. Cambridge: Cambridge University Press, 1992.

————. *The Living Text of the Gospels*. Cambridge: Cambridge University Press, 1997.

Parker, D. C., Taylor, D. G. K., and Goodacre, M. S. "The Dura-Europas Gospel Harmony." *Studies in the Early Text of the Gospels and Acts*. D. G. K. Taylor, ed. SBLTS 1. Atlanta: Society of Biblical Literature, 1999: 192–228.

Parker, D. C. and Amphoux, C.-B., eds. *Codex Bezae: Studies from the Lunel Colloquium, June 1994*. Leiden: E. J. Brill, 1996.

Parson, Mikeal C. "A Christological Tendency in P75." *JBL* 105 (1986): 463–79.

Parvis, Merrill M. "The Nature and Tasks of New Testament Textual Criticism: An Appraisal." *Journal of Religion* 32 (1952): 165–74.

Patrick, John. *The Apology of Origen in Reply to Celsus: A Chapter in the History of Apologetics*. Edinburgh, 1892.

Petersen, William L. *Tatian's Diatessaron: Its Creation, Dissemination, Significance, and History in Scholarship*. Leiden: E. J. Brill, 1994.

————., ed. *Gospel Traditions in the Second Century: Origins, Recensions, Text, and Transmission*. Notre Dame: University of Notre Dame Press, 1989.

Petzer, Jacobus H. "The History of the New Testament Text–Its Reconstruction, Significance, and Use in New Testament Textual Criticism." In *New Testament Textual Criticism, Exegesis and Church History: A Discussion of Methods*, ed. B. Aland and J. Delobel. Kampen, The Netherlands: Pharos, 1994: 1–32.

Pichler, Karl. *Streit um das Christentum: Der Angriff des Kelsos und die Antwort des Origenes*. Frankfurt-am-Main, 1980.

Plooij, D. "A Fragment of Tatian's Diatessaron in Greek," *ExTim* 46 (1934/5): 471–76.

Plummer, A. *Luke*. ICC 29. Fifth Edition. Edinburgh: T&T Clark, 1922.

Porter, C. L. "Papyrus Bodmer XV (P 75) and the Text of Codex Vaticanus," *JBL* 81 (1962): 363–76.

Price, R. M. "'Hellenization' and Logos Doctrine in Justin Martyr," *VC* 42 (1988): 18–23.

Quasten, Johannes. *Patrology.* 4 volumes. Utrecht-Antwerp: Spectrum, 1950–86.

Quispel, G. M. *Minucii Felicis Octavius.* Leiden: E. J. Brill, 1973.

———. "Marcion and the Text of the New Testament," *VC* 52 (1998): 349–60.

Rankin, David. *Tertullian and the Church.* Cambridge: Cambridge University Press, 1995.

Rendall, Gerald H. *Minucius Felix: Octavius.* LCL. Cambridge, MA: Harvard University Press, 1960.

Rice, George. "Western Non-Interpolations: A Defense of the Apostolate," in *Luke–Acts: New Perspectives from the SBL Seminar,* edited by Charles H. Talbert. New York: Crossroad, 1984: 1–16.

Riddle, D. W. "Textual Criticism as a Historical Discipline," *Anglican Theological Review* 18 (1936): 220–33.

Roberts, C. H. *Manuscript, Society and Belief in Early Christian Egypt.* London: Oxford University Press, 1979.

Ross, J. M. "Floating Words: Their Significance for Textual Criticism." *NTS* 38 (1992): 153–156.

———. "The Rejected Words in Luke 9:54–56," *Expository Times* 84 (1972–73): 85–88.

Rougier, Louis. *Celse Contre les Chretiens: la réaction païenne sous l'empire romain.* Theoriques, Vol. I; Alain de Benoit, ed. Paris: Copernic, 1977.

Royse, James R. "Scribal Tendencies in the Transmission of the Text." *The Text of the New Testament in Contemporary Research: Essays on the Status Quaestionis.* Bart D. Ehrman and Michael W. Holmes, eds. Grand Rapids, MI: Eerdmans, 1995: 239–52.

Ryan, Rosalie. "The Women from Galilee and Discipleship in Luke," *Biblical Theology Bulletin* 15 (1985): 56–59.

Samain, P. "L'Accusation de magie contre le Christ dans les Évangiles." *Ephemerides Theologicae Lovanienses* 15 (1938): 449–90.

Sanders, E. P., ed. *Jewish and Christian Self-Determination. Volume 1: The Shaping of Christianity in the Second and Third Centuries.* Philadelphia: Fortress, 1980.

———. *Tendencies of the Synoptic Tradition.* Cambridge: Cambridge University Press, 1969.

Sawyer, Deborah F. *Women and Religion in the First Christian Centuries.* London: Routledge, 1996.

Scheidweiler, F. "The Gospel of Nicodemus, Acts of Pilate and Christ's Descent Into Hell." Edgar Hennecke and Wilhelm Schneemelcher, eds. *The New Testament Apocrypha.* 2 Volumes. R. McL. Wilson, trans. Philadelphia: Westminster, 1963–66: I.444–84.

Schnackenburg, Rudolf. *The Gospel According to John.* New York: Seabury Press, 1980.

Schoedel, W. R. "In Praise of a King: A Rhetorical Pattern in Athenagoras." *Disciplina Nostra: In Memory of Robert F. Evans,* ed. D. F. Winslow. Cambridge, MA: Philadelphia Patristic Foundation, 1979: 69–90.

———. "Christian Atheism and the Peace of the Roman Empire," *CH* 42 (1973): 309–19.

———, ed. and trans. *Athenagoras: Legatio and De Resurrectione.* Oxford: Clarendon Press, 1972.

Schüssler Fiorenza, Elizabeth, ed. *Aspects of Religious Propaganda in Judaism and Early Christianity.* South Bend, IN: University of Notre Dame Press, 1976.

Schweizer, Eduard. *The Good News According to Mark.* Donald H. Madvig, trans. Atlanta: John Knox Press, 1977.

———. *The Good News According to Matthew.* David Green, trans. Atlanta: John Knox Press, 1975.

Shelton, Jo-Ann. *As the Romans Did: A Sourcebook in Roman Social History.* New York: Oxford University Press, 1988.

Sherwin-White, A. N. *The Letters of Pliny: A Historical and Social Commentary.* Oxford: Clarendon Press, 1985.

———. "The Early Persecutions and the Roman Law Again," *JTS* n. s. III, 2 (October, 1952): 199–213.

———. "Why Were the Early Christians Persecuted?—An Amendment," *Past and Present* 27 (1964): 23–7.

Simpson, A. D. M. *Minucii Felicis Octavius: Prolegomena, Text and Critical Notes.* New York: Columbia University Press, 1938.

Skeat, T. C. "Irenaeus and the Four-Gospel Canon," *NovT* 34 (1992): 194–99.

Smith, D. Moody. *Johannine Christianity: Essays on Its Setting, Sources, and Theology.* Columbia, SC: University of South Carolina Press, 1984.

———. *The Composition and Order of the Fourth Gospel.* New Haven: Yale University Press, 1965.

———. *John.* Abingdon New Testament Commentaries. Nashville: Abingdon, 1999.

Smith, Morton. *Jesus the Magician.* New York: , 1978.

———. *Clement of Alexandria and a Secret Gospel of Mark.* Cambridge, MA: Harvard University Press, 1973.

Snodgrass, Klyne. "Western Non-Interpolations." *JBL* 91 (1972): 369–79.

Ste. Croix, G. E. M. de. "Why Were the Early Christians Persecuted?" *Past and Present* 26 (1963): 6–38.

———. "Why Were the Early Christians Persecuted?—A Rejoinder," *Past and Present* 27 (1964): 28–33.

Stendahl, Krister. *The School of St. Matthew and Its Use of the Old Testament.* Philadelphia: Fortress, 1968.

Sterling, Gregory E. *Historiography and Self-Definition: Josephos, Luke–Acts and Apologetic Historiography.* Leiden: E. J. Brill, 1992.

Stewart-Sykes, Alistair. *Melito of Sardis: On Pascha.* Crestwood, NY: St. Vladimir's Seminary Press, 2001.

Streeter, B. H. *The Four Gospels: A Study of Origins Treating of the Manuscript Tradition, Sources, Authorship, and Dates.* Eleventh Edition; New York: St. Martin's Press, 1964. First edition published in London: MacMillan, 1924.

Talbert, Charles H. *Reading John: A Literary and Theological Commentary on the Fourth Gospel and the Johannine Epistles.* New York: Crossroad, 1994.

———. *Reading Luke: A New Commentary for Preachers.* London: SPCK, 1982.

Taylor, Vincent. *The Gospel According to St. Mark.* Second Edition. New York: St. Martin's Press, 1966.

Tetlow, Elizabeth. *Women and Ministry in the New Testament.* New York: Paulist Press, 1980.

Thayse, André. *Matthieu: L'Évangile Revisité.* Brussells: Éditions Racine, 1998.

Theissen, Gerd. *Sociology of Early Palestinian Christianity.* Eng. trans. John Bowden. Philadelphia: Fortress, 1978.

———. *The Miracle Stories of the Early Christian Tradition.* SNTW. Edinburgh: T&T Clark, 1983.

Titus, E. L. "The Motivation of Changes Made in the New Testament Text by Justin Martyr and Clement of Alexandria: A Study in the Origin of New Testament Variation." Unpublished Ph.D. Thesis, University of Chicago, 1942.

Torjesen, Karen Jo. *When Women Were Priests*. San Francisco: HarperSanFrancisco, 1993.

Trigg, Joseph Wilson. *Origen: The Bible and Philosophy in the Third-Century Church*. Atlanta: John Knox Press, 1983.

———. *Origen*. London: Routledge, 1998.

Turner, C. H., "A Textual Commentary on Mark I," *JTS* 28 (1926–27): 145–58.

———. "Théophile d'Antioche contre Celse: *A Autolycos* III." *Revue des Études Augustiniennes* 17 (1971): 203–25.

Visotsky, Burton L. "Overturning the Lamp," *JJS* 38 (1987): 72–80.

Walzer, Richard. *Galen on Jews and Christians*. London: Oxford University Press, 1949.

Westcott, B. F., and Hort, F. J. A. *Introduction to the New Testament in the Original Greek*. New York: Harper & Brothers, 1882. Reprinted Peabody, Massachusetts: Hendrickson, 1988.

Whittaker, Molly, ed. and trans. *Tatian: Oratio ad Graecos and Fragments*. Oxford: Clarendon Press, 1982.

Wilken, Robert. *The Christians as the Romans Saw Them*. New Haven: Yale University Press, 1984.

———. "Toward a Social Interpretation of Early Christian Apologetics." *CH* 39 (1970): 437–58.

———. "Alexandria: A School for Training in Virtue." *Schools of Thought in the Christian Tradition*. Patrick Henry, ed. Philadelphia: Fortress, 1984: 15–30.

Williams, C. S. C. *Alterations to the Text of the Synoptic Gospels and Acts*. Oxford: Basil Blackwell, 1951.

Winter, Paul. "The Trial of Jesus as a Rebel Against Rome," *Jewish Quarterly* 16 (1968): 31–37.

———. *On the Trial of Jesus*. Berlin: Walter de Gruyter, 1961.

Wisse, Frederick. "The Nature and Purpose of Redactional Changes in Early Christian Texts: The Canonical Gospels." *The Gospel Traditions in the Second Century: Origins, Recensions, Text, and Transmission*. William L. Petersen, ed. South Bend, IN: University of Notre Dame Press, 1989: 39–53.

Wisselink, Willem F. *Assimilation as a Criterion for Establishing the Text*. Kampen: Uitgeversmaatschappij J. H. Kok, 1989.

Witherington, Ben, "The Anti-Feminist Tendencies of the 'Western' Text in Acts," *JBL* 103 (1984): 82–84.

———. "On the Road with Mary Magdalene, Joanna, Susanna, and Other Disciples—Luke 8:1–3," *ZNW* 70 (1979): 243–48.

———. *The Gospel of Mark: A Socio-Rhetorical Commentary*. Grand Rapids, MI: Eerdmans, 2001.

Wolf, G., ed. *Porphyrii de Philosophia Ex Oraculis Haurienda*. Hildesheim: Georg Olms, 1962. Original edition, 1856.

Wrede, William. *The Messianic Secret*. J. C. G. Grieg, trans. Greenwood, SC: Attic Press, 1971. German edition *Das Messiasgeheimnis in den Evangelien*. Göttingen: Vanderhoeck & Ruprecht, 1963. Original German publication, 1901.

Wright, Leon E. *Alterations to the Words of Jesus as Quoted in the Literature of the Second Century*. Cambridge: Harvard University Press, 1952.

Zeegers-Vander Vorst, N. "Les Citations du Nouveau Testament dans les livres à Autolycus de Théophile d'Antioche." *Texte und Untersuchungen* 115 (1975): 371–82.

Zuntz, Günther. *The Text of the Epistles: A Disquisition upon the Corpus Paulinum*. London: Oxford University Press, 1953.

GENERAL INDEX

272   APOLOGETIC DISCOURSE AND THE SCRIBAL TRADITION

Taylor, V., 67, 69, 110, 114, 118, 123, 126,
    131, 133, 134, 168, 175, 179, 184,
    189, 190, 195, 227, 228, 247, 248,
    258, 261, 263
temporal priority, viii, 49, 78, 79, 82
Tendenzkritik, 14
Tertullian, vii, 27, 45, 46, 50, 54-56, 59, 62,
    112, 122, 148, 149, 151, 154, 155,
    159, 162, 164-166, 173, 192, 203,
    205, 212, 213, 220, 222, 225, 251,
    252, 262
textual criticism, 4-8, 10-18, 67, 87, 88, 92,
    131, 164, 184, 238, 242, 243,
    246-248, 251-259, 261, 262
Textus Receptus, 7, 193
Theodosius, 24, 32
Theophilus of Antioch, vii, 48, 49, 55, 60,
    62, 84, 89, 90, 112, 180, 193, 209,
    256, 257
Thyestean feasts, 35
Tischendorf, Constantine von, 7
Titus, E. L, 12, 87, 97, 264
Torjesen, Karen Jo, 16, 178, 228, 238, 264
Trajan, 1, 2, 20, 25, 36, 141, 142, 147,
    199-201, 204-206, 222
transcriptional probabilities, 14, 71, 73, 88,
    92, 94, 116, 136, 157, 245, 247
treason, 24, 50, 55, 56, 104, 109, 207, 209,
    215
True Doctrine, 19, 27, 31, 40, 44, 86,
    101-103, 247, 258
True Logos, 27, 31, 239
Tune, E. W., 9, 78, 88
Turner, C. H., 228, 264
Valentinian, 32, 51
Vaticanus, 8, 11, 80, 92, 214, 227, 261
versions, 73, 77, 78, 118, 127, 150, 159,
    160, 170, 193, 245, 248, 252, 253, 260
Vulgate, 6, 71, 73, 160
Walzer, R., 2, 264
Washingtonianus, 190
Westcott, Brooke Foos, xiii, 4, 8, 10, 11,
    71, 156, 190, 195, 238, 242, 252, 264

"Western", 8, 72, 91, 92, 106, 131, 133,
    135, 137, 139, 156, 159, 163, 164,
    168, 171, 179-181, 194, 211, 225,
    231, 232, 248
Western non-interpolations, 8, 156, 183,
    194, 262, 263
Wilken, R., 3, 24, 32, 51, 83, 134, 141, 143,
    208, 264
Williams, C. S. C., 12, 87, 195, 251, 264
Wisse, F., 191, 264
Wisselink, W., 86, 87, 89, 90, 264
Witherington, Ben, 16, 114, 168, 172, 180,
    181, 238, 264
Wright, Leon, 13, 264
Zuntz, Günther, 12, 88, 265

INDEX OF TEXTUAL VARIANTS

Printed in the United States
68206LVS00003B/91